WITHDRAWN
UTSA Libraries

Beyond DiMaggio

Beyond DiMaggio

Italian Americans in Baseball

LAWRENCE BALDASSARO

Foreword by DOM DIMAGGIO

University of Nebraska Press | Lincoln and London

© 2011 by Lawrence Baldassaro
Foreword © 2011 by Dom DiMaggio

Acknowledgments for the use of copyrighted
material appear on page 455, which
constitutes an extension of the copyright page.

All rights reserved
Manufactured in the United States of America

Library of Congress Cataloging-in-Publication Data
Baldassaro, Lawrence.
Beyond DiMaggio : Italian Americans in baseball /
Lawrence Baldassaro, foreword by Dom DiMaggio.
p. cm.
Includes bibliographical references and index.
ISBN 978-0-8032-1705-8 (cloth: alk. paper)
1. Italian American baseball players—Biography.
2. Italian American baseball players—History. I. Title.
GV865.A1.B3216   2011
796.3570922—dc22
[B]
2010026060

Set in Minion by Bob Reitz.

Library
University of Texas
at San Antonio

To my grandparents,
Vincenzo and Amelia Baldassaro
and Orazio and Rosa Nubile,
for their courage and their gift of opportunity

Contents

Illustrations

Foreword

Dom DiMaggio

This book is about the long and distinguished history of Italian Americans in Major League Baseball, a tradition I am proud to be a part of.

Like so many of the players discussed in this book, I and my brothers, Joe and Vince, were the children of Italian immigrants, people who came to this country to make a better life for their families. Giuseppe and Rosalia DiMaggio came to America from Isola delle Femmine, near Palermo, and raised nine kids. Dad worked for forty years as a fisherman in the waters of San Francisco Bay and off Catalina Island. (I joined him one year during school vacation.)

We lived in the North Beach area of San Francisco, and as kids we spent a good deal of our time at the North Beach playground, which was very near our house. There was baseball, basketball, tennis, and soccer, and we played checkers. In fact, when I was about twelve or thirteen years old, I was the champion checkers player for some period of time. We played a lot of baseball, and Joe and Vince played a little tennis.

Joe was an outstanding ballplayer from practically day one. Vince, being the oldest, played around the sandlots. Dad thought he was wasting his childhood. The Italian families always had a strong work ethic, and they thought you should be working. But as fast as Dad used to throw Vince's glove and spikes into the trash can, Mom would retrieve them and hide them until Vince played again. Finally, when Vince signed a Minor League contract and went to Tucson, Dad said, "You mean they pay you for playing this game?" Then, after Joe started playing pro ball, one day Dad came to me and said, "And when are you going to start playing baseball?"

We had a whole slew of baseball fields around the San Francisco area, and, of course, several of the ballplayers featured in this book came from the Bay Area. I knew many of them. Dario Lodigiani lived just a few blocks from our house on Taylor Street. I met Tony Lazzeri a few times during the off season. He was kind of shy, but he was a very, very knowledgeable baseball player. In fact, everybody thought he was one of the smartest baseball guys they'd seen.

Frankie Crosetti was an outstanding shortstop. When he was coaching for the Yankees, he really gave it to me when I first came up to the Majors. He called me all the names a guy who wore glasses could be called, and he'd yell, "Four eyes! How many balls do you see?" Of course, it was good-natured, but it wasn't all that great to hear it. I sort of returned the ribbing just before I retired.

Another Italian ballplayer from San Francisco, Joe Orengo, drove cross country with me on my first trip to spring training in 1940. That was an experience in itself; we had a barrel of fun. When I got to the Red Sox camp at Sarasota, I met everybody in the clubhouse, and they were all very nice. Jimmie Foxx came over to my locker and said, "Glad to have you aboard. Welcome to the big leagues, kid." On the other hand, it took almost three weeks before Lefty Grove and I spoke to each other, but we ended up as very close friends.

There were three of us DiMaggio brothers playing in the Major

Leagues at the same time, all outfielders. Joe started with the Yankees in 1936, Vince broke in with the Braves the next year, and I made it to the Majors in 1940. The San Francisco papers were running a "DiMaggio Digest" every day, showing what each of us had done the day before. Vince spent ten years in the Majors with three clubs, all in the National League. Joe was with the Yankees for thirteen years, and I played for the Red Sox throughout my eleven-year career, so we were part of that great rivalry.

I'll forever be grateful that I was privileged to play baseball in the Major Leagues. There were only four hundred people in the United States playing Major League baseball; it was an honor. Anybody that does anything detrimental to baseball might as well be doing it to me.

I was in an enviable position, not only because I was capable of playing to the extent I did, but also because I had a brother and a teammate who were two of the greatest players in the history of the game. I was privileged to be Joe's brother and a teammate of Ted Williams my entire career, and I loved both of those guys. I was also privileged to be picked for seven All-Star teams and to start in three of them with those two guys next to me. Remember, there was only one outfield position open in the All-Star game each year because those two guys monopolized two of the positions.

I'm also proud of my Italian heritage. My dad's strong work ethic and his determination to succeed, regardless of the obstacles he faced, and Mom's determination for a better life for her family obviously had a great impact on the three of us who went on to become Major League ballplayers and, each in our own way, to realize the American Dream.

Preface

Athletes of Italian descent have achieved distinction in virtually every American sport. Joe Montana and Dan Marino rank among the greatest quarterbacks in football history, and Vince Lombardi remains the standard by which football coaches are measured. From featherweight Willie Pep to undefeated heavyweight champion Rocky Marciano, Italian Americans were preeminent in boxing for several decades. Even those sports in which fewer Italian Americans participated produced some of the all-time greats: five-time Kentucky Derby winner Eddie Arcaro, racing legend Mario Andretti, hockey Hall of Famer Phil Esposito, Grand Slam–winning golfer Gene Saracen, and fifteen-time world's pocket billiard champion Willie Mosconi. And generations of boys grew up dreaming of changing from ninety-pound weaklings to he-men after seeing comic book ads featuring pioneer body builder Charles Atlas, born Angelo Siciliano.

But in no sport has their success been more enduring or more significant than in baseball. Once, after I had given a talk at my school to the inductees of Phi Eta Sigma, the freshman honors society, one of the students approached me and said, "You've had a great life: Italian food and baseball." Without knowing it, that young man had summarized, in a nutshell, the genesis of this book. Since I am the grandson of four Italian immigrants, have been passionate about baseball as long as I can remember, and began writing about the game almost thirty years ago, this book would almost seem inevitable. However, there was a time when I could not have imagined writing about Italian American ballplayers.

This book is born of my lifelong love of baseball but, oddly enough, not of a childhood devotion to players with Italian names. I was aware, of course, of Joe DiMaggio and Yogi Berra, and my first glove was a Phil Rizzuto model, but to me those Yankees were adversaries, not role models. Geographic loyalties, not ethnic affinity, determined my earliest baseball allegiance. Growing up in western Massachusetts, I rooted for the Red Sox, as did my father and even my Italian-born mother. It would be many years before I became dispassionate enough to appreciate not only the greatness of those ballplayers whose heroics had saddened me as a child by beating my beloved Red Sox year after year, but also their significant role in promoting ethnic awareness and understanding.

Beyond DiMaggio is a chronological history of the evolution of Italian Americans in professional baseball, from the turn of the twentieth century, when a handful of pioneers first broke in, to the turn of the twenty-first century, when Italian Americans were prominent in all aspects of the game. For several reasons, my emphasis is on those who were active through the 1950s. In most cases, their stories are less well known than those of contemporary players whose careers, and lives, are more fully documented by the media. One of the main issues addressed in the book is how and when the early players gained entry to a game that was then dominated by Anglo, German, and Irish Americans. Also, the impact of Italian American players peaked in the forties and fifties. After that period, there were fewer prominent players of Italian descent, and their ethnicity, like that of others of South and East European lineage, became less obvious and less noteworthy because of increasing assimilation and intermarriage.

Any book that deals with baseball history is at least implicitly about ethnic succession, which is as much a part of the game's history as it is of the nation's. This book is more explicit than most in its focus on ethnicity, but it remains, first and foremost, a book about baseball or, more specifically, about the men who played the game. While statistics are a part of any baseball narrative, I have tried to adhere as much as possible to Red Smith's premise that in writing about sports, it is not the score of the game that is important but the people who play it. In preparing this book, I have had the good fortune, and pleasure, of interviewing more than fifty players (including some whose careers began in the 1930s), coaches, managers, and executives. In addition, I have relied on general histories, autobiographies, biographies, and newspaper and magazine articles.

In most cases, especially in the first half of the twentieth century, the individuals discussed in this book are readily recognizable as Italian Americans from their surnames. But this is not so in the case of those whose mothers but not fathers are of Italian origin or whose surnames were changed. Surnames can also be misleading. Any number of players have been wrongly identified in print as being of Italian descent, including, just to name a few, Eddie Cicotte, Lew Fonseca, Mike Mussina, and Lou Piniella. In cases where no definitive proof of ethnic background was available, I have chosen to err on the side of caution. Frank Demaree, a Major Leaguer from 1932 to 1944, is one case in point. In various publications, Demaree's birth name is listed as Joseph Franklin Dimaria. However, the native of Winters, California, is listed as Franklin J. Demaree in the 1920 census, and there is no Dimaria or DiMaria listed in California in either the 1920 or 1930 census. Also, on both his Hall of Fame questionnaire, signed by his widow, and his American League questionnaire, filled out by Demaree himself, his nationality is listed as German-Irish.

When there was uncertainty about an individual's ethnic background, two invaluable resources, both in the Baseball Hall of Fame Library, were the Lee Allen Research Papers (which contain Allen's record of the ethnic origin of Major League recruits between 1871 and 1980) and the individual player questionnaires, which ask players to identify their nationality. Especially in cases where a player began his career after 1980, Maxwell Kates was another reliable source of information.

My goals in writing this book were to fill a gap in the existing body of literature on baseball history and to produce a work that would appeal to the general reader as much as to the baseball aficionado. But this story was also written, in part, to honor the memory of my four grandparents, and the millions of others like them, who left behind everything that was familiar to them and came to America in search of a better life. A few of the men portrayed in this book found unimaginable fame and fortune by playing baseball. Most found more modest success. But they all had one thing in common in addition to their ethnic heritage: they all made a living playing the quintessential American game that for many was the very symbol of the values and promises of the country to which their forebears had immigrated.

Acknowledgments

Research for this book began in earnest when I spent two weeks at the Baseball Hall of Fame Library in 1999 as a scholar in residence. No one could have asked for a more supportive environment in which to work. Thanks to Library Director Jim Gates for extending the invitation. Director of Research Tim Wiles was always available for consultation, and Senior Research Associates Scot Mondore and Bruce Markusen generously shared their knowledge of all things baseball on a daily basis. Senior Researcher Bill Francis was, and continues to be, a swift and reliable source of information. Thanks also to Jeff Idelson, Pat Kelly, Bill Burdick, Eric Enders, and Helen Stiles for their assistance during my stay. I am also grateful to Jeff Arnett and Amanda Pinney for inviting me to be part of the Hall of Fame's "Celebration of Italian Americans in Baseball" in November 2005.

I am deeply indebted to Bob Gormley and Paul Salsini, who read the entire manuscript in draft form, and to Marcie Hoffman, who read significant portions of the draft; thanks to each of them for their honest critiques and invaluable suggestions and for saving me from myself. An additional note of gratitude to Bob for his wise and patient counsel from start to finish. Thanks also to those who read and critiqued various segments of the draft: Jules Tygiel, Richard Crepeau, Sal LaGumina, Carolyn Alfvin, Carolyn Kott Washburne, Sue Shemanske, Terry Kumakura and Jack Pearson. Matt Follett, my student research assistant in 2007–8, was attentive to detail, accurate, and diligent; I couldn't have asked for more. Whatever errors may remain in the text are my sole responsibility.

Many of the most rewarding and enjoyable moments I had in preparing this book were those I spent speaking with the more than fifty individuals I interviewed, most in person, a few by phone. Their names appear in the text. Whether they were players, coaches, managers, or executives, I was always impressed by both their obvious love of the game and the vivid detail with which they could recall even long past baseball experiences. I thank them all for enriching this book with their memories and insights. A special note of gratitude to the late Dom DiMaggio, one of the true gentlemen of the game, for writing the foreword and for so generously and patiently sharing his memories.

Dick Johnson, curator of the Sports Museum of New England, and Mario Ziino, former publications director with the Milwaukee Brewers, have been helpful in many ways throughout the course of this project, and I thank them for their friendship and support. My friends Irwin and Sandy Herlihy were particularly helpful in putting me in touch with West Coast baseball people, not to mention providing many hours of baseball camaraderie during visits to spring training.

Members of the Society for American Baseball Research (SABR) can always be counted on for their willingness to help a colleague and for quickly and graciously responding to questions. My thanks to Dave Smith (whose Retrosheet Web site is an invaluable research tool), Roland Hemond, Maxwell Kates, Evelyn Begley, Judith Testa, Bill Deane, Fred Ivor-Campbell, John Thorn, Bill Nowlin, James Odenkirk, Lee Lowenfish, Bob Richardson, Newt Weaver, Gil Bogen, Sean Lahman, Michael Mancuso, Neal Pease, Rick Schabowski, Bob Buege, and Alan Kaufmann.

My sincere appreciation to others who provided research assistance, leads, or moral support, including Larry Freundlich, George Randazzo, Ira Berkow, Dick Bresciani, Murray McGee, Rudolph Vecoli, Michael Bauman, Tom Heitz, Steve Lehman, Rick Cerrone, David Kaplan, Jess Prochilo, Dominic Candeloro, Paul Bosque, John Grippo, Bobby Tanzilo, Gil Becker, Paola Sensi-Isolani, Mike Vassallo, Michael McCoy, William McColly, Ed Hartig, Diane Lodigiani, and my friend since childhood Judy Domingos Porter. I am grateful to the following members of the Abbaticchio family for providing biographical information on Ed Abbaticchio: Albert, William, and William J. Abbaticchio; Edward F. Abbey; Jerome Frecon; and James Shinn.

Sadly three friends who helped me in various ways—Jules Tygiel, Bill Kirwin, and Larry Ritter—are no longer with us, and their loss is felt by everyone in the baseball community. Three different personalities, they were alike in their love of the game, their major contributions to scholarship, and their generosity of spirit. I will always be grateful for their support and encouragement.

In addition to the Hall of Fame staff, other librarians and curators provided essential assistance: Steve Gietschier, former archivist of the *Sporting News*; Dave Kelly of the Library of Congress; and George Rugg, curator of the Joyce Sports Collection in the Notre Dame Library. Also of great help were the staffs at the University of Wisconsin-Milwaukee and Milwaukee Public Libraries.

Pat Kelly at the Hall of Fame Library provided invaluable assistance in assembling the photos for this book, as did Mark Rucker of Transcendental Graphics, Megan LaBella of the Boston Red Sox, and Brooke Bohling of Getty Images.

I am grateful to Dean Richard Meadows of the College of Letters and Science at the University of Wisconsin (uw)-Milwaukee for providing released time to work on the book, to the Office of Undergraduate Research at uw-Milwaukee for funds to support a student assistant, and to the uw System Institute on Race and Ethnicity for helping fund my stay at the Hall of Fame Library. Thanks also to the Terry Family Foundation for inviting me to be a resident fellow at Edenfred in Madison, Wisconsin, and to Jan Terry and David Wells for being such gracious hosts during my stay in November 2008.

I'm greatly indebted to Joeth Zucco, Cara Pesek, Katie Neubauer, and Courtney Ochsner at the University of Nebraska Press for their invaluable support and assistance. Special thanks to Rob Taylor for believing in this project and for his patient guidance. This book also benefited greatly from the stellar work of copy editor Bojana Ristich; her sure-handed catches saved me from a number of errors.

Introduction
At Home in America

I am never more at home in America than at a baseball game.

—Robert Frost

Before the first game of the American League (AL) Championship Series on October 10, 2000, Yankee legends Yogi Berra and Phil Rizzuto both threw out the ceremonial first pitch. In the Yankee dugout was manager Joe Torre, a former Most Valuable Player (MVP), as were Berra and Rizzuto. On that same day, the Associated Press reported that the North Beach Playground in San Francisco would be renamed in honor of the late Joe DiMaggio, who had played there as a child.

The two National League (NL) playoff teams that year were also managed by Italian Americans: the New York Mets by Bobby Valentine and the St. Louis Cardinals by Tony La Russa, then a three-time winner of the Manager of the Year Award. Prior to the third game of the World Series between Valentine's Mets and Torre's Yankees, the first pitch was thrown out by Hall of Famer Tommy Lasorda, who had managed the Los Angeles Dodgers for twenty-one years, winning two World Series in four appearances. That summer he had coached the U.S. baseball team that won the gold medal at the 2000 Olympics in Sidney. Catching Lasorda's ceremonial toss was Mike Piazza, the mainstay of the Mets lineup who was already acknowledged by many as the greatest hitting catcher of all time. In the Mets bullpen was reliever John Franco, who at the time ranked second all-time in saves.

The presence of all these prominent figures in postseason play provided a vivid reminder of the legacy of Italian Americans in Major League Baseball, a legacy that includes some of the most notable figures in the history of the game. In addition to Hall of Fame players (Tony Lazzeri, Ernie Lombardi, and Roy Campanella as well as DiMaggio, Berra, and Rizzuto), there are legendary managers such as Lasorda, Torre, La Russa, and Billy Martin. Italian Americans have gained prominence off the field as well. Paul Gallico was acknowledged as one of the best sportswriters during the Golden Age of sports in the 1920s, and Harry Caray (born Carabina) and Joe Garagiola are two of the most celebrated names in baseball broadcasting. And A. (for Angelo) Bartlett Giamatti left his job as president of Yale University in 1986 to become president of the National League and then, in 1989, the seventh commissioner of Major League Baseball.

The roots of the legacy can be traced back a century and more, to the mass migration of almost 4 million Italians who came to the United States between 1880 and 1920—more than from any other country in that period. Most of those who made the trip across the Atlantic, including my four grandparents, left their home in the old country with the hope of finding a new and better home in America. None of them could have imagined that their sons and grandsons would realize the American Dream by playing baseball, a game that was as foreign to them as the language of their newly adopted home. Yet that is exactly what happened. Today the names of DiMaggio,

Berra, and Lasorda are as much a part of the game's lore as those of Ruth, Cobb, and Wagner. This book traces the evolution of Italian Americans in Major League Baseball. Its purpose is not to foster ethnic pride but to examine the history of their participation in the national pastime, a history that more or less mirrors the general experience of Italian Americans.

Even before he assumed his administrative positions in baseball, Giamatti, the grandson of two Italian immigrants, had written eloquently about the role of the game in American society. He expressed intellectually what some immigrants and most second-generation Italian Americans had understood intuitively: baseball was not only a specific manifestation of the American Dream, but also a metaphor of the American experience as a whole.

Central to Giamatti's vision of baseball is the metaphor of the quest for home, the goal of every Western hero descended from Odysseus. The search for home, he argues, is fundamental both to the nature of the game and to those who came from other lands in search of a new home. In a 1985 speech to the Massachusetts Historical Society, he said, "For what is baseball, and indeed much of the American experience, about but looking for home? *Nostos*, the desire to return home, gives us a nation of immigrants always migrating in search of home." In a later essay he wrote, "The concept of home has a particular resonance for a nation of immigrants, all of whom left one home to seek another."[1]

The obvious question is: why did so many Italians leave their homes in Italy, the land of the Renaissance, the "cradle of civilization" that produced Leonardo da Vinci and Michelangelo? The answer lies in both the dual nature of Italy and the specific conditions that existed late in the nineteenth century. The vast majority

of immigrants—around 85 percent—came not from the regions
of northern and central Italy where the Renaissance flourished but
from the impoverished south, which was, in many ways, a separate
country. Historically the Mezzogiorno (the seven regions south and
east of Rome) had endured centuries of conquest and subjugation,
reaching back to the Greeks and Romans and continuing into the
nineteenth century, when the Bourbons ruled the Kingdom of the
Two Sicilies. Two of the primary consequences of that history were
a stagnant agrarian economy that left little hope for economic improvement and the southerners' deep-seated distrust of all institutions outside the family. In his 1945 landmark book about the Italian
south, *Christ Stopped at Eboli*, Carlo Levi wrote, "No one has come
to this land except as an enemy, a conqueror, or a visitor devoid of
understanding."[2] In those words, Levi essentially defined the history
of southern Italy and the reasons for mass emigration.

Even after the unification of Italy, when the south nominally became part of the Kingdom of Italy, the differences not only continued but increased. The movement to unify Italy was centered in the
northwestern region of Piedmont, whose king, Vittorio Emanuele
II, became the monarch of the new nation in 1861. Not surprisingly,
rather than invest resources in the impoverished south so as to establish a greater balance in the national economy, the new government chose to further industrialize the north. By the last decades
of the nineteenth century, the worsening economy and increasing
population in the south coincided with the rapidly developing in-
dustrialization of America and its need for cheap labor, together with
the ready availability of steamship travel. With little or no hope for
improving their lives at home, Italians began to cross the ocean in
ever-increasing numbers.

Between 1881 and 1890 approximately 307,300 Italians immigrated to the United States. In the following decade, the number reached 652,000, then peaked in the first decade of the twentieth century, reaching 2,136,000. Another 651,893 came between 1911 and 1920. For most of those immigrants it was not easy to feel at home in America. They came to this country because it held out a great promise for a better life than the one they had left behind in the old country. But for a long time that promise came with a high price.

On the one hand, immigrant labor was needed to help build a rapidly developing nation. The great majority of Italians who came in the mass migration were unskilled farm workers from the rural south. In the United States they shunned agricultural work (which was the hopeless labor that had engendered the poverty they were hoping to escape) and settled primarily where the jobs were, in the large cities of the Northeast and Midwest, areas that were totally alien to their rural background. The bosses welcomed them because they were needed to run the machines in the factories and to provide the labor to build the nation's infrastructure. (One of my grandfathers worked for the railroad in New Hampshire, the other in construction in Massachusetts.)

But to many, these new immigrants posed a threat, both economic and moral. Along with their hopes for a better life and their rope-tied suitcases, Italian immigrants (along with others from Eastern and Southern Europe) unwittingly brought with them their ethnic baggage, all of which was generally unwelcome in the United States. Earlier ethnic arrivals and old-stock Americans resented them as threats to their jobs and to traditional American values. They were looked at suspiciously because they were different from those who had preceded them: they were Mediterranean, not Anglo-Saxon or Celtic, with darker skin and curlier hair, and they were Catholic, not Protestant. (The Irish may have been Catholic, but they at least had the advantage of speaking English and looking more like North Europeans.) In his 1906 essay "The Coming of the Italians," John Foster Carr noted, "They are charged with pauperism, crime, and degraded living, and they are judged unheard and almost unseen. These short and sturdy laborers, who swing along the streets with their heavy stride early in the morning and late at night, deserve better of the country. They are doing the work of men, and they are the full equals of any national army of peasant adventurers that ever landed on our shores."[3]

It was an uneasy dance between economic expediency and xenophobic anxiety. The massive arrival of foreigners created a culture of suspicion and fear, a distrust of those who did not fit the mold of how Americans were supposed to look, talk, and behave. Those who had overcome their fear of the unknown to make the journey to America in turn became the unknown that engendered fear of the unknown among those who had arrived before them.

For the first two decades of mass emigration, it is estimated that between one-third and one-half of the immigrants returned to Italy. For these "birds of passage," many of whom had been recruited in Italy by labor agents known as *padroni*, the goal was to earn money to send back to their families in the old country, then return. But by 1900 more and more families were coming to America, often settling in the same towns or cities as other family members or *paesani* who had come before them. The cultural roots of Italian immigrants were regional rather than national; they identified with their town, city, province, or (at most) their region, not with what was to them the more abstract notion of "Italy." Their dialects, dress, and customs differed greatly from one region to another, often from one city to another. Consequently, especially if they settled in large cities—as

the great majority did initially, living in crowded, dark tenements—
it was comforting to live near others from their own area, people
who spoke the same dialect, ate the same food, worshiped the same
patron saints. Even when they formed mutual aid societies to offer
aid to families that had fallen on hard times, regional differences
often led them to restrict membership to those from the same area
of Italy. It was precisely their tendency to live in ethnic enclaves and
maintain vestiges of their life in the old country that led Italians to
be branded as clannish and unlikely to assimilate.

While all immigrant groups from Southern and Eastern Europe
were subject to prejudice and discrimination, Italians, more numerous than others, were the targets of the most persistent and
virulent attacks. The stereotypical portrayal of Italians ranged from
the image of the fruit peddler and organ grinder to the more sinister image of the volatile, knife-wielding criminal, prone to settling
differences with violence. They were routinely characterized by the
press as criminals and political radicals. Early on, the stigma of the
Mafia was attached to the new immigrants, and it was suggested
that Italy was exporting from its south a criminal element as a way
of cleaning its own house. A front-page story in the June 14, 1887,
issue of the *New York Times*, with a Memphis dateline, suggests that
the stereotypical image of Italian immigrants was established soon
after mass migration began. It told the story of "Dago Joe," a "half
breed" accused of murder who was lynched by a mob while he was
being transported back to prison following his escape. The *Times*
story described him as the son of "a Sicilian father and a mulatto
mother," with "the worst characteristics of both races in his makeup. He was cunning, treacherous, and cruel, and was regarded . . .
as an assassin by nature."

The level of discrimination Italians encountered upon arrival was evident in an announcement published in newspapers in 1895 to recruit workers for the Croton Reservoir, being built to provide water for New York City. The daily wages being offered were as follows:

Common labor, white $1.30 to $1.50

Common labor, colored $1.25 to $1.40

Common labor, Italian $1.15 to $1.25[4]

Wherever Italians settled, ethnic tensions and conflict were often part of everyday life. Especially in urban environments, the geographical boundaries that separated Italians from earlier immigrant groups constituted a dividing line that was crossed at some peril. In his study of Italians in St. Louis, Gary Mormino cited a resident of the Italian neighborhood known as "Dago Hill" who recalled the danger of venturing beyond the ethnic boundaries: "If you got caught on the other side of Southwest Avenue, you got the heck kicked out of you."[5]

This hostile response to the new immigrants was in marked contrast to the image of Italy that had been fostered by nineteenth-century American intellectuals, many of whom were fervent Italophiles. Such major figures as James Fenimore Cooper, Nathaniel Hawthorne, and Henry James all celebrated Italy as the fountain of artistic and cultural sophistication, the repository of what was best in the Old World, even as they were at times disturbed by what they perceived as the decadent behavior of contemporary Italians.

But when large numbers of Italians landed in America late in the nineteenth century, nativists saw them not as the inheritors of a great cultural tradition but as uneducated, illiterate peasants who were morally and intellectually inferior to the Nordic immigrants who had preceded them. Social scientists "documented" the genetic and moral inferiority of southern Italians, classifying them as part of the Mediterranean race and taking care to distinguish them from northern Italians, part of the Alpine race, who exhibited the positive traits of the Germanic and Scandinavian peoples. In 1922 Arthur Sweeney, a physician, wrote, "We have no place in this country for the 'man with the hoe,' stained with the earth he digs, and guided by a mind scarcely superior to the ox, whose brother he is." In the words of historian John P. Diggins, "Americans reacted to the last wave of immigration with an outburst of nativism that was as neurotic as it was narcissistic."[6]

Even some of the most prominent Americans spoke out openly against the wave of new immigrants who threatened to destroy an American way of life established by their Anglo-Saxon predecessors. In a speech at New York's Carnegie Hall in October 1915, former president Teddy Roosevelt said, "There is no room in this country for hyphenated Americans." And in that same year President Woodrow Wilson announced that "hyphenated Americans . . . have poured the poison of disloyalty into the very arteries of our national life. . . . Such creatures of passion, disloyalty and anarchy must be crushed out."[7]

The sentiments that Roosevelt, Wilson, and others expressed fueled resentment and hostility toward the new immigrants that was usually verbal but at times turned violent. It has been estimated that between 1885 and 1915 at least fifty Italians were lynched in states ranging from New York to Mississippi. The most notorious incident of anti-Italian violence occurred in New Orleans on March 14, 1891, when an armed mob killed eleven Italians, some of whom had been suspected of killing police chief David Hennessy but had been acquitted by a jury. It was the largest mass lynching in U.S. history. Following the incident, articles and editorials in magazines and newspapers, including the *New York Times*, justified the killings as the response of reasonable men to the wrongful acquittal of the accused, who were labeled as members of the Mafia.

Especially in the South—but not only in the South—Italians were often not considered to be white. "'You don't call an Italian a white man?' a construction boss was asked. 'No sir,' he replied. 'An Italian is a dago.'"[8] Before they were known as the Pirates, one of the nicknames applied to the Pittsburgh baseball team was "Smoked Italians," an apparent reference to the ballplayers' dark skin caused by the smoky atmosphere created by the city's steel mills. A story in the September 13, 1890, issue of *Sporting Life* noted that John Montgomery Ward, recruiting players for his newly formed renegade Players League, was "trying out, informally, a couple of 'smoked Italians.' The men were almost certainly black."[9]

It was nativist opposition to immigration that motivated Congress to establish the Dillingham Commission, which in its 1911 report concluded that the wave of immigrants from Southern and Eastern Europe posed a grave threat to American society. That, in turn, led Congress to establish immigration quotas based on countries of origin. Both the Emergency Quota Act of 1921 and the Immigration Act of 1924 severely limited the annual number of immigrants from South and East European countries.

My Name Is My Enemy

Juliet said to Romeo, "'Tis but thy name that is my enemy," but for many Italian immigrants who faced hostility in America, the phrase would have been, "'Tis but *my* name that is my enemy." For most immigrants their names were one of the few possessions they brought with them from the old country. But that most obvious and personal form of self identity proved to be a liability for those whose names were considered difficult to pronounce and spell. In an effort to slip quietly into the American mainstream or simply to avoid the hassles associated with names that unmistakably marked their otherness, many chose to shorten, anglicize, or totally change their names.

The complex history of name changes in my own family may serve to illustrate. My paternal grandparents immigrated to North Walpole, New Hampshire, early in the twentieth century. In that distinctly Yankee environment, where names like Bailey, Baker, Ball, Bancroft, and Barber surrounded that of my grandfather in the town directory, a long name ending in a vowel stood out like coal in a snowbank. In an attempt to appear more American, two of my father's siblings legally changed their surname to the obviously Anglo-Saxon Bowen. They were simply following the lead of my grandfather, whose will begins, "I, Vincenzo Baldassaro, sometimes known as James Bowen. . . ." While my father retained his surname, he legally changed his first name from Ruggiero to Gerald. Meanwhile, in Massachusetts, my maternal grandfather anglicized his surname from Nubile (pronounced NEW-bee-lay and meaning the same in Italian as in English) to the more masculine and majestic sounding Noble.

The pressure to modify names was even more intense for those whose professions exposed them to media coverage. It was common for Italian American prizefighters to abandon their birth names, as it would be in later years for entertainers. The same was true for ballplayers. Beginning in 1897, when Ed Abbaticchio became, in all likelihood, the first Italian American to play in the big leagues, sportswriters (and typesetters) struggled with Italian names. In many cases, they shortened the names to fit them into box scores or gave the ballplayers English-sounding nicknames (Abbaticchio becoming Abby, for example). In other cases, the players themselves shortened their names (Paolinelli choosing to play as Pinelli) or changed them completely (Mercantelli becoming Rye).

If Italian Americans felt compelled to change their names, it was in response to names that others imposed on them: "guinea," "dago," "wop." Their names were the markers of the original sin they had brought with them from the old country, what Americans saw as an inherent otherness—evident in their appearance, language, customs—which was easily equated with inferiority.

Name changes were just the most obvious consequence of the discrimination that many of the immigrants and their children encountered and of the pressure they felt to deny their ethnicity. Leonard Covello, who immigrated with his parents in 1897 at the age of nine, would become a noted education reformer in New York City. In his memoir, *The Heart Is the Teacher*, he described his experience in elementary school: "I do not recall one mention of Italy or the Italian language or what famous Italians had done in the world with the possible exception of Columbus, who was pretty popular in America. We soon got the idea that Italy meant something inferior." That stigma would not soon disappear. In a 2005 interview, Joe Torre told me that when he asked his mother, a native of Naples, where in Italy the family had come from, she said, "We're American." Said Torre, "I felt that there was something shameful about being Italian."[10]

Baseball: The Common Denominator

Though some chose to change their names, most immigrants felt the need to cling to the familiar, to hold on to what they had brought with them—their language, customs, beliefs—as a way of coping with the often menacing life they found in the New World. Their children, though, were caught in the middle, between parents eager to protect them against the alien ways of America that threatened to destroy the family unit and their own desire to become a part of the culture into which they were born. They lived a dual existence, with one foot in the Old World customs of their parents and the other in the world that existed outside their homes in the streets and in the schools.

Even when I was growing up in the 1950s, school was still the main purveyor of cultural values. (Television was in its infancy and had not yet homogenized American culture.) Every morning my classmates and I recited the pledge of allegiance to the flag and sang "My Country, 'Tis of Thee." Multiculturalism as a prescribed cultural concept was far in the future, but I lived it every day in my small western Massachusetts town. Our neighbors were of French Canadian, Greek, Polish, and Irish extraction, and we all knew the ethnic background of our friends' families, in many cases because their parents still spoke their native language or spoke English with heavy accents. But at school we were taught to become American, "one nation, indivisible."

It was up to the second-generation Italian Americans to find a way of navigating between these two shores, one tying them to the past, the other beckoning them to a new life that was in many ways so different from that which their parents lived. If their parents had left one home behind, they had to discover a new home in a new land.

The answer to the stigma of being outsiders was to find a way to become less different, to assimilate into the larger culture that found their differences to be unsettling, if not unacceptable. Baseball, one of the most obvious and visible signs of mainstream American life, offered them one avenue of entry, either as fans or as participants. By the late nineteenth century, when Italians began coming to America in large numbers, baseball had already established itself as the national pastime. And by the early years of the twentieth century the game had been endowed with metaphorical significance as a true symbol of the American values of fair play and opportunity. Journalists were touting baseball not only as the grand expression of American democracy, but also as a means of teaching the children of immigrants how to become Americans. In 1912 sportswriter Hugh Fullerton declared that "baseball is the melting pot at a boil, the most democratic sport in the world." In 1923 Frederick G. Lieb, president of the Baseball Writers' Association of America, concluded that "next to the little red school house, there has been no greater agency in bringing our different races together than our national game, baseball. Baseball is our real melting pot."[11]

Not only was baseball proclaimed a didactic tool for imparting American values, it was also hailed as an equal-opportunity employer. In the same year that Lieb's article appeared, the *Sporting News* proclaimed the game's professed indifference to the ethnic background of its players (with the obvious exception of blacks): "The Mick, the Sheeny, the Wop, the Dutch and the Chink, the Cuban, the Indian, the Jap or the so-called Anglo-Saxon—his 'nationality' is never a matter of moment if he can pitch, hit, or field."[12]

According to this and other public statements, all were welcome to participate in the national pastime, with its promise of equal access to the American Dream. But those noble sentiments were in stark contrast to the vitriolic anti-immigrant proclamations that became more prevalent following World War I. And in 1924, one year after Lieb proclaimed baseball as the nation's melting pot and the *Sporting News* praised baseball's love for all ethnic groups, the new immigration law was passed that restricted the entry of East and South Europeans to 2 percent of persons from those regions living in the United States in 1890.

It would be naive to believe that baseball was somehow immune to the ethnic bias that led to the new immigration laws. For all the noble declarations of the game's inherent democratic nature, there was a considerable gap between theory and practice, at least at the professional level. Regardless of the prevailing rhetoric of the time, Italians, like others of South and East European background, were not welcomed into professional baseball with open arms. For them the professed democratic ideals of Major League Baseball were enacted slowly and sparingly. When the above-mentioned *Sporting News* story appeared in December 1923, only twelve players of Italian descent had ever played in the Major Leagues. And it would not be until the late 1930s that the proportion of Italian American Major Leaguers would approach their proportion of the American population.

Even though very few children of the early twentieth-century immigrants were able to make a living playing America's game, there is no question that for a long time baseball helped newcomers to this country become American, or at least think they knew what it meant to be American. Ralph Fasanella, born in 1914 in New York City to immigrant parents, became a well known "primitive" painter whose subjects included labor history, urban life, and baseball. He recalled what baseball meant for the children of immigrants: "We [Italians] were foreigners. We were the ginzos from the other side, and the only thing that made the connection was the baseball game. Baseball was America."[13]

I got to witness this process of acculturation firsthand in my own family. Two of my maternal grandmother's brothers came to America as teenagers early in the twentieth century. In some ways they were similar: both worked as hod carriers in the construction trade and neither married. And like those of many first-generation Italians, their names were Americanized by others. The older brother was Nunzio, but everyone outside our family called him Charlie, for no apparent reason. Enrico (the Italian equivalent of Henry) was known as Andy.

For all their outward similarities, the American experiences of Nunzio and Enrico were dramatically different. It was obvious that Nunzio never felt completely at home in America. He was respected and liked by his bosses and co-workers, but he never learned English well and kept to himself most of the time. There was always an air of sadness about him, perhaps a lifelong homesickness for the old country. For him America meant an escape from poverty but an otherwise drab existence of lonely apartments and relative isolation. Enrico, on the other hand, was much more comfortable in his American world. He was a garrulous good old boy—he even worked part time as a bartender—who happened to speak with an Italian accent. The surest mark of his Americanization, and of the difference between him and his brother, was his passion for baseball; he was a devoted and knowledgeable Yankee fan. Whatever else set him apart as an immigrant, baseball was the common language that connected him to his non-Italian acquaintances and made him seem less foreign.

For all the discrimination and hostility they faced, immigrants like my grandparents found opportunities in America that were not available in the old country. They came from places where, for generation after generation, there was little if any hope of improving or even changing their destiny. Whatever circumstances they had been born into would be their lot in life. Most of those immigrants struggled at first in blue-collar jobs, hoping to work their way up the ladder gradually. But for that small minority blessed with athletic skill, baseball—a game that their parents generally considered a foolish diversion and a waste of time—offered a shortcut to relative economic success and some measure of social status. It was their ticket to the American Dream.

Just as their parents or grandparents had embarked on a difficult journey to the New World, the ballplayers chronicled in this book undertook their own difficult journey, one that took them away from the Old World ways of their forebears to the unknown territory of mainstream American life. They did not play to send a message nor to break barriers; they played because they loved the game and because it was a way to make a living in a society that for a long time did not provide them with a wide range of opportunities. Nevertheless, they were unwitting pioneers. Both by their success in that most American of endeavors and their demeanor, they began to break down stereotypes that had plagued Italian Americans since the 1880s. It was baseball that enabled them to enter the public consciousness as something other than organ grinders, unskilled laborers, or mustachioed Mafiosi.

But like their immigrant parents or grandparents, the ballplayers received mixed messages. When Italian Americans began to appear in the Major Leagues in increasing numbers in the 1930s, media portrayals of their arrival betrayed a curious mixture of welcome and apprehension. Stories that claimed to celebrate the sudden surge of Italian players were sometimes written in a style that was at once patronizing and slightly derogatory. In other words, praise mingled easily with a barely masked smirk that was frequently apparent in stereotypical depictions that suggested that these athletes, talented though they might be, were not yet fully assimilated Americans. The terms "wop" and "dago," unimaginable today, appeared routinely in even the most prestigious publications.

When, in the late 1920s, Tony Lazzeri became the first Italian to achieve star status in the Major Leagues, fans would wave Italian flags in the stands of Yankee Stadium to cheer for their new hero.

They did the same in the thirties, when Joe DiMaggio surpassed Lazzeri in talent and star power. It is likely that a good number of those cheering for Lazzeri and DiMaggio had not been baseball fans before they had these *paesani* to root for. It is even likely that at least some of them never came to care about the game that their heroes were playing. What mattered to them was that one of their own was at center stage of the national pastime of their adopted homeland, making them both proud to be Italian and giving them some sense of belonging in the country that so often had told them, in various ways, that their ethnic background made them something other than fully assimilated Americans.

That ethnic heroes like Lazzeri and DiMaggio could evoke such a powerful response from immigrants might seem, in what we like to think of as our more enlightened time of multicultural awareness, like an antiquated concept. But anyone who has been in Fenway Park or, even more so, Yankee Stadium or Shea Stadium when Pedro Martinez was pitching has seen fans walking through the stands waving the flag of the Dominican Republic. They were motivated by the same sense of ethnic pride and allegiance that motivated those Italian fans eighty years earlier. The success of Martinez, like that of Lazzeri and DiMaggio, told them that it was possible to achieve at least some measure of acceptance.

I think it is fair to say that the early ballplayers, those of the 1920s and 1930s, did more to counter public hostility and demeaning stereotypes than any other Italian Americans to that time. Tony Lazzeri was being praised for his intelligence and character during his rookie year of 1926, only two years after strict immigration laws were aimed at limiting the influx of South and East Europeans. Stereotypical portrayals by the press notwithstanding, these players garnered national attention in the game that more than any other sport and more than most social institutions defined an American way of life. Even before the labels of "dago" and "wop" faded from the pages of newspapers and magazines, baseball players were sending a subtle message to the public that regardless of ingrained biases, these children of immigrants were succeeding in the national pastime—and becoming more and more American in the process.

To most people, Joe DiMaggio remains *the* representative ballplayer of Italian descent, and there is no question that he rose to unprecedented heights, both as an athlete and as a cultural phenomenon. For Italian Americans, DiMaggio was quite simply the single greatest hero. But there were many others who came before him, paving the way and making it possible for a Joe DiMaggio to evolve from an ethnic hero to an American icon.

Others have since carried on the tradition with distinction, including players of the caliber of Rocky Colavito, Ron Santo, and Tony Conigliaro. Yogi Berra, Phil Rizzuto, and Tommy Lasorda have followed DiMaggio into the Hall of Fame, and at least two others (Mike Piazza and Craig Biggio) are likely to do the same. Gradually Italian Americans have moved into executive roles as managers, general managers, owners, and even commissioner of baseball. It is all part of the American pattern of ethnic succession, but like the rest of the process of assimilation and acculturation, the evolution was neither quick nor easy, and it was not without a price. By succeeding in America's game, the men portrayed in this book realized the dream that had motivated their parents or grandparents to leave the old country in the first place. But for both players and executives, assimilation has come at the cost of relinquishing at least some part of the culture they inherited from their Old World roots in order to become something new. Like those who left Italy in search of a better life, they too had to leave one home to seek another.

1. The *Italian Immigrants*, by Rudolph Torrini, stands in front of St. Ambrose Church in the heart of the Italian neighborhood of St. Louis known as "the Hill." Photograph by Lawrence Baldassaro.

Beyond DiMaggio

One

THE PIONEERS

1

Ed Abbaticchio
Forgotten Pioneer

In one of the first stories on Joe DiMaggio to appear in a national publication, Quentin Reynolds, associate editor of *Collier's* magazine, recounted the following exchange among baseball writers covering spring training in 1936: "'He says you pronounce it Dee-Mah-gee-o,' one of the sports writers said gloomily. 'That's a very tough name to pronounce and also tough to spell,' another added. 'DiMaggio sounds like something you put on a steak,' one writer said in disgust."[1]

That same spring, following several letters from readers offering the correct pronunciation of the DiMaggio name, an editorial note pointed out that in a recent interview with a *New York Times* reporter, DiMaggio himself said that "if there is any further argument on this point he will have to change his name to Smith."[2]

From the time Italian Americans first appeared in the Major Leagues, sportswriters and typesetters were baffled by their names. Compared to the more familiar Anglo-Saxon and Celtic names that dominated baseball rosters, Italian names seemed long and confusing; they did not trip off the tongue like "Tinker to Evers to Chance." Both phonetically and culturally, their foreign-sounding names set Italians apart, a reminder that they were somehow not quite as American as those who had come before them.

Since so many Italian immigrants changed their names precisely to be less "different," it is impossible to identify with absolute certainty the first Major Leaguer of Italian descent. There is no question, however, as to who was the first to have a significant career. Between 1897 and 1910, Ed Abbaticchio spent all or part of nine seasons playing for Philadelphia, Boston, and Pittsburgh in the National League. And for one year at least he was one of the highest-paid players in baseball. In many ways he was atypical of the early Italian American ballplayers who would follow him in the Major Leagues, most of whom would be second-generation sons of unskilled working-class immigrants who came to the United States after 1880.[3]

Unlike most of the Italians who would immigrate in later years, Abbaticchio's father, Archangelo, came to America out of curiosity, not necessity. Born in 1842 near Naples, where he became a well-established and prosperous barber, Archangelo was convinced by a sea captain friend to sail to the New World. He arrived in 1873, at the age of thirty-one, almost a decade before the large wave of Italian immigration would begin. His initial curiosity turned to desperation when his money was stolen in New York City. Armed with a letter of introduction from his uncle, a priest in Naples, he made his way to St. Vincent's Monastery in Latrobe, Pennsylvania. There, with the help of the local Benedictines, he was able to open a barber shop. A shrewd businessman, he soon had a chain of shops and began to acquire property, including a tavern/hotel. By 1875 he felt secure enough to bring his wife and four children to the United States.

The first of four additional children to be born in America, Edward James Abbaticchio was born in Latrobe on April 15, 1877. At a time when only about 5 percent of Americans even finished high school, Abbaticchio received a master of accounts degree in 1895 from St. Mary's College in North Carolina. His education would suggest that

2. Ed Abbaticchio of the Philadelphia Phillies, 1898. National Baseball Hall of Fame Library, Cooperstown NY.

he was preparing for a career in business, but he chose instead to be a professional baseball player. For the son of Italian immigrants baseball was a most unlikely and unpromising career choice in the 1890s. Nevertheless, after playing semi-pro ball in Greensburg, Pennsylvania, Abbaticchio, a twenty-year-old five-foot-eleven, 170-pound infielder, began his Major League career with a brief three-game stint with the Philadelphia Phillies in September 1897.

Two-Sport Star

Even before he appeared in his first Major League game with the Phillies, Abbaticchio already had made his debut as a professional athlete, but as a football player. In 1895 the town of Latrobe fielded what is generally acknowledged as the first professional football team in the country. Abbaticchio was its star fullback and kicker, earning fifty dollars a game. According to coaching legend Fielding Yost, Abbaticchio also made a historic contribution to football: he created the spiral punt. Yost claimed that he saw Abbaticchio kick the spiral in Latrobe, learned the technique from him, then taught it to his kickers at the University of Michigan.[4] Abbaticchio, who continued to play football until 1900, was not only in all probability the first Italian American to play in the Major Leagues, but he was also the first two-sport professional athlete.[5]

In 1898 Abbaticchio appeared in twenty-five games for the Phillies, but it would be five years before he would return to the Major Leagues. In 1899 he played for Minneapolis of the Western League and in 1900—the year the circuit changed its name to the American League—for Milwaukee, where his manager was Connie Mack. He then spent the next two years with Nashville in the newly organized Southern League.

There is ample evidence that Abbaticchio was highly regarded by knowledgeable baseball people of that era. In 1901, the year that the American League declared itself a major league, the legendary Connie Mack became manager of the Philadelphia Athletics, a post he would hold for fifty years. In 1902, Abbaticchio's second season with Nashville, Mack sought to lure his former Milwaukee infielder to Philadelphia. On June 11, he sent Abbaticchio a telegram: "What can your release be secured for and what salary do you want?" Abbaticchio, who was making $250 a month in Nashville (the league limit at the time), declined Mack's offer. A Nashville paper reported in 1901 that Abbaticchio was the highest paid player in the Southern League, adding that "Abbaticchio comes of wealthy parentage, and plays the game merely because he loves it."[6]

At the end of the 1902 season the Boston Beaneaters of the National League purchased Abbaticchio's contract for $1,200, and from 1903 to 1905 he was a starter at both shortstop and second base. Then, even though several teams were anxious to sign him, the twenty-eight-year-old infielder suddenly retired from baseball after the 1905 season. According to a *Pittsburgh Post* story of January 2, 1905, Abbaticchio's father offered to turn his hotel over to his son on condition that he never play baseball again: "His father has always been opposed to his playing in the big leagues and has stipulated that the hotel will revert to him if the well-known short stop ever again dons a league uniform." It is not surprising that his father, a successful businessman, was opposed to his son's chosen career. Abbaticchio, after all, broke into professional baseball when it had not yet gained widespread respectability and ballplayers were generally regarded by the public as undisciplined rowdies. Whatever the reason, Abbaticchio did in fact retire from baseball after the 1905 season to run the hotel in spite of Boston's efforts to resign him.

Connie Mack was not the only big-name manager who wanted

Abbaticchio in his lineup. John McGraw, whose Giants had won the 1905 World Series, tried to lure him out of retirement in 1906. McGraw and Giants president John T. Brush both went to Latrobe in an unsuccessful attempt to sign Abbaticchio. It is possible that Mack and McGraw so eagerly sought Abbaticchio for more than his proven ability as a ballplayer. Both managers were actively seeking to improve the image of baseball, and one way to do that was to recruit college-educated athletes who would presumably bring new prestige to the game by raising the level of decorum. The most famous example is Christy Mathewson, the blond, blue-eyed alumnus of Bucknell University who, as the star pitcher of McGraw's Giants, did more than anyone else to enhance the reputation of professional ballplayers during this era. Abbaticchio, Mathewson's former rival in professional football, was likely viewed by both managers not only as a valuable ballplayer who would improve their respective teams on the field, but also as a well-educated gentleman with a college degree who would help better the reputation of both his own team and the game as a whole.

Abbaticchio turned down all offers and announced that if he were to play again, it would be only for the Pittsburgh Pirates, apparently for business reasons. State law required that the owner of a liquor license could not reside outside the state for more than three consecutive months. By playing for the Pirates, Abbaticchio could stay near his hotel and retain his liquor license. So anxious were the Pirates to secure the rights to Abbaticchio that they sent three frontline players to Boston in what would today be considered a blockbuster deal. Claude Ritchey, the Pirates' starting second baseman; outfielder Ginger Beaumont, who had led the National League in hits from 1902 through 1904; and pitcher Patsy Flaherty, who had won twenty-nine games for the Pirates in 1904–5, were all traded for the rights to Abbaticchio in December 1906.

Not only did the Pirates trade away three players for their new second baseman, but they also gave him what was at the time the extraordinary salary of $5,000. To put this figure into perspective, consider that three years later, in 1909, the average Major League salary was under $2,500. In that year two of the greats of that era, Christy Mathewson and Nap Lajoie, made $6,000 and $7,500 respectively.[7] It is even more remarkable that in 1907 Abbaticchio was being paid $800 more than teammate Honus Wagner, who had been a Pirates star since 1900. Wagner, the "Flying Dutchman," had led the National League in hitting in 1900, 1903, and 1904, and in 1906, the year before Abbaticchio joined the team, he led the National League in batting average, doubles, runs, and total bases. The scales quickly tipped in Wagner's favor, however; after holding out, he was given a $10,000 contract in 1908.

Abbaticchio's salary for 1908 remained at $5,000 but not because he hadn't lived up to Pittsburgh's expectations in 1907. He was the starting second baseman, forming the double play combination with Wagner, and drove in eighty-two runs, tying Wagner for second place in the National League. Abbaticchio was the regular second baseman again in 1908, but his offensive production slipped as he hit .250 and drove in sixty-one runs. In that year the Pirates, Cubs, and Giants were involved in one of the closest pennant races in history, and Fred Merkle's base-running blunder, ever after known as "Merkle's boner," led to a one-game playoff in which the Cubs beat the Giants.

At the end of that season, eleven days after Merkle's boner, Abbaticchio himself was involved in one of the more bizarre controversial plays in baseball history that supposedly lost the pennant for the Pirates, who finished one game behind the Cubs. The incident occurred on October 4, in the last game of the season, in Chicago before 30,247 fans, which *Sporting Life* termed "the largest crowd that ever witnessed a base ball contest in America."[8] With the Pirates trailing the Cubs 5–2, Abbaticchio came to bat in the ninth inning. The traditional account of the story has Abbaticchio hitting an apparent grand slam against the Cubs—which would have won the game for the Pirates and given them the pennant—only to have home plate umpire Hank O'Day overrule the base umpire and call the ball foul. When a fan subsequently sued the Pittsburgh team, claiming that Abbaticchio's drive had hit and injured her, her ticket stub allegedly showed that she had been seated in fair territory.

While this colorful account has appeared in several publications, it has proved to be inaccurate. According to information compiled by Mike Kopf for Bill James's *The Baseball Book*, the hit was a double, not a home run; the ball was hit not into the stands but into an overflow crowd standing in the outfield; and no record has been found of such a law suit.[9] The only thing that is certain is that the Pirates did not win the game or the pennant.

The following year the Pirates bounced back and won the World Series, but Abbaticchio, now thirty-two years old, lost his starting job and became a utility player. His career ended in 1910, when, after appearing in three games for the Pirates, he returned to Boston, playing in only fifty-two games. He continued to run his hotel in Latrobe until 1932, then retired to Fort Lauderdale, Florida, where he died on January 6, 1957.

The Name Doesn't Fit

Ed Abbaticchio played in an era when Major League rosters were dominated by players of Irish descent. In September 1906 Timothy Sharp wrote the following in the *Sporting News*: "The foundation stone, superstructure and even the base ball roof is as Irish as Paddy's pig. . . . The finest athletes in the world are Irish and it is due to the predominance of the Irish in base ball that the American nation's chosen pastime is the most skillful in the world."[10]

Abbaticchio's teammates on the 1908 Pirates team bore names like Shannon, Clarke, O'Connor, Kane, and Leach; only his surname stretched beyond two syllables. From his early days in professional baseball Abbaticchio's polysyllabic name posed problems for sportswriters, who spelled it in a variety of ways. In one game story in a Nashville paper it appeared as both "Abbatticcio" and "Abbittico." Abbaticchio was also the first in a long line of Italian names to fall victim to box-score shorthand; in the box scores of his first three Major League games, his name appeared as "Abbatchio."

Writers soon resorted to abbreviating his name to "Abby" and "Batty." Nicknames are an integral part of baseball lore, ranging from the merely descriptive (Three-Finger Brown) to the whimsical (Dizzy and Daffy Dean) to the derogatory (Dick "Dr. Strangeglove" Stuart). While not exceptional in themselves, "Abby" and "Batty" obviously mask Abbaticchio's Italian origins and may indicate that some compromise of his ethnic background was a necessary condition of his acceptance in professional baseball. At the very least, they suggest a need to anglicize Abbaticchio's identity at a time when fans and the media were not yet accustomed to seeing Italian surnames in the box score.

Newspapers continued to identify Abbaticchio as both "Abby" and "Batty" during his Major League career, and one of those nicknames even became the legal name of one of his three sons. Edward, a physician who taught at Yale, anglicized his surname to Abbey. According to Abbey's son, Edward F. Abbey, the doctor changed his name while a medical student at Georgetown because he thought he would have

11

a better chance to succeed in American society without the burden of a long and difficult surname.

Apart from abbreviating his name, the press paid little attention to Abbaticchio's ethnicity. There were occasional references to his Italian background—he was a "son of sunny Italy" and a "son of Caesar"—but for the most part his nationality was ignored. On one occasion, however, Abbaticchio's presence on a Major League diamond raised an interesting question for one Boston newspaper. On June 7, 1903 (Abbaticchio's first season with the Beaneaters), the *Boston Sunday Journal* ran a story under the headline "Boston May Contribute to Italian Supremacy in Baseball." The story began by posing a sociological question: "Does the entrance of an Italian into baseball presage another great ethnological movement such as has taken place in the American labor world?" The anonymous writer then wondered if Abbaticchio, "believed to be the first Italian that ever played in a major league," might be the "forerunner of the movement" and if Boston was to be "the headquarters of the movement," as if to suggest that Abbaticchio was the standard-bearer of an organized plan to infiltrate baseball. Noting that while a decade earlier "the large majority of laborers seen in the city streets were Irish" but now "the majority are Italians," the writer posed yet another question: "Will the Italians supplant the Irish on the diamond as they have supplanted them with the pick and the shovel?" The writer then revealed his real concern with the broader implications of "Batty's case." With ever-increasing numbers of Italians ("the most clannish of all the nationalities that emigrate to the United States") settling in Boston, the city "grows more Italian every year."

It is revealing that the appearance of a single Major Leaguer of Italian descent would prompt such a story. Though the piece is ostensibly about the implications of Abbaticchio's arrival for the baseball world, the issues and questions it raises reflect the growing nativist concern with the rapidly increasing numbers of immigrants from Southern and Eastern Europe, in particular the Irish-Italian tensions that existed in the large urban centers of the Northeast.[11]

By 1900 there were more than seventeen thousand Italians in Boston. In a pattern common to many American cities, they moved into neighborhoods inhabited predominantly by the Irish, the previously dominant immigrant group. Settling primarily in the North End, they were met with resentment, not only because they had invaded Irish territory, but also because, as the story in the *Boston Sunday Journal* suggests, they were perceived as competitors for jobs. Italians also became the targets of the American nativist movement, which was particularly zealous in Boston, where the Immigration Restriction League was formed in 1894. In a 1909 speech, "The Restriction of Immigration," Senator Henry Cabot Lodge, a Bostonian and the public voice of the league, warned that the tide of foreign immigrants from Southern and Eastern Europe threatened to bring about "nothing less than the possibility of a great and perilous change in the very fabric of our race."[12]

As a Major Leaguer, Ed Abbaticchio, with a lifetime batting average of .254, never matched the hitting prowess he had shown at Nashville. Nevertheless, no less an authority than Honus Wagner confirmed Abbaticchio's reputation as one of the most respected players of his time. On the occasion of a dinner given by the Justinian Society of Philadelphia in 1953 honoring Ray Abbaticchio (a nephew of Ed and the head of the local FBI office), Wagner wrote a letter, presumably meant to be read at the dinner, that provided a glowing tribute to his former teammate. Because the letter provides insight into

Abbaticchio's personality as well as his athletic ability by one of the legends of the game, it deserves to be quoted at some length:

> "Batty" was one of the best of his day as a player and one of the finest of any baseball era as a man and a true friend. . . . No one was in a better position than myself to see and realize his worth as a player, and nobody ever had a better partner around that part of the diamond. He was an everlasting credit to baseball, to Pittsburgh, and to his home section of Latrobe, and it is a great pleasure to me to be able to greet him again at the Justinian dinner, if only by means of this long-distance letter.
>
> John Honus Wagner

The length and warmth of Wagner's 880-word letter make it obvious that this was no perfunctory exercise in response to a request for a favor. His assessment of Abbaticchio's stature as a ballplayer cannot be dismissed since it effectively confirms the reason he was so highly sought by Connie Mack and John McGraw and why Pittsburgh traded away three starters and gave him such a lucrative contract.

Ed Abbaticchio was certainly not a pioneer in the way that Jackie Robinson would be a half century later, breaking down blatantly discriminatory practices. There is no indication, either from Abbaticchio himself or from surviving relatives, that he encountered open prejudice during his career. Nevertheless, by demonstrating that an Italian American could be a successful and respected Major League ballplayer at a time when anti-Italian sentiment was widespread, he opened the door for all those that would follow. And his display of skill and character on the highly visible stage of America's pastime may have helped in some small way to alter the public's perception of Italian Americans in general.

Baseball historians have not been as kind to Abbaticchio as were his contemporaries. On the rare occasions when his name appears in print, it is only to note his place in baseball history as the first player of Italian origin to appear in the Major Leagues. Occasionally he is described, somewhat dismissively, as a "journeyman ballplayer" or, less frequently, as a "slick-fielding infielder." But the evidence indicates that in the eyes of his peers, he was hardly an anonymous role player. In the era of Mack and McGraw, Mathewson and Wagner, Abbaticchio's contemporaries obviously considered him to be a valuable asset. For a brief period he was one of the most highly sought-after players of his time. Except for 1907, his statistics were modest enough, yet several teams were offering unusually high salaries for his services, and he was courted by two of the game's legendary managers. Given all of that, as well as his two-sport versatility, Ed Abbaticchio deserves to be remembered as more than a historical footnote.

The First Italian Name in Baseball

Even before Abbaticchio appeared on the scene, another Italian name proved to be problematic. According to noted baseball writer Dan Daniel, writing in the July 1936 issue of *Baseball Magazine*, "The first Italian name in baseball was that of N. T. Apolonio, who was president of the Boston club in 1876, when the National League got under way." Daniel further explained: "On the playing field, an Italian would have been eyed with intense curiosity in those days. In fact, he might have been lured from the diamond to Phineas T. Barnum's American Museum of Curiosities in New York."[13]

The same name had appeared in print twenty-five years earlier in *America's National Game*, A. G. Spalding's 1911 history of the formative years of baseball. In that book it was the only Italian name that appeared: "N. T. Appolonio, then [1876] president of the Boston Club."[14] Spalding also noted that the Boston president was one of the club owners present at the Chicago meeting at which the National League was formed on February 2, 1876. Spalding and Daniel spelled the "first Italian name in baseball" differently, and they both got it wrong; the correct form is Apollonio. In *Total Baseball*'s "Owners and Officials Roster," the man Spalding identified as "N. T. Appolonio" became "Nathaniel Taylor Appolonio."[15] But his obituary in the April 7, 1911, issue of the Winchester (MA) *Star* identified him correctly as Nicholas Taylor Apollonio.

Apollonio was first elected as president of the Boston franchise in 1874, when the team was in the National Association, the forerunner of the National League. The grandson of an Italian immigrant, he served essentially a ceremonial function, presiding over the annual stockholders' meeting. The club was in fact run by Harry Wright, the legendary pitcher who had organized the Cincinnati Red Stockings in 1869 as the first openly all-professional baseball team. Apollonio served as president through 1876, the year that Boston became one of the charter members of the National League.[16]

It is ironic that the individual who was in all likelihood the first Italian American to be associated with Major League Baseball was an executive. Following Apollonio's election in 1874, many decades would pass before anyone of Italian descent would rise even to the level of coach in Major League Baseball. And it would be twenty-three years before a player with an Italian name appeared on a Major League roster. Dan Daniel's suggestion that in 1876 an Italian on a Major League diamond would have been a candidate for Barnum's freak show may have been offensive, but it was also true.

Other Pioneers

The first player of obvious Italian descent to follow Abbaticchio to the Major Leagues was Willie Garoni, a right-handed pitcher born in

Fort Lee, New Jersey, in 1887. Signed by the New York Giants, Garoni's career consisted of ten innings pitched in three games in September 1899, with no wins and one loss. The Giants offered him a $1,200 salary for the 1900 season, twice what he was paid the previous year, but for reasons lost to history he returned the contract unsigned and never returned to the Major Leagues. Instead he played for various clubs in New Jersey and worked as a sewer contractor until his death in 1914 at the age of thirty-seven.

As well known as Ed Abbaticchio was in baseball circles, Garoni's family was apparently unaware of Abbaticchio's career. In an undated letter, Garoni's daughter, Mildred, wrote to Hall of Fame historian Lee Allen: "I would like to inform you that my father was the first major league ball player with an Italian name."[17] She was wrong, but at least her father was the first Major League *pitcher* with an Italian name.

The distinction of being the first Italian American to make his Major League debut in the twentieth century, and the only one to debut in the entire first decade of the century, belongs to Lou Schiappacasse, whose name must have confounded sportswriters at least as much as did that of Abbaticchio. (He was in fact referred to as "Shippy," according to his obituary in an Ann Arbor, Michigan, newspaper.) Not that they had to worry about it for very long; the outfielder's Major League career consisted of two games for the Tigers in 1902, in which he went hitless in five times at bat. Born in 1881 in Ann Arbor to immigrant parents, Schiappacasse, like Garoni, died young, the victim of typhoid fever at the age of twenty-nine.

The Boston writer who predicted that the appearance of Ed Abbaticchio signaled the beginning of an Italian invasion of baseball need not have worried. In spite of Abbaticchio's strong performance and positive contributions to the game, his arrival was not the beginning of a trend but an isolated case. After Garoni and Schiappacasse (who together appeared in a total of five games), no player of Italian descent other than Abbaticchio would appear on a Major League roster until 1911, and only six would play in the big leagues in the teens. By the end of the twenties, two decades after Abbaticchio had ended his career, only twenty-two players identifiable as Italian Americans had played in the Major Leagues. With few exceptions, most had brief, unremarkable careers.

2

The Boys from San Francisco

Italian Americans are traditionally associated with Eastern cities, especially New York, where a large percentage of the early immigrants initially settled. Even Italian American ballplayers are likely to be thought of as New Yorkers since so many of the prominent players—such as Joe DiMaggio, Yogi Berra, Phil Rizzuto, Carl Furillo and (more recently) Mike Piazza—have played for New York teams over the years. Yet after Pennsylvania native Ed Abbaticchio ended his career in 1910, it was to be a long time before another Italian American from the East Coast would have a significant Major League career.

Ironically for many years virtually all the important Italian American Major Leaguers were to come from the San Francisco Bay Area, but they played in the East since there were no Major League teams west of St. Louis until 1958. Of the six Italian players who made their Major League debuts between 1910 and 1920, three were from San Francisco, and two of the other three were also from California (Napa and Santa Barbara).

By 1930 only one Italian American born in New York City—Harry Riconda, an infielder who played for five teams between 1923 and

1930—had made it to the Major Leagues. Even by 1940, by which time more than forty Italian Americans had appeared on Major League rosters, only four were from metropolitan New York. By that time at least sixteen players from the San Francisco Bay Area had played in the big leagues, as had at least four others from other parts of California. Several of them had long and successful big league careers, and three (Tony Lazzeri, Ernie Lombardi, and Joe DiMaggio) are in the Hall of Fame. Their journey east, to make a living playing the game that for many was the very symbol of America, was an ironic reversal of the long westward journey their parents had made from Italy a generation earlier in search of the American Dream.

Why did such an apparently unlikely place as San Francisco prove to be so fertile a breeding ground for Major Leaguers of Italian descent? At least two elements account for the city's prominent place in Italian American baseball history: a large Italian population and a strong baseball tradition that fostered, more than in large eastern cities, the development of players from that population.

The origins of baseball have always been associated with the East Coast, where the "New York Game" and the "Massachusetts Game" vied for supremacy in the mid-nineteenth century. (Ultimately it was the New York version that gained prominence, primarily because of the rules set down by the Knickerbocker Club of New York City in 1845.) But baseball made its way to the West Coast prior to the Civil War. According to baseball historian Charles Alexander, it was none other than Alexander Cartwright, the man usually identified as the principal designer of the Knickerbocker rules, who introduced the game to California. Cartwright went to California during the gold rush of 1849 but left less than two months later and spent the remainder of his life in Hawaii. According to Alexander, Cartwright and a man named Frank Turk organized the first baseball club in San

Francisco. Cartwright in fact brought Knickerbocker baseball to San Francisco before it reached Boston, Philadelphia, or Chicago.[1]

There are varying accounts as to which was the first baseball club in San Francisco and when it began, but it is clear that baseball flourished there soon after the Civil War. By 1866 several Bay Area teams had formed the Pacific Base Ball Convention. By 1867 there were about one hundred organized clubs in California, and by 1868 San Francisco had the first enclosed ballfield on the West Coast.[2]

Whatever the historical details, California became a hotbed of amateur and semi-professional baseball, particularly in San Francisco. As in other cities and towns across America, youth teams were sponsored by civic and fraternal groups, businesses, and churches. The semi-pro Pacific Base Ball League was established in 1878, and the following year the rival California League was formed in Oakland. By the mid-1880s there were two professional leagues in the state, the California League and the California State League, each with three franchises in San Francisco. The Pacific Coast League (PCL) was recognized by organized baseball in 1904 as a Class A league, at that time the highest minor league classification, and it soon became a major force in California sports. Several franchises had farm teams, enabling them to develop their own home-grown talent. For those living on or near the West Coast, the PCL was their major league.

Italians in California

At the same time that baseball was planting its roots on the West Coast, Italians were settling in California in increasing numbers. In many ways their experience differed from that of their counterparts in the East. As previously noted, the great majority of Italian immigrants after 1880 were from the impoverished southern regions of Italy, and they settled in the large cities of the East and Midwest. There they mainly found entry-level jobs in factories, on the railroads, or in public works, and they often lived in crowded tenements.

Those who made their way to California, on the other hand, were primarily from the north of Italy. During the gold rush era, between 1850 and 1870, there was a steady influx of Italian immigrants. When the promises of the gold rush went unfulfilled, many settled in northern California, finding work in agriculture and fishing. Others moved to San Francisco, where an Italian community of merchants had already been providing services to the miners. By 1890 there were more than fifteen thousand foreign-born Italians in the state, approximately one-third living in San Francisco. By 1910 the city had more than twenty-nine thousand first- and second-generation Italians.[3]

In California the early Italian immigrants found a more cosmopolitan society than their later counterparts in the East. In *The Italians of San Francisco, 1850–1930*, historian Deanna Paoli Gumina noted that "California offered immigrants a share in the process of building, molding, developing, and institutionalizing a new state that bore the stamp of Italianism. . . . Italians felt they were competing on a par with their American counterparts, with an equal chance for advancement."[4] Italians in San Francisco encountered a less hostile environment than did those in the East (in part because Chinese immigrants bore the brunt of nativist resentment) and found greater opportunity for economic and social mobility. More than in other cities, the hard-working and frugal Italians were acknowledged as solid citizens. Before the turn of the century the Italian community of San Francisco was prosperous enough to support opera and theater companies, as well as several Italian language newspapers. For those with an entrepreneurial spirit the city even offered a chance for great wealth. Following the gold rush, Domenico Ghirardelli made a fortune selling chocolate. In 1904 Amadeo Giannini, the son of immigrants, formed the Bank of Italy to serve the local Italian community. Later he provided financing for the construction of the Golden Gate Bridge and for Hollywood films. By 1930 the Bank of Italy had become the Bank of America and was soon the world's largest commercial bank. In 1931 Angelo Rossi became the first American of Italian descent to be elected mayor of a major city.

While an increasing number of southern Italians arrived after the turn of the century, San Francisco remained different from most American cities in that northern Italians continued to outnumber southerners. By the time the new immigrants arrived, earlier settlers had established a strong foothold in the local economy, controlling the garbage collection business, the produce markets, and the fishing industry. Newcomers from southern Italy—fishermen like Joe DiMaggio's father, for example—struggled at first to make inroads against the Genovesi who controlled the waterfront.

By 1920 San Francisco had the sixth largest Italian community in the United States, with twenty-four thousand immigrants and another twenty-two thousand American born; there were more than eighty thousand in California as a whole. Italians accounted for 16 percent of the city's foreign-born population; only New York City had a higher percentage. Italians in San Francisco were also less segregated than in other cities, though the heaviest concentration lived in the North Beach area, not far from Fisherman's Wharf.[5] While North Beach was a low-rent neighborhood, it was a far cry from the squalid tenement districts that so many immigrants occupied in the large urban centers of the East. Even for struggling newcomers, the American experience in San Francisco was generally less oppressive than it was for so many Italians elsewhere.

Baseball in San Francisco

In *City Games: The Evolution of American Urban Society and the Rise of Sports*, historian Steven Riess concluded that the primary reason why so few children of East and South European immigrants played professional baseball in the first three decades of the century was the lack of facilities in the inner cities of the East and Midwest where they lived. It was difficult to acquire the experience and skills needed to play at the professional level by just playing in streets and alleys.[6] Unlike those crowded inner cities, San Francisco had numerous playgrounds where boys could play baseball. The availability of such facilities, together with a relatively mild climate, undoubtedly contributed to the development of baseball talent among young Italian Americans. One of the city's playgrounds sat right in the middle of the Italian quarter of San Francisco. It was at the North Beach Playground (now called the Joe DiMaggio Playground) that many of the Italian American children who later became professional ballplayers first learned to play the game. There they played on blacktop. Nearby, however, on the western edge of North Beach, was Funston Playground, another training ground for young Italian American ballplayers, but one that had two authentic baseball diamonds.

For the Italian American kids in the North Beach neighborhood, playing ball was their primary form of recreation. Dario Lodigiani, who grew up a few blocks from the DiMaggio family and played in the Major Leagues for six years beginning in 1938, was one of those kids. He played on the local playgrounds with both Joe and Dom DiMaggio. "Things were kind of tough," he told me. "We played a lot of ball. There was nothing else to do. A lot of us couldn't afford the price of going to different places, so we stuck around Funston Playground, North Beach Playground, and the different playgrounds around San Francisco. Of course, the Italian ballplayers came out of mostly Italian neighborhoods, like all of North Beach and the Marina. At that time we were just a bunch of friends playing, not knowing that we were going to have one of the most famous players of all time [DiMaggio] playing with us."[7]

Lodigiani recalled the amateur baseball scene in San Francisco in the 1920s and '30s. "No matter what park you went to, there was a ballgame going on. There was always some place to play. On Sunday, they started at eight in the morning, then ten, twelve, two, and four. If you showed any kind of ability, you always had a place to play. San Francisco had the best semi-pro programs in the country."

Well aware that he was part of the Italian American baseball tradition of San Francisco, Lodigiani could name all the local players who made it to the big leagues, as well as those who never got beyond the PCL. But as a kid playing at the North Beach Playground, he never dreamed that he or any of his friends would become big league players. "The Coast League was really the big thing out here when we were kids," he said. "We never thought of New York, Philadelphia, Chicago, or anything."

Most of the Italian American ballplayers from California who did make it to one of the big league cities played in the PCL on their way up. The vitality of the minor leagues in California was possible because of the rich pool of talent that was nourished first on the local sandlots and then in the amateur and semi-pro leagues that flourished in California, nowhere more so than in the San Francisco area. In fact, in the first three decades of the twentieth century, several players who got their start on San Francisco Bay Area sandlots made it to the big leagues, including such notables as Harry Heilmann, Lefty O'Doul, Joe Cronin, and Lefty Gomez.

In his 1994 history of professional baseball in San Francisco, *Nuggets on the Diamond*, Dick Dobbins, who grew up in Oakland, confirmed Lodigiani's assessment of the local amateur baseball scene. "The early phenomenon of sandlot baseball—a term that originated in San Francisco—became an institution here," he wrote. Dobbins, in fact, was convinced that as children playing on those sandlots, he and his buddies "were growing up in the richest baseball center in the world. The game may have been 'invented' in upstate New York and played professionally for the first time in Ohio, but the true heart of American baseball is right here in the Bay Area."[8]

The availability of playing facilities, the large number of amateur teams and leagues, and a moderate climate enabling year-round play were all factors that contributed to a high level of competition that in turn enabled young players to hone their skills. Only the most talented and dedicated players could succeed as they grew into their teens and faced stiffer competition from the best players in the Bay Area. At the same time, the increase in the number of organized teams at the amateur level made it more likely that outstanding players would be seen and recommended by local scouts. And the increase in the number of minor leagues after the turn of the century (including the PCL) meant that there were more opportunities for young men to make a living playing the game. It was because of that baseball-rich environment that San Francisco, and not New York, Philadelphia, or Chicago, produced the preponderance of early Italian American Major Leaguers.[9]

Still the chances for an Italian American kid to play at the professional level remained slim. Another San Francisco native, Dolph Camilli, made it to the Majors before Lodigiani (in 1933), but he too had thought it was an impossible dream. "When I was a kid I suppose I hoped to be a ballplayer," he said, "but I thought it was too far out of reach. I mean pro ballplayers were men."[10] And since when Camilli was still playing sandlot ball so few of those men had Italian names, there wasn't much encouragement for him to follow his dream. Indeed there weren't many San Francisco boys who had made it to the big leagues before Camilli, but there were a few.

Ping Bodie

The first San Francisco native of Italian descent to make his way from the sandlots to the Major Leagues was also the first Italian American after Ed Abbaticchio to have a notable big league career. He would also prove to be one of the most colorful characters in baseball history, but fans would not have known from his name alone that he had a drop of Italian blood in his veins. He played his entire professional career as Ping Bodie, but he was born Francesco Pezzolo.

Francesco's parents, Giuseppe and Rosa, had emigrated in the early 1870s from a small town near Genoa to New York City, where Giuseppe worked on the construction of the Brooklyn Bridge. By 1876 the family had moved to Bodie, California, a booming and lawless gold-mining settlement that is now a ghost town near the Nevada border. In the early 1880s they moved to what was then known as the Cow Hollow district of San Francisco and opened a grocery store. It was there that Francesco, one of five brothers, was born on October 8, 1887.

In September 1908 Francesco (now playing under the name of Ping Bodie) was signed by the San Francisco Seals of the Pacific Coast League. After modest success in his first two seasons, Bodie made the front pages when, in 1910, he hit the then remarkable total of thirty home runs, setting the PCL record. The following year he made his Major League debut with the Chicago White Sox, initially playing only in a reserve role. Unhappy about sitting on the bench, Bodie, who was never shy, went to see Charles Comiskey after reading that the club owner was displeased with the team's lack of hitting. Bodie boldly promised Comiskey that if he put him in the starting lineup, "I'll show you some hitting of the old apple."[11] Comiskey ordered Manager Jimmy Callahan to play the rookie, and Bodie went on to hit .289 and finish fourth in the American League with ninety-seven runs batted in (RBIs). The slugging outfielder hit only four homers, but that year Frank "Home Run" Baker led the league with the majestic total of eleven.

The 1912 *Spalding Guide*, commenting on young players who had done well in the previous season, provided colorful commentary on Ping's rookie year. Bodie, it said, "made both place and name for himself although he found the concrete walls of most American League parks too hard and too far away to be deeply dented by the war club that damaged so much timber on the Pacific Coast."[12] In fact, in nine seasons in the Major Leagues, Bodie hit a total of forty-three home runs, with a career-high of eight in 1913. In the dead-ball era those were respectable numbers, and in two of his nine seasons (1913 and 1917) Bodie finished third in the league in homers.

One White Sox fan who was impressed by Bodie was Chicago-born novelist James T. Farrell, the author of the Studs Lonigan trilogy. In his 1957 book *My Baseball Diary*, he recalled going to see the White Sox play in 1911, when Bodie was a rookie and Farrell was not yet ten years old. The "burly, barrel-built player" became one of his first heroes. "I talked of Ping Bodie more than I did of any other player," he wrote, "and in my neighborhood I acquired the nickname of 'Young Ping.'"[13]

After Bodie's average plummeted to .229 in 1914, he found himself back with the Seals in 1915, then returned to the Majors in 1917, this time with Connie Mack's Philadelphia Athletics. Impressed by his performance that year (.291 average, seventy-four RBIs, seven home

runs [only two fewer than the nine hit by league-leader Wally Pipp]),
the Yankees bought Bodie from Connie Mack, who was cleaning house
in one of his cost-cutting campaigns. The New York press heralded
the arrival of Bodie, who by then had established a reputation as
both a hard-hitting outfielder and a colorful character.

The *Sporting News*, adopting Bodie's own jargon, commented on
March 18, 1918 that "Bodie may not be a Speaker or a Cobb, but he
can hammer the old apple." Bodie was indeed no Speaker or Cobb
in the field. With his squat body—he stood at five-foot-eight and
weighed 195 pounds—Bodie was no sleek ballhawk. Dario Lodigiani
said that Bodie was "built like a six-footer somebody dropped a
safe on."[14]

Bodie was variously described in the press as stout, rotund, and
even roly poly; one writer called him "one of New York's most famous
spaghetti destroyers."[15] In the April 6, 1919, issue of the *New York
Tribune*, W. O. McGeehan wrote a tongue-in-cheek story describing
a contest reputedly sponsored by the Jacksonville, Florida, Chamber
of Commerce "for the heavyweight eating championship of the world
between Percy the Ostrich and Ping Bodie." According to McGeehan,
Bodie won the title in eleven rounds, when Percy, unable to eat any
more spaghetti, dropped to his knees. Bodie relinquished his unofficial title as the Yankees' biggest eater when Ruth joined the team in
1921. "Anybody who eats three pounds of steak and a bottle of chili
sauce for a starter has got me," he admitted.[16] Not surprisingly, given
his ample physique, Bodie was not the swiftest of base runners. His
lack of speed led to one of the more memorable lines in baseball lore.
Following a failed stolen base attempt, sportswriter Bugs Baer wrote,
"Ping had larceny in his heart, but his feet were honest."[17]

When it was announced in January 1920 that Babe Ruth had been
sold to the Yankees, Bodie reportedly said, "I suppose this means I'll

3. Ping Bodie with Yankee teammate Babe Ruth, 1920. Transcendental Graphics.

be sent to China."[18] But 1920 proved to be his best year with New York; he hit .295 and drove in seventy-nine runs, and his slugging average of .446 was second among Yankee players, trailing only Ruth's astronomical .847, the highest of his career. Bodie, who roomed with Ruth in the Babe's first year with the Yankees, will forever be linked with the Babe because of one of the most frequently quoted lines in baseball literature. When a reporter asked Bodie what it was like to room with the freewheeling Ruth, who rarely spent time in his hotel room when on the road, he replied, "I don't room with him, I room with his suitcase."[19] When Bodie was traded to the Red Sox in August 1921, rather than report to Boston, he went home and spent the next seven seasons playing minor league ball in the Pacific Coast, Western, and Texas Leagues. In 1928, at the age of forty-one, he finished his career by hitting .348 while playing for the two San Francisco franchises in the PCL, the Seals and the Missions. Following his retirement from baseball, he worked for thirty-two years as an electrician on Hollywood movie sets. Bodie died in 1961, one year after retiring at the age of seventy-three.

Though obviously not in the same league as the Babe on or off the field, Ping Bodie was quite a celebrity in his own right. His *Sporting News* obituary called him "one of the most colorful characters the game ever produced." Bodie was well aware of his popularity with fans, even when he played for Connie Mack in Philadelphia. When Mack asked him to take a pay cut before the 1918 season, Bodie was reported as saying, "Now I ain't bragging or anything like that, but I got to admit I'm the only real ball player Connie's got. I and the Liberty Bell are the only attractions left in Philadelphia."[20]

Long before Yogi Berra and Phil Rizzuto came along, Bodie was well known for his colorful approach to the English language and has even been credited with adding some new terms to the baseball lexicon. The ball was not only an apple but a "stitched apricot" and a "spheroid"; he didn't just hit the ball, he "whaled the onion." A home run was a "four-ply swat." And when someone asked Bodie, then in his seventies, if he thought he could still hit, he replied, "Give me a mace and I'll drive the pumpkin down Whitey Ford's throat."[21]

Bodie has even achieved a quirky place in literary history. He was reportedly a major inspiration for Jack Keefe, the protagonist of Ring Lardner's classic book of fictional letters, *You Know Me Al.* (Lardner was a Chicago sportswriter when Bodie played for the White Sox.) Keefe, a brash, eccentric ballplayer who chronicles his big league experiences in letters to a hometown friend, is a semi-literate pitcher who is part bombastic soldier from Roman comedy and part country bumpkin out of Mark Twain.

What's In a Name?

Names like Abbaticchio and Schiappacasse may have baffled sports-writers, but Ping Bodie's name presents more of a dilemma than those of his predecessors because of both its disputed origins and the variety of versions that have appeared in print. The Bodie name riddle is unusual in that both his first and last names were assumed. And not only did Bodie abandon his Italian name, but there is also disagreement as to the origin of his pseudonym and his actual birth name.

How did Francesco Pezzolo become Ping Bodie? In the *Sporting News* obituary, he was quoted as saying that the nickname was given to him when he was two years old by a family friend who was also called "Ping." Another, more commonly cited, version was that "Ping" came from the sound that his bat made when it hit the ball. Whether or not Bodie himself was the source of this version, he apparently never refuted it.[22] The origin of the adopted surname, on the other hand, would seem to be more obvious since Bodie was the name of the mining town where the family had lived before moving to San Francisco. According to Joseph Pezzolo, the son of Ping's brother Jack, when Ping and his brothers played ball on the sandlots of San Francisco, the other players, who had trouble pronouncing Italian names, would call them "the kids from Bodie."[23]

The oddities regarding Bodie's birth name are more baffling. Amazingly there seems to have been confusion about the family name within the family itself. In a letter published in the February 4, 1912, issue of *Sporting Life* (a weekly publication devoted to baseball and trap shooting), Bodie's own brother Dave wrote, "Frank's correct name in our language (Italian) is Franceto Sanguenitta Pizzola; he took the name of Bodie from our uncle—my mother's brother—when he started to play ball because he thought all the fans would josh him." When informed of the letter, which he had never seen, Bodie's nephew Joseph expressed doubt as to its authenticity. "That letter doesn't sound like it came from anybody in the family," he said. "I am stunned that Uncle Dave would write a letter with so much misinformation. I really doubt that he would have written that letter." Regardless of the authenticity or accuracy of the letter, the *Sporting Life* version of Bodie's name has survived over the years as one of many variations seen in print.

What is clear amid all the confusion over Bodie's name is the reason he chose to change it: "He thought all the fans would josh him." Realizing that his name branded him as an outsider, he chose to mask his ethnic identity so as to appear less foreign and more American. The bias against "odd" names was so blatant that in the May 12, 1918, issue of the *New York Tribune* reporter Wood Ballard could write of Bodie, "Ping needs a stage name. Pezzolo wouldn't look well in a box score." Little wonder that Bodie, like many other immigrants and their children, thought it necessary to assume a new, more acceptable identity.

Given all these versions, what is the proper form of Bodie's birth name? Joseph Pezzolo referred to a notebook kept by Ping's mother in which she had written the given names, in Italian, of her surviving children. The last-born son is listed as Francesco Stefano. As for the family surname, Pezzolo cited a mortgage his grandparents had taken with the Hibernia Savings and Loan Society in San Francisco in June 1896. It lists their names as Joseph and Rose Pezzolo. (Giuseppe and Rosa had obviously chosen to Americanize their first names.) And on Ping's death certificate, which gives his name as Frank S. Bodie, his father's name is listed as Joseph Pezzolo. Ping Bodie, then, was born Francesco Stefano Pezzolo, the only form possible in standard Italian.

Of the five Pezzolo brothers only Ping and Dave kept Bodie as their legal name. Their father was never pleased that his sons abandoned the family name, so much so that he kept them out of his will. According to Joseph Pezzolo, his grandfather said of Ping and Dave, "If my name isn't good enough for them, neither is my money."

It is ironic that the first of what was to be a large number of Italian American players to have an impact in New York, with its huge Italian population, played under an assumed name. To add to the irony, even though Ping Bodie abandoned his family name, he was proud to think of himself (mistakenly) as the first Italian to play in the big leagues. In the *Sporting News* obituary, Bodie is quoted as acknowledging that his father had been angry about the name change "because I became a national figure and the first player of Italian descent to reach the majors." Bodie's claim is particularly curious since his Major League career began in 1911, only one year after Ed Abbaticchio's ended. He was either ignorant of, or chose to ignore, Abbaticchio's role as a pioneer. Or perhaps Bodie simply didn't recognize other players as Italians from their names. When Babe Pinelli, who was playing for Detroit, asked Bodie, "What's the idea of claiming you're the only Italian ballplayer in the big leagues?," Bodie replied, "I am." At which point Pinelli said, "What do you think I am, a Chinaman?"[24]

Though his claim of being first was inaccurate, Bodie was no less a pioneer than Ed Abbaticchio. He was the first Italian American ballplayer from the West Coast to gain national attention, and he was the first to break into the big show out East. In that way he opened the door for the many others from San Francisco and other parts of California who would make a living playing baseball, either in the Major Leagues or in the Pacific Coast League.

Babe Pinelli

Babe Pinelli was not the first San Francisco native to follow Ping Bodie to the Major Leagues. That distinction belongs to Joe Giannini, a shortstop who appeared in exactly one game for the Boston Red Sox on August 7, 1911, the same year Bodie broke into the Majors. Giannini hit a double in his two times at bat, compiling a "lifetime" average of .500. Pinelli, who made his debut seven years later, had a somewhat longer and more distinguished career.

Unlike Bodie, Pinelli did not play under a pseudonym, but he did abbreviate his birth name. Born Rinaldo Angelo Paolinelli, he became Ralph Pinelli in order to accommodate the media bias of his time. "I shortened it to Pinelli when I began to play ball and my name began to appear in box scores," he explained in his autobiography, *Mr. Ump.* "Pinelli was easier for sports writers."[25] The nickname of Babe was given to him by friends of his older brother because, they said, he cried like a baby when his brother wouldn't let him tag along.

Pinelli was born on October 18, 1895, the son of immigrants from Lucca, in Tuscany. He was ten years old when his father, who ran a fruit and vegetable store on Fillmore Street, was crushed by a telephone pole during the 1906 earthquake. His mother had to sell the store, then work for twenty-five cents an hour cleaning houses. In order to help her support the family (two brothers and a sister), Pinelli left school and worked at various jobs. He also earned a reputation as a tough kid on the streets, where he fought to get a good corner on which to sell newspapers or just to fight. He had, in his words, "firecrackers in my blood."[26]

Pinelli had a few bouts as an amateur fighter, but more than anything he loved to play baseball. "The baseball bug had bitten me early," he wrote, "as in those days it seemed to bite many San Francisco boys."[27] At Hamilton Park he came under the tutelage of the legendary Spike Hennessy, a baseball coach who taught San Francisco boys the fundamentals of the game, offered guidance, and tipped off scouts about promising prospects.

In 1917 Pinelli began his professional career playing third base for Portland in the Pacific Coast League. Except for a brief stay with the White Sox near the end of the 1918 season, he was in the PCL through 1919, spent one year with the Tigers in 1920, then returned to the PCL. After hitting .339 with fifty stolen bases for the Oakland Oaks in 1921, he was signed by Cincinnati, where he had the unenviable task of replacing third baseman Heinie Groh, a favorite of the city's large German fan base. But Pinelli himself had support in Cincinnati from the local Italian population, which formed the Pinelli Rooters Club, whose slogan was "Viva Pinelli." The local Italian language newspaper, *La Falce*, also expressed its support for the Reds in general and for Pinelli in particular. On April 12, 1924, the paper ran an announcement of the upcoming opening day and concluded, "The

4. Babe Pinelli in the uniform of the San Francisco Seals of the Pacific Coast League, 1928. California Historical Society, FN-32101.

Pinelli Rooters Club will be in attendance to encourage and welcome our dear friend Babe Pinelli and all the players of the Cincinnati Base Ball Club" (my translation).[28]

The starting third baseman for the next four years, Pinelli became the first Italian American ballplayer to receive consideration for what was then the equivalent of the Most Valuable Player Award in 1924, finishing thirteenth in the league after hitting .306 with seventy RBIs. Pinelli's eight-year Major League career came to an end in the middle of the 1927 season when the Reds released him and sent him to the San Francisco Seals of the Pacific Coast League.

Throughout his career Pinelli struggled with the "firecrackers" in his blood. He stood five-foot-nine and weighed 165 pounds, but he was a fiery player who on occasion fought with teammates as well as opposing players. Dolf Luque, a teammate with the Reds, was a star pitcher from Cuba with a temper at least the equal of Pinelli's. In one clubhouse encounter, he challenged Pinelli to a duel, saying, "We get two taxicabs. You get in one, I get in one. We get guns. We go away. We fight duel."[29] One of Pinelli's fights was with Bob Smith, a reserve infielder for the Boston Braves who taunted him from the dugout, calling him a "dago." That was not the only time Pinelli heard that epithet. "From 1922 to 1925 I was the only Italian in the National League," he wrote. "I'd taken a riding from the bench jockeys and I'd had to keep my fist cocked."[30]

Media references to Pinelli's Italian heritage were common and at times stereotypical. But in 1926 F. C. Lane took a different approach in a story entitled "'Babe' Pinelli, a Colorful Descendant of the Ancient Romans." Lane waxed poetic in his portrayal, describing the ballplayer as "this product of Old Rome transplanted to the fertile soil of a New World." Pinelli, he wrote, was "the only Italian of prominence in the Major Leagues, and though from an ancient race, with many brilliant heritages from the past, speaks to a new order as exemplified in the vast fabric of a modern sport."[31] Such references to the cultural heritage of Italy were uncommon in stories about Italian Americans players, who were typically identified as "sons of sunny Italy" and frequently characterized as "fiery" and "colorful." Even when Pinelli became a Major League umpire, the ethnic characterization continued. In a 1934 article announcing his hiring, the *Sporting News* reported that "he is a genial, likable fellow with innumerable friends, but he always was a hot-tempered, cocky young fellow whose Latin blood boiled over easily."[32]

When, near the end of his playing days in the Major Leagues, Pinelli thought about becoming an umpire, he consulted Bill Klem about his future plans; the legendary umpire had one piece of advice: "Get rid of that chip on your shoulder."[33] In 1933, the year after he ended his playing career, Pinelli got the chance to prove he could heed Klem's advice when he was hired by the Pacific Coast League, thus beginning "the transition from fiery player to self-controlled umpire."[34] After two seasons in the PCL Pinelli became the first Italian American umpire in Major League history when he was hired by the National League prior to the start of the 1935 season. He would remain in the big leagues for the next twenty-two years.

Pinelli's ability to control his temper was tested early and often in the Majors. One of the testers in his first year was none other than Babe Ruth, who was winding up his career with the Boston Braves. Pinelli recalled that when Ruth came to bat in the first inning, he greeted the umpire with the same "Hi ya, Wop" salutation he had used when they had played against each other in the American League. "As I was the only Italian in the American League at the time," wrote Pinelli, "'Wop' seemed to him appropriately distinguishing." When

Pinelli called him out on strikes in his first at bat, Ruth came at the rookie ump. "He bulged with wrath. He started with 'Wop' and called me everything."[35] But Pinelli, who had been so volatile as a player, simply walked away. On another occasion, when Pinelli called Ruth out on strikes, the Bambino turned and said, "There's 40,000 people here who know that last one was a ball, tomato head." Pinelli replied, "Maybe so, but mine is the only opinion that counts."[36]

Pinelli went on to have a distinguished career as an umpire, winning the respect of players and managers with his even-handed, and even-tempered, demeanor. So cautious was he in ejecting people from games that he earned the nickname of "the Soft Thumb." Over a span of twenty-two years and some 3,400 games Pinelli never missed a single umpiring assignment. His career ended in historic fashion when, in his very last appearance as a home plate umpire, he called Don Larsen's perfect game in the fifth game of the 1956 World Series. Following his retirement, Pinelli settled in Sonoma County, California, and worked as a scout for the Cincinnati Reds. He died on October 22, 1984, at the age of eighty-nine.

The playgrounds of San Francisco produced many other players of Italian descent who would enjoy lengthy big league careers that began in the twenties and thirties. In addition to future Hall of Famers Tony Lazzeri, Ernie Lombardi, and Joe DiMaggio, there were Vince and Dom DiMaggio, Frank Crosetti, Dolph Camilli, Cookie Lavagetto and Dario Lodigiani. But it was Bodie and Pinelli, who made their debuts in 1911 and 1918 respectively, who paved the way for all others who would make the journey east, from the Pacific Coast League to the Major Leagues. If Bodie was the first Italian American Major Leaguer to capture public attention, it was Pinelli who had the greater long-term impact. By becoming the first Italian to reach the prominent position of a Major League umpire and performing with dignity and skill for more than two decades, he gained the respect of everyone connected to the game and projected a positive image of his ethnic heritage.

3

Where Are the Italians?

O! greata game ees basaball
For yo'nga 'Merican.
But, O! my frand, ees not at all
Da theeng for Dagoman.

—T. A. Daly, "Da Greata Basaball"

In the years following World War I, as urban Americans adapted to a more regimented lifestyle in an increasingly industrialized society, their appetite for diversion and entertainment increased. In the exuberant era of the Jazz Age, with more money and more free time to spend it, the American public developed a passion for sports that has never abated. Grantland Rice, among others, would call it the golden age of sport. One event that may be said to have ushered in this golden age symbolized both the prosperity of the period and the increasing popularity of sports. On July 2, 1921, more than 80,000 fans paid $1.8 million to watch the heavyweight title fight between Jack Dempsey and Georges Carpentier in Jersey City, creating the first million-dollar gate. Six years later the public passion for spectacle reached a new high when 145,000 people paid $2.6 million to watch Dempsey fight Gene Tunney in Chicago.

The new enthusiasm for sports was both reported and fostered by rapidly expanding newspaper coverage, and the exploits of the superstar athletes were chronicled, and heightened, by a generation of sportswriters who themselves became legendary figures. Writers such as Damon Runyon, Ring Lardner, Heywood Broun, Paul Gallico, and Rice reflected the excitement of the period in their accounts of the great athletes. Some were swept up in the youthful enthusiasm of the Jazz Age and glorified the stars in prose that embellished athletic prowess to mythic heights. It was Rice, after all, who elevated the 1924 Notre Dame backfield to biblical proportions by christening it "the Four Horsemen." In the words of historian Frederick Lewis Allen, it was a time "when pockets were full and the art of ballyhoo was young and vigorous."[1]

Regardless of their level of enthusiasm or restraint, these and other writers managed to create an impressive array of legendary heroes who in their own right redefined their respective sports and raised them to unprecedented levels of popularity and acclaim. This was the era of Dempsey, Red Grange, Bobby Jones, Bill Tilden, and, towering over all of them, the incomparable Babe Ruth. The perfect icon for an age of consumption, Ruth transformed baseball forever while resurrecting it from its darkest days of the Black Sox scandal. While college football, boxing, and horse racing became big draws, baseball remained the undisputed national pastime.

In the celebrity-hungry atmosphere of the twenties, athletes were not the only lionized figures. In 1927, four months before Babe Ruth hit his sixtieth homer, Charles Lindbergh crossed the Atlantic and became an international icon. The film industry created movie idols such as John Barrymore, Douglas Fairbanks, Mary Pickford, and Charlie Chaplin.

While Italian Americans as a whole were not exactly equal-opportunity participants in this phenomenon, a few individuals did achieve celebrity status, though not always for the most desirable reasons. Prior to the twenties, the Italian name best known in the United States was that of Neapolitan opera star Enrico Caruso. Between his debut in 1903 and his final performance in 1920, Caruso, acclaimed as the greatest singer of his time, was the primary attraction at the Metropolitan Opera in New York. (In his biography of Babe Ruth, Robert Creamer notes that the caption of a photo of Caruso in the *New York Times* called the singer "the Babe Ruth of operatic tenors.")[2]

Prior to the 1920s no American of Italian descent had achieved national fame. That changed with the controversial trial of Nicola Sacco and Bartolomeo Vanzetti, the Italian immigrants charged with the murders of two men during a robbery at a shoe factory in South Braintree, Massachusetts, in April 1920. In what was probably the most politically charged homicide case in American history, the two were convicted after a six-week trial in 1921 and sentenced to death. The trial took place in the midst of the patriotic fervor lingering from World War I and the "Red Scare" that followed the Russian Revolution, all of which contributed to renewed hostility toward European immigrants. That hostility became the law of the land in 1924, when the National Origins Act was passed, severely restricting immigration from Southern and Eastern Europe by setting an annual quota of 2 percent of a given nationality based on the 1890 census. Within that context the political activities of both Sacco and Vanzetti—Sacco, a worker in a shoe factory, was a socialist supporter of the labor movement, and Vanzetti, a fish peddler, was an outspoken anarchist—made them all the more suspect at a time when such activism was seen as a threat to American democracy. In spite of limited evidence and conflicting testimony, they were found guilty and sentenced to die. After six years of fruitless appeals for a new trial, Sacco and Vanzetti, who proclaimed their innocence to the very end, were electrocuted on August 23, 1927. Their execution, which triggered protests in North and South America and Europe, served as a vivid reminder of the high level of animosity within the United States toward immigrants in general and Italian Americans in particular.

The other Italian American to achieve nationwide notoriety in the 1920s was Al Capone, the most famous of the Prohibition-era gangsters. Born in Brooklyn, Capone took control of the bootlegging industry of Chicago after moving there in 1920 and created an intricate and profitable syndicate. While his crime organization employed members of many different ethnic groups, it was the flamboyant Capone who became one of the most famous personalities in America.

Meanwhile, a much different Italian American image swept across the country on its movie screens. Rodolfo di Valentina d'Antonguolla had emigrated from his native Italy in 1913 at the age of eighteen. After working as a professional dancer, he went on to Hollywood, where, as Rudolph Valentino, he became a national phenomenon with the release in 1921 of *The Sheik*. His performance as a smoldering lover set the standard and the stereotype for all Latin lovers to follow and made him the most celebrated sex symbol of the era. He went on to star in several other films until his career was cut short by his untimely death, due to peritonitis, in 1926 at the age of thirty-one. His early death, which was mourned nationwide—more than one hundred thousand fans lined up in New York City to view his body in state—made him an instant screen legend.

In the midst of the glamour and hype of the twenties, the few other Italian Americans who achieved celebrity status were athletes. But until the appearance of Tony Lazzeri in 1926, they were not baseball players. Italian Americans found it much easier to find their way into professional boxing, the preferred sport of those at the bottom of the socioeconomic ladder who saw little other hope for success. The development of prize fighters was an almost inevitable consequence of life in the ethnic enclaves of big cities, where kids learned to fight to protect neighborhood turf in interethnic gang disputes or to secure a good corner on which to sell newspapers. Street fighters discovered that if they trained, they could make money with their fists. For those who had the discipline to learn the craft of the "sweet science," it was a relatively short road from the mean streets to the professional ring.

As in other areas of American life, the pattern of ethnic succession applied in prize fighting. Irish fighters had dominated professional boxing since the late nineteenth century, but by 1920 hungry newcomers, especially second-generation South and East Europeans, were providing increased competition. Boxing promoters, anxious to exploit the ethnic rivalries prevalent in large cities, often recruited street fighters from low-income, heavily populated ethnic neighborhoods, then set up bouts in which Irish, Italian, and Jewish fighters were pitted against each other. In 1924 Frederick G. Lieb, who was president of the Baseball Writers' Association at the time, wrote an article entitled "The Italian in Sport" for *The Ring* magazine, the unofficial bible of boxing. "The fight game has proved especially attractive to our young Italians," he wrote, "with the result that today the Italians and Hebrews have almost dislodged the Irish as the most powerful race in the ring."[3]

During the twenties no fewer than ten Italian Americans held world titles, though their ethnicity was not always obvious from their ring names. Whether to escape discrimination, to adopt Irish or Jewish names that may have had more box office appeal, to hide their activities from disapproving parents, or simply to adopt "easier" names, fighters changed their identities even more frequently than did baseball players. Italian Americans in the twenties fought under such names as Bogash, Conley, Corbett, Graham, Kelly, and Sullivan. Fireman Jim Flynn, the only fighter ever to knock out Jack Dempsey—he dropped him in the first round in a 1917 bout in Utah—was born Andrew Chiariglione.

The first Italian to hold a title was Peter Gulotta, who fought under the name of Pete Herman, the bantamweight champion from 1917 to 1920. Johnny Dundee, born in Sciacca, Sicily, as Giuseppe Corrara and known as "the Scotch Wop," held both the junior lightweight and featherweight titles between 1921 and 1924. Salvatore Mandala, fighting under the name of Sammy Mandell to appeal to Jewish fans, became lightweight champion in 1926, when he beat veteran Rocky Kansas (real name: Rocco Tozzo), then held the title until 1930.

Since most Italian American fighters were in the lighter weight classes, they did not receive the same level of acclaim and adulation that was primarily reserved for heavyweights like Dempsey and Tunney. One of the best-known Italian American fighters of the era, however, was one who did not change his name. Tony Canzoneri defeated an aging Johnny Dundee in 1927, at the age of nineteen, to win the featherweight title. In 1930 he won the lightweight title and in 1931 the junior welterweight title to become a champion in three weight classes. Considered one of the best lightweights ever, Canzoneri was also one of the most popular fighters of his time.

No matter how many world champions came from the ranks of Italian Americans in the twenties, no fighter became *the* hero who would enhance the public image of Italian Americans. Although boxing had become enormously popular, for the general public it remained suspect; its association with the harsh life of the ethnic ghetto, as well as with gamblers and mobsters, made it somewhat less than a wholesome, all-American sport. Moreover, no Italian took the ultimate crown, the heavyweight championship. That wouldn't happen until Primo Carnera won the title in 1933, and that proved to be an embarrassment when Mussolini's hero turned out to be a palooka whose fights, it was alleged, had been fixed.[4] No Italian American would win the title until 1952, when Rocky Marciano, who turned to boxing after a failed tryout with the Chicago Cubs, defeated Jersey Joe Walcott. In other words, no Italian American sports figure in the first half of the 1920s achieved the same level of public adulation as Valentino or the notoriety of Sacco, Vanzetti, and Capone.

If the prominence of Italian Americans in boxing in the 1920s is understandable from a socioeconomic point of view, it is less obvious why so few baseball players made it to the Major Leagues during the golden age of sport. Only sixteen players identifiable as Italian Americans, including Babe Pinelli and Ping Bodie (whose career ended in 1921), appeared in the Major Leagues in the entire decade of the twenties.

Of the twelve players who made their debuts in the twenties, four barely stayed long enough for a cup of espresso. Jess Cortazzo, an outfielder, appeared in one game for the White Sox in 1923. Paddy Smith, who was of Irish and Italian descent, played in two games for the Boston Red Sox in 1920. Al Pierotti pitched in a total of eight games for the Boston Braves in 1920–21, and Joe Mellana appeared in four games as an infielder with the Philadelphia Athletics in 1927. Two others managed to hang on a little longer. Patrick Simoni, who played under the name of Pat Simmons, had a record of 0-2 while appearing in thirty-three games for the Red Sox in 1928–29, and Joe

Martina went 6-8 pitching for the Washington Senators in 1924.

Certainly baseball players were no less hungry than boxers; virtually all of those who did make it to the Majors in the first three decades of the twentieth century came from the same economic environment as did the fighters. But whereas Italian Americans entering the ranks of professional boxing faced competition primarily from Irish and (to a lesser extent) Jewish fighters, those interested in playing baseball encountered a much wider range of competitors. In the first decade of the century baseball attendance increased by 70 percent. The game's growing popularity and consequent financial success made it more attractive as a means of making a comfortable living. As historian Steven Riess noted, baseball, with its "intrinsic and extrinsic rewards," appealed to men in all social classes, but boxing drew primarily from those "at the nadir of the social ladder."[5]

While the competition may have been stiffer in baseball at the professional level, there is no question that Italian American boys had opportunities to play baseball at the amateur level, even at a young age. By the late nineteenth century, there were town teams in every part of the country. After the turn of the century, when social reformers made a concerted effort to provide recreational activities for children, there were more opportunities to play baseball even for children living in the ethnic enclaves of large cities. The reformers built playgrounds and advocated participation in organized sports both as a deterrent to juvenile delinquency and as a means of acculturating children to American ideals and mores. By 1906 there were playground programs in forty-one cities. Spurred in part by the Progressive movement, which sought to counter the negative effects of urban life and instill middle-class values in the children of European immigrants, fraternal, civic, and church groups, as well as businesses, sponsored youth baseball teams and organized leagues, and the number of public and parochial high schools offering baseball programs increased greatly.[6]

Like the children of other immigrant groups, second-generation Italian Americans took quickly to the national pastime. As one contemporary observer noted in 1906, "The children [of Italian immigrants] almost immediately become Americans. The boy takes no interest in 'Boccie.'... Like any other American boy, he plays marbles, and when there is no policeman about, baseball."[7]

The fascination with baseball among Italian Americans, as both spectators and players, was noted in the 1912 edition of *Spalding's Official Base Ball Guide*: "One of the most noticeable characteristics of the game in the last two years is the avidity with which many of the Italian race have entered into the game. Although there is no Base Ball in Italy, the younger Italians who come to the United States are quick to grasp its fine points."[8]

The scarcity of Italians in the Major Leagues cannot be satisfactorily explained, therefore, by a lack of interest in the game. And while the majority of Italians did settle initially in the larger Eastern cities, Italians soon lived in virtually every part of the United States. From early in the century, sandlot and amateur teams made up primarily if not exclusively of Italian Americans could be found in towns across the country.

With such widespread participation in baseball, why did so few Italian Americans make it to the big leagues? The reasons appear to be many. As noted in chapter 2, Steven Riess, in *City Games*, concluded that the main factor was the lack of playing space in the crowded inner cities, making it difficult for second-generation youth to acquire the skills and experience needed to make it as professionals. While this offers a plausible argument why the inner cities did not produce Italian American Major Leaguers, it does not explain why there were almost none from anywhere else since we know that Italian American boys were playing baseball, as was virtually everyone else, wherever they lived. It is not clear that Italian American boys in rural or smaller urban areas had any less opportunity to develop their skills, at least at the amateur level, than other American youth.

Generational Conflict

Implicit in the movement to teach the children of South and East European immigrants how to behave as Americans was the need to reject the "foreign" customs of their parents.[9] One example of the consequences of the Americanization effort at the turn of the century can be seen in the rules posted in the North Bennet Street Boys' Club in Boston, which catered primarily to Italian and Irish teens. According to the rules, the boys "mustn't get excited, chew gum, spit, swear, cheat or talk Italian."[10] Apparently, speaking the native language of your parents was as much an offense as swearing or cheating; denying your heritage was part of the price you paid to gain entry into the mainstream.

Such efforts to "purify" their children were seen by many Italian immigrants as a threat to their way of life. Most felt the need to cling to the familiar, to hold on to what they had brought with them from the old country: their language, customs, beliefs. That was their way of coping with the often threatening life they found in the New World. The immigrant generation was wary of institutions in general, a lesson learned in the old country, where centuries of foreign domination had bred a deep-seated distrust of all forms of authority. From this distrust was born the sanctity of the family, both nuclear and extended, a tradition that held true in America as much as it had in Italy. The immigrants were skeptical, therefore, of both the motives and consequences of the efforts of urban reformers. Many were also skeptical of the value of education, seen as yet another threatening public institution. In his study of Italians and Jews in New York City from 1880 to 1915 titled *The Golden Door*, Thomas Kessner concluded that as a consequence of this attitude, second-generation Italian Americans tended to work in jobs similar to those held by their fathers and to live in the same ethnic neighborhoods. It was this emphasis on family unity that led to the widely held assumption that Italians were less assimilable than other ethnic groups and therefore fated to remain in the lower socioeconomic strata.

Eventually, however, the children of immigrants could hardly resist the allure of the world in which they were born. It was an almost inevitable clash between Old World fatalism—the expectation, nourished for generations, that tomorrow would be the same as today—and New World optimism, the infectious American conviction that one could make a better life. It was ultimately impossible for parents to shield their children from the "subversive" forces they encountered outside the home. Even for those children who did not care for school, the models they encountered there—classmates and teachers who were more assimilated into the mainstream and textbooks that portrayed an American way of life—made them aware of a world different from that of their parents.

The following statement, written in 1897 by Frederick O. Bushee of South End House, a Boston settlement house, illustrates the pressures faced by the children of Italian immigrants: "The schools, the street life, and especially the use of the English language bring them into closer touch with American life. Their dread of appearing strange before their playmates stimulates them to imitate American ways and soon their home becomes the single link which binds them to Italy. Even their euphonious names become distasteful to them, and a Marandotti wishes he were a Smith or a Brown."[11] The question was how to find the passport to that promising new world.

Baseball seemed to offer one avenue of entry; as the game that all true Americans played as children or at least followed as fans, it provided some common ground for newcomers. But precisely because baseball was so American, many immigrants saw it as one of the many institutions that threatened to destroy their children's ties to Old World traditions and to weaken the all-important family structure. For the children of immigrants, family—that most enduring and ambiguous of Italian stereotypes—was a double-edged sword. It provided a safety net and protection from the dangers your parents were certain lay in wait beyond the front door, but it also did its best to keep you close to home, physically and emotionally, and not only as a child. Leaving home was not only difficult, it could border on the treasonous. John Fante succinctly captured the essence of this intergenerational conflict in his 1938 novel, *Wait until Spring, Bandini*. Embarrassed by his name and the "Italianness" of his parents, young Arturo Bandini longs to assimilate: "His name was Arturo, but he hated it and wanted to be called John. His last name was Bandini, and he wanted it to be Jones. His mother and father were Italians, but he wanted to be an American. His father was a bricklayer, but he wanted to be a pitcher for the Chicago Cubs."[12]

The experience of growing up in a world divided between the traditional values of parents and the American culture encountered outside the home was not unique to the Italian enclaves of large cities. It took place everywhere that Italians settled. A vivid account of this phenomenon was provided by Jerre Mangione, a second-generation son of Sicilian immigrants, in his 1942 fictionalized memoir, *Mount Allegro*. Mangione, whose family lived in Rochester, New York, tells of his struggle to come to terms with the divided world in which he grew up. The opening line of the book, spoken by the narrator's sister, sums up the dilemma: "WHEN I GROW UP I WANT TO BE AN AMERICAN." When the narrator points out that his teacher has told the class that "If you're born here you're an American," the father responds, "Your children will grow up to be *Americani*. But you, my son, are half-and-half."[13]

Often participation in sports was a source of tension between second-generation Italian Americans anxious to assimilate into the mainstream and their immigrant parents. With the exception of *bocce*, the great majority of the Italians who immigrated between 1880 and 1920 had almost no tradition of participation in sports. And their struggle to survive afforded them little time to pursue leisure activities other than family gatherings on weekends. Games were for the *Americani* who could afford to waste their time. When they weren't in school, sons should be working to help support the family.[14]

Inevitably the immigrant generation was in general not supportive of its children's participation in baseball, especially if they expressed an interest in playing professionally. The necessity to work hard to provide for their families, combined with their lack of a sporting tradition, made parents skeptical of their sons' interest in a game they considered frivolous. How, they asked, could an adult make a living playing a boy's game? They distrusted any institution that threatened the stability and security of the family, and here were their sons asking to leave home to play a game they did not understand, a game that was so very *americano*. Their children, who followed the Major Leagues, knew that men could indeed make a living that way, but throughout the twenties they had very little evidence that this was an avenue to success for Italian Americans.

There is little indication, judging from the experiences of the early Italian American ballplayers, that second-generation boys had a great deal of leisure time to devote to their pursuit of baseball. Instead those who made it to the Major Leagues usually did so in spite of parental opposition. Those who concluded, either out of love for the game or simply out of a desire to make a living, that baseball was to be their chosen profession made the game their top priority; all other concerns, such as school or working at other jobs, became secondary. Given the fierce competition, only with that level of commitment could second-generation athletes acquire the skills necessary to make it to the big leagues.

Parental opposition began with the earliest Italian American players, as we saw in the case of Ed Abbaticchio's father. Any number of Italian American Major Leaguers have acknowledged that their parents, or at least one of them, were opposed to what they considered to be the foolish impulse to play baseball. Some players have noted that while their fathers were firmly opposed, their mothers were more supportive of their desire to play. Dolph Camilli, a San Francisco native who made his Major League debut in 1933, said, "My mother encouraged me to play as a kid, but my father did not get too excited over it. He thought we kids should go to work." Phil Rizzuto noted the same dichotomy in his family. "My mother was all for it, but my father was dead against it," he told me. "He wanted me to get a job, to follow in his footsteps."[15]

In the case of Frank Crosetti, who began his Major League career with the Yankees in 1932, it was his mother who objected when he was invited to leave home in California to play semi-pro ball in Butte, Montana, at age sixteen. "In those days the old folks thought you were a bum if you played ball," he said. "Some friends came over and tried to talk my mother into letting me play ball. My father was quiet, but finally he stepped in and said, 'Let him go.'" Crosetti quit school and headed to Montana.[16]

Most parents dropped their opposition when the paychecks started coming in. When the Giants wanted to sign Joe Amalfitano in 1954, as a minor he needed his parents' signature on the contract. His father, a commercial fisherman in San Pedro, California, who had emigrated from the island of Ischia near Naples, agreed to sign, then had a glass of wine with the Giants scouts. "Then I took him back to the boat," said Amalfitano, "and he asked me, 'How much money did you sign for?' I told him $35,000. He looked at me and said, in Italian, 'Isn't this a great country?'"[17]

External Obstacles

Though there appears to be no overt evidence to suggest outright discrimination against Italian American ballplayers (as well as others of East and South European descent), it seems unlikely that the hostility expressed against these immigrant groups by the general population did not play a role in delaying their entry into the big leagues. How else to explain that there were so few of them in the Major Leagues in the twenties? In 1921 less than 3 percent of Major League rookies were of South or East European descent (Italians, Slavs, Hungarians). By the end of the decade their numbers had risen to no more than 6 percent.[18] Those figures must be examined in the context of the postwar period, when anti-foreign sentiment resurfaced with a vengeance and the restrictive immigration laws were enacted. Baseball, as the national pastime, was inevitably linked to patriotism, and it is unlikely that the widespread impetus toward "Americanization" in the postwar period did anything to create a more welcoming atmosphere in professional baseball for players of non-West-European descent.

The absence of Italian Americans from Major League rosters is particularly striking given the large number of immigrants since

5. Italian Athletic Club of Barre, Vermont. State Amateur Champions, 1909.
Courtesy of the Aldrich Public Library, Barre, Vermont.

the 1880s. Italians constituted the largest single segment of the new immigration wave; by 1920 more than 1.5 million people born in Italy were living in the United States, and by that time they were outnumbered by second-generation Italian Americans. One might argue that even through the first decade of the century they simply had not been around long enough to acquire the skills necessary to succeed in pro ball, but that argument carries less weight by 1920. By that time large numbers of Italian Americans had been playing baseball at the amateur and semi-pro levels in many parts of the country for many years—and playing it well. In 1909 the Italian Athletic Club team of Barre, Vermont, won the state amateur championship. In 1912 the predominantly Italian Telegraph Hill–Montgomery St. Baseball Club won the city championship of San Francisco. Also, virtually all the Italian American players who made it to the big leagues, even through the thirties, were second generation, suggesting that no transitional generation was necessary. Those players did not inherit their baseball talent from fathers who had played the game.

In light of the statistics, the claims made by various sources that baseball reflected the democratic and unbiased posture of America seem particularly ironic in retrospect. Declarations of the open-arms policy of baseball were made early in the twentieth century. In 1912, a year after A. G. Spalding published his history of baseball, *America's National Game*, there appeared a volume with the same title edited by sportswriter Will Wroth Aulick. A quirky combination of statistics, humor, and odd features, Aulick's book included a cartoon with the caption "Sources from which Ball players are drawn." To illustrate the diverse backgrounds of baseball players, the cartoon portrayed stereotypical sketches of men in "native" costumes from Ireland, Germany, Spain, Sweden, France, and Poland, as well as an American Indian (brandishing a tomahawk) and a college boy. Italy, however, was conspicuously absent.[19]

In 1923, a year before his story on Italians in sports appeared in *The Ring*, Frederick G. Lieb published an article entitled "Baseball—The Nation's Melting Pot." Referring to the 1921 immigration laws that "have been passed with the purpose of keeping the North of Europe races predominant in our national make-up," Lieb noted that some of the "races" that had migrated to America "have been easier to assimilate than others." Other than the schoolhouse, Lieb concluded, "there has been no greater agency in bringing our races together than our national game, baseball. . . . The diamond brings together all races, Anglo-Saxon, Celt, Teuton, Slav and Latin. In the language of the two-base hit, and out-curve, there is no racial prejudice nor jealousy." To prove his point, Lieb listed an "All-Star Team of All Nations." His Italian representative was Babe Pinelli, but Lieb failed to mention that Pinelli was one of only three Italian Americans playing in the Major Leagues that year.[20]

That same year the *Sporting News* proclaimed baseball "a democratic, catholic, real American game" and insisted that for the fans at least the nationality of a ballplayer, be he a Mick, Sheeny, Wop, Chink, or Jap, "is never a matter of moment if he can pitch, hit, or field. . . . In Organized Baseball there has been no distinction raised except tacit understanding that a player of Ethiopian descent is ineligible."[21] Like Lieb, the *Sporting News* did not note that the number of players representing some of the various ethnic "pools" identified in the story was very small. If, as this article suggested, players were judged strictly on their ability, then one must conclude that very few Italian Americans, as well as players of certain other nationalities, had ever learned to pitch, hit, or field well enough to make it to the Majors.

Eight years later, in the January 26, 1931, issue of the *Sporting News*, Tommy Holmes, noting the Italians' passion for baseball, expressed surprise that there were so few in the Major Leagues. "Strange that the Italians, with all of their vast enthusiasm for baseball, should have produced so few outstanding players," he wrote. "Apart from Lazzeri, Oscar Melillo, Ernie Orsatti and Tony Cuccinello are about the only other Italians established in the Major Leagues at present."[22]

Some analysts of the game have suggested that there were factors other than player ability that determined the makeup of Major League rosters early in the twentieth century. According to Robert Burk, even in the mid-nineteenth century baseball management was concerned that the "intrusion" of ethnic players (that is, German and Irish) threatened to undermine the gentlemanly behavior that had typified the play of the Anglo-American originators of the game. When it became clear that it was impossible to exclude these new elements from the game, "an increasingly centralized and segregated managerial hierarchy would regulate player behavior while vigilantly guarding its own reins of power from intrusion." Then, late in the nineteenth century, when the game was dominated by players of English, Irish, and German heritage, owners failed "to invest in systems of youth training so as to more rapidly generate skilled players from other, non-Western European backgrounds."[23]

In *Diamonds in the Rough*, Joel Zoss and John Bowman suggest there may have been a subtle form of prejudice that accounts in part for the small number of "ethnic" players in the Majors. After citing the claim made by "official spokesmen for organized baseball" that baseball was a great assimilator of players of East and South European heritage, they conclude as follows:

> What emerges from a close reading of the roster of all who have made the Majors since 1876, however, is how exclusive baseball long was. To that extent, the Irish-Americans who were so much a part of the earliest years of baseball have to take some of the responsibility for the slow assimilation of Americans of other ethnic and national persuasions; they were part of the Baseball Establishment and they did not let others in. . . . Perhaps the motives are more economic than anything else, more a case of positive fraternity than negative prejudice, more unconscious decisions than deliberate, but the end result for those left out is much the same.[24]

As noted above, by 1929 players of South and East European descent still made up only 6 percent of Major League rookies. So while the social reformers were providing more opportunities for immigrant children to participate in sandlot and amateur baseball, there was little support for them to move into the professional ranks. And the problem apparently was not limited to the Major Leagues. Even in California, where there was a large Italian American population and conditions were relatively favorable, surprisingly few players of Italian descent were found on the rosters of the prestigious Pacific Coast League, which offered young players the best opportunity short of the Major Leagues.

In *Barbary Baseball: The Pacific Coast League of the 1920s*, R. Scott Mackey commented on the background of the players in the PCL: "Most of the talent in the league came from the West, a preponderance from the baseball-rich San Francisco Bay Area. Players were white, quite often the sons of Italian and Irish immigrants."[25] However, the rosters of the PCL clubs in the twenties, which appear in Mackey's book, seem to contradict the conclusion that the players were "quite often" the sons of Italian immigrants. Of the approximately nine hundred players listed on those rosters, only twenty-seven can be clearly identified as Italian American. While there may have been a few more who, like Ping Bodie, played under assumed names, Italian Americans in all likelihood represented little more than 3 percent of all PCL players in the twenties. This is all the more revealing since the preponderance of PCL players came from the San Francisco area, where in 1920 there were nearly fifty thousand Italian immigrants and first-generation Italian Americans.[26]

Considering the ethnic biases evident at the time (as witnessed in the Sacco and Vanzetti case, as well as the immigration restriction law of 1924), it is not unreasonable to conclude that there was some level of discrimination, no matter how subconscious, within professional baseball. At the very least, it may have been one of the factors that accounted for the small number of Italian Americans in the Major Leagues throughout the twenties. In any case it appears that Italian American youth hoping to play professional baseball were frequently subjected to obstacles that might come from within their own families, from personal and institutional bias outside the family, or both. Given the lack of documented evidence of discrimination, it is impossible to reconstruct with any accuracy a clear pattern of the factors that accounted for the relatively late entry of Italian Americans in Major League Baseball. Nor is it possible to estimate the relative weight of the various elements that may have retarded their entry. What is clear is that by the end of the third decade of the century, in spite of the large numbers of Italian American boys playing baseball across the country, only a small number of individuals with a combination of innate talent and a strong commitment to the demands of the game were able to reach the Major Leagues. Perhaps they just weren't up to Major League standards. Or perhaps they were held to a higher standard. Whatever the subtleties of social and economic factors, there was without question a gulf between the established American groups, including the German and Irish, and the more recent newcomers.

4

The Tony Lazzeri Era

On October 3, 1926, *Il Progresso Italo-Americano*, the nation's largest-circulation Italian language newspaper, printed a story on the opening game of the World Series between the Yankees and Cardinals. Noting the enthusiasm of the more than sixty thousand fans in attendance, the story commented on the growing interest in baseball among Italian Americans: "Even Italians, especially those of the second generation, are following with interest the shifting events of the American national game in which, for some time now, outstanding players of our race have been participating."[1]

A major reason for the growing interest in baseball among Italian Americans was the appearance in the Yankee lineup that season of a rookie second baseman from San Francisco. Tony Lazzeri, who had set a new professional record by hitting sixty home runs the previous season in the Pacific Coast League, quickly established himself as a leader of the Murderers' Row lineup. In the process he became the first major star of Italian descent, winning accolades and tributes from Italian American organizations in every city in which the Yankees played. He would be joined in 1932 by shortstop Frank Crosetti, another San Francisco native. As the Yankees double play combination for the next six years, Lazzeri and Crosetti were key figures on the team that won three World Series. Together they came to represent Italian players in the big leagues—at least until 1936, when yet another San Franciscan, Joe DiMaggio, would become the third member of the Yankee triumvirate and soon overshadow both of his teammates.

Prior to the 1920s baseball games were attended mostly by relatively affluent white-collar workers who had the leisure time to attend games that were played primarily on weekday afternoons. In the twenties a higher standard of living and the curtailment of blue laws that had prohibited Sunday games resulted in a broadening of the fan base. Now people from all social classes were going to ball games, including the working-class children and grandchildren of immigrants. Baseball executives, recognizing the potential audience among ethnic populations, eagerly sought heroes that would draw new fans to the ballparks. Since the two largest ethnic populations in the nation's largest city in the twenties were Jews and Italians, New York's Major League franchises logically focused their marketing strategies on those groups.

The Giants, whose home field Polo Grounds was in the middle of a fast-growing Jewish neighborhood, made the most concerted effort to find an outstanding Jewish ballplayer. In the same year that Lazzeri made his debut, Andy Cohen showed great potential to be the star that Manager John McGraw was hoping to find. Before thirty thousand opening day fans in 1928, Cohen drove in two runs and scored twice to lead the Giants to victory. At the end of the game Jewish fans rushed onto the field and carried Cohen on their shoulders. McGraw had found his ethnic hero. Jewish fans everywhere celebrated Cohen's success and honored him with special "days."

Cohen went on to enjoy modest success on the field in both 1928 and 1929, but by 1930 he was back in the minor leagues, his Major League career finished. More than one contemporary observer speculated that Cohen's demise as a ballplayer was hastened by the demands made on him as the "Great Jewish Hope." He was expected to single-handedly overcome the stereotypical characterization of Jews as non-athletic and to be a role model of assimilation. Nevertheless, according to historian Peter Levine, Cohen's brief career in the national pastime "helped diminish stereotypes about Jewish weakness and encouraged immigrants and their children to feel comfortable both as Americans and as Jews."[2]

At the same time that the Giants were promoting a Jewish star, the Yankees were scouting for a hero who would appeal to the largest Italian American community in the United States. They found him not in New York but on the West Coast. Anthony Michael Lazzeri was born in the Cow Hollow district of San Francisco on December 6, 1903, the son of immigrant parents. Like his predecessor, Babe Pinelli, Lazzeri was a tough kid from the streets. "The neighborhood wasn't one in which a boy was likely to grow up a sissy," Lazzeri recalled in 1930, "for it was always fight or get licked, and I never got licked."[3]

Lazzeri's success on the streets grew into an ambition to be a prizefighter, but he also liked to play baseball, initially as a pitcher for his school team. Nothing else about school interested him, and he thanked officials when they expelled him at the age of fifteen. He then went to work as a helper at the Maine Iron Works, where his father, Agostino, was a boilermaker. While continuing to train for a career as a prizefighter, Lazzeri also played shortstop for a local semi-pro team. In 1922, his dream of becoming a professional fighter long gone, Lazzeri was signed to his first pro baseball contract by the Salt Lake City Bees of the Pacific Coast League. After playing one year for the Bees and another with Peoria of the Three-I League, he split the 1924 season between Salt Lake City and Lincoln in the Western League, hitting a total of forty-four home runs, a forecast of the breakout season that was to come in 1925.

And what a season it was. At the age of twenty-one, in his first and only full year in the Pacific Coast League, Lazzeri put together one of the greatest offensive performances in professional baseball history. In 197 games, he had a .355 average and hit sixty home runs, the first time that number had ever been reached in organized baseball. (Babe Ruth had hit fifty-nine for the Yankees in 1921.) Lazzeri also scored 202 runs and drove in 222. All three records remained unsurpassed throughout the history of the PCL, which was active until 1957.

Some would argue that Lazzeri's home run mark is tarnished by the length of the PCL season and the fact that he played in the friendly confines and high altitude of Bonneville Park, where he hit thirty-nine of his home runs. Yet in the eleven-year existence of the Salt Lake City franchise (1915–25), no other Bees player ever hit more than forty-three homers. No matter where he hit them, the fact remains that Lazzeri had done something no one else had ever done in professional baseball.

It was while he was playing in Salt Lake City that Lazzeri was given the nickname that would stick with him throughout his career. Cesare Rinetti, co-owner of the Rotisserie Inn in Salt Lake City, was a big fan of his fellow Italian American. One day, when Lazzeri was at the plate, Rinetti reportedly shouted out, "Poosh 'em up, Tony." The next day, May 24, 1925, sports editor John C. Derks ran the following headline in the *Salt Lake Tribune*: "'Poosh Um Up, Tone,' Yella Da Fan, an' Tone She Poosh." From then on Lazzeri was known to the fans as "Poosh 'Em Up." Derks continued to run the "dialect" headlines as Lazzeri's home run production mounted. When on October 18

Lazzeri surpassed Ruth with his sixtieth home run, Derks offered this headline: "Gooda da Tone, She Poosh Um Up for Beat Bambino."[4]

Notwithstanding Derks's patronizing, if affectionate, portrayal, Lazzeri was a favorite of fans and the press in Salt Lake City. That may seem to be stating the obvious, but in fact his popularity at that time and in that place was quite remarkable. The long-standing anti-foreign sentiment in Utah, especially against South and East Europeans, was at its peak in the 1920s, leading to the establishment of the Ku Klux Klan. At the very time that Lazzeri was hitting all those home runs for the Bees, "Klan activity reached a high point in Salt Lake City in 1925" so that "Many immigrants lived in a state of uncertainty."[5] In other words at a time when Italian Americans in Utah were living in a hostile environment, Lazzeri's success in the national pastime earned him an uncommon level of respectability. At the same time, the media, by their stereotypical depiction of the local hero, reminded the public that he was, after all, an outsider. It was a pattern that would continue throughout Lazzeri's career, as well as those of other Italian American ballplayers prior to World War II.

In spite of Lazzeri's awesome performance in 1925, Major League teams were not breaking down his door to sign him. Perhaps they were skeptical of his performance in the thin air of Salt Lake City, but the standard explanation was that they were afraid to take a chance on Lazzeri because he was an epileptic. Lazzeri would eventually play in the Majors for fourteen years, and the fans would never know of his affliction. He never had a seizure while on the field, and the Yankees never revealed his illness publicly. Writers who did know about it were true to the unwritten code of the day that kept information about a ballplayer's private life out of the papers.

Whatever the reason for the reluctance of other teams to pursue Lazzeri, it was the Yankees who finally signed him. General Manager (GM) Ed Barrow sent five players to Salt Lake City and paid the club $50,000 for Lazzeri's contract, a remarkable sum for that time.[6] Lazzeri then signed with the Yankees for a salary of $5,000, the same amount the Pirates paid Ed Abbaticchio in 1907.

Great Expectations

Lazzeri's spectacular performance in 1925 and the lofty price the Yankees paid for his contract ensured plenty of media scrutiny as he entered his rookie year. Given the team's dismal seventh-place finish the previous year, Manager Miller Huggins's decision to start two rookies (Lazzeri and Mark Koenig, another San Francisco native) at second and short in 1926 was met with skepticism. Both rookies were under pressure to perform, but Lazzeri faced additional challenges. Primarily a shortstop in the Minors, he was now being asked to play second base. And there was the big question as to whether he would be able to live up to the expectations created by his incredible performance the previous year in Salt Lake City. Others, the writers noted, had done well in the thin air of Salt Lake City only to fizzle out in the big leagues. So there he was on opening day, a twenty-two-year-old former boilermaker's assistant and street fighter who had never even seen a Major League game, in the starting lineup with Babe Ruth and Lou Gehrig, in front of the biggest crowds and the toughest press in all of baseball.

The greatest burden Lazzeri bore that rookie year was his role as the showcase Italian, the player the Yankees were counting on to bring new fans to the stadium. In that regard he faced the same pressure as Andy Cohen; whether he liked it or not, he represented an entire ethnic group, and he did so in the media capital of America. If he failed, it would not be just another promising rookie who flopped, but the most highly touted Italian American ever to appear in the big leagues.

If Cohen's challenge was to overcome the stereotypical view of Jews as non-athletic, Lazzeri faced a different, unspoken challenge. From the time Italians began immigrating to the United States in large numbers, they were subject to vilification. Newspapers and popular magazines routinely portrayed them as swarthy knife wielders prone to violence, Mafiosi who posed a threat to public safety. By the time Lazzeri stepped into the spotlight in 1926—only two years after anti-immigrant sentiment had led to restrictive immigration laws and one year before the execution of Sacco and Vanzetti—that image was firmly established in the public mind. If Lazzeri were to let the pressure unsettle him and get into scraps with other ballplayers, he would only contribute to intensifying the negative image of Italian Americans everywhere.

From the beginning the press took note of Lazzeri's ethnicity. Several months before his first big league game, a story ran on the front page of the *Sporting News* under a headline that featured various spellings that had appeared in print when Lazzeri was in the minor leagues: "LA ZERRE, LIZZERIA OR LI ZERRI! NO, IT'S NOT THE MUSSOLINI YELL."[7] Unlike "Ping Bodie," Lazzeri's name did not mask his Italian roots. And just as Ed Abbaticchio's name stood out in the midst of the Pirates lineup, so did Lazzeri's among the Irish and German names of the Yankee lineup: Koenig, Meusel, Combs, Ruth, Gehrig, Dugan.

When Lazzeri hit his first home run in a preseason game against the Dodgers, a subhead in a *Sporting News* story read, "Walloping Wop Comes Through," establishing an alliterative nickname that other writers would borrow in the future.[8] Other references to Lazzeri's ethnic identity were common during his rookie season; he was variously identified as "Signor Lazzeri," "the bronze Italian," "the popular Italian," "the hard-hitting Italian," and the "favorite son of Italy."

The rookie more than met the high expectations. In that first, closely scrutinized season, Lazzeri played in every game, hit a respectable .275, played solid defense, and stole sixteen bases. Though he did not come close to duplicating his record-setting Salt Lake City statistics, he did hit eighteen home runs—only Ruth (forty-seven) and Al Simmons (nineteen) hit more in the American League. Keep in mind that the era of power hitting, sparked by the Ruthian revolution, was still relatively new, and it was even more uncommon for a middle infielder like Lazzeri to hit the ball out of the park. Lazzeri initially surprised observers with his power; at five-foot-eleven and 170 pounds, he did not have the imposing physique of either Ruth or Gehrig. But his work in the boiler factory as a teenager had given him powerful forearms and wrists, enabling him to drive the ball to all fields.

Barrow's gamble in signing Lazzeri and Huggins's in starting the rookie had paid off as Lazzeri played a key role in bringing the Yankees back to a first-place finish. In his autobiography Barrow recalled Lazzeri's contributions in his rookie year: "In our comeback from a calamitous seventh-place finish in 1925 to a championship in 1926 there is one man who stands out above all others—Tony Lazzeri. He was the making of that ball club, holding it together, guiding it, and inspiring it. He was one of the greatest ballplayers I have ever known."[9] The gamble also paid off at the gate. Just as the Yankees had hoped, the young star drew large numbers of Italian fans—and not only in New York. In his history of the Yankees, Frank Graham wrote, "[Lazzeri] was almost as big a drawing card as Ruth. Italian societies in New York, Boston, Detroit, almost everywhere the Yankees played, held banquets in his honor and showered him with gifts."[10]

After such a spectacular debut in the regular season, no one could have imagined the disaster that awaited the rookie in the World Series against the Cardinals. In the seventh inning of the seventh game, Lazzeri stepped to the plate with the bases loaded and the Yankees trailing 3–2. St. Louis player/manager Rogers Hornsby went to the mound and brought in the veteran Grover Cleveland Alexander to relieve starter Jesse Haines. Alexander, thirty-nine at the time and well beyond his prime, was already a baseball legend. Then in the sixteenth year of his career, he had won 327 games. That year he had won nine games for the Cardinals after they picked him up from the Cubs in midseason. The previous day, in Game 6, he had pitched a complete-game, 10–2 win, his second complete-game win in the Series.

Like Lazzeri, "Alex" was an epileptic. He was also a notorious drinker. After winning the sixth game, he reportedly went out to celebrate, assuming he would not be asked to pitch in the finale. Bob O'Farrell, who was the Cardinals' catcher in that seventh game, told Lawrence Ritter that when Hornsby made the pitching change, "Alex is tight asleep in the bullpen, sleeping off the night before."[11]

Whatever his condition, Alexander came to the mound to face Lazzeri. It was the classic showdown between pitcher and batter—bases loaded, two out, game on the line—but heightened by the contrast between the protagonists: the battle-tested veteran trying to recapture past glory, facing the twenty-two-year-old rookie coming off a great season. And there was a touch of irony in that both suffered from epilepsy, though few knew about Lazzeri's condition at the time. The *New York Times* described the scene: "Throughout the park there came a silence. The fans slid forward to the edge of their seats. Hardly a mother's son of them seemed to be moving a muscle."[12] All that was needed for the moment to become baseball legend was a dramatic ending.

Alexander's first pitch was a ball, outside. Lazzeri took a strike; then on the 1-1 count he hit a vicious drive down the left-field line. Some accounts have the ball landing in the stands, a near-miss homer; others record it near the line, a sure double that would have driven in the lead run. Either way, the ball landed foul. Lazzeri's fate was decided on the next pitch, a low, outside curve that he couldn't resist. He swung and missed and the threat was over.

That strikeout has become one of the most famous moments in World Series history. It is even immortalized on Alexander's Hall of Fame plaque, which reads in part: "Won 1926 world championship for Cardinals by striking out Lazzeri with bases full in final crisis at Yankee Stadium." The reference to the "final crisis" perpetuates the misconception that Lazzeri's strikeout ended the Series when in fact the Yankees had two more innings to come from behind. But Alexander shut them down. The ninth inning, and the Series, ended when Babe Ruth was thrown out trying to steal second.

Whatever psychological impact that 1926 World Series strikeout may have had on Lazzeri, it did not affect his play the next year. He again hit eighteen homers (third best in the league), drove in 102 runs, raised his batting average to .309, and stole twenty-two bases. On June 8 he hit three home runs against Chicago, becoming only the sixth man in American League history to do so. But then, it was an extraordinary year for the entire Yankee team, still considered by many to be the greatest in Major League history. Six players from that roster that won 110 games and swept the World Series are in the Hall of Fame, as well as Manager Miller Huggins and General Manager Ed Barrow.

The references to Lazzeri's Italian background continued in 1927. In the April issue of *Baseball Magazine* F. C. Lane published a story whose title modified Lazzeri's nickname: "'Poosh-Em-Out' Tony Lazzeri and His Colorful Record." Lane began by noting that baseball "has attracted comparatively few from sunny Italy." Calling Lazzeri "a sort of Babe Ruth of the Rockies," Lane recalled that in the previous year "fabulous tales floated eastward from the mountains of a slugging Wop in Salt Lake City who could hammer the ball a mile." Lane then reported that on one occasion Ty Cobb happened to walk by when he, Lane, was asking Lazzeri the secret of his ability to hit the ball so hard. According to Lane, Cobb said, "It comes from eating spaghetti and drinking wop wine."[13]

In another feature on Lazzeri in the December issue of *Baseball Magazine*, Lane focused on Lazzeri's natural abilities. But again Lane indulged in casual ethnic characterization, if only to distinguish Lazzeri from the author's stereotypical perception. "Italians," he wrote, "are noted for their volatile nature and excitability. In the main they are a joyous race. Lazzeri, however, moves in an atmosphere of settled calm, verging upon melancholy." To demonstrate Lazzeri's calm demeanor, Lane recalled a conversation with him in the Yankee dugout. At one point Babe Ruth called to him from the other end of the bench, and when Lazzeri did not reply, Ruth said, "Here, you spaghetti eating Dago Wop." As if to confirm Ruth's characterization, the photo that accompanies the story shows Lazzeri and heavyweight fighter Roberto Roberti vigorously engaged in a spaghetti-eating contest. The ethnic references would continue throughout Lazzeri's career. Not even Paul Gallico, the first important sportswriter of Italian descent, could resist, calling Lazzeri "the Wonderful Wop."[14]

Lazzeri's performance in 1927, on the heels of his great rookie year, established his credentials as one of the most dangerous hitters in baseball and as a star on the best team in baseball. The Italian American community, no doubt delighted to have someone other than Al Capone or Sacco and Vanzetti generating newsprint, continued to acknowledge and celebrate its new hero. On June 22 the Italian-American Society of Boston held a testimonial dinner at which Babe Ruth was one of the speakers. According to the *New York Times*, Lazzeri "heard himself compared with Columbus, Marconi, and Mussolini." On September 8 the Yankees honored their young star with Lazzeri Day at Yankee Stadium. In its July 25 issue the *New York Graphic* had announced that all the owners of Italian restaurants in greater New York had agreed "to serve Poosh 'Em Up Tony's favorite dish, spaghetti with mushrooms" on Lazzeri Day, which would be "a half-holiday for Italian-Americans of New York and vicinity." That night more than one thousand people attended a banquet in his honor at the Commodore Hotel. The *Times* reported that "speeches lauding the brilliant work of the popular infielder and his exemplary conduct both on and off the field rang through the grand ballroom" at the dinner sponsored by "his Italian-American friends."[15]

Lazzeri continued to excel on the field as well as attract fans to the ballpark in subsequent years. He had his best all-around season in 1929, with career highs in average, home runs, hits, on-base percentage, and slugging percentage. In the years that followed, Lazzeri's average slipped somewhat, never exceeding his .303 mark in 1930, but he continued to be a dangerous power hitter. On May 24, 1936, in a 25–2 rout of the Philadelphia Athletics, Lazzeri became the first player in Major League history to hit two grand slams in one game, and he set the still-standing American League record with eleven runs batted in. He also hit a third home run and a triple for fifteen total bases. Added to the three home runs he hit the previous day in a doubleheader, his six home runs in three consecutive games set a Major League record (later tied).

Lazzeri was the Yankees' second baseman for twelve years, from

1926 through 1937. In 1938 he was a player/coach for the Cubs, then returned to New York in 1939, finishing his playing career by appearing in twenty-seven games for the Dodgers and Giants. Released by the Giants in June, Lazzeri then managed the Toronto Maple Leafs of the International League through the 1940 season. After playing for the San Francisco Seals in 1941, he went back East as player/manager for Portsmouth of the Piedmont League, then ended his career in 1943 as player/manager for Wilkes-Barre of the Eastern League. He returned to San Francisco, where he became a partner in a local tavern. On August 6, 1946, four months shy of his forty-third birthday, Tony Lazzeri died in his home of a heart attack.[16]

A Forgotten Star

Tony Lazzeri is one of the best "forgotten" players in Major League history. As both the statistics and the testimony of his contemporaries confirm, he was a key player on a Yankee team that won six pennants and five World Series in his twelve years in New York. In fact Lazzeri's home run and RBI statistics between 1926 and 1937 put him in the company of the game's most elite sluggers of that time. Over that period only five players in the American League, all Hall of Famers, drove in more runs: Gehrig, Al Simmons, Jimmie Foxx, Ruth, and Goose Goslin. In that same span Lazzeri hit more home runs than all but six American Leaguers: Ruth, Gehrig, Foxx, Simmons, Earl Averill, and Goslin. (The free-swinging slugger was also among the top five in strikeouts in six of those twelve years.) Lazzeri's name stands out in that list because as a second baseman, he played a position typically associated with defensive prowess. All the others played at the traditional power-hitter positions of first base or the outfield.

It should also be noted that right-handed hitters like Lazzeri were typically at a disadvantage in Yankee Stadium, which is more favorable to left-handed power hitters like Ruth and Gehrig. Between 1924 and 1936 the average outfield distance in left field at Yankee Stadium was 401 feet, compared to an average of 346 feet in right field. Baseball historians have often wondered, for example, how many home runs Joe DiMaggio would have hit had he played in a park more friendly to right-handed sluggers. In any case, Lazzeri's power was such that he did not suffer greatly from the home park disadvantage; in his twelve years as a Yankee he hit seventy-seven home runs at home and eighty-eight on the road.

Lazzeri was also an excellent base runner, three times finishing in the top five in stolen bases. A sure-handed if not flashy fielder, from his rookie year on he proved to be a steadying influence in the Yankee infield. Baseball historians generally rate Lazzeri as an average defensive player, presumably on the basis of statistical analysis. But his contemporaries considered him an outstanding fielder, capable of playing equally well at any infield position. In 1927 Frank Graham, then a Yankee beat writer for the *New York Sun*, assessed Lazzeri's defensive play: "He stands out as the league's best second baseman only because he plays second base most of the time. He is just as good at short or third base as he is at second."[17]

In spite of an outstanding career that eventually earned him a place in the Hall of Fame, Lazzeri's legacy is haunted by his 1926 World Series strikeout. To his contemporaries, however, Tony Lazzeri was anything but a loser. He was recognized by his peers and the press as a natural leader who possessed one of the keenest baseball minds of his time. When Lazzeri died, *New York Times* columnist Arthur Daley wrote, "He evoked infinitely greater admiration from the other athletes than he ever did from the fans." He was "a money

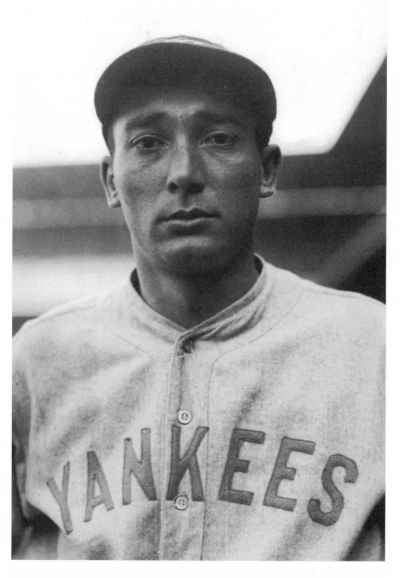

6. Tony "Poosh 'Em Up" Lazzeri, ca. 1928. National Baseball Hall of Fame
Library, Cooperstown NY.

player almost without equal and one of the smartest athletes ever to patrol the diamond."[18]

Tony Lazzeri was an unlikely hero for the Jazz Age, whose prototypical idol was the gregarious and self-indulgent Babe Ruth. But as an ethnic hero, the laconic slugger was the right person at the right time. He was the perfect role model for the children of immigrants who inherited their parents' stern work ethic. Photos of Lazzeri are frequently reminiscent of those of Italian immigrants at the turn of the century; he gazes straight into the camera with doleful eyes and shows little or no trace of a smile, looking somewhat apprehensive, even insecure. Even in his early photos he does not look like a boy playing a game for the fun of it, but a man going about the serious business of working to make a living.

True to the image conveyed in those photos, Lazzeri was also a man of few words. As one writer put it, "Trying to interview Tony Lazzeri is like trying to mine coal with a comb and a nail file."[19] Stories of Lazzeri's laconic nature have become legendary. Probably the most famous example is the often-told anecdote regarding a 1936 cross-country drive from San Francisco to the Yankees' spring training site in Florida by Lazzeri and Yankee teammates Frank Crosetti and rookie Joe DiMaggio. In a telephone interview Crosetti confirmed the story. "It was Joe's first year, and we invited him to go with us," said Crosetti. "We pooled our money, and I would pay for the gas, food, and hotels. We got to about Florida, and Tony and I were doing all the driving. So Tony says, 'Let's ask this guy to drive,' and Joe said, 'I don't drive.' We didn't say much on the whole drive. The three of us were quiet."[20]

But lurking behind the serious facade was a surprisingly mischievous spirit. Lazzeri was a notorious locker room prankster who

7. Joe DiMaggio, Tony Lazzeri, and Frank Crosetti about to drive to spring
training, 1936. California Historical Society, FN-32203.

liked to give a hotfoot or put a match to the corner of a newspaper
a teammate was reading. One of his favorite targets was none other
than Babe Ruth. In addition to nailing the Babe's shoes to the floor
of his locker, Lazzeri liked to "doctor" Ruth's eye drops. Crosetti
recounted that when Ruth would come into the clubhouse after a
long night on the town, he would clear his eyes with the drops, saying
"These are what makes the Babe hit." But before Ruth would come
in, Lazzeri would empty the solution from the bottle and fill it with
water. Ruth apparently never knew the difference.

Lazzeri was as stoic on the field as he was in his private life, but
as many have testified, he was the leader of the Yankee infield from
his rookie year on. He was the archetypal hard-nosed blue-collar
second baseman—no flash, no frills, just steady, dependable work
every day. (Only three times in his twelve-year run with the Yanks
did he appear in fewer than 130 games.) He backed down from no

one, but for all his street-hardened toughness, he never got into a fight, possibly because other players, knowing of his strength, were reluctant to challenge him. According to his *Sporting News* obituary, "He had half the league afraid of him." At the same time, his *New York Times* obituary called him "one of the most popular men in modern baseball."[21]

While he obviously does not belong in the same class as Ruth or Gehrig, Lazzeri was the third most dangerous hitter in one of the most potent lineups in the history of baseball and one of the most feared clutch hitters of his era. Playing in that formidable Yankee lineup was a mixed blessing. On the one hand, he got to play for the best team in baseball in the city with the largest Italian American population in the country, and he got more media coverage than he would have had he played in any other city. On the other hand, playing for the Yankees meant that he played in what F. C. Lane termed "the gigantic shadows of Ruth and Gehrig," the most potent one-two punch in baseball history. He was no match for either their statistics or their star power.

Ruth was in a class by himself, the lovable bad boy who captivated the entire nation. Lou Gehrig was the strong, silent hero, the kind of enigmatic figure that invites fans to impose on him whatever meaning they wish. For all that he did on the field, Lazzeri could never have been an equal member of that trinity of Yankee stars. Even though Gehrig, like Lazzeri, was the son of immigrants, he had gone to Columbia University, an automatic passport to American respectability. As an Ivy Leaguer, he was the embodiment of the fully assimilated second-generation ethnic. And because he was German American, his ethnicity was never a matter of note. Like the Irish, Germans had been so prevalent in Major League Baseball for so long that their ethnic background was no longer remarkable.

Lazzeri, on the other hand, was identified as an *Italian* ballplayer throughout his career and was never able to transcend his role as an ethnic hero. That identity was perhaps inevitable, at least initially, since he was the star the Yankees had sought to draw Italian American fans to the ballpark. But continuing references to his ethnicity were also a sign of the times, when anti-immigrant feelings were still widespread. Ruth was the "Babe," Gehrig the "Iron Horse"; neither was identified as "the German," much less as "the kraut." In contrast, for many, both in the media and in the stands, Lazzeri was always the "wop" and therefore not qualified to be an authentic American hero no matter how well he played.

Perhaps because he played for so long in the twin shadows of Ruth and Gehrig or perhaps because the memory of that 1926 strikeout was what everyone seemed to remember most about his career, ultimate recognition of Lazzeri's achievements was slow in coming. It was not until 1991, forty-six years after his death, that he was inducted into the Baseball Hall of Fame. For the school dropout who worked as a boilermaker's assistant and dreamed of becoming a boxer, the road from the sandlots of San Francisco to the House that Ruth Built had been a long one. The journey to Cooperstown proved to be even longer.

The Crow Flies East

In 1932 the Yankees introduced New York fans to another Italian American sensation from San Francisco. Like Lazzeri, Frank Crosetti had been a star with the San Francisco Seals, and there was fierce competition among Major League clubs to sign him. As they had done with Lazzeri, the Yankees paid a hefty price for the young shortstop: $75,000, a phenomenal sum in the midst of the Depression. "In those days," Crosetti told me, "they were looking for Italian ballplayers."

Frank Peter Crosetti was born in San Francisco on October 4, 1910. His father had come to the United States from a town near Genoa at the turn of the century, then married a California-born girl whose parents had also emigrated from the same area. Because Frank was afflicted with various childhood illnesses, when he was two the family moved to a farm in Los Gatos, south of San Jose, where his father started a scavenger business. On the farm Frank and his older brother would play what he referred to as "one o'cat," a term that typically applied to a bat and ball game for three players. "We used the big end of a corn cob as a ball," he told me. "For a bat we'd take a board and shave it down." No matter what form it took, he liked nothing better than to play ball. "Baseball came naturally to me," he said. "I wanted to play as long as I can remember."

By the time the family moved back to San Francisco when Frank was in his early teens, he was playing so well in local sandlot leagues that he caught the attention of local scouts. In 1927 he was invited to play semi-pro ball in the Butte (Montana) Mines League, and the next year, at the age of seventeen, he was playing for the Seals. One of his teammates in his rookie year with the Seals was Ping Bodie, who had ended his Major League career seven years earlier. The forty-one-year-old San Francisco legend had some advice for the youngster: "He told me, 'Go to the butcher shop and get a large meat bone. Have your mother boil the meat off and use that to bone your bats.' I did that; then when I went to the Yankees I took the same bone with me." It was while playing for the Seals that Crosetti first met Tony Lazzeri, who was already a star for the Yankees as well as a local hero. "He was really good to me," Crosetti recalled. "I looked up to him. He was really a hell of a hitter, but you'd never know it from him. He was a humble person."

In the standard baseball sources such as *Total Baseball*, Crosetti's nickname appears as "Crow" or "Cro," for obvious reasons. But those sources do not list the nickname he was given when he joined Lazzeri on the Yankees' roster. "They used to call Tony the 'Big Dago,' and I was the 'Little Dago,'" he recalled. "Then Joe [DiMaggio] became the 'Big Dago.' We didn't mind that name then. It was good-natured ribbing." One of his teammates had yet another tag for Crosetti. "Babe Ruth used to call me 'Dago Bananas,'" he said, "probably because he couldn't remember my name." Crosetti didn't object to that name either. "Babe was a wonderful person," he said. "He did more for the game of baseball than anybody."

Crosetti, a right-handed hitter who stood five-foot-ten and weighed 165 pounds, played for the Yankees from 1932 until 1948. His career batting statistics were modest (.245 average, 98 home runs, 649 RBIs), but as a sure-handed shortstop he was a mainstay of the Yankee lineup from 1933 to 1940, a period in which the Bronx Bombers won four straight World Series (1936–1939). Always among the leaders in fielding, Crosetti led American League shortstops in putouts and double plays in 1938 and 1939.

Crosetti specialized in a couple of relatively obscure aspects of the game. Like Babe Pinelli before him, he was an acknowledged master of the hidden ball trick. It was Pinelli, in fact, who taught him the technique when they played together in the San Francisco Seals infield from 1928 to 1930. He also led the league in being hit by pitches eight times. Phil Rizzuto, who ultimately replaced Crosetti as the Yankee shortstop, said that the master taught him the art of how to get hit gently by a pitch. According to Rizzuto, "When Crosetti would get hit his shirt would blossom out, or he'd just get a flick on the arm."[22]

It has already been established that both Lazzeri and Crosetti were men of few words. But in contrast to the quiet Lazzeri, Crosetti was the "holler guy" in the Yankee infield, constantly jabbering to the pitcher and yelling out instructions to other players. Off the field, however, Crosetti was a reserved, private man. Never a media darling, he shied away from reporters—to him they were unwelcome intruders in his workplace—and they in turn largely ignored him. He refused to attend banquets or give speeches, claiming that the public should not make a fuss over ballplayers. "We're just doing a job, like the butcher, baker, or plumber," he argued. "Doctors, scientists and people who really do important work aren't bothered this way. I can't see it at all."[23]

Unlike his double play partner, Crosetti did not soften his stern facade with whimsical locker room pranks. To some, in fact, he was a humorless curmudgeon. In *Ball Four*, Jim Bouton's iconoclastic look at the inside world of baseball, Crosetti (who was then a coach with the Seattle Pilots) is portrayed as a dour taskmaster. Bouton described Crosetti's "twin fortes" as a coach as "saving baseballs (he's a strong company man) . . . and chasing photographers off the field." He then concluded, "Don't get the idea that I consider Cro a lovable old man, butt of little jokes but a heart of gold. Like most coaches he's a bit of a washerwoman and sometimes a pain in the ass."[24]

No matter what people thought of Crosetti personally, no one questioned his professionalism. He never lost his childhood love of the game; to him baseball was to be taken seriously and treated with the utmost respect. He had little patience for young players who took the game lightly. Even Bouton admitted to a grudging respect for Crosetti's indefatigable work ethic.

Few benefited as much from Crosetti's professionalism as did a rookie named Rizzuto. After Crosetti hit only .194 in 1940, the Yankees decided to give the young Brooklyn native a chance to win the job at short. Rizzuto had a rough time in spring training, spurned by Yankee veterans who were fond of Crosetti. Rizzuto felt uneasy too since "Cro" had been a childhood hero. Crosetti, however, did not shut out his potential replacement. Instead he did all he could to groom the youngster to take over at short, teaching him where to play the hitters that the veteran knew so well.

Even before his playing days ended in 1948, Crosetti began his second career, serving as a player/coach in his final two seasons with the Yankees. Following his retirement as a player, he remained as the Yankees third base coach through the 1968 season. Crosetti then coached for the Seattle Pilots in 1969 and for the Minnesota Twins in 1970–71 before retiring from the game.

Frank Crosetti wore a Yankee uniform for thirty-seven consecutive years, from ages twenty-one to fifty-eight, a record unmatched by anyone in franchise history. As a player and coach, he was involved in 23 World Series, or a total of 122 Series games—more than anyone else in Major League history—and came away with the winners' share in 17 of those Series, also a record. More than anything, he was a Yankee loyalist; in his six-page, hand-written letter of resignation in 1968 he wrote, "Once a Yankee, always a Yankee."[25]

Lazzeri, and later Joe DiMaggio, far surpassed Crosetti in talent and fame. But finally it was Crosetti who, by his very longevity in a New York uniform, would come to symbolize the long tradition of Italian American ballplayers who wore the Yankee pinstripes. When Lazzeri ended his career with the Yankees in 1937, Crosetti was there to carry on, as he was when DiMaggio retired in 1951. He was still there through the fifties when Rizzuto, Berra, Martin, and Raschi were stars of a new era of Yankee domination. And he was still there in the sixties when first baseman Joe Pepitone carried on the tradition. It was a tradition that had begun in 1918 with Ping Bodie, the first Italian American Yankee and the man who taught

Crosetti how to harden the grain in his bats with a meat bone, the same bone the young infielder carried with him when he went to New York in 1932.

Not Just Yankees

It was not until the 1930s that there was a notable increase in the number of Italian Americans appearing in the Major Leagues. And no player would eclipse the impact of Tony Lazzeri until Joe DiMaggio made his meteoric debut in 1936. Nevertheless, at the same time that Lazzeri was making his mark, a small number of other players who broke into the Majors in the twenties were enjoying varying degrees of success, most of them away from the spotlight of the New York media.

In 1926, the same year that Lazzeri made his debut with the Yankees, Oscar Melillo, a five-foot-eight, 150-pound second baseman, broke into the Majors with the St. Louis Browns. He would remain in the big leagues for the next twelve years, establishing a reputation as an outstanding defensive player. He was also the first Italian American to serve as manager of a Major League team and one of the first two to receive Most Valuable Player votes in the American League.

The youngest of five children of immigrants from Tuscany, Melillo was born in the Chicago suburb of Pullman on August 4, 1899. While working for International Harvester after leaving high school, his outstanding play as captain of the company baseball team earned him a contract with Winnipeg of the Western Canadian League in 1920. He moved up to the American Association in 1922, playing for the Milwaukee Brewers. It was there, in the middle of the 1923 season, that he became an infielder. When Fred "King" Lear, the Brewers starting second baseman, went out with an injury, Melillo came in from the outfield and proved to be a defensive wizard. Without that transition it is unlikely that the light-hitting Melillo would have made it to the Majors.

While Lazzeri was putting up dazzling numbers in his rookie year for the pennant-winning Yankees, Melillo got off to a more modest start for the seventh-place Browns, hitting .255 in ninety-nine games. Still his defensive play was so impressive that he earned six votes in the balloting for the American League Trophy, at that time the equivalent of the Most Valuable Player award. That was a remarkable showing since Lazzeri, who played for the pennant winner and was a far more productive hitter, received only one more vote. It marked the first time Italian Americans had received MVP votes in the American League.

The next year Melillo's career, and life, almost came to an end. In midseason he was diagnosed as having Bright's disease, a life-threatening kidney ailment that would ultimately become the source of a new nickname. (As a child Melillo was called "Ski" by his friends because he idolized a local football hero, Frank "Ski" Fiske.) Doctors prescribed a bland diet heavy on vegetables, especially spinach and raw carrots. Newspapers focused on the spinach angle to the point that Melillo became known as "Spinach."

Melillo himself enjoyed embellishing the odd cure that was credited with saving his life. "They told me I'd have to eat nothing but spinach for the next few months if I wanted to live," he said. "I tried to talk them into letting me have a steak, spaghetti, ravioli or goulash once in a while, but they said nothing doing. When I told them I couldn't stand the monotony of spinach three times a day, they told me I could have some variety by boiling it for breakfast, making a salad of it for lunch and baking it for dinner."[26]

After missing the remainder of the 1927 season and playing in only 51 games in 1928, "Spinach" came back strong in 1929, hitting .296 in

141 games. In each of the next five seasons he played in at least 132 games, hitting a career-high .306 in 1931 and finishing eighth in the MVP balloting. Traded to Boston in 1935, he remained with the Red Sox until he retired at the end of the 1937 season.

In 1938 Melillo began a new career as a coach with the Browns. Toward the end of the season he became the first Major League manager of Italian descent when he replaced Gabby Street as skipper of the Browns, whose record to that point had been 53-90. Under Melillo the Browns went 2-7 and finished the season in seventh place. It would be his only experience as a manager. From 1939 until his retirement in 1956, he was a coach for Cleveland, Boston, and Kansas City. He continued to live in the Chicago area until his death in 1963.

Melillo never approached Lazzeri as an offensive threat; his lifetime average was a modest .260, and he hit a total of twenty-two home runs in twelve seasons. While he did enjoy a brief run as a celebrity thanks to his spinach cure, he never came close to Lazzeri's level of national fame. But when it came to fielding his position, the man of many nicknames was second to none. In 1930 he set the still-standing American League record for assists by a second baseman in a season with 572. He led the American League in assists by a second baseman for four consecutive seasons beginning in 1929, in putouts three times, and in fielding percentage twice. His obituary in the *Sporting News* rated him as "one of the top defensive second basemen of all time," and in *Best of Baseball*, Paul Adomites and Saul Wisnia ranked Melillo as one of the ten best defensive second basemen in baseball history. "In the 1920s and '30s," they wrote, "when big sluggers dominated baseball, the slick Oscar ("Ski" or "Spinach") Melillo was a genuine fielding superstar."[27]

One year after Melillo broke in with the Browns, Ernie Orsatti made his debut across town with the more successful and flamboyant

8. Oscar "Spinach" Melillo, 1935. National Baseball Hall of Fame Library, Cooperstown NY.

Cardinals. Whereas Ping Bodie had gone to work for a Hollywood studio when his baseball career ended, this California native got to the big leagues *because* he worked for a Hollywood studio. Born in Los Angeles to immigrant parents on September 8, 1902, Ernest Ralph Orsatti caught the movie bug at an early age, spending all his spare time hanging around the studios and doing odd jobs. "I wanted to be an actor, a director, a camera man," he said, "anything that would identify me with motion pictures."[28] He quit school at the age of sixteen to work full time at the studios, first as a "gofer," then as a stunt man. He walked on the wings of airplanes, dived off cliffs, and did automobile and boat stunts.

In 1922 Orsatti went to work as a prop man and bit player at the studio of the great silent film comedian Buster Keaton, who also happened to be part owner of the Vernon franchise in the Pacific Coast League. Orsatti also played first base and caught for Keaton's indoor baseball team. When "Turkey" Mike Donlin, a former Major Leaguer turned Hollywood supporting actor, saw Orsatti play, he told Keaton that the young man could make more money playing baseball than by working in the studio. In 1925 Keaton told Orsatti he was going to be a professional ballplayer and presented him with a Vernon contract. His contract was later purchased by the St. Louis Cardinals, who called him up late in 1927.

After spending most of the 1928 season in the Minors, Orsatti hit .332 for St. Louis in 1929. Yet the left-handed outfielder/first baseman was never able to nail down a starting job in the powerful Cardinal lineup. (In the years Orsatti played in St. Louis, the Cards won four pennants and two World Series.) In only four of his nine years with the club did he appear in more than one hundred games, even though he hit .300 or better in six seasons, twice hit over .330, and finished with a lifetime average of .306. Orsatti attributed his failure to crack the starting lineup to bad timing. "In one way, I came along at the wrong time," he said. "Every year I'd go to camp thinking I finally had a regular job wrapped up, when some phenom would come along—like Joe Medwick or George Watkins."[29]

While he played a utility role on the field, Orsatti led his team in fashionable attire. This was the era of the Gashouse Gang, a collection of talented but rowdy and eccentric players who would have been at home in a Ring Lardner novel. Good old country boys like Dizzy Dean and Pepper Martin, they were never slaves to fashion. Unlike most of his teammates, Orsatti was a big-city boy, a colorful character who brought a touch of Hollywood to the Cardinal lineup. His movie background had given him a flair for glamorous clothing, in obvious contrast to most of his Cardinal teammates, and earned him the nickname of "Showboat." A 1932 *Sporting News* feature, in which Orsatti was called "the Dashing Dago" and a "colorful wop," described his attire: "His flashy sweaters, golf hose, knickers and sports suits are Hollywood importations, and his wardrobe is the envy of most of the younger players." In its obituary of Orsatti the *Sporting News* concluded that "Ernie's ensembles made him stand out like a peacock in the ranks of the Gashouse Gang."[30]

Even before his baseball career ended, Orsatti returned to his Hollywood roots by becoming a talent agent, teaming up with his brothers, Frank and Vic. His two sons, Ernie F. and Frank, followed in their father's footsteps by becoming Hollywood stunt men.[31]

When Tony Lazzeri joined the Yankees in 1926, an Italian in a Major League lineup was still something of an anomaly, as evident in the struggle by sportswriters to get his name right. Only three players—Abbaticchio, Bodie, and Pinelli—had made much of a mark, and the four players other than Lazzeri, Melillo, and Orsatti who entered the Majors between 1926 and 1929 made only brief appearances.

The time may not have been right for the son of Italian immigrants to be recognized as a full-fledged national hero, but it is difficult to exaggerate Lazzeri's significance in the evolution of Italian American participation in Major League Baseball. He was the first to draw large numbers of Italian fans to the ballpark, and he was the first to achieve star status. Nor was his celebrity limited to the local Italian American community or to those in other cities with Major League teams. The rapid expansion of the media in the twenties—radio, movie newsreels, magazines—made baseball players more immediately and widely recognizable to the public than ever before. Fans all over the country could see images of ballplayers in action within a few days of the actual event. This meant that Lazzeri, one of the stars of baseball's most highly publicized team, became more widely known to a national audience than any other Italian American player before him.

Before Lazzeri came along, baseball had already provided Italian immigrants and their offspring a means of connecting to the patterns of American life. However, his emergence as a genuine hero of the game provided them with a more personal link to the national pastime by demonstrating that one of their own could excel in a distinctly American venture. And with his stoic demeanor, strong work ethic, and quiet leadership, he helped counter the stereotypical media portrayal of Italian ballplayers as hot-blooded and temperamental. Both by his accomplishments and his conduct, Lazzeri established, more than anyone before him, the credibility of Italian Americans in Major League Baseball.

That credibility was further enhanced when Frank Crosetti joined Lazzeri in the Yankee infield in 1932. As great as Lazzeri was in his own right, he and Crosetti were also important as a duo. They were both classic representatives of the self-effacing, team-oriented ballplayers who (with the notable exception of Ruth) characterized the Yankees in the first half of the century. Moreover, they were the first Italian American players to play important roles together on a Major League team. And not just any team. Their presence in New York

City on baseball's most successful and highly publicized team made them an even more visible symbol of Italian American success in the national pastime.

The era of the pioneers was coming to an end. The door had been opened and soon Italian Americans would enter the big leagues in unprecedented numbers. Now the stage was set for the appearance of yet another young star from San Francisco who would become the greatest player of Italian descent and would ultimately transcend his ethnic identity to become one of the most famous celebrities of the twentieth century.

Two

ARRIVAL

5

The Turning Point
1930–1935

Riding the wave of Babe Ruth's revolutionary home run productivity and the subsequent upsurge in offense throughout the Majors, baseball enjoyed unprecedented financial success in the 1920s. In 1930 attendance reached a then all-time high when more than 10 million fans paid to watch the national pastime. All that changed in the thirties, when baseball, like the rest of the nation, suffered the effects of the Great Depression. The impact was not immediate, but by 1932 attendance dropped precipitously, falling below 7 million for the first time since 1919, and in 1934 baseball attracted fewer than 6 million fans, a drop of 40 percent from the record crowds of 1930. Even though owners cut salaries dramatically, several teams, including the Browns, Reds, Phillies, and A's, were foundering. Connie Mack's A's won three straight pennants between 1929 and 1931 with one of the great teams in history. But declining attendance forced him to sell off several of his best players, including future Hall of Famers Al Simmons, Mickey Cochrane, Lefty Grove, and Jimmie Foxx.[1]

It was during this dark period in baseball's history that two major demographic shifts occurred. More and more players were coming from rural areas, especially from the South, and an increasing number of second-generation players of South and East European heritage, primarily Italians and Slavs, were making it to the Major Leagues.[2] Together with Orsatti, Mancuso, and Puccinelli, names such as Comorosky, Swetorich, and Vosmik appeared on 1930 rosters alongside the still predominant Irish, German, and Anglo-Saxon names. By the end of the decade the trend was such that the *Sporting News* trumpeted, as it had done in the past, the democratic nature of baseball as a symbol of the melting pot. In the baseball equivalent of multiethnic army platoons that would become so common in World War II movies, the front page of its July 13, 1939, issue featured photos of seven players under the caption "Typographical Errors to be Found on Major Scorecards."

Even though large numbers of players of South and East European heritage had come into the big leagues since 1930, their names continued to be regarded as something of a curiosity, still a mark of their "otherness." Three of the players represented on the *Sporting News* front page were of Italian descent: Angelo Giuliani, Lou Chiozza, and Dario Lodigiani. The other four were Lithuanian (Joe Krakauskas), French (Stanley Bordagaray), Greek (Alex Kampouris), and Cuban (Robert Estalella). Beneath their photos was the assurance that "the boys with the names of many letters are just so many sons of the nation's greatest forces of democracy—baseball, the National Game—the melting pot of the sons of all languages, the caldron of equal big opportunity."

By a curious quirk of history, it was in the first year of the new decade that the number of Italians entering the Majors began to increase significantly, a trend that would continue throughout the decade. While only twenty-two Italians had ever played in the Majors by 1929, at least fifty-four entered the big leagues in the thirties. Some made brief appearances, then disappeared from the Major

League scene. Many, however, had lengthy if unspectacular careers, some turning into baseball "lifers" as coaches and managers, and two—Joe DiMaggio and Ernie Lombardi—are enshrined in the Hall of Fame.

There was also a greater diversity of geographical origins, which was true of Major Leaguers in general. California continued to be a primary source, providing approximately one-third (nineteen) of the fifty-four players clearly identifiable as Italian American. Of those, nine were from the San Francisco Bay Area. Another third was from the northeastern states, but many now came from the Midwest (Illinois, Indiana, Minnesota, and Missouri) and South (Alabama, Florida, Georgia, Louisiana, Tennessee, and Texas.)

1930

In 1930 as the nation was heading into the Depression, there were six rookies of Italian descent: Tony Cuccinello (Cincinnati), George DeTore and Sal Gliatto (Cleveland), Gus Mancuso and George Puccinelli (St. Louis Cardinals), and Lin Storti (St. Louis Browns).[3] By comparison, only thirteen Italian Americans had entered the Majors between 1920 and 1929. Of the nine Italian Americans in the Majors in 1930, five were playing in St. Louis; in addition to the three rookies, Oscar Melillo was with the Browns and Ernie Orsatti with the Cardinals.

It appears unlikely that the St. Louis franchises purposely sought Italian ballplayers to attract ethnic customers to the ballpark as the Yankees had done with Lazzeri. For one thing, the Italian community of St. Louis was relatively small, numbering three thousand in 1920. Also, the Italians did not live in close proximity to the Major League parks as did those in New York City. Instead they were concentrated in an area they called "the Hill" (known as "Dago Hill" to non-Italians), which was located several miles away from downtown. Furthermore, none of the Italians recruited by the St. Louis franchises was of the caliber to inspire intense ethnic loyalty. Of the five, only Oscar Melillo was a starter, and only he and Orsatti spent more than four seasons in the city. Two of the second-generation Italian Americans growing up on the Hill in the thirties were future big leaguers Yogi Berra and Joe Garagiola; their boyhood hero was not Oscar Melillo but Joe "Ducky" Medwick, the son of Hungarian immigrants.

Gus Mancuso, the Texas Italian

Of the rookie class of 1930 only Mancuso and Cuccinello went on to have notable careers. August Rodney "Blackie" Mancuso offers proof that Italians settled in places other than the East, Midwest, and West Coast. He was born in Galveston, Texas, on December 5, 1905, and died in Houston on October 26, 1984. (Many Italians who had originally immigrated to Louisiana to work on sugar plantations eventually moved west to Texas, some drawn by the possibility of owning their own farmland, others to work in railroad construction.)

A burly catcher who stood five-foot-ten and weighed 185 pounds, Mancuso was signed by the Cardinals in 1925, then languished in Branch Rickey's farm system for five years. Finally, in 1930 Commissioner Kenesaw Mountain Landis directed St. Louis to keep him on the Major League roster or lose him to another franchise. After two years in a backup role, he was the starting catcher in 1932, hitting .284, then went to the Giants in a six-player deal. He hit a respectable .264 in 1933 and finished sixth in the National League MVP vote as the Giants won the World Series. But his real contribution was in his skillful handling of the pitching staff, which was led by future Hall of Famer Carl Hubbell. In September 1933 the Sporting News reported that Mancuso, "the Texas Italian," deserved much of the credit for the improvement of the entire pitching staff, which led the league in earned run average (ERA).[4]

In 1937, when Manager Bill Terry named Mancuso team captain, the *New York Times* reported that Mancuso was rated "as one of the smartest catchers in the major leagues" and that his manager "frequently has attributed the Giants' uniformly successful pitching to Mancuso's skillful handling of his hurlers."[5] In fact the Giants staff would lead the league in ERA in three of the four years Mancuso was the starting catcher.

After falling out of favor with Terry, reportedly for going public with the news that the Giants' manager had cut his salary, Mancuso was traded to the Cubs after the 1938 season. Over the next three years Mancuso played for Chicago, Brooklyn, and St. Louis before returning to the Giants in May 1942. After one season with the Phillies, he retired in 1945 at the age of thirty-nine. A two-time All-Star (1935 and 1937), Mancuso compiled a lifetime average of .265 over his seventeen-year career, the longest of any Italian American player to that point.

Following his playing days, Mancuso managed in the minor leagues at Tulsa and San Antonio and was a coach for the Cincinnati Reds in 1950. He then moved to the broadcast booth, calling Cardinals games from 1951 to 1953 alongside another Italian American, Harry Caray, whose birth name was Carabina.

Tony Cuccinello

A native of Long Island City in Queens, New York, "Cooch" was signed by the Cardinals at the age of seventeen, in spite of the initial objections of his father. "I liked baseball so much I wanted to see if I could make the big leagues," he said. "At first my father wasn't very happy about it because he's an old timer from Italy and he thought baseball was a passing fancy. Finally, when I told him what I was going to get, he agreed."[6] This would become a standard response in the Depression years by immigrant parents whose initial objections suddenly turned into delight when they saw what their sons would be earning by playing baseball.

By 1930, after his contract had been purchased by Cincinnati, the five-foot-seven second baseman was in the Reds starting lineup. In his first two seasons he hit .312 and .315, but when he then held out for more money, he was traded in 1932 to Brooklyn, where in four seasons he never hit higher than .292. Ironically his lowest average as a starter (.252) came in 1933, the year he was selected to represent the Dodgers in the first-ever All-Star Game.

In Brooklyn the New York native was playing in front of hometown fans. According to the 1933 edition of *Who's Who in Major League Baseball*, "This bright-eyed son of sunny Italy [was] quite the hero of the Brooklyn fans."[7] But in 1936 he was traded to the Boston Bees. Three years later the *Sporting News* reported that Italian fans in Brooklyn were still upset that the Dodgers had traded Cuccinello, especially since they had also traded away another favorite, Ernie Lombardi, in the deal that brought Cuccinello to Brooklyn in the first place: "'They give up Schnozz [Lombardi], one great Italian player, to get another, Cuccinello, and then they give Tony to Boston,' is the wail of Long Island's Italian fan colony. 'What a club we'd have now if we had Tony working with Durocher at second base, and big Lombardi behind the plate.'"[8]

Cuccinello was traded to the Giants in 1940, spent the '41 season as player/manager for Jersey City of the International League, then returned to Boston as a player/coach in 1942. (He was exempt from military service because of chronic laryngitis.) Traded to the White Sox in '43, he retired after the 1945 season. He went out in style, almost winning the American League batting title in his final year—at the age of thirty-seven—when, admittedly, Major League talent was depleted by World War II. Going into the final day of the season, Cuccinello held a two-point lead over George "Snuffy" Stirnweiss of the Yankees. The White Sox doubleheader was rained out on the final day, and all Cuccinello could do was wait and see how Stirnweiss did. The Yankee infielder went 3 for 3, but only after the official scorer changed an initial ruling of an error to a hit for Stirnweiss when he learned about the Chicago rainout. That ruling made the difference, giving Stirnweiss a final average of .309, one point higher than Cuccinello's .308. Had he won, "Cooch" would have become the oldest player to win a batting title.

A .280 hitter over his fifteen-year career, Cuccinello was also a solid defensive player, leading National League second basemen in double plays four times and in assists twice. He was especially adept at the hidden ball trick. According to Dick Bartell, a Major League infielder for eighteen years, "Tony Cuccinello was probably the champion trickster in the National League." Bartell tells the story of the time Ernie Lombardi became angry when Cuccinello caught him off base: "You tag me and I'll punch you right in the nose," Lombardi told him. "I never tagged him," said Cuccinello. "He just walked back to the dugout."[9]

After managing and coaching in the Minors for three years, Cuccinello coached in the Majors from 1949 until 1969, then retired to Tampa. Even then he kept his hand in baseball by serving as a scout for the Yankees in Florida until 1985. (Since 1926 he had been out of baseball for only one year; in 1946 he stayed home with his wife to help care for a newborn child who was ill.) Cuccinello, who died in 1995 at the age of eighty-seven, was involved in professional baseball for fifty-nine years.

"Baseball was at its peak in the 1930s," Cuccinello was quoted as saying. "You really had to be good to play then. Why, they used to send guys who hit .320 and .330 back to the Minors because they couldn't field." Of his long career in baseball he said, "I enjoyed every minute of it. I don't think you could ask for a better way to spend a lifetime."[10]

1931–33

Four players of Italian descent entered the Majors in 1931, including future Hall of Famer Ernie Lombardi. The others were Joe Palmisano, Johnny Scalzi and Gene "Half-Pint" Rye, whose birth name was Eugene Mercantelli. Of this group only Lombardi was still in the Majors in 1932. Rye/Mercantelli, however, deserves to be remembered for one record-breaking day in the minor leagues. On August 6, 1930, his Waco team in the Texas League beat Beaumont by the score of 22–4. In the eighth inning of that game Rye set organized baseball records for a single inning with three home runs, twelve total bases, and eight RBIs. That single-inning rampage surpassed his entire Major League production; in seventeen games as a Red Sox outfielder in 1931 he had seven hits, all singles, and drove in one run.

In addition to Frank Crosetti, three other rookies made their debut in 1932. Louis Americo "Crip" Polli—his nickname stemmed from a high school injury that put him on crutches—was one of six Major Leaguers born in Italy (on July 9, 1901, in Baveno, a small town on Lago Maggiore in northern Italy). At the age of seven months Polli immigrated with his mother to Barre, Vermont, where his father worked in the granite quarries. Barre, "the granite capital of the world," which had attracted a large number of Italian stonecutters at the turn of the century, was the home of the Italian Athletic Club team that had won the state amateur baseball title in 1908. Polli toiled in the minor leagues from 1927 to 1945, with two brief appearances in the Majors in 1932 and 1944, going 0-2 in twenty-four games. The other 1932 rookies each spent one year in the Majors: Andrea Ettore (Andy) Spognardi, an infielder, appeared in seventeen games for his hometown Boston Red Sox, and Pete Daglia won two and lost four pitching for the White Sox.

Nineteen thirty-three was the only year in the decade when there were fewer than three Italian American rookies, but one of the two newcomers was Dolph Camilli, a future MVP. The other rookie, Mike Meola of New York City, pitched in three games for the Red Sox with no decisions, then returned in 1936 and finished his career with a record of 0-3 for the Red Sox and Browns.

1934: A Special Crop

The 1934 crop of six rookies was probably the richest of the decade in terms of overall quality. Nick Tremark, an outfielder who appeared in thirty-five games for Brooklyn over three years, had the shortest career. Lou Chiozza of the Phillies holds the distinction of having been the first batter in the first Major League night game on May 24, 1935, at Crosley Field in Cincinnati. (Dolph Camilli was the cleanup hitter for the Phillies, and Babe Pinelli was the third base umpire.) Chiozza, who compiled a .277 lifetime average over six seasons as an infielder/outfielder for the Phillies and Giants, was a favorite of actress Tallulah Bankhead. In her autobiography she wrote that when Chiozza was hospitalized with a broken ankle suffered in an outfield collision, she "banked his bed with flowers." When two of his teammates went to visit him, they were "paralyzed with fright" upon entering his room. "They found their white-clad comrade asleep in a profusion of lilies and came to the conclusion he was dead," she wrote.[11] Why was the famous Hollywood star fascinated by Chiozza? He was a native of Tallulah, Louisiana.

Joe Cascarella, who posted a 27-48 record pitching for four teams over five years, secured a unique spot in baseball history. After winning twelve games in his rookie year, Cascarella was invited to participate in a world tour with a team that included Ruth, Gehrig, and Foxx and was managed by Connie Mack. On December 6, 1934, Cascarella was the winning pitcher in the first and only Major League game ever played on the Chinese mainland. The Major League squad beat a team of U.S. Marines and missionaries in Shanghai by a score of 22–1.[12]

Phil Cavarretta, a future MVP, and Zeke Bonura went on to have notable careers, and Cookie Lavagetto's ten years in the Majors culminated in one of baseball's unforgettable moments.

Zeke Bonura

Born in New Orleans on September 20, 1908, Henry John "Zeke" Bonura was one of the first Italian Major Leaguers to come out of the deep South. (The first was another native of New Orleans, "Oyster Joe" Martina, who pitched for the Washington Senators in 1924.) Bonura's parents, Giovanni and Rosa, had left Sicily at the turn of the century and settled in the Louisiana city that was the destination of many Italian immigrants. By the time he was a teenager Bonura had distinguished himself as one of the best all-around athletes in the South. At St. Stanislaus College, a prep school in Bay St. Louis, Mississippi, he was captain of the football, basketball, track, and baseball teams. In 1925, while representing his school at an international track meet in San Francisco, the sixteen-year-old stunned everyone by beating Jon Myrra of Finland, the world record holder in the javelin, while setting a new American record.

Bonura's athletic achievements caught the attention of Notre Dame football coach Knute Rockne, who went to the National Catholic

9. Zeke Bonura, Chicago White Sox rookie, being welcomed to Comiskey Park on April 18, 1934. Transcendental Graphics.

Youth basketball tournament in Chicago in an attempt to recruit the young star. According to one account, it was Rockne who was responsible for Bonura's nickname. After seeing the muscular athlete in action, he told Bonura's coach, "I want that young man with that magnificent physique to play for me." His teammates started calling him "Physique," which eventually became "Zeke."[13] His other nickname, "Bananas," came from the fact that his father was in the fruit business in New Orleans.

Zeke passed up the opportunity to play football for Notre Dame and enrolled instead at Loyola University in New Orleans, where he lettered in baseball, track, basketball, and football. After beginning his professional career with the New Orleans Pelicans of the Southern League in 1931, he was sold in 1933 to Dallas in the Texas

League, where he hit .352 and was the league MVP, good enough to get a contract with the Chicago White Sox.

In 1934 the twenty-five-year-old right-handed hitter had the best rookie season of any Italian American player since Lazzeri, hitting .302 and leading the team in home runs and RBIs. He moved to another level in 1936, hitting .330 and driving in 138 runs, which stood as the White Sox single-season record until 1998. Bonura's best year came in 1937, when he had career highs in batting average (.345, fourth best in the AL) and slugging average (.573, fifth best).

Traded to the Washington Senators in 1938 (presumably because of his defensive weaknesses), Bonura drove in more than 100 runs (114) for the fourth time in five years. He hit .321 for the Giants in 1939, then split his final year in the Majors between the Senators and the Cubs. In his seven-year career he averaged 100 RBIs and seventeen home runs a year and compiled a .307 batting average and a .487 slugging average. Even in the offense-oriented 1930s, his .307 lifetime average was an impressive achievement for a power-hitting first baseman.

Like other first basemen before and after him, Bonura hit a ton and fielded as if he weighed that much. Given the versatile athletic skills he had displayed in high school and college, he proved to be surprisingly immobile. His defensive performance offered proof that baseball statistics can be misleading, especially when it comes to fielding. Three times in seven years he led the league in fielding percentage at first base, but that was because he had so little range he only touched balls hit right at him. He should have been credited with inventing the concept of "defensive indifference." In 1936 he made only seven errors in handling 1,614 chances, but his manager, Jimmy Dykes, put that figure in perspective by noting, "You can't miss what you can't get to." Then Dykes added, "He's not exactly my favorite first baseman, but he is my favorite character."[14]

Dykes's opinion was shared by both his fellow players and fans. Not since Ping Bodie had there been an Italian American player with the size and personality of Zeke Bonura. When the first baseman was traded to the Senators, the *Washington Post*'s Shirley Povich wrote that White Sox fans were fond of "big, loud, bumptious Bonura." In his four years in Chicago, "they have voted him the most popular player on the club, have presented him with two automobiles, four radio sets and several wardrobes of clothes." Then, in a column published during spring training of the 1938 season, Povich noted that Bonura "has infected the Nats with a fire and dash that is downright remarkable considering the traditional dullness of Washington teams. . . . They are submitting with pleasure to the dominance of the large Italian."[15]

Bonura may have lacked the verbal eccentricities of a Ping Bodie, but on the field he was a nonstop talker, chatting with teammates, opponents, umpires, and even the paying customers. A congenial, fun-loving character, Zeke had a smile for everyone and was not afraid to laugh at himself, especially about his defensive play at first base. His enthusiastic approach to the game and infectious personality inspired one contemporary observer to suggest that this second-generation Italian was the embodiment of the American Dream: "Zeke, if he is anything, is the eternal symbol of Youth and Ambition and Success. Nobody who loves the spirit of America will ever forget Mr. Bonura as he leaps from the dugout and races to his position, full of vigor and determination, full of zest and good spirits and courage."[16]

Bonura was the kind of character who generated any number of anecdotes, several of which involved Dykes and most of which were probably at least partly apocryphal. As much as Dykes liked his iron-gloved first baseman, he was often exasperated by him. On one occasion the slow-footed Bonura startled everyone by stealing home in the ninth inning to win a game. When he got to the dugout, he proudly announced to Dykes that he had seen the steal sign, which consisted of the manager waving the scorecard. Dykes replied that he had been waving the scorecard to brush a fly off his nose.

One of Bonura's biggest fans was Vice President Jon Nance Garner, who was delighted when Zeke went to the Senators. He reportedly had been lobbying Washington owner Clark Griffith for years to acquire the slugger. When Bonura stopped by the vice president's box during his first game with the Senators, Nance urged him to hit a home run. Bonura obliged, then stopped on his way to the dugout to accept a congratulatory hug from the vice president.

A different kind of official recognition awaited Bonura after his Major League career ended. In September 1941 he became one of the first Major Leaguers drafted into the army. Assigned to Special Services, he was sent to North Africa to organize recreational programs for troops waiting to be sent to the front lines. The personable Bonura proved to be a resourceful and effective administrator. In addition to organizing boxing, basketball, and touch football programs, by 1943 he had set up twenty baseball diamonds and ten leagues for GIs throughout North Africa and organized an African World Series. Bonura recalled how he used "volunteers" to build the baseball diamonds: "The Italian prisoners of war we had did the work. They didn't know a baseball diamond from Adam and Eve but I could speak a little Italian. I showed 'em what we had to do and I stayed out there with 'em till we got it organized, dragging the infield and marking it off. I'd get a detail of forty-five or fifty men, they had a helluva time, they all wanted to come out."[17]

On New Year's Day 1944 Bonura staged a GI football championship dubbed the Arab Bowl, which drew ten thousand spectators. He also established baseball teams for children in both Italy and France. In recognition of Bonura's many contributions, on October 23, 1944, General Dwight D. Eisenhower personally awarded him the Legion of Merit medal.

Cookie Lavagetto

It was right at the end of a solid if undistinguished ten-year run in the Majors that Harry "Cookie" Lavagetto did something that earned him an indelible place in baseball lore. At one time it seemed unlikely that the Oakland native would ever play professional baseball. Unlike so many other Italian American boys in the Bay Area, Lavagetto did not distinguish himself on the local sandlots, and his father, who was in the trash collection business, wanted his son to go to work with him. But in the spring of 1933 Harry happened to be in the right place at the right time.

During a benefit game between a group of Major League players from the area and local sandlotters, Lavagetto emptied the bases with a double. One of the spectators was Cookie DeVincenzi, owner of the Oakland franchise of the Pacific Coast League. He signed Harry, who became known as "Cookie's boy" and then just "Cookie." Signed by the Pittsburgh Pirates in 1934, the six-foot, 170-pound infielder spent three seasons as a part-time player before being traded to Brooklyn in 1937. For the next five years he was the Dodgers' starting third baseman and, beginning in 1938, was selected to play in the All-Star Game four consecutive years.

In a 1943 column Shirley Povich told of a widely rumored incident during the 1941 season involving Lavagetto and Dodgers teammate Ducky Medwick. According to Povich, Lavagetto "beat the daylights out of Medwick in the dressing room late in the season" after Medwick complained about the presence of Lavagetto's two sons in the dressing room. "There was also something said about Lavagetto's Italian ancestry," wrote Povich.[18]

Following the '41 season, Lavagetto enlisted in the navy, one of the first big leaguers to sign up, and spent the next four years in the service, a stint that effectively put an end to his career. He returned to the Dodgers in 1946 but appeared in only eighty-eight games that year and forty-one in 1947, his final season in the Majors. It was in the fourth game of the 1947 World Series that Cookie Lavagetto found his moment of glory when his ninth-inning double broke up a no-hit bid by the Yankees' Bill Bevens, but that is a story to be told in a later chapter. In ten years Lavagetto compiled a modest average of .269 but was considered a reliable clutch hitter. According to teammate Whitlow Wyatt, the ace of the Dodgers pitching staff before World War II, "with men on base he was about the toughest man to get out that we had on the club."[19]

Though not in the same league as Bodie or Bonura, Cookie was something of a character. One sportswriter was quoted as saying that he looked like he always needed a shave, his shirt would hang out of his pants, and he wore his hat at a funny angle. Lavagetto himself admitted that he liked to wear one sock up, the other down, for no particular reason.[20] Cookie's casual style and solid play appealed to the Brooklyn faithful, but no one rooted for him with as much gusto as a Brooklyn restaurant owner named Jack Pierce. Seated in box seats near the third-base dugout, Pierce would drape over the railing banners with "Cookie" written on them and cheer loudly every time his hero came up. When Lavagetto did something special, Pierce would inflate a balloon, release it, and shout Cookie's name for all to hear.

When Lavagetto was released by the Dodgers in May 1948, the

thirty-five-year-old veteran wasn't ready to hang up his spikes, so he returned to his roots and played once again for his hometown Oakland Oaks in the PCL. Lavagetto's 1948 Oakland team, a curious collection of former Major Leaguers, merits some mention here. Under Manager Casey Stengel, the Oaks, known affectionately as the "Nine Old Men," won their first PCL pennant since 1927. In addition to Lavagetto the team featured several other Italian American Major League veterans, all natives of the San Francisco Bay Area. Ernie Lombardi, the National League MVP in 1938, was the oldest on the team at forty. He shared the catching duties with thirty-four-year-old Billy Raimondi, a fixture in the PCL since 1933. Infielders Dario Lodigiani and Les Scarsella were thirty-two and thirty-four years old respectively. The pitching staff included Rinaldo "Rugger" Ardizoia, a career minor leaguer born in Oleggio, Italy, who had appeared in one game for the Yankees in 1947. The youngster on the team was Billy Martin, who, at the age of twenty, was two years away from his Major League debut.

After serving as a coach for the Dodgers and Senators, Lavagetto was named manager of the Senators in 1957, a post he held for four-plus years. He finished his career as a coach for the New York Mets and the San Francisco Giants. When Lavagetto retired in 1967 after thirty-one years in professional baseball, Bob Stevens, writing in the *Sporting News*, noted that Cookie—an "entirely good guy" and "as warm a personality as ever lifted a bat"—had enjoyed "one of the longest and most honorable careers in baseball."[21]

The First All-Italian Team

By 1934 enough players had made it to the Majors that Samuel Merin, writing in the March issue of *Baseball Magazine*, could offer his list of an "All-Italian-American Baseball Team," probably the first such list to appear in print. (In 1930 only three teams had Italian Americans in their starting lineups; by 1934 there were nine.) Of the five players in Merin's lineup playing in the Minors at the time, only Jack La Rocca never made it to the Majors.

First base	Dolph Camilli	Chicago, NL
Second base	Oscar Melillo	St. Louis, AL
Third base	Tony Lazzeri	New York, AL
Shortstop	Ernest [sic] Crosetti	New York, AL
Right field	Ernest Orsatti	St. Louis, NL
Center field	Joe Di Maggio [sic]	San Francisco, PCL
Left field	George Puccinelli	Newark, IL
Catcher	Gus Mancuso	New York, NL
Catcher	Ernest Lombardi	Cincinnati, NL
Pitcher	Joe Cascarella	Jersey City, IL
Pitcher	Salvatore Gliatto	Dallas, Texas League
Pitcher	Jack La Rocca	Binghamton, NY-PL
Utility	Tony Cuccinello	Brooklyn, NL
Utility	Frank [sic] Storti	St. Louis, AL

Noting that Italian names "may not furnish the happiest moments in the lives of announcers or linotype operators," Merin adds that "Minor league records reveal that many another disciple of Mussolini and Uncle Sam is on his way to the big time.... In the Minors there is a good supply of dashing Latins who hope to advance. Italian boys mature early, due to their huge fund of surplus nervous energy and the enthusiasm with which they embrace the sport."[22]

1935

Although 1935 produced the second-largest number of recruits of any year in the decade, none of the ten had a particularly distinguished career. Only three—Les Scarsella, Mel Mazzera, and Italo Chelini—spent more than two seasons in the Majors. A few, however, did have interesting names. Chelini's nickname was, for obvious reasons, "Chilly." According to Arch Ward, the *Chicago Daily Tribune* columnist responsible for establishing the first All-Star Game in 1933, that was not his only nickname. In the July 21, 1936, issue of the *Tribune* he wrote, "Even [teammate] Zeke Bonura calls Italo Chelini of the White Sox Dago. Nickname experts, however, are striving for a less delicate moniker, now that the 21 year old lefty has achieved some fame." A few weeks later a story in the September 6 issue of the *Los Angeles Times* reported that the Hays Office, as the film censorship administration was known, had established an informal list of words that "must be excluded from all movies." Among the words listed were Chink, Dago, Frog, and Hun.

John Pezzullo, a left-handed pitcher with the Phillies, was known as "Pretzel" Pezzullo. Guido Martini, a pitcher with the Philadelphia A's, obviously owed his nickname of "Southern" to his birthplace of Birmingham, Alabama. In addition, his first name appears in the record books in the oddly anglicized form of Wedo. Al Cuccinello, a one-season infielder with the Giants, would undoubtedly have been called "Cooch" if the nickname hadn't already been taken by his older brother Tony, who debuted in 1930. Prospero Bilangio, a reliever for the Boston Braves in '35 and '36, chose to play under the name of Al Blanche.

Media Response

The unprecedented influx of Italian American ballplayers in the 1930s triggered an equally unprecedented response from the media, which treated their arrival with an ambiguous attitude not unlike that which had greeted Italian immigrants since the late nineteenth century. While other players of East and South European heritage, who were also entering the big leagues in unprecedented numbers, were subject to stereotypical portrayals, Italians were the most frequently targeted group.[23] For example, in the 1936 edition of *Who's Who in Major League Baseball*, which provided a brief biographical sketch of each player, very few references are made to the ethnic background of any but the Italian players. Ernie Lombardi is "one of numerous Italians who won major league renown." DiMaggio is "a giant Italian," Lazzeri a "lanky Italian," Hank Coppola "a rangy Italian," and Mel Mazzera a "husky young Italian." Players of Italian descent received greater media attention because they represented a significant percentage of the newcomers, both in baseball and in society as a whole, and because their names more readily identified their ethnic origin.

When Ernie Lombardi was signed by the Dodgers in 1931, Tommy Holmes, writing in the *Sporting News*, proclaimed that the "acquisition of Signor Ernesto Lombardi . . . makes the Brooklyn ball club a sort of a baseball melting pot." The team would now include Spanish American, Cuban, Czech, French Canadian, Teutonic, Jewish and Irish players, "and Anglo-Saxons will be all over the premises." Lombardi, the story concluded, was the piece that made the puzzle complete: "Only an Italian was necessary to convert this menage into a team of all nations and Lombardi fits the bill." But Holmes was puzzled by the relative scarcity of Italians in the big leagues. "Apart from Lazzeri, Oscar Melillo, Ernie Orsatti and Tony Cuccinello are about the only other Italians established in the major leagues at present," he wrote. "Strange that the Italians, with all of their vast enthusiasm for baseball, should have produced so few outstanding players."[24]

A *Sporting News* article that appeared less than six months later took a different approach to the Italian presence in baseball. Appearing under the title "The Sons of Caesar," it saw the growing number of Italian players as a threat to the traditional domination of Irish players, thus invoking the ethnic tensions that had existed for so long between these two groups. The writer hinted at the kind of ethnic epithets that have been noted elsewhere in this volume: "Many and many an interesting bit of repartee flashed across the diamond as some Irish wit challenged the skill of another player whose forbears had not been born where the shamrock lies in its emerald green. . . . The Irish are good ball players with their alertness and avidity of mind, but they are being challenged right under their noses." The challenge was coming from players whose names "ring with the musical vowels of the familiar names of the sons of the Caesars. . . . The Italians have found baseball and they like it. Little by little they are making their way into the foreground. In those cities in which there is a large Italian population there are many boy teams made up of sons of the United States whose parents were born in sunny Italy." The threat is clear and imminent: "The Irish would better beware. They will be challenged to prove their racial superiority one of these days." Considering what would occur in Europe within a few years, that statement is particularly chilling in retrospect. But in its most telling remark, the article ends with a comment that suggests that neither the Irish nor the Italians represent the real America: "There are still Smiths and Browns playing and there always will be. They represent Uncle Sam."[25]

One year later a strikingly similar piece titled "How Tony Gives a Latin Tone to Our National Game" appeared in the *Literary Digest*. In what was essentially a summary of a Consolidated Press dispatch by George Chadwick, the piece began by asking, "Will Tony nose Pat out of the national game?" After listing the names of several Italians then playing in the big leagues, Chadwick quoted an unnamed manager: "They take to baseball quicker than they take to spaghetti. . . . These Tonies walk right into baseball if they take to it a bit. . . . Nowadays I can't even get a player on my team with the nickname of Pat. Once they were all Pat. Better look out for these Garibaldis who are born in the United States. When they get baseball good, they are some good, and they are getting that way fast.[26]

In the opening weeks of the 1934 season the play of three of the Italian American rookies prompted *Boston Globe* sports cartoonist Gene Mack (a cousin of Connie Mack) to write a story titled "Some New Baseball Dishes, Done Italian Style." It began as follows: "Early returns on the 1934 baseball season indicate that spaghetti may soon become the national dish of the national game. Oscar Melillo will vary the diet now and then with large helpings of spinach but Cuccinello, Puccinelli, Crosetti, Lazzeri, Bonura, Orsatti, Di Maggio [*sic*] and a host of other "walloping Wops" can't be wrong. The Italians are in this business to stay."[27] There was a time when "Abbaticchio was about the only Italian big leaguer," but now "the Italians are running all over the organized baseball field." Mack even included a reference to New York's Italian American mayor, Fiorello La Guardia, who threw out the first pitch on opening day at Yankee Stadium: "Mayor La Guardia surprised the crowd by stepping out to the pitching hill with a cap and glove, winding up, and burning a fast one past Col. Ruppert [the Yankees' owner], who was going through the motions with a bat. Baseball seems to be in the Italian blood of the Fusion Mayor."

Mack concluded with a reference to Ping Bodie. "Strong, ambitious boys, these Italian ballplayers, and they love to hit. As Bodie used to say, 'Gimme a bat. I'll knock down all the fences.' Viva, Ping! And another order of spaghetti." In his accompanying cartoon, which includes a caricature of Mussolini giving a Fascist salute and saying

"Viva baseball," Mack illustrated his benign stereotypical portrayal by depicting thirteen Italian ballplayers, past and present, seated around a large table. In the middle of the table sits a large bowl labeled "spaghetti," while several cloves of garlic hang above the table.

Mack's stereotypical depiction illustrates the mixed response to the unprecedented influx of players of Italian descent in the first half of the thirties, a combination of praise for the ability of these newcomers and concern for their impact on the national pastime. On the one hand, the growing numbers of Italian Americans (as well as Slavic Americans) gave journalists the opportunity to flaunt the democratic nature of professional baseball, a symbol of the American melting pot. At the same time, there was an undercurrent of concern that these newcomers threatened to upset the traditional nature of the game, which had for so long been the domain of the English, Germans, and Irish. That concern would linger, and even intensify, as the Italian "invasion" of the game continued for the remainder of the decade.

6

Viva Italia!
1936–1939

Baseball had long been acknowledged as the national pastime, but in 1936 its integral place in American folklore took on an even more palpable form when on February 2 baseball writers selected the first inductees for the newly established Hall of Fame. Babe Ruth, Ty Cobb, Walter Johnson, Honus Wagner, and Christy Mathewson were the first to be sanctified, three years before their red brick shrine would open its doors in Cooperstown.

That same year also proved to be something of a watershed for Italian Americans in baseball, and not only because of the sensational debut of a twenty-one-year-old rookie named Joe DiMaggio. The press was paying particular attention to Italian American ballplayers, both because of their growing numbers and because of their impact on the field. While players of Slavic origin were entering the Majors at about the same rate as Italians in the thirties, they did not receive the same media attention. For one thing, they were a less homogenous group than the Italians, consisting of Poles, Czechs, Serbs, Croats, and others. Also, their names, unlike those of most Italian players, did not always identify their ethnic origins. There was no question about the ancestry of someone named DiMaggio, but a name like Musial or Lopat or Stanky was less obviously "ethnic."

There were Italians playing at every position in 1936, and with the exception of Cleveland and Detroit every Major League team had at least one player of Italian descent on its roster. Among the Italian Americans in the Majors by 1936 were three future Hall of Famers (Lazzeri, DiMaggio, and Ernie Lombardi) and four future MVP Award winners (DiMaggio, Lombardi, Phil Cavarretta, and Dolph Camilli). In addition, Babe Pinelli was in his second year as a National League umpire.

For the first time three Italian Americans were starters on the same team, as DiMaggio joined Lazzeri and Crosetti in the Yankees lineup. As usual it was the Italian Yankees who stole the spotlight. DiMaggio was the big story of the season, but Lazzeri also made headlines when on May 24 he became the first player in Major League history to hit two grand slams in one game and set the still-standing American League record with eleven runs batted in. Crosetti, the third member of the triumvirate, hit a career-high .288 and made the AL All-Star team, as did DiMaggio.

But there were also non-Yankees making news in 1936. Giants catcher Gus Mancuso had a career-high .301 average and finished eighth in the NL MVP vote. Four other Italian American players (Camilli, Lombardi, DiMaggio, and Bonura) received MVP votes that year, more than in any previous season. If nothing else, those MVP votes meant that the press was paying attention to Italian American ballplayers.

Of course events of more monumental import than the presence of Italians on baseball diamonds were unfolding in 1936. The American economy was beginning its slow recovery from the Depression—unemployment was "down" to 17 percent—and Franklin Roosevelt was reelected in a landslide. But overseas there were ominous signs of what was to come. The Spanish Civil War began, and German troops occupied the demilitarized zone of the Rhineland. Hitler and Mussolini joined forces to establish the Rome-Berlin Axis and Italy, which had invaded Ethiopia in October 1935, annexed the African nation as Mussolini began to unfold his plan to create a new Roman Empire.

There were political implications even on the world sports scene. When Max Schmeling won the heavyweight championship on June 19 by knocking out Joe Louis, Nazi Germany touted the victory as proof of Aryan physical superiority. But in August another black athlete, Jesse Owens, embarrassed Hitler by winning four gold medals and setting two world records and equaling a third at the Berlin Olympics.

"Viva Italia!," by Daniel M. Daniel, in the July 1936 issue of *Baseball Magazine*, illustrated the growing awareness among the media of the presence and prestige of Italian Americans in the Major Leagues, as well as the tendency to portray them in stereotypical terms. It also revealed how in an increasingly turbulent time the worlds of international politics and sports could collide. Daniel's article, which attempted to trace the history of Italian Americans in the big leagues, began with a curious comparison between Mussolini's troops and Italian American ballplayers: "The legions of Rome march across the deserts and the mountains to an African triumph. And here in America, sons of men who immigrated from Italy march across the diamonds of the Major Leagues to glories of their own. This surely is Italy's year. And no matter how we may look upon the Ethiopian adventure of *Il Duce*, no matter what our sentiments on the political aspects of the African grab, the fact remains that Italy has finally invaded baseball with a bang. And this invasion is a wholesome—a most welcome one."[1]

Daniel's somewhat ambiguous reference to Mussolini's invasion of Ethiopia reflects the changing attitude in America toward the Italian dictator. From the time he came to power in 1922 the American press was generally supportive of Mussolini, who was credited with restoring order in postwar Italy and revitalizing its economy. Not surprisingly, the majority of Italian Americans, who had been subjected to accusations of inferiority for decades, saw Mussolini as a heroic figure who had given Italy international respectability. His image as a strong and effective leader was welcomed as an antidote to long-standing nativist stereotypes.

But Mussolini's imperialistic ambitions, previously limited to bombastic rhetoric, were suddenly made tangible by the attack on Ethiopia in 1935, and most of the goodwill that remained in America evaporated. Inevitably the old suspicions and stereotypes about Italians as being hot-tempered and prone to violence resurfaced. Daniel's metaphoric description of the Italian "invasion" of baseball, a theme that permeated the entire article, fed off that prevailing stereotype.

Though his story was not primarily about DiMaggio, Daniel admitted that the rookie's brilliant performance had driven home the "sudden importance of players of Italian descent in our major leagues." There was also a hint that not everyone had welcomed the change in baseball's demographics, which Daniel again characterized as an invasion: "The time was when it was considered an oddity for any club to have an Italian ballplayer. For a team to boast two sons of Italy, as did the Yankees with the establishment of Crosetti as a regular, was considered phenomenal or bizarre, according to the way you looked at it, and the manner in which your psychology responded to the invasion of baseball by the sons of immigrants from Europe." Now with three Italians in their lineup, the Yankees were attracting new fans everywhere they played. "The exploits of Di Maggio [sic], in combination with those of Lazzeri and Crosetti, have intrigued Italians all over the country. They have established in every city visited by the Yankees—most particularly in New York, of course—a new school of fans, who heretofore evinced little or no interest in major league baseball."[2] (In a *Sporting News* story that appeared on May 21, Daniel had adopted a military image in identifying the trio as "the Three Musketeers of the Roman Legion of the Yankees." The cartoon accompanying the story portrayed the three Italians singing, "Oh, the miners came in '49—th' wops in '51.")[3]

Daniel identified more than twenty Italian American ballplayers, from Abbaticchio to Bonura and Cavarretta. While he seemed to be genuinely enthusiastic about the arrival of Italians on the Major League scene, he could not refrain from stereotypical characterizations. His insistence on the military analogy throughout—Italian players are "sons of the legions of Rome [who] have fought their way into the current rosters of the major leagues"—hints at the author's ambiguous attitude toward the group he apparently intended to praise. This becomes overt in his general conclusion that Italians are "an agile race, a sturdy, enduring and durable people, quick to learn and aggressive in the highest degree."[4] What purports to be a complimentary portrayal is ultimately a portrait painted with a very broad, and not entirely flattering, brush. (Two years later, in the short-lived publication *Jack Dempsey's All Sports Magazine*, Daniel would publish another summary of Italian American Major Leaguers, this time with the intriguing title "Watch Those Walloping Wops.")

There is even a suggestion of "racial" bias in Daniel's conclusion that Italians are not well suited to be pitchers: "They go well in the infield, they have the power needed for outfield success, but they do not develop the sort of talent which is required for pitching achievement. Whether this is just a coincidence, or a quirk of Fortune or race, let Time tell."[5] Daniel's not-so-subtle suggestion that perhaps Italians didn't have the qualities needed to be pitchers would be echoed years later by commentators noting the lack of black pitchers in baseball and black quarterbacks in football. The implication of course was that they lacked the brains to play those key positions.

Three months before his *Baseball Magazine* story appeared, Daniel had published a feature story on DiMaggio, the most highly touted rookie to come along in years. Such were the expectations placed on the kid from San Francisco that "Yankee fans regard him as the Moses who is to lead their club out of the second-place wilderness."[6] DiMaggio's arrival in fact generated much more publicity than had that of Tony Lazzeri ten years earlier. Lazzeri had created a sensation by hitting sixty homers in the Pacific Coast League, but he had done it in the relative obscurity of Salt Lake City. DiMaggio, on the other hand, put on his show on the much larger stage of San Francisco. And it was an impressive show, including a record-setting sixty-one-game hitting streak for the Seals in 1934 and a .398 batting average in 1935. Furthermore, when Lazzeri arrived, the Yankees had not yet become a dynasty, having won only one World Series (in 1923), and Lazzeri was hardly expected to carry a team with Babe Ruth and Lou Gehrig in the lineup.

By the time DiMaggio came on the scene, expectations were much higher since the Yanks had won three Series titles between 1927 and 1932, and DiMaggio was now expected to lead them back to the promised land. While Daniel refrained from the more blatant stereotyping evident in the *Baseball Magazine* story, he referred to DiMaggio as

"Giuseppe" (as he would often do in subsequent stories) and pointed out that Joe "likes spaghetti, even though his new teammate, Tony Lazzeri, doesn't care much for Italy's favorite dish." (Incidentally, Daniel's frequent use of the Italian version of DiMaggio's first name—an obvious way to call attention to his ethnicity—is ironic since Daniel himself wrote under a pseudonym after he had been denied a byline because of his Jewish birth name, Daniel Margowitz.)[7]

Other Italian American players were making the front page of the *Sporting News* early in the 1936 season. The March 19 issue featured a photo of pitcher Mike Meola and catcher Angelo (Tony) Giuliani of the St. Louis Browns. The caption read, "Italian Battery Moves Up," and the story below the photo began, "The firm of Meola and Giuliani, which sounds somewhat like a wholesale spaghetti business, promises to produce an interesting phase of the Browns' battery bill-of-fare this year."[8]

Meola would appear in nine games for the Browns in 1936, going 0-1, then finish the season (and his two-year career) with an 0-2 record in six games with the Red Sox. Giuliani, on the other hand, stayed in the Majors for seven years, working mainly as a backup catcher for the Browns, Senators, and Dodgers. The first Italian American from Minnesota to reach the big leagues, he played for his hometown St. Paul Saints of the American Association before joining the Browns. His name appears in *Total Baseball* as Tony Giuliani, but that was simply one of those names arbitrarily given to Italian Americans, apparently because it seemed less foreign than a name like Angelo. "They called me Tony, which had no connection to my name at all," he told me. "'Tony' was an Italian-type greeting." Giuliani, whose parents immigrated from a town near Lucca, in Tuscany, spoke only Italian until he went to grade school. He recalled playing against Tony Lazzeri. "He took a shine to me because I was Italian," said Giuliani.

"We would speak our native tongue. '*Come stai*, Antonio?,' I would say to him." He also recalled what the fans would say to him: "The fans would holler out, 'dago,' 'wop,' 'guinea.' You got a little bit sizzled at that, and maybe you'd holler back a little."[9]

Following his playing career, Giuliani scouted for San Francisco and Minnesota for many years, retiring in 1980. When I visited him at his St. Paul home in June 2001, Giuliani, still spry at eighty-eight years, proudly wore his World Series ring from the Twins. He also pointed out two photos that hung side by side on the wall of his basement recreation room. One was of him as a baby, the other was of Babe Ruth. "There's the two babes," he said, a big smile lighting up his face. "The two bambinos."

In 1936 the Italian language press in America also began to devote more coverage to baseball, presumably because of the immediate impact of DiMaggio. Prior to '36 even *Il Progresso Italo-Americano* of New York, the largest of the Italian-language papers, paid little attention to sports. In its "Cronaca dello Sport," a minor section appearing near the end of the daily paper and occupying no more than two columns, boxing was by far the dominant sport, followed by cycling and soccer. There were only occasional stories on baseball, mostly brief game summaries and usually when the Yankees were involved in the World Series. Even by 1932, when Tony Lazzeri had established a reputation as one of the best players in the game, there was minimal coverage until the end of the season. The World Series generated headlines in the sports section, but the game stories were brief and there was no particular focus on the Italian American players.

In 1936 boxing continued to dominate the sports section of *Il Progresso*, and it is not surprising, given the predominance of Italian

American fighters. But there was a marked increase in baseball coverage. There were frequent, though not daily, stories, and one indication of growing interest in the sport was that not all the articles were about Italian ballplayers. On March 21, for example, the lead story in the sports section was about Dizzy Dean's salary dispute with the Cardinals.

The big story of course was the highly anticipated arrival of the young sensation from San Francisco; even as a rookie, DiMaggio received more attention than any Italian American player before him. The DiMaggio watch continued throughout the season, and on August 27 *Il Progresso* proclaimed him the best rookie in the past ten years. In that same story DiMaggio, Lazzeri, and Crosetti were dubbed (in language that echoed that of Dan Daniel in his May 21 *Sporting News* story) "the three Italian-Californian musketeers" and "the Roman legion of the Yankees."

On September 30, the day of the first game of the World Series, the lead sports story noted that for the first time in the history of baseball four players of Italian descent—DiMaggio, Lazzeri, Crosetti, and Mancuso—would play for the two contending teams. Mancuso was hailed as the linchpin of the Giants squad who saved many games with his flawless technique, while the thirty-two-year-old Lazzeri was described as "*la vecchia volpe*" (the old fox). In addition to the stories that were appearing in *Il Progresso*, cartoons by Dan Martinelli were a regular feature of the sports page in 1936. (The text within the cartoons was in English, while the captions above were in Italian.) In addition to DiMaggio, several other Italian American ballplayers were sketched by Martinelli that spring, including Mancuso, Camilli, Crosetti, and Lombardi, "the most formidable Italian American hitter."[10]

The increased attention given to baseball by *Il Progresso*, and in particular to players of Italian descent, reflected a growing sense of awareness of, and pride in, the heroes of the national pastime on the part of the Italian American community. But it was clearly DiMaggio who spurred the most interest, both in the Italian language press and the American press in general.

1937

On the whole the rookie class of 1937 was as notable for its demographics as for its baseball prowess. Whereas both parents of almost all of the previous players had been first-generation Italian immigrants, three of the nine recruits in 1937 (Jimmy Bloodworth, Hank Steinbacher, and Emil "Hill Billy" Bildilli) were the offspring of mixed marriages. On the other hand, Julio Giacomo Bonetti, a native of Genoa, was one of the few Major Leaguers born in Italy. A pitcher, he won six and lost fourteen in three seasons with the Browns and Cubs. In 1941, after spending three seasons with Los Angeles in the Pacific Coast League, Bonetti was banned from baseball after being seen giving money to known gamblers.

None of the nine newcomers came close to duplicating Joe DiMaggio's rookie year performance, but one of them did share his name. Although he made his Major League debut a year after his younger brother, as we shall see below, it was Vince DiMaggio who opened the door to a career in baseball for both Joe and their brother Dom by defying his parents.

The only other rookie to spend more than a handful of games in the Majors was Nicholas Dominic "Dim Dom" Dallessandro. In eight seasons with the Red Sox and Cubs, mostly as a backup, the left-handed-hitting outfielder compiled a .267 average. He attributed his brief, one-year tenure with the Red Sox to his diminutive stature. "The Boston ball club was always stressing on ballplayers six feet or better," he said. "Just about everyone on that ball club was six feet or better. I am, right today, the smallest ballplayer that ever played in the big leagues. Rizzuto was three or four inches taller. I'm five-foot-five; he's about five-foot-eight.[11] (For the record, *Total Baseball* lists both Dallessandro and Rizzuto at five-foot-six. Freddie Patek, who played from 1968 to 1981, is listed at five-foot-five.)

1938

Two of the five rookies of 1938, Johnny Rizzo and Johnny Lucadello, were born in Texas. Lucadello, a native of Thurber, spent six years as an infielder with the Browns and Yankees, primarily as a utility player. Rizzo, on the other hand, had one of the more perplexing careers of any Italian American Major Leaguer. A native of Houston—his grandfather was reportedly the town's first blacksmith—Rizzo was one of the many players who languished in the Cardinals' farm system, spending six years in the Minors before getting a shot in the big leagues. In 1938 the Cardinals sent Rizzo to Pittsburgh in exchange for three players and $75,000, a huge figure in those Depression years.

Rizzo's long stay in the Minors apparently did nothing to diminish his self-confidence. When Pittsburgh sent him his first Major League contract, he wrote to the team president, Bill Benswanger, and asked for more money. "You have heard of Joe DiMaggio of the American League," he wrote. "I am going to be the Johnny Rizzo of the National League."[12] At first it appeared that he would make good on his boast. He got off to a spectacular start with the Pirates in 1938 and seemed destined to become one of the stars of the National League. A feature story on the "broad-shouldered lad of Italian extraction" appeared in the May 5 issue of the *Sporting News*, identifying him as part of the growing ethnic competition in the Major Leagues: "The story of John Costa Rizzo is another chapter in the record of the new generation of Italian athletes, since the Latins came over the diamond horizon to vie with the Germans, the Irish, the Poles and the Vikings. With boys like Joe and Vince DiMaggio, Cookie Lavagetto . . . and several other young luminaries in their ascendancy, Il Duce's boys are doing fairly well by themselves." The story also noted the apparent irony of a Texas Italian. "Although Johnny was born in Texas, when you look at his thick chest, his pearly teeth and his raven locks you might surmise that he had landed with one of the late Italian quotas, although he has yet to see the land of Mussolini."[13]

In 143 games the burly outfielder (six feet, 190 pounds) hit .301 with twenty-three home runs, a Pittsburgh record that stood until 1947, when Ralph Kiner hit fifty-one. He finished sixth in the NL MVP balloting with ninety-six votes, the most any Italian American player had ever received except for Ernie Lombardi, who that same year became the first Italian American to win the award.

But Rizzo's fast start proved to be the beginning of a five-year roller coaster ride. The next year he fell victim to the sophomore jinx (.261, six homers, fifty-five RBIs), then came back strong in 1940, hitting twenty-four home runs with the Pirates, Reds, and Phillies. In his next two seasons he played in fewer than one hundred games each year and hit a total of eight home runs. Rizzo then spent three years in the service and never returned to the Major Leagues. His downward spiral may have been linked to his volatile temperament. When he died in 1977, his *Sporting News* obituary noted that from 1939 on, "it was all downhill for Rizzo, whose temper tantrums alienated teammates and fans."[14]

Dario Lodigiani

Frank Angelo "Creepy" Crespi, who hit .263 in five years as a second baseman with the Cardinals, may have had the most interesting name of the 1938 newcomers, but it was Dario Lodigiani who had the longest and most notable career. A San Francisco native, he was a neighbor and teammate of the DiMaggio brothers, was tutored by Ping Bodie, and played against Frank Crosetti when he got to the big leagues. His recollections provide a glimpse of life inside the San Francisco Italian baseball community.

Lodigiani, whose parents, Carlo and Antoinetta, had emigrated from a town near Milan, was born on June 6, 1916, in the North Beach neighborhood, where his father worked as a baker. The family moved to Napa for a time, then returned to North Beach, where their home at 469 Greenwich Street was just four blocks from the DiMaggio home on Taylor Street. He recalled that everyone in the neighborhood, including the children, spoke Italian. "My brothers and I spoke Italian with our parents," he said. "When I went away to play ball, my dad would write to me in Italian, and I'd write back in Italian. Everybody in North Beach spoke Italian, at least the dialects their parents spoke. We spoke Milanese; the DiMaggios were Sicilian. George Puccinelli's family was from Lucca, so they spoke Tuscan." Like so many North Beach Italian kids, Lodigiani grew up playing baseball, either at the North Beach Playground or at Funston Playground. "There was nothing for us to do as kids other than play baseball," he said. One of his teammates at Francisco Junior High was Joe DiMaggio. "Joe was the shortstop, and I was the second baseman," he recalled. "Then I played two years in high school with Dom."[15]

After making all-star teams in baseball, basketball, and football at Galileo High, Lodigiani was offered a scholarship to St. Mary's College (a baseball powerhouse in the West) but decided to take a shot at pro ball instead. "I played my first year out of high school with Oakland and made $150 a month. I was tickled to death; it was during the Depression. Dad was kind of hesitant about my not continuing school and playing ball. He said, 'You want to become a ballplayer? You'll become a bum.' But when I got to the point where I was making more money than he was, he said, 'Boy, you've got a good job.'"[16]

While playing for Oakland, Lodigiani received a batting tip from an unlikely source. His father knew almost nothing about baseball ("he thought bocce was the national pastime"), but he did listen to the radio broadcasts of his son's games. At times he would hear the announcer say that Lodigiani hit a popup. "One time," Lodigiani said, "I came home after a game and he asked me, 'What's this poppa-up I hear on the radio?' 'Pop,' I said, 'that's when I hit the ball under the center and it goes straight up in the air.' Then he said, 'I know what you do. Put one of those inner soles in your shoe, then you'll be taller and you'll hit the ball in the middle.'"

After three years with Oakland, the five-foot-eight, 170-pound second baseman went east to play for Connie Mack's Philadelphia Athletics in 1938. It proved to be a new experience for the kid from San Francisco. "When I first went to Philadelphia, some of the writers wanted to shorten my name to Lodi, but I said, 'No, use the whole thing. You'll get used to it.' The only person who couldn't pronounce my name was Connie Mack. He'd just call me 'young man.' Playing for Mr. Mack was like playing for your father. If you made a mistake, he would never say anything at the time, but he'd write it down in his notebook. Then the next day he'd call you over and let you know about it in a quiet way."

The Philadelphia fans, however, were not so quiet. "If you played in front of those fans, the toughest fans in the world, you could play anywhere," Lodigiani said. "They had these cups filled with ice. They'd suck the lemonade out of [the cup] and, if you made a boot,

10. Dario Lodigiani with Connie Mack, owner and manager of the Philadelphia Athletics, ca. 1938. Courtesy of Diane Lodigiani.

whoom!, it would come down on you. One day I made an error late in the game and somebody took off a shoe and threw it at me. I went over and picked it up and saw it was a brand new Florsheim shoe, size 8.5, and I thought to myself, 'Throw the other one down and I've got a pair of shoes.'"

Lodigiani also picked up some new vocabulary in the city of brotherly love. "They didn't call you a wop or a dago; they called you a guinea. I didn't know what a guinea was; what the hell's a guinea?" The local Italian community was more hospitable. "South Philadelphia had the big Italian settlement," he said, "and they'd invite me down there to the different functions they had. I remember one time I was invited to an Italian sports club and I got into a bocce ball tournament with them."

When the Athletics played the Yankees, Lodigiani would talk to DiMaggio and Crosetti during batting practice. One day Commissioner Landis was sitting in the front row and motioned to Lodigiani to come over. "I went over there, and he said, 'Did you read that bulletin about not fraternizing? The next time I see you talking to those fellows, it's going to cost you some money.' I told him they were friends at home, and he said, 'I don't care whose friends they are, you don't talk to them.'"

After two seasons as a starting infielder with the Athletics and one year with Toronto in the International League, Lodigiani played for the White Sox in '41 and '42 before serving for three years in the Army Air Corps with a B-17 squadron in the South Pacific. Following the war, he returned to the White Sox in 1946 for one final season.

Lodigiani's career in professional baseball was hardly over, however. Like so many before him, he returned to the Pacific Coast League, playing with the Oakland Oaks and the San Francisco Seals until 1952. He managed in the Minors for two years, then worked as a coach for the Indians and A's and as a scout for the White Sox. At the time I interviewed him in October 2000, he was still serving as a part-time White Sox scout in northern California. It was his sixty-fifth year in professional baseball. In recognition of his service to the franchise, the White Sox awarded him a ring following their 2005 World Series win. Lodigiani, who was inducted into the Pacific Coast League Hall of Fame in 2006, died in 2008 in Napa.

What did all those years in the game mean to him? "Baseball has been real great to me," he said. "It's given me a job that I've loved all my life, taken care of me and my family. I've been very, very lucky. I still get a big kick out of sitting in the stands and watching those high school and college kids play. I'd give anything if 1935 could roll around again and I could play again."

Nino Bongiovanni

Of the five rookies who made their debut in 1938, Anthony "Nino" Bongiovanni had the shortest Major League career—sixty-eight games in '38 and '39—but he made up for that in personal longevity. When I spoke with him in November 2005, he was a few weeks shy of his ninety-fifth birthday and held the distinction of being the oldest surviving Major Leaguer of Italian descent. The son of immigrants from Palermo, he was born on December 21, 1911, in Donaldson, Louisiana, about fifty miles from New Orleans. Unable to make enough money picking sugar cane, when Nino was two, his father moved the family to San Jose, California. Nino and his two sisters were examples of the reluctance of second-generation Italian Americans to identify fully with their parents' culture. When I asked if they spoke Italian with their parents, he said, "They used to tell us to answer in Italian, but we never did."[17]

In a January 2005 interview Bongiovanni recalled what he did to play baseball early in the twentieth century. "We used to cut the weeds in the field and make our own baselines, and that was our ballpark," he said. "The rest of the infield and outfield was all weeds. I wanted to play ball so badly, I took a two-by-four that was about two feet long and a pocket knife and I made a bat out of it. I took a round stone and wrapped it with all kinds of string and then wrapped it with bicycle tape, and you don't know what it felt like to hit that kind of ball with that kind of bat."[18]

Like so many Californians, the left-handed hitting outfielder began his professional career in the Pacific Coast League, joining Seattle in 1933. There he was known as "Bongi" because "they didn't have room to put the name in the newspaper," he told me. In 1934 he was traded to Portland, where he stayed until being drafted by the Cincinnati Reds in 1938. In 1939 he appeared in sixty-six games with the Reds, but he had trouble with Manager Bill McKechnie. "I didn't like him," he said. "He didn't like me because he always called me 'dago,' and I didn't care for that. But I was too shy to tell him not to do it."

Bongiovanni recalled that in his first season in Portland, he hit in forty-three straight games. In the forty-fourth game he reached base on a bunt and a bad-hop grounder, both of which were ruled as errors, then went on to hit safely in twelve more games. "The scorekeeper took two hits away from me in the forty-fourth game, so I say in my book I hit in fifty-six straight games; I would have tied Joe DiMaggio." Amazingly Bongiovanni still remembered the scorekeeper's name, seventy years after the fact: "Screwball Gregory was his name."

At the end of our conversation in 2005 the nearly ninety-five-year-old Bongiovanni said, "People ask me sometimes to what do I owe all of my longevity, and I say four things: I never smoked, never drank any alcohol, never took any dope, and never had any sex until I was ten years old." At which point he laughed heartily.

1939

The last group of rookies in the thirties was also the largest of the decade. While none of the eleven was to have an outstanding career, nine remained in the Majors for four or more years, and three had careers ranging from eleven to thirteen years. And one would go on to achieve greater fame as a television soap opera star after his Major League career ended.

Marius Russo

Born in 1914, Marius Ugo Russo was signed by the Yankees after pitching for Brooklyn College and Long Island University. Near the end of Russo's rookie year, when he went 8-3 with a 2.41 ERA, Fred

Lieb wrote a feature story for the *Sporting News*. The headline, with a play on Lazzeri's "Poosh 'Em Up" nickname, read, "Viva Russo! Southpaw Poosh 'Em Downer of Yankees Promises to Give Italians Their First Major Hill Star."[19]

Lieb, following the lead of Dan Daniel's 1936 story, "Viva Italia!," pointed out the paucity of Italian pitchers before Russo. Noting that "within the past decade these sons of the sunny Mediterranean peninsula have become more and more numerous," he then added, "In one department, boys of Italian origin seem to be backward. Perhaps they develop more on the line of the offense than the defense, as the great race of Cicero and Marc Anthony has given us no pitchers of the first class." But in Russo "an Italian boy bids fair to become the first real big league pitcher of that race." According to Lieb, Russo played pro ball "to help earn some of the family spaghetti." The cartoon accompanying the story showed a line of eleven Italian American Major Leaguers, from Bodie to DiMaggio, with Russo looking on and saying, "Guess I'll have to tell 'em I'm a Swede—or else play in the outfield." Below, a batter swinging at, and missing, one of Russo's pitches, is saying, "He's a traitor to his country."[20]

Russo, whose 1939 performance earned him a spot in the starting rotation, continued to pitch well in the next two seasons (14-8 and 14-10) and was named to the 1941 All-Star team. He was never as effective again; injuries limited him to nine games in '42, and in '43 he fell to a 5-10 record. After missing two years to World War II, Russo returned for one final season in 1946 but appeared in only eight games. In six seasons he won forty-five and lost thirty-four, with a solid 3.13 ERA, and in both the '41 and '43 World Series he pitched complete game wins, giving up a total of one run and eleven hits.

Johnny Berardino, Soap Star

Like Ernie Orsatti, John Berardino was a native of Los Angeles who was involved in the movie industry from an early age. Born in 1917, Berardino appeared in a few of the "Our Gang" comedies as a child actor. He was also a talented athlete who attended the University of Southern California on a football scholarship, then turned to a career in baseball.

A right-handed-hitting second baseman, Berardino was a starter in his first three seasons with the St. Louis Browns, played in a reserve role in 1942, then missed three seasons while serving in the navy. After regaining his role as a starter for St. Louis in 1946, he was almost traded to the Washington Senators. According to Shirley Povich, Berardino was traded to Washington for Gerry Priddy but refused to report, claiming he had an offer to act in Hollywood. When Berardino told Washington owner Clark Griffith to deal with his agent, Griffith called off the deal.[21]

Following the 1947 season, Indians' owner Bill Veeck bought Berardino from St. Louis, then had the part-time actor's face insured for $100,000.[22] Berardino auditioned for a role as a ballplayer in *The Stratton Story*, a film about White Sox pitcher Monty Stratton, who lost his leg in a hunting accident, but he was passed over by director Sam Wood. "The son of a bitch had never heard of me," Berardino said years later, "and said I didn't look like a major league ballplayer."[23] Berardino spent seven seasons as a utility player for the Indians, Browns, and Pirates before being released by Pittsburgh in 1952. In eleven years he compiled an average of .249 with thirty-six home runs and 387 runs batted in.

Berardino, who would recite excerpts from Shakespeare to entertain his roommates, then returned to Hollywood and resumed his acting career.[24] He appeared in several television shows, but his niche in entertainment history was established when, in 1963, he became one of the original cast members of the ABC soap opera *General Hospital.* (His name had appeared in credits at various times as Barardino and Berardino, but by this time he had dropped the second "r" in his name and become John Beradino, presumably because he thought it easier to pronounce.) For more than thirty years he played the role of Dr. Steve Hardy and was nominated three times for an Emmy as best actor in a daytime drama. He died in 1996 at the age of seventy-nine.

Berardino was one of six 1939 rookies whose careers were interrupted by military service in World War II. Of those six, three returned to play only one or two more years in the Majors. Other than Berardino, only two played beyond 1947: Herman Franks and Sibby Sisti.

After immigrating from Cloz, a small town north of Trento, Celeste Franch went to photography school, settled in Price, Utah, married Edith Dozzi, and changed his surname to Franks. Not long after Herman was born in 1914, the family moved to Salt Lake City. When his parents divorced in 1920, Franks stayed in Salt Lake City with his mother. Although he lettered in four sports, Franks admitted that he encountered some prejudice when he was in high school. "In the twenties and early thirties, when you were Italian, you didn't talk about eating spaghetti and garlic," he said. But even if his Anglicized name concealed his ethnic background, Franks insists that he never did: "I have always been Italian and proud of it."[25]

As a youngster, Franks had the chance to see at least one famous Italian who served as a role model. "When I was a kid, I used to watch Tony Lazzeri in Salt Lake," he recalled. (Lazzeri was with the Bees in 1922, '24, and '25, the year he hit sixty home runs.) "He was very popular," said Franks.

When Franks was growing up, there was not much of a baseball tradition in Utah. "Baseball wasn't played here that much because of the winter," he said. "I was one of the very first guys to come out of Utah to play Major League Baseball." (He was in fact only the ninth Utah native to play in the Majors.) But he did play amateur ball and recalls playing for the first American Legion team in the state. He attended the University of Utah but did not graduate. "I got too smart and I knew more than the professors," he joked. One stop on his road to the Majors was in Los Angeles, where he played for a meatpacking company in 1934. "That was in the Depression," he said. "I was making big wages, twenty-six dollars a week."

Franks was a backup catcher for three years with the Cardinals and Dodgers before entering the service in 1942. He returned to the Majors in 1947 but appeared in only 49 games for the Athletics and Giants over the next three seasons. In his six-year career he played in only 188 games and compiled a lifetime average of .199, but he obviously learned the game from his vantage point on the bench. He served as a coach for the Giants from 1949 to '55, then again in 1958 and 1964 after they moved to San Francisco. In 1965 he was named manager of the Giants, leading them to a second-place finish in each of the next four years. A decade later he managed the Cubs in 1977, '78, and part of '79.

Throughout his baseball career Franks also pursued business interests in and around Salt Lake City and in the process became a wealthy man. "All the time I was in baseball, I was in different businesses," he said. "A chain of grocery stores, we made mobile homes, I developed a very exclusive area here in Salt Lake." With all that money and all those business pursuits, why did he return to baseball as a manager? "I love baseball," he said. "I retired about five or six times. The Cubs called me in '77. I kind of missed it, so I went back. Then

[Cubs owner William] Wrigley called me again in '81 and asked me to be general manager. Then I retired, and I've been retired ever since." Franks died on March 30, 2009, at the age of ninety-five.

Sebastian "Sibby" Sisti, whose grandparents immigrated from central Italy, grew up in an Italian neighborhood on the west side of Buffalo, New York. After graduating from high school, he signed with the Boston Braves in 1938, then made his Major League debut the next year at the age of eighteen. He started at third and second for three years before entering the service in 1943, then returned to Boston in 1946. In his remaining nine years in the big leagues he played in more than one hundred games only twice before retiring with a lifetime batting average of .244.

Like most ballplayers of his era, Sisti worked during the off-season. "Every year after the season was over I'd have to go out and get a job," he said. "My first year in the big leagues, my salary was $400 a month, and I got a big raise my second year; I made $450 a month. When you talk about the salaries these guys are making today, it's enough to make you sick. Guys who knew I was a Major League ballplayer would say, 'What are you doing working?' I used to have a stock answer. I said, 'I've got a very bad habit; I like to eat in the winter time like I do in the summer.' I was a truck driver for a good twenty-five years during the off-season, and after I quit managing in baseball, I stuck with driving all the time."[26]

Sisti managed in the Braves organization for seven years after his release in 1954. He donned a baseball uniform one more time, appearing as a manager in the 1984 film *The Natural*. "Baseball," he said, "earned me a living and earned me recognition throughout the United States. I'm very proud to be Italian and represent the Italian heritage." Sisti, who still lived in a suburb of Buffalo, died on April 24, 2006, at the age of eighty-five, survived by his wife, Norine (Barone), five children, eleven grandchildren, and sixteen great-grandchildren.

One of the 1939 rookies who did not lose time to World War II was Phil Masi, a catcher from Chicago who spent fourteen years in the big leagues. His was an unremarkable career except for its unusual progression. A teammate of Sisti's with the Braves, Masi was a reserve through his first six years in the Majors, never playing in more than 89 games even during the war, when the talent pool was deleted. Then in 1945, at age twenty-nine, the longtime bench player suddenly became a regular and achieved unprecedented success. From 1945 to 1948 he appeared in at least 113 games, was named to the All-Star team each year, and received votes for MVP in '45 and '46. Johnny Antonelli, who was a teammate of Masi's in 1948, recalled the catcher's durability: "He caught doubleheaders, day games after night games," said Antonelli. "He was never tired."[27]

Masi was also the source of a classic baseball anecdote. One day the Braves were facing the Giants when Al Javery, the Boston pitcher, gave up hits on the first three pitches he threw. Manager Casey Stengel came out of the dugout, called Masi to the mound, and asked his catcher what kind of pitches Javery was throwing. "I don't know," Masi reportedly said, "I haven't caught one yet."[28]

All-Italian-American Baseball Team

In its August 13, 1939, issue, the *New York Times* published the All-Italian-American baseball team as selected by the National Italian-American Civic League. When compared to the All-Italian-American team that appeared in *Baseball Magazine* in 1934, in which five of the fourteen players were minor leaguers, this list of twenty players indicates the growing number of notable Italians playing in the Majors by the end of the thirties. (The *Times* list does include two minor leaguers, both with the Kansas City Blues: Phil Rizzuto, who would make his Major League debut in 1941, and Vince DiMaggio, who had been a starter for the Boston Bees in '37 and '38 and would return to the Majors as a regular in 1940.)

First base	Bonura, Giants	Camilli, Dodgers
Second base	Cuccinello, Bees	Berardino, Browns
Third base	Lavagetto, Dodgers	Lodigiani, Athletics
Shortstop	Crosetti, Yankees	Rizzuto, KC Blues
Left field	Rizzo, Pirates	Chiozza, Giants
Center field	J. DiMaggio, Yankees	V. DiMaggio, KC Blues
Right field	Bongiovanni, Reds	Cavarretta, Cubs
Catcher	Lombardi, Reds	Giuliani, Senators
Pitcher	Russo, Yankees	Salvo, Giants
Utility	Sisti, Bees	Mancuso, Cubs
Umpire	Babe Pinelli	

Just as it was difficult to determine with absolute certainty why so few Italian Americans appeared in the Majors by the end of the 1920s, it is no less difficult to offer conclusive reasons for the sudden increase in their numbers in the 1930s. It does not appear that the attitude of Italian parents had changed significantly. Anecdotal evidence gathered from interviews with players indicates that parents of aspiring ballplayers continued to doubt that their sons could make a living playing a boy's game. As we have seen, however, parental opposition usually evaporated when the first paychecks were brought home, especially during the Depression years.

The main factor contributing to the increase would appear to be a simple matter of demographics. The number of foreign-born

Italians in America reached its peak in 1930, numbering about 1.8 million. Since the peak of Italian immigration came in the first decade of the twentieth century, it is obvious that by the mid- to late twenties there were more Italian Americans reaching the age when they could become professional ballplayers. This conclusion would seem to be supported by the fact that Slavs, whose peak immigration years roughly coincided with those of Italians, also entered the Majors in increasing numbers in the thirties.

Also, an increasing number of Italians were living in various parts of the country, away from the large cities of the Northeast and Midwest. With a greater number of youngsters living away from the crowded urban centers (where fewer diamonds meant fewer opportunities to learn the game), presumably more Italian Americans were honing their baseball skills. In turn, there was a greater likelihood that youngsters who displayed talent would be seen by scouts, signed to pro contracts, and begin working their way through the minor league system.

In fact, as we have seen, there was much greater geographical distribution of Italian Americans entering the big leagues in the thirties than had been the case previously. Of the twenty-two players who had made it to the Majors by 1929, eight came from California, three from New York,) and three from Pennsylvania. While a third of those entering in the thirties came from California, an increasing number were coming from the Midwest, the South, and the Southwest. All in all eighteen states other than California were represented, from Alabama to Minnesota, from Indiana to Utah.

Another possible reason for the increase was the continuing interest on the part of management to recruit ethnic players, at least in cities with large ethnic populations. In a reversal of the pattern we have noted throughout, Herman Franks thought it would have improved his chances of getting to the big leagues had his name been more obviously Italian. "I would have really liked to have had more of an Italian name," he said. "It would have been beneficial to me. They wanted Jewish players, Italian players, to draw fans."[29]

In his history of the business side of baseball since 1921, *Much More Than a Game*, Robert Burk offered another explanation for the owners' interest in recruiting ethnic players. In the twenties, when Irish and German Americans continued to dominate Major League rosters, "the continued overall reliance on the Minors meant that the ethnic and regional composition of the major league playing force changed only modestly."[30] According to the data compiled by Hall of Fame historian Lee Allen, by 1929 only 6 percent of Major League rookies were of South and East European heritage.[31] Obviously the efforts of a few franchises to recruit players who would appeal to their ethnic fan base had little impact on the overall makeup of Major League rosters.

With the onset of the Depression and the need to economize, owners were selling off many of their players, thus opening the door to new recruits. Prior to the 1931 season a new National Agreement establishing a universal, compulsory draft gave Major League clubs greater control over the Minors and the ability to lower the cost of signing new players. "In their push to acquire and control a larger pool of low-cost playing labor, baseball owners in the 1930s opened wider the doors of ethnic and regional access," wrote Burk. "Despite the rising tide of immigration to U.S. shores in the late nineteenth and early twentieth centuries, entry by these Southern and Eastern European sons into a major league career had been bottlenecked as late as the 1920s by the draft controversies with the high minors."[32] According to Lee Allen's data, by 1940 the proportion of Major League rookies of South and East European heritage was close to 20 percent of the total, as compared to only 6 percent in 1929.

While Burk's analysis is not always substantiated by hard evidence or precise documentation of sources, it does provide a reasonable supplement to the simpler explanation that credits the sudden rise of the new ethnics to demographics alone: there were more Italian and Slavic Americans in the Majors in the thirties because there were more of them in the general population. Demographics notwithstanding, it is noteworthy that the sudden surge coincided more or less with the economic crisis of the Depression. In such harsh circumstances, when jobs of any kind were hard to come by, wouldn't players from the previously established ethnic groups (English, German, Irish) be just as likely to want Major League jobs as anyone else? And given their well-established foothold, wouldn't they have been more likely to get them unless other circumstances had intervened? Of course Burk's assertion that the ethnic makeup of the game was changing because of the owners' desire to hire cheaper labor, as plausible as it is, would be more compelling had the sudden increase not begun in 1930, before the full impact of the Depression had taken effect. Nevertheless, it seems reasonable to conclude that both economics and demographics played a role in the dramatic changes in Major League personnel that occurred in the thirties.

As we have seen, the emergence of several prominent Italian American players, most notably Joe DiMaggio, spurred more intense media coverage in the thirties. The language adopted by some writers was in itself revealing of ongoing societal attitudes toward immigrants and their children. The entry of increasing numbers of Italian American players was an "invasion," a metaphor occasionally linked directly to Mussolini's assault on Africa. At other times Italians were said to be "threatening" to replace the Irish on the diamond.

Whatever the tone, media coverage suggested that Italian Americans were entering the Majors in large numbers, even supplanting other ethnic groups. In fact that was never the case. Lee Allen's data on rookies indicate that players of Irish, German, and English descent continued to dominate the game. Each of those groups still represented a larger percentage of players than any other ethnic group. The following list indicates the number of rookies from the four ethnic groups for selected years, including players who listed multiple nationalities (for example, Irish-Scotch), followed by their percentage of all rookies in that year. In cases in which two of the target groups are listed (for example, English-German), players were identified according to the first nationality listed.

	English	Irish	German	Italian	Total
1920	22 (16%)	37 (27%)	29 (21%)	2 (1%)	135
1930	19 (19%)	30 (31%)	. 18 (18%)	5 (5%)	98
1935	22 (19%)	37 (32%)	18 (16%)	9 (8%)	116
1939	38 (30%)	28 (22%)	28 (22%)	11 (9%)	127[33]

Though their numbers were increasing dramatically relative to previous decades, Italian American players continued to be greatly outnumbered by those of the dominant ethnic groups. In 1930, '35, and '39 there was an average of twenty-six rookies of English descent, thirty-two of Irish descent, and twenty-one of German descent. By comparison, no more than eleven Italian rookies entered the Majors in any one year in the thirties, and the average number per year was six. Although the proportion of rookies of Irish descent dropped from 32 percent in 1935 to 22 percent in 1939, that decline was offset by the increase in the number of English and German rookies. In 1939 players of Irish, English, and German descent represented 77 percent of all rookies, compared with 67 percent in 1935.

Similarly while the proportion of all Italian American Major

Leaguers, not just rookies, increased throughout the thirties, it never surpassed 6 percent of the total number of players in any given year. In 1930 Italian Americans comprised 2.0 percent of all Major Leaguers; by 1935 the figure had risen to 4.5 percent, and by 1939, 5.6 percent.[34]

In the decade that ended in 1939 the number of Italian Americans who entered the Major Leagues was more than double the number who had ever played in all previous years. Whatever the reasons for the increase, the door had been opened wider than ever before. While their arrival was not always met with enthusiasm, their impact on the game was undeniable, most notably, but not exclusively, because of the sudden stardom of Joe DiMaggio. But just as DiMaggio's greatest achievements, and fame, were still to come, so too with Italian Americans in general, who would reach unprecedented heights in the postwar era.

7

The First MVPS
Lombardi, Camilli, and Cavarretta

The Most Valuable Player Award, which has existed in its current form since 1931, represents Major League Baseball's official recognition of its best players. There could be no more visible and public proof, therefore, that Italian American ballplayers had reached the pinnacle of America's game than to receive that honor. The first four to win the award all made their Major League debuts in the thirties. Joe DiMaggio, who won the award three times, will be discussed below. This chapter is devoted to the other three earliest recipients of baseball's most prestigious accolade: Ernie Lombardi (1938), Dolph Camilli (1941), and Phil Cavarretta (1945).

Ernie Lombardi

Lombardi was one of the more tragic figures in big league history. His statistics and the judgment of his peers clearly identify him as one of the best hitters of his era. No less an authority than Ted Williams considered him to be one of the best ever. An eight-time All-Star and one of only two catchers to win two batting titles, he hit over .300 ten times during his seventeen-year career and compiled a lifetime average of .306. In 1938, the year he won his first batting title,

11. Ernie Lombardi, 1938 National League MVP, with his trademark overlapping grip. National Baseball Hall of Fame Library, Cooperstown NY.

he became the first Italian American to win the MVP Award. Yet for all that, Lombardi was remembered less for his prodigious hitting than for his comic nickname ("the Schnozz"), ungainly physique, lead feet, and a single lapse in a World Series game. In the pantheon of baseball heroes Lombardi plays the role of a comic figure, a Falstaff among so many Prince Hals. Increasingly despondent after his retirement, in part because of his failure to be elected to the Hall of Fame, he once attempted suicide, and his life ended in isolation and bitterness.

Another of the many players from the San Francisco Bay Area, Ernesto Natali Lombardi was born in Oakland on April 6, 1908. A standout on the local sandlots, he quit school as a teenager to work in the grocery store run by his father, Dominic, an immigrant from Piedmont. But he continued to play amateur and semi-pro ball, and when he was offered a contract to play for the Oakland Oaks in the PCL, he gladly moved out from behind the grocery counter.

It was while playing for Oakland (from 1926 to 1930) that Lombardi adopted his unorthodox batting grip. When a blister on the little finger of his right hand made it painful to swing the bat, he locked the little finger under the index finger of his left hand in the manner of an interlocking golf grip. The grip not only alleviated the pain but improved his hitting so much that Lombardi never went back to the traditional way of holding the bat.

When the Dodgers purchased his contract at the end of the 1930 season, the *Sporting News* reported that Lombardi "would appeal greatly to the Italian vote, which makes up a comparatively large portion of the summertime customers at Ebbets Field."[1] But he reportedly did not get along with Brooklyn manager Wilbert Robinson, and after one year he was traded to Cincinnati. In his ten years in Cincinnati he played in an average of 120 games a year, hit over .300 seven times, and was selected to the All-Star team each year from 1936 to 1940.

Lombardi's best all-around season came in 1938, when he hit .342 to become only the second catcher (after Bubbles Hargrave in 1926) to win a batting title.[2] Perhaps the most remarkable detail from that season is that he struck out only fourteen times in 489 times at bat. It was also the year he caught Johnny Vander Meer's back-to-back no-hitters. Following the season, the Baseball Writers' Association of America named him the National League's Most Valuable Player.

In his 1948 history of the Cincinnati Reds, Lee Allen wrote the following: "In the summer of 1938, when the ominous clouds of war were growing ever darker, the people of Cincinnati, one slice of the isolationist Midwest of America, were cheering the names of Johnny Vander Meer and Ernie Lombardi, the sons, respectively, of a Dutch stonecutter and an Italian grocer, living testimony as to the value of the melting-pot tradition and the glory of a game."[3]

After hitting only .264 in 1941, Lombardi was traded to the Boston Braves. Whether rejuvenated by the change of scenery or motivated by revenge, he came back to hit .330 in 1942 and win his second batting title. It is one of the unchallenged axioms of baseball that catchers are unable to sustain a high batting average over the course of the season because of the unique physical and mental demands of the position. The constant crouching, the foul tips that smash into fingers, the bone-bruising collisions with runners, calling the right pitches and handling the sometimes delicate psyche of a pitching staff—all these drain the body and mind so that by August and September the productivity of even the best-hitting catchers is likely to fall off. It is both proof of that axiom and a testimony of Lombardi's remarkable skill as a hitter that no other catcher won a batting title until Joe Mauer in 2006. (Mauer then became the only catcher to win three batting titles by repeating in 2008 and 2009.)

A salary cap imposed during World War II forced the Braves to trade Lombardi to the Giants in 1943. Exempt from military service as the sole support of his father and sister, he spent his last five seasons in New York, making the All-Star team in both 1943 and 1945 before being released in September 1947.

In part because of his size and the appearance of clumsiness, Lombardi has never been ranked among the outstanding defensive catchers. At six-foot-three and 230 pounds, he was routinely described in the press as "lumbering" and "cumbersome," but the consensus was that he was a solid receiver who handled pitchers well and possessed one of the strongest and most accurate throwing arms in the Majors. His major weakness was his lack of mobility, which meant that he was not particularly adept at fielding bunts or pop flies or at preventing passed balls. In fact he holds the Major League record for most years leading the league in passed balls (ten).

Whatever his abilities as a catcher, it was with his bat, not his glove, that Ernie Lombardi made his mark in the Major Leagues. His lifetime average of .306 is third highest among the sixteen catchers in the Hall of Fame, trailing only Mickey Cochrane and Bill Dickey. In spite of his size, Lombardi was not the prototypical power hitter, never hitting more than twenty homers in a season. He was, however, an outstanding contact hitter; in 5,855 times at bat, he struck out only 262 times. What Ernie Lombardi did better than just about anyone was hit blistering line drives that terrified opposing pitchers and infielders. Giants pitcher Carl Hubbell once said, "I thought he might hurt me, even kill me, with one of those liners. They were screamers."[4] In fact in 1937 one of Lombardi's line drives did break three fingers on the right hand of Cubs pitcher Larry French.

Lombardi's lifetime average of .306 is all the more remarkable given his legendary slowness on the base paths; there were few if any "leg hits" in his career. In baseball lingo a "piano man" is someone who runs as if he were carrying a piano on his back. By that standard

Lombardi, considered the slowest runner of his time, lugged a large pipe organ. It was common for infielders to play on the outfield grass when he came to the plate, knowing they had plenty of time to throw him out. Lombardi once told Dodger shortstop Pee Wee Reese, "It was five years before I learned you weren't an outfielder." Sibby Sisti, a Braves infielder for thirteen years, recalled playing against Lombardi. "I played deep on the grass, like every other infielder," he told me. "It was amazing to see that a guy could hit so well that couldn't run a lick. He was the slowest man I've ever seen in baseball."[5]

Lombardi's greatness as a hitter was widely acknowledged by his peers and the press. Lee Allen, the late historian of the Hall of Fame, recalled the scene as Ted Williams toured the baseball shrine on the morning of his own induction. As he looked at an exhibit listing the game's lifetime batting leaders, Williams said to former teammate Bobby Doerr, "Do you know who was one of the greatest batters of all time? Ernie Lombardi! If he had had normal speed, he would have made batting marks that would still be on the books."[6]

At the same time he was being praised for his hitting, Lombardi was also subject to ridicule because of his appearance. Wearing the baggy uniform of the era, he gave the impression of being lumpy rather than burly. And atop his ungainly body sat a doughy face dominated by a large, bulbous nose. Never camera-friendly, he simply did not look like an athlete. Even in his prime Lombardi looked more like a rumpled manager than a batting champion.

The 1930s was a decade marked by colorful nicknames, many of which appear insensitive by today's standards: Stinky Davis, Fat Freddie Fitzsimmons, Twinkletoes Selkirk. One of the more disparaging nicknames based on appearance was hung on Lombardi, whose conspicuous nose earned him the handle of "the Schnozz." Other, less offensive, nicknames were used by teammates and those afraid to call him "Schnozz" to his face, including "Lom," "Lumbago," and "Bocce," a name he acquired as a child because of his skill at the Italian bowling game. But it was his best known nickname that most clearly identified him as an object of ridicule. Lombardi was a gentle man who took the ribbing in good humor. But the time would come when his outlook changed.

The "Snooze" Play

From Fred Merkle in 1908 to Bill Buckner in 1986 "goats" have been a staple of baseball lore. A source of nostalgic anecdotes for fans, the label can leave an indelible stain on an otherwise stellar career. It was in the fourth and final game of the 1939 World Series that Lombardi was involved in the play that would forever tarnish his reputation.

With the Yankees leading three games to none, Game 4 was tied 4–4 after nine innings. In the top of the tenth Joe DiMaggio came to the plate with Frank Crosetti on third and Charlie Keller on first. DiMaggio hit a single to right, scoring Crosetti with the go-ahead run. When right fielder Ivar Goodman bobbled the ball, Keller rounded third and headed for home. As Lombardi took the throw and applied the tag, Keller bowled him over, leaving the catcher momentarily stunned. DiMaggio, seeing Lombardi lying on the ground and the ball a few feet away, headed for home. Before Lombardi could recover, DiMaggio slid across home plate and was signaled safe by Babe Pinelli.

Grantland Rice, then the dean of American sportswriters, set the tone for future accounts of the play: "You won't believe what I am telling you—and I don't blame you. But it happened this way—the greatest World Series anticlimax I've ever seen in 35 years of close inspection." According to Rice, the stunned catcher lay on his back as DiMaggio raced home, "with Lombardi still at rest, a stricken being" with "no idea the roving DiMaggio was on his way to the plate."[7]

The problem is that it didn't happen "this way." Film of the play, as well as still photographs, clearly reveal that Lombardi did not lay "at rest." The film shows Lombardi getting knocked down by Keller, then lying face down on the ground as the ball rolls a few feet away. As a Yankee player waves DiMaggio home, Lombardi regains his senses and picks up the ball. He then makes a lunging tag that DiMaggio gracefully eludes with a perfect hook slide away from Lombardi's outstretched glove.

Regardless of its inaccuracy, it was Rice's typically colorful version of the play that stuck and apparently became the source of virtually all future accounts. Apart from the blatant inaccuracy, which survives to this day, the question remains: Why has this play assumed mythic proportions in the annals of baseball history? Since his was the final run in a 7–4 victory, DiMaggio's tally was meaningless; the play had no effect on the outcome of the game or the Series. Was it because there was so little else of dramatic interest in the Series that this one episode became its signature play? Would the play have received so much attention if the player sliding across home plate had been anyone other than Joe DiMaggio? Would the same play have received so much attention had it been made by a catcher whose physical appearance had not already made him an object of ridicule? Had it not been for his well-established image as a clumsy backstop, it is unlikely that the "snooze" play would have gained the prominence that it did, thereby cementing Lombardi's reputation as a comic character.

By all accounts Lombardi was a gentle giant during his playing days, a friendly, quiet guy who was well liked by teammates and adored by Cincinnati fans. But in the years following his retirement Lombardi became embittered and depressed. Perhaps the indignities he had quietly endured throughout his career, together with the stigma of the "snooze," had done more damage than he knew or was willing to admit. Whatever the reasons, Lombardi's mental state deteriorated to the point where, on the night of April 8, 1953, he succumbed to his inner demons. While he and his wife were visiting friends, Lombardi excused himself, went into a bedroom and slit his throat with a razor. Rushed to a hospital, he soon recovered, then checked into a sanitarium to be treated for depression. In subsequent years Lombardi grew even more despondent and reclusive. Nothing did more to fuel his bitterness than his failure to be elected to the Hall of Fame, first by the Baseball Writers' Association and then by the Hall of Fame Veterans Committee.

Following his retirement, Lombardi operated a liquor store in San Leandro, California, then worked as an attendant in the San Francisco Giants press box from 1957 to 1963. He then disappeared from public view until 1974, when Ed Levitt, a sportswriter for the *Oakland Tribune*, found him working at a local gas station. For years Lombardi had remained silent as players he considered less worthy were elected to the Hall of Fame while he was left out. But he told Levitt, "If they elected me, I wouldn't show up for the ceremony. They've waited too long and they've ignored me too long. That sounds terrible. But every year I see my chances getting smaller and smaller. Sure, who wouldn't be bitter?"[8]

After spending his final years as a virtual recluse, Ernie Lombardi died on September 26, 1977. Nine years later, in 1986, he was elected to the Hall of Fame by the Veterans Committee. Sadly his legacy was undermined by a combination of genetics and bad press. The fans loved him, but writers and the baseball establishment were less generous. His flaws were routinely noted by the media, which treated him more as a pathetic than a heroic figure. And the "snooze" play provided the perfect opportunity to perpetuate his image as a comic character, an image that, over time, diminished the memory of the screaming line drives, two batting titles, an MVP Award, and his stature as one of the most feared hitters in the game.

At least in Cincinnati, however, Lombardi's greatness has not been forgotten. The Reds' MVP Award is named in his honor, and he was one of four heroes of the Crosley Field era (along with Joe Nuxhall, Ted Kluszewski, and Frank Robinson) to be honored with statues outside the Great American Ballpark that opened in 2003. Lombardi would no doubt have appreciated this symbol of the recognition and respect that had been denied him for so long, just as he would have appreciated his belated entry into the Hall of Fame, in spite of his long-standing resentment. Would he have maintained his vow to boycott his own induction ceremony? Not according to Johnny Vander Meer, who was a vocal advocate of his teammate's selection. "He'd have been there," he said at the time of Lombardi's posthumous induction in 1986. "The thing you have to know about Lom was that baseball was his life."[9]

Dolph Camilli

In 1941 for the first time two Italian American ballplayers, both natives of San Francisco, won the MVP Awards in their respective leagues: Joe DiMaggio in the AL and Dolph Camilli in the NL. DiMaggio had previously won the award in 1939, only his third year in the Majors. Camilli, on the other hand, was in his ninth season in 1941, having played for the Cubs and Phillies before going to the Dodgers in 1938. Known as a productive if unspectacular power hitter, he had never come closer than twelfth in the MVP balloting. Then, in '41, the left-handed first baseman suddenly distinguished himself by leading the league in both home runs and RBIs.

Camilli's career year was overshadowed by any number of spectacular and newsworthy events in what was one of the most memorable seasons in baseball history. The big story, of course, was the DiMaggio streak. But it was also the year Ted Williams hit .406 and won the All-Star Game with a dramatic three-run homer with two out in the bottom of the ninth inning to give the American League a 7–5 win. On June 2 Lou Gehrig died at the age of thirty-seven, and on July 25 Lefty Grove won his 300th game, becoming only the sixth pitcher in the modern era to reach that mark. All the while, Americans were reading and hearing about the war that was raging in Europe.

Against that backdrop Camilli fashioned his MVP season in relative obscurity. Although he failed to garner national attention, he did become the darling of Dodger fans by leading Brooklyn to its first pennant in twenty-one years. Like those Dodger fans whose legendary slogan was "Wait 'til next year," Adolph Louis Camilli was used to waiting for a chance at glory. An amateur boxer as a youngster, Camilli soured on the sport when his brother, Francesco, a heavyweight fighting under the name of Frankie Campbell, died of head injuries after being knocked out by Max Baer in 1930. After starring for Sacred Heart High School, Camilli was signed in 1926 by his hometown Seals of the Pacific Coast League. Other than appearing in sixteen games with the Cubs at the end of the 1933 season, he spent eight years with four Minor League teams.

Traded to the Phillies in June 1934, Camilli was their starting first baseman for four years. From 1935 to 1937 he averaged twenty-seven home runs and eighty-eight RBIs a season. That caught the attention of the Dodgers' new general manager, Larry MacPhail, who was hired to revitalize a floundering franchise that was on the brink of bankruptcy. MacPhail, who lived by the philosophy that the only way to make money was to spend money, moved quickly to refurbish a shoddy Ebbets Field and to rebuild the ball club.

The first player he went after was Camilli, acquiring him in a trade with the Phillies in March 1938. That same season MacPhail also hired Babe Ruth as the first-base coach. As usual Ruth had trouble remembering the names of players. "Babe didn't pay much attention to names," Camilli recalled later. "He called me 'Cameo.' Once I was with Cookie Lavagetto and we met Ruth with Claire, his wife. He introduced me as 'Cameo' and then looked at Cookie and couldn't think of his name. He just said, 'And this is the dago.' There was no resentment because that was the Babe."[10]

MacPhail continued to wheel and deal, naming fiery shortstop Leo Durocher as player/manager in 1939 and adding Pee Wee Reese, Pete Reiser, and "Ducky" Medwick to the lineup. It all came together for the resurgent Dodgers in 1941, when they edged the Cardinals for the pennant. No one did more to end the Dodgers' twenty-one-year pennant drought than Camilli. By 1941 the man around whom MacPhail had rebuilt the franchise was not only the team captain, but also a fan favorite. Playing in 149 games, Camilli led the league in home runs (34) and RBIs (120) and finished second in total bases, slugging average, and walks. At the end of the season Camilli was selected as the league's Most Valuable Player, winning by a wide margin over runner-up Reiser and becoming the first player ever to be named on all ballots.

Camilli had another outstanding season in 1942, finishing second in the league in RBIs and third in home runs, but it would prove to be his last productive year. When the thirty-five-year-old infielder struggled in 1943, the Dodgers traded him to the Giants in July, but Camilli refused to report. In 1944 he returned to the Pacific Coast League as player/manager of the Oakland Oaks, but in June 1945 the wartime shortage of players induced him to return to the Majors

12. Dolph Camilli, 1941 National League MVP. National Baseball Hall of Fame Library, Cooperstown NY.

with the Boston Red Sox. It proved to be an anticlimactic comeback; in sixty-three games he hit .212 with two homers and nineteen RBIs. He later managed Minor League teams in Spokane, Dayton, and Magic Valley (Idaho) and coached at Sacramento before working as a scout for the Yankees and Angels.

In his twelve-year career Camilli hit 239 home runs, drove in 950 runs, and had a slugging average of .492. He was both dependable and durable, hitting at least 23 homers in eight straight seasons (1935–42) and averaging over that same period 99 RBIs while playing in an average of 148 games. Considered one of the strongest players of his time, Camilli was also blessed with soft hands and was acknowledged as an outstanding first baseman. When he was traded to the Dodgers in 1938, a story in the *Sporting News* said of the "muscular, long-hitting Italian" that "No first baseman in the league is a superior stylist around the bag."[11]

In his later years Camilli became actively involved in the legal battle to secure pension payments for players who, because they had played before 1947, were excluded from the pension plan created that year by the owners. "I never received a dime from baseball outside of my salary," he was quoted as saying. "The owners treated us lousy. They didn't give us any credit for making money for them by putting fans in the parks. The new owners are not responsible for that, but when they came in they ignored us. Eventually, it was turned over to the baseball union, and they ignored us, too."[12] The battle remained unsettled at the time of Camilli's death, at the age of ninety, on October 21, 1997.

Phil Cavarretta

The typical path to the Major Leagues takes a ballplayer through at least a few years of Minor League apprenticeship before he gets a shot at the big leagues. By that time he is usually in his early to mid-twenties. When Phil Cavarretta made his debut with the Chicago Cubs on September 16, 1934, he was less than two months past his eighteenth birthday, making him the youngest Major Leaguer since Mel Ott joined the Giants in 1926 at the age of sixteen. Just a year earlier Cavarretta, who threw and hit left-handed, had been a star pitcher and first baseman for Lane Tech High School in his hometown of Chicago and had pitched the local American Legion team to a national championship. But the effects of the Depression quickly turned the youngster from a teenager playing for the love of the game into a professional trying to earn a living.

Angelo and Josephine Cavarretta had emigrated from Palermo, Sicily, to Chicago, where Phil was born on July 19, 1916. At home everyone spoke Italian. "That's all we spoke at home," recalled Cavarretta in a telephone interview. "That's the only language mom and dad knew and, naturally, going to school I learned to speak English. I'm very proud of that, really." He described the Near North Side neighborhood where he grew up. "When I was there, it was mostly Italian, Irish, and German people. Real good people, very family-oriented. If you ever needed a hand, they'd come over and help you. They all respected their neighbors."[13]

At Lane Tech, which was located less than two miles from Wrigley Field, Cavarretta was a phenom, both as a pitcher and as a hitter, leading the team to three consecutive city titles. By the spring of 1934 the Depression was at its worst, and Angelo, who worked as a school janitor, had lost his job. "We had a tough time getting anything to eat," Cavarretta recalled. "My dad couldn't get a job; my brother couldn't get a job. Things were so tough I'd go down to the coal yards and pick up the droppings [from the coal cars] and take them home to put in the pot-bellied stove."

Angelo Cavarretta had not always been supportive of his son's love for baseball. "Base-a-ball, what the hell is base-a-ball? You go to school," he told him. But now that the family was in a desperate situation, Angelo didn't object when Phil decided to leave school and try to earn some money to help the family by playing professional baseball, even if he couldn't imagine how someone could make a living playing ball.

Cavarretta's high school coach arranged for the Cubs to give the seventeen-year-old senior a tryout. Cavarretta recalled that day at Wrigley Field: "I went out there, and I must have weighed all of about 150 pounds. I'm walking around and, geez, all these players are looking at me and they thought I was a bat boy. Someone came up and said, 'Hey, kid, what are you doing here?,' and I said, 'I'm here for a tryout.' [Cubs pitcher] Pat Malone, he was a tough guy, he came up and said, 'A tryout? You oughtta go get something to eat and put some weight on, kid.' I was scared to death. Finally, Charley Grimm, who was their first baseman and manager, came over and said, 'Go get yourself a bat, take a few swings, and we'll look at you.' Anyway, I had a real good batting session. One I hit out of the park. They were saying, 'Look at this guy; he's whacking that pea pretty good. We'd better sign this kid.'"

They did sign him—for $125 a month—and after spending the summer playing in the Minors, the youngster was called up to the parent club at the end of the 1934 season. In his first start at Wrigley Field in front of his hometown fans, he hit a game-winning home run to beat Cincinnati, 1–0. The following May, Grimm, who had been the starting first baseman, took himself out of the lineup and gave the job to the new kid. Cavarretta remained a fixture with the Cubs for the next nineteen years.

In 1945 Cavarretta reached the pinnacle of his career, winning the

13. Phil Cavarretta, 1945 National League MVP. National Baseball Hall of Fame Library, Cooperstown NY.

NL batting title with an average of .355 and driving in a career-high ninety-seven runs in leading the Cubs to the pennant. At the end of the season he was voted the league's Most Valuable Player by a comfortable margin. "It was the kind of a year you dream of," said Cavarretta. "Everything has to go your way, your line drives have to drop, your broken-bat hits have to drop. To hit .355, you know, that's a bundle. I was a disciplined, patient hitter."

Unlike many of the Major Leaguers who played between 1942 and 1945, Cavarretta did not disappear from the radar screen when those who served in World War II returned in 1946.[14] An All-Star each year from 1944 to 1947, he spent his final two seasons (1954–55) across town with the White Sox. A line-drive hitter with limited power—he never hit more than ten homers in a season—he finished his twenty-two-year career with a lifetime average of .293, with ninety-five home runs and 920 RBIs.

It was in the 1938 World Series that Cavarretta got to meet his hero, fellow first baseman Lou Gehrig. "I got on base, I think it was the third game," he recalled. "He's holding me on first—this was when he was first starting to get ill—and I'm peeking at him, thinking, 'My God, this is my man.' He finally said, 'I've been watching you, and I like the way you play. You're always hustling.' Then he said one more thing, and I'll never forget this as long as I live. He said, 'Don't change.' The rest of my career I always remembered that because I always gave 100 percent; I always hustled, regardless of the score."

Cavarretta was a favorite of his hometown Cubs fans, especially the Italians. In 1935 the local Knights of Columbus sponsored "Phil Cavarretta Day" at Wrigley Field and presented their local hero with "a nice automobile and a sixteen-gauge shotgun, which I still have." Even his parents became fans. "Once I went to the Cubs, they took a little interest 'cause I was bringing in some money," he said. For Phil Cavarretta baseball not only provided a way to make a living, it also enabled him to help support his family at the height of the Depression. "I'd get paid on the first and the fifteenth," he said, "and I'd bring the check to my mom and dad."

Eighty games into the 1951 season Cavarretta was named the Cubs player/manager, replacing Frankie Frisch. The next year Cavarretta became the first Italian American to manage a Major League club for a full season. When I asked Cavarretta, then eighty-four years old, if he was aware of this distinction, he said, "I feel honored. I didn't know that. That's great."

The Cubs moved up to fifth place in 1952 with a 77-77 record, but then dropped back to seventh place the following year. Cavarretta's tenure as manager came to an abrupt end during spring training in 1954 after he told owner Phil Wrigley that the Cubs weren't very good and would probably finish in the second division. Within a few days Cavarretta became the first manager ever fired during spring training.

The standard explanation is that Wrigley didn't want to hear what his manager told him and fired him out of anger, but almost half a century later Cavarretta remained convinced that it was the Cubs' general manager, Wid Matthews, who persuaded Wrigley to dismiss him. "I guess my general manager got to Mr. Wrigley, and he [Matthews] didn't like what I said," Cavarretta explained. "We didn't get along together. I was just being honest with Mr. Wrigley, telling him the truth. We needed a center fielder, a catcher, and a first baseman. Before the meeting was over, Mr. Wrigley said, 'This is the first time in all the time I've owned the club that any manager has spoken to me on these grounds. I'm really glad that we talked.' I felt pretty good."

Soon after, when the Cubs were in Dallas to play an exhibition game against the Giants, Cavarretta was told to see Matthews. "I figured we were going to go over the roster and see who we were going to keep and who we were going to release. Well," said Cavarretta with a chuckle, "he released me. I couldn't believe it." Cavarretta proved to be a reliable judge of the team's prospects. His replacement, Stan Hack, led the Cubs to a seventh-place finish with a record of 64-90. After the Cubs finished last in 1956, Wrigley fired both Matthews and Hack.

Cavarretta remained in the game for many years after his playing days ended, working as a scout, coach, and Minor League manager. From 1973 to 1977 he was the Minor League hitting instructor for the New York Mets, then completed his career by serving as the Mets hitting coach in 1978 under manager Joe Torre.

Looking back on his long career, Cavarretta, then living in retirement in Georgia, reflected on what baseball meant to him. "I don't know what I would have done if it hadn't been for baseball," he told me. "It was a game that I was proud to be a part of, proud of so many things that I learned from the game itself and the people that were affiliated with the game."

8

To War and Back

The 1940s were a tumultuous and eventful period in baseball history. Soon after the end of the memorable 1941 season, the game was disrupted when dozens of players were called to military duty following the attack on Pearl Harbor. Inevitably the quality of play declined dramatically as replacement players filled the void left when more than five thousand Major and Minor Leaguers ultimately went into the service. After the war the national pastime moved a step closer to meriting that title when Jackie Robinson paved the way for African Americans and other minorities, especially Latin players. It was a decade marked by fierce competition on the field. The Yankees won five pennants and the Cardinals four, but ten different teams went to the World Series. Eight times the pennant was decided by two or fewer games, and in the final year of the decade both races were determined on the final day of the season. Two pennants ended in dead heats and forced the first-ever playoffs: a best of three series in 1946 in which the Cardinals beat the Dodgers and a one-game playoff in 1948 in which the Indians beat the Red Sox.

The number of rookies of Italian descent continued to rise in the early forties, particularly during the war years, when the departure of many established players opened up roster spots for newcomers as well as those with 4-F deferments (unfit for military service but fit enough to meet the diminished standards of wartime baseball). Of the thirteen Italian American rookies who broke into the Majors between 1940 and 1942—the final seasons before the war took so many players away from the game—two were destined to have significant careers. In 1940 Dominic DiMaggio, the youngest of the three brothers to play in the big leagues, made his debut with the Red Sox. That same year Phil Rizzuto was the MVP in the American Association and the Minor League Player of the Year. The following season Rizzuto began a thirteen-year career with the Yankees that would ultimately take him to the Hall of Fame.

1941: The Year of the Streak

In the final summer before the United States entered the war, fans enjoyed what baseball historian Robert Creamer has called "the best baseball season ever."[1] It was the year the Dodgers won their first pennant in twenty-one years, after a hard-fought, season-long struggle with the Cardinals, then saw their hopes die (yet again) with Mickey Owens's infamous passed ball in the fourth game of the World Series. But the season is best remembered for two individual performances: Joe DiMaggio's fifty-six-game hitting streak, which riveted the attention of the public for weeks and established what many consider to be the most remarkable record in baseball history, and Ted Williams's .406 batting average, a mark that has grown in magnitude with each passing year. All of these events unfolded as Hitler continued his march across Europe, tensions between the United States and Japan were intensifying, and there was a growing sense that it was a question of when, not if, America would be drawn into what was looking more and more like another world war.

On May 15 neither the Yankees nor DiMaggio seemed headed for a big season. The Yanks, coming off their third-place finish in 1940, were in fourth place, five and a half games behind Cleveland. And Joltin' Joe was anything but, mired in a slump and hitting .194 over the previous three weeks. That day the Yankees were humiliated by the White Sox, 13–1, their fifth straight loss. But that contest would ultimately assume historic import as the day that DiMaggio, who went 1 for 4 with a single off Edgar Smith, began his streak.

As DiMaggio and other Yankees started hitting, the team slowly climbed up the standings, but at first the press paid little attention to DiMaggio's nascent streak. On June 3, the day the streak reached twenty games, news of Lou Gehrig's death hit the front pages. That same day the *New York Times* ran this headline: "Hitler and Mussolini Chart War Moves in 5-Hour Talk." For the next several weeks DiMaggio and Il Duce—the two faces of America's perceptions of Italians—would be sharing space in newspapers and magazines. This odd juxtaposition was nothing new. The same *Time* magazine issue of July 13, 1936, that had featured the rookie DiMaggio on its cover also had reported the speech of Ethiopian leader Haile Selassie, in which he asked the League of Nations to assist his country in its struggle against Mussolini's invading army. The very next week it was Mussolini's picture that appeared on the cover of *Time*.

On June 17 in an 8–7 loss to the White Sox, DiMaggio broke the Yankee hitting-streak record of twenty-nine games, set by Roger Peckinpaugh in 1919 and equaled by Earle Combs in 1931. The record most widely recognized at that time was George Sisler's forty-one-game streak, set in 1922. Sisler's mark was commonly referred to as the "modern record" to distinguish it from Wee Willie Keeler's forty-four-game streak, the "all-time record," which many considered suspect because it was set in 1897, when batters weren't charged with a strike for a foul ball. Both marks seemed remote when DiMaggio set the new Yankee record. But as he inched closer, the drama intensified and interest, among both fans and non-fans, grew until the streak became a national obsession and a subject of daily conversation. Before the age of television saturation, when news came by way of newspaper and radio, the same question was asked day after day across the country: "Did he get one today?"

On June 29 more than thirty-one thousand sweltering fans endured 98-degree heat and a doubleheader in Washington hoping to see DiMaggio tie and break Sisler's record. In the sixth inning of the first game he doubled to tie Sisler. Then in the seventh inning of the second game DiMaggio lined a single to left to set a new modern record. It was purely incidental to the Senator fans that the home team lost both games; the *New York Times* reported that they "roared thunderous acclaim" to "one of the greatest players baseball has ever known," while his teammates, "to a man, were as excited as schoolboys over the feat."[2]

On July 1 the Yankees played another twin bill, this one at home against the Red Sox before 52,832 fans. In the fifth inning, when DiMaggio reached first on a bad throw by third baseman Jim Tabor, official scorer Dan Daniel ruled it a hit. Had that been the "hit" that extended the streak, the record might have always been suspect because of that controversial call. DiMaggio came up again in the sixth, and in recounting the incident in his column in the July 17 issue of the *Sporting News*, Daniel quoted noted cartoonist Willard Mullin as saying the following: "I suppose you are praying for another hit for the big Wop, so it will take the weight off you."[3] And DiMaggio did take Daniel off the hook by lining a clean single to left. Joe's brother Dom, the Red Sox center fielder, recalled the moment in his book *Real Grass, Real Heroes*: "The noise was ear-splitting as the

52,000 fans in the 95-degree heat made themselves even hotter with a standing ovation that lasted several long minutes."[4]

In the second game DiMaggio wasted no time, lining a single to left in the first inning to tie Wee Willie Keeler's all-time record. Syndicated columnist Bob Considine, in citing DiMaggio's historic contribution to the national pastime, made note of his ethnic background, suggesting, as had so many before him, baseball's role as an instrument of assimilation: "Joe DiMaggio, son of an immigrant Italian fisherman, scaled a peak in the great American game of baseball here today."[5] The next day DiMaggio was hitless in his first two times at bat, then hit a 2-0 pitch from rookie Dick Newsome over the left field wall to pass Keeler's record. By the time the Yankees faced the Indians on July 17, the streak had reached fifty-six games. Then, before 67,468 fans in Municipal Stadium, the largest crowd to date for a Major League night game, third baseman Ken Keltner made two spectacular plays to rob DiMaggio of hits and bring the streak to an end. (The very next day he started a new streak in which he hit safely in sixteen straight games; in other words, he got a hit in seventy-two of seventy-three games.)

DiMaggio's average during the streak was .408, and in his 223 official times at bat he struck out only five times. (In the entire season he struck out a total of thirteen times.) According to noted Harvard paleontologist and essayist Stephen Jay Gould, DiMaggio's streak defies all laws of probability; Gould called it "one sequence so many standard deviations above the expected distribution that it should not have occurred at all" and "the most extraordinary thing that ever happened in American sports."[6]

When the streak began, the team was in fourth place, six and a half games behind Cleveland; when it ended, the Yankees were six games

14. Joe DiMaggio with young fans, ca. 1940. National Baseball Hall of Fame Library, Cooperstown NY.

ahead of the Indians and went on to win the pennant by seventeen games. DiMaggio's teammates showed their respect and appreciation by presenting him with a Tiffany-designed silver humidor that featured an engraving on its cover of the classic DiMaggio swing. The inscription on the front read, "Presented to Joe DiMaggio by his fellow players of the New York Yankees to express their admiration for the world's consecutive game hitting record—1941." Even before the '41 season began, Joe DiMaggio was widely acknowledged as the best player in the game. But the streak elevated him to an entirely new plane of heroism and made him the most popular celebrity in the country.

Indicative of the public's fascination with DiMaggio's daily pursuit was the popularity of "Joltin' Joe DiMaggio," the song that immortalized the streak. Written by Alan Courtney and Ben Homer and recorded by Les Brown and his Band of Renown three weeks after the streak ended, the tune shot to the top of the charts. Framed by the refrain of "Joe, Joe DiMaggio, we want you on our side," the lyrics went in part as follows:

> He started baseball's famous streak,
> That's got us all aglow.
> He's just a man and not a freak,
> Joltin' Joe DiMaggio.
>
> He'll live in Baseball's Hall of Fame,
> He got there blow by blow.
> Our kids will tell their kids his name,
> Joltin' Joe DiMaggio.

That refrain—"Joe, Joe DiMaggio, we want you on our side"—took on a curiously patriotic overtone given the ever-increasing likelihood of American involvement in the war. Ironically such a refrain, with its suggestion that DiMaggio was embraced as an American hero, would have been unimaginable not long before. It had been only five years earlier, at the start of his rookie year, that sportswriters at spring training had ridiculed his name as being "very tough" to pronounce and sounding "like something you put on a steak." Suddenly it had become downright lyrical.

In its July 14 issue *Time* magazine described the magnitude of DiMaggio's celebrity but felt compelled to note his ethnicity even as it compared him to the all-time greats: "In 102 years of baseball, few feats have caused such nationwide to do. Ever since it became apparent that the big Italian from San Francisco's Fisherman's Wharf was approaching a record that had eluded Ty Cobb, Babe Ruth, Lou Gehrig and other great batsmen, Big Joe's hits have been the biggest news in U.S. sport. Radio programs were interrupted for DiMaggio bulletins."[7]

That summer Joe DiMaggio probably did more to enhance the image of Italian Americans than anyone before him. He offered the American public a positive counterpoint to Benito Mussolini, that other Italian who was making news at the time: the consummate professional performing at the highest level under intense scrutiny with quiet dignity versus the bombastic, increasingly foolish figure posing on his balcony in Rome. DiMaggio's achievement transcended baseball, providing a welcome but, as it turned out, brief distraction to a nation preoccupied by the ominous developments overseas. He momentarily lifted the minds of America's citizens above the banal, if disconcerting, daily reports on the war in Europe and mounting tensions between the United States and Japan.

Five years earlier, in 1936, DiMaggio's rookie season, players of Italian descent had first received significant media attention, highlighted by Dan Daniel's "Viva Italia!" article in *Baseball Magazine*. The 1941 season was a no less significant landmark in the evolution of Italian American participation in Major League Baseball. DiMaggio's remark-able streak was only the most dramatic and memorable achievement in a season in which players of Italian descent were in the spotlight as never before.

In an unsigned column that appeared in the *Washington Post* the day after DiMaggio broke George Sisler's record, the Yankee star was said to be "merely the most illustrious among the steadily increasing group that is finding in baseball a new form of expression for the serene and heroic Latin genius." (After naming several of the current crop of Italian players, the writer concluded, "Sometimes it seems a great pity that Benito [Lippy] Mussolini never went in for baseball.

177

... What a beautiful umpire baiter he would have made!") When DiMaggio, Rizzuto, and Russo led the Yankees to an early season win over the Senators, Jack Munhall, writing in the *Washington Post*, went so far as to refer to "the growing Italian domination of the great American pastime of baseball."[8]

There were thirty-seven Italians in the big leagues in 1941, representing 6.8 percent of all Major Leaguers. More significant than the sheer number of players was their unprecedented prominence in the game. Apart from DiMaggio's streak, the most notable achievement was that for the first time Italian Americans were officially recognized as the top players in both leagues, with both DiMaggio and Camilli winning MVP Awards. In a one-paragraph announcement at the end of its sports section, the November 24 issue of *Time* magazine reported, "Second-generation Italians made a clean sweep of U.S. baseball honors in the season just past." In addition to citing the MVP winners, the story also noted that "Phil Rizzuto, New York Yankee shortstop, was the outstanding rookie of the year." (There was no official Rookie of the Year Award until 1947.)

A total of eight Italian American players (including all three DiMaggio brothers) received votes in the MVP balloting, more than in any previous year. It was a good year all around for the DiMaggio family. Dom not only played in the All-Star Game, but he also hit .283 in his sophomore season and was considered by many virtually equal to Joe as a center fielder. Meanwhile, Vince, playing for the Pirates in his fifth year in the Majors, had what was probably his best all-around season, with career highs in home runs (twenty-one) and RBIs (one hundred).

At the other end of the record-setting spectrum Al Brancato, a twenty-two-year-old shortstop then in his third season with the Philadelphia A's, made sixty-one errors in 139 games. No Major League player has made as many errors in a single season since. One year later another shortstop would fumble his way into the Major League record books. Len Merullo was one of twelve children born to Carmen and Angelina Merullo, who had emigrated from a small town outside Naples and settled in Boston, where Carmen worked on the railroad. A standout baseball player at East Boston High School, Len was awarded a baseball scholarship to Villanova University. During his senior year he was taken to Chicago, where Cubs owner Phil Wrigley gave him a check for $1,500, with the understanding that when Merullo returned to Chicago in June, after completing his senior year, he would receive another check.

Angelina Merullo could never understand why her sons wasted so much time playing ball when they should have been earning money to support the family. Then Len came home with the tangible sign of the American Dream. "When I got home," said Merullo in a telephone interview, "I just threw the check on the table. They didn't know what it was; they couldn't read or write. My older brother picked it up and read it to them. From that day on, my mother kicked the others out of the house, saying, 'Get out and play ball!'"[9]

Merullo was the Cubs' starting shortstop from 1942 to 1947, when a back injury forced him to retire. His road roommate throughout his time with the Cubs was Phil Cavarretta. "We were two Italian kids, about the same age and we got along great," said Merullo. "Our teammates called us 'the Grand Opera Twins.' I called him 'Buck,' short for *baccalà*" (literally dried cod, but in Italian slang it refers to a foolish person). Asked if he thought that was the origin of Cavarretta's more commonly known nickname of "Philabuck," he answered, "I don't know, but I had something to do with it." Cavarretta's nickname for Merullo was "Moose," for Mussolini. "That didn't bother me at all," said Merullo. "The only thing that would bother you was if someone called you a 'guinea.'"

Merullo's day of infamy came on September 13, 1942, in the nightcap of a doubleheader against the Braves (in his hometown of Boston). In the second inning he made four errors to tie the record for most errors by a shortstop in one inning. The next day the *Chicago Tribune* offered some consolation, explaining that "the Merullo jitters were pardonable, however, for he had just become the father of a son born in a Boston hospital a few hours before the game."[10] The son, Len Jr., became known as "Boots" in "tribute" to his father's record-setting performance. A classic baseball "lifer," Merullo served as a Cubs scout for many years and then worked for the Major League Baseball Scouting Bureau as an area scout responsible for New England. He retired in 2002 after sixty-four years in professional baseball.

1942: Casualties of War

Sixty-one days after the 1941 World Series ended, what had been an ominous threat suddenly became a startling reality. The bombing of Pearl Harbor made the glorious baseball season a distant and trivial memory. Some even wondered if Major League Baseball would be played in 1942. In response to a query from Commissioner Kenesaw Mountain Landis, President Roosevelt wrote in January 1942 what has come to be known as the "green light letter," saying that "it would be best for the country to keep baseball going."

So baseball would continue during the war years, but the loss of many players would alter the game dramatically. A total of seventy-one Major Leaguers did not play in 1942 because of military service, but most players were deferred with 3-A classifications, meaning that they were sole providers for dependents. However, most of those would be reclassified by the end of '42 and subject to call-up. In 1943, 219 Major Leaguers were in uniform; the number increased to 242 in 1944 and 384 in 1945.[11]

It is estimated that as many as 1 million Italian Americans served in the military during World War II—no other ethnic group would contribute as many members of the armed services—but even before Pearl Harbor the ever-darkening image of Mussolini and his Fascists and the entrance of Italy into the war on the side of Germany had made many suspicious of Italian American loyalties. In the immediate aftermath of Pearl Harbor those suspicions were translated into public policy.

Italian Americans were the largest group of foreign-born U.S. residents, numbering about 5 million, and all but six hundred thousand had become citizens. Like their Japanese and German counterparts, those noncitizen Italian Americans were declared "enemy aliens" and as of January 1942 were required to register at post offices, be fingerprinted, and carry photo identification cards at all times. They also had to surrender cameras, shortwave radios, and firearms. Those living along the California coast were subject to a curfew that confined them to their homes between 8 p.m. and 6 a.m. and were not allowed to travel more than five miles from home. About ten thousand who lived near the coast in areas considered sensitive military zones were required to leave their homes and move inland. Resident alien fishermen along the California coast were prevented from fishing in prohibited zones, and many had their boats confiscated by the coast guard. In addition, the FBI arrested approximately 250 Italian aliens and interned them (some for as long as two years) in military camps in various states.

The treatment of resident-alien Italians was obviously moderate compared to the internment of more than 120,000 Japanese Americans during the war, and the order declaring Italians to be enemy aliens was rescinded by President Roosevelt on October 12, 1942. Nevertheless, the policies enacted, however short-lived, served to reignite long-standing attitudes among the American public. If nothing else, the sanctions served to remind Italian Americans that they were still perceived by many as pretenders to full citizen status.

One San Francisco Italian whose travel was restricted was retired fisherman Giuseppe DiMaggio, who was unable to visit DiMaggio's Grotto, the restaurant owned by his son, Joe, because it was located on Fisherman's Wharf, one of the waterfront areas off limits to enemy aliens. Dominic DiMaggio, who served for three years in the navy, learned of this on his return home. "My dad was very disappointed, and it hurt me when I found out about it," DiMaggio said of his father. "He loved America, and had lived here since about the turn of the century."[12]

There is evidence that one season after his streak established him as a national hero, even Giuseppe's son Joe was the target of anti-Italian sentiment fueled by the war. The thunderous cheers of 1941 suddenly turned into boos when he came to the plate in 1942. Undoubtedly part of the reason was his disappointing performance on the field; the Yankees were winning and leading the league, but by the end of May DiMaggio's average was around .250. There was also the fact that DiMaggio had not signed up for military service; as a husband and the father of Joe Jr. (born in October 1941), he was classified 3-A. Hank Greenberg and Bob Feller were in uniform, and many other Major Leaguers (including Joe's brother Dom) had enlisted or announced plans to do so, but Joe remained silent on the subject. (DiMaggio would enlist in the army on February 17, 1943.)

Shirley Povich, in his *Washington Post* column of May 11, 1942, noted that Italian flags ("which Italian admirers of Joe DiMaggio used to break out for their hero before Italy's stab-in-the-back war against France") were now missing from Yankee Stadium and that "elements of Yankee fans are booing DiMaggio." One week later, mystified by the continued booing of DiMaggio, Povich wrote, "Could be, of course, that his hecklers are the sort of morons who remember for no reason at all that Dimag is of Italian parentage and permit that to prejudice them against the Yankee star." In his biography of DiMaggio, Richard Ben Cramer paraphrased the kind of letters the fallen hero was receiving: *Why didn't he go back to Italy with the rest of the coward wops?*[13]

1943–1945

Major League Baseball changed dramatically in 1943 when scores of players, including approximately sixty starters, traded their white and gray flannels for army khaki and navy blue uniforms, forcing teams to rely on players too young or too old for the draft and those classified as 4-F. With the talent pool diminished drastically the quality of play inevitably declined, but Major League Baseball continued to do what President Roosevelt had asked it to do: sustain the nation's morale by providing entertainment and diversion.

The war took many Italian American players away from the game, including standouts such as Joe and Dom DiMaggio, Phil Rizzuto, and Dolph Camilli. For those who, for whatever reason, were exempt from service, it provided an opportunity to play Major League Baseball that in all likelihood they otherwise would not have had. Following rookie classes of three, seven, and three in the first three years of the decade, the number jumped to seventeen in '43—the highest single-season number to that time—and twelve in '44, then dropped back to seven in '45, presumably because rosters had stabilized by that point. Of those thirty-six players, twenty-six disappeared from Major League rosters when the war ended, as did the majority of wartime replacement players.

Of the seventeen rookies who debuted in 1943, thirteen never played in the Majors after the war ended, and only two—Al Zarilla and Milo Candini—played beyond 1947. Zarilla, an All-Star in 1948, was a left-handed-hitting outfielder with a lifetime average of .276 in ten years with the Browns, Red Sox, and White Sox. Mario "Milo" Candini, a right-handed pitcher, posted a 26-21 record in eight years with the Senators and Phillies. One player who did not play after the war deserves mention for his name alone. Arthur Joseph "Cookie" Cuccurullo, appeared in sixty-two games for the Pirates between 1943 and 1945 and compiled a 3-5 record.

Only five of the twelve Italian American players who made their debuts in 1944 played beyond 1945, and only two—Ralph Branca and Tommy Brown—had extended careers. Brown, of Irish and Italian descent, personified the youth movement forced upon Major League teams by the wartime player shortage. He was one of the three dozen boys too young for military service that the Brooklyn Dodgers invited to their 1944 spring training camp. The Dodgers sent Brown to their Minor League affiliate in Newport News, Virginia, but when shortstop Pee Wee Reese entered the navy, they brought him up in late July. On August 3 the Brooklyn native made his Major League debut at the age of sixteen years, seven months. Branca, another of the Dodgers' kiddie corps, had made his debut on June 12 at the ripe old age of eighteen. The ultimate example of the wartime youth movement was Cincinnati pitcher Joe Nuxhall, who made his debut two days before Branca at the age of fifteen years, ten months, eleven days. Nuxhall, however, appeared in only one game and did not return to the Majors until 1952, when he resumed what would be a sixteen-year career.

Nuxhall's brief appearance in 1944 made him the youngest player in Major League history. But Tommy Brown, who appeared in forty-six games for the seventh-place Dodgers, became the youngest player ever to play on a regular basis. On August 20, 1945, the seventeen-year-old infielder became the youngest player ever to hit a home run in the Majors when he hit a round-tripper off Preacher Roe of the Pirates. Brown, who also played for the Phillies and Cubs, was in the Majors for a total of nine seasons, appearing in an average of fifty-five games a year.

At the other end of the age spectrum were the old-timers, who were approaching or had exceeded the draft age limit of thirty-eight. Some were extending their careers, while others came out of retirement for one last fling in the big show, including former MVP Dolph Camilli. In 1945 Gus Mancuso, the Texas Italian then in his seventeenth and final big league season at the age of thirty-nine, caught seventy games for the last-place Phillies, hitting only .199, well below his .265 career average. Mancuso's younger brother, Frank, was a rookie catcher for the St. Louis Browns in 1944, the year they won their only pennant. Other than 1945, when he was the Browns' starting catcher, he was used sparingly in his four-year career.

One of Frank Mancuso's teammates on the '45 Browns' squad was Pete Gray, the one-armed outfielder who epitomized the plight of wartime baseball. While Gray, who hit .218 in seventy-seven games, admirably overcame his handicap, his presence on the Browns' roster underscored the lengths to which some clubs had to go to put even the semblance of a Major League lineup on the field. All that would change in 1946, when most of the prewar regulars returned and Major League Baseball enjoyed a tremendous resurgence, both in quality and attendance. Not only was baseball back, but it was also about to enter one of its most memorable and historic eras.

Three

POSTWAR BOOM

9

Postwar New York
The Golden Age

After the sacrifice and anguish of the war years, baseball provided a comforting return to normality for a nation both exhausted and exhilarated. It was, after all, still the undisputed national pastime. The NFL and NBA were struggling to establish a foothold, and hockey was a "foreign" sport. While sportswriters had dubbed the 1920s the golden age of sport, for many the period from 1947, when Jackie Robinson broke the color line, to 1957, the final season before the Dodgers and Giants headed west, was the golden age of baseball. Others downplay this claim as being too New York-centric, but there is no question that the postwar period was the golden age for Italian Americans in Major League Baseball.

Even though Major League attendance in 1945 set a new record at 10.8 million, attendance nearly doubled in 1946, reaching 18.5 million, followed by 19.8 million and 20.8 million in the next two years. Admittedly the boom didn't last long. By 1953 total attendance had fallen to 14.3 million. Not even New York teams were exempt. In 1947 the Yankees, Dodgers, and Giants drew a combined 5.5 million fans; by 1957 the number had dropped to 3.2 million. The decline in attendance would seem to suggest that the golden age of baseball was short-lived, but it must be noted that the average per-game attendance of 13,366 between 1950 and 1959 was about double that of the decades prior to the war. The bump in postwar attendance, concluded Jules Tygiel, was an aberration, not a new benchmark: "The decline of the 1950s represented a correction to baseball's postwar bull market."[1]

Historians have generally attributed the drop in attendance to factors other than a dwindling interest in the game itself: the suburbanization of affluent customers and their reluctance to drive to downtown ballparks with inadequate parking and decaying infrastructures; the growing popularity of television (all three New York teams offered TV coverage by the early fifties); a greater array of leisure activities. While fewer people were walking through the turnstiles, more and more were following the game on television.

Nowhere was the resurgence of postwar baseball more evident and prolonged than in New York City. Anyone who grew up in that period or who has even a passing knowledge of baseball history knows that in the 1950s New York was not only the financial and media capital of the United States, but also the center of the baseball universe. There had never been anything like it in the history of Major League Baseball; it seemed that the World Series had taken up permanent residence in the boroughs of Brooklyn, Manhattan, and the Bronx. Between 1947 and 1958 at least one of the three New York teams appeared in all but two of the World Series, with the Yankees and either the Dodgers or Giants facing off seven times. In those twelve years the Yankees won ten pennants and eight World Series, including five in a row, the Dodgers six pennants and one Series. The Giants were relative bridesmaids, winning two league titles and one Series. In 1951 the Dodgers and Giants met in one of the most storied matchups in baseball history, a three-game playoff that ended with Bobby Thomson's epic home run off the Dodgers' Ralph Branca. And in 1956 Don Larsen pitched the only perfect game in World Series history.

It was a time of exciting baseball and impassioned rivalries, as much among fans as among franchises. And it was a time of engaging and sometimes outrageous personalities, when any number of major figures burst onto the scene, led (in terms of both chronology and social significance) by Robinson's history-making debut. There were Mays, Mantle, and Snider, the outfield triumvirate that sparked endless debates among fans of the three New York franchises. There was Leo "The Lip" Durocher, the fiery bench jockey who managed both the Dodgers and Giants and was suspended for a year following a series of incidents considered detrimental to baseball. And there was Casey Stengel, suddenly transformed from a clownish manager with a poor track record to the brilliant leader of a Yankee dynasty.

It was during this heady period that Italian American ballplayers, who played key roles on all three New York teams, achieved unprecedented visibility and prominence, thanks in part to playing in the nation's media center. The previous high point had come in 1941, when both Joe DiMaggio and Dolph Camilli won MVP awards, both the Yankees and Dodgers had two Italian Americans in their starting lineups in the World Series, and Marius Russo pitched a complete-game win in Game 3. But in the years following the war there were more outstanding players than ever before, and their success was sustained over a longer period. The Yankees had DiMaggio, Berra, Rizzuto, Raschi, and Martin; the Dodgers had Campanella, Furillo, and Branca; and the Giants had Maglie and Antonelli.

Between 1947 and 1957 eight of the twenty-two MVP Awards went to players of Italian descent playing for New York City teams, and five times Italian Americans finished second in the balloting. Seven times in that period Italian American pitchers (Antonelli, Branca, Maglie, and Raschi) won twenty or more games in a season. From 1948 to 1951 six Italian Americans were named to the All-Star team each year. In 1952 there were seven All-Stars, more than ever before or since, with an unmatched five in the starting lineup.

Italian Americans were also key figures in some of the most memorable moments of the postwar era: Cookie Lavagetto breaking up Bill Bevens's no-hitter and Al Gionfriddo robbing Joe DiMaggio with a spectacular catch, both in the '47 World Series; Ralph Branca surrendering the pennant-winning homer to Bobby Thomson in '51; Billy Martin making the catch that saved the '52 Series for the Yankees, then driving in the Series-winning run in '53 with his record-setting twelfth hit; Yogi Berra catching Don Larsen's perfect game in the '56 Series, with Babe Pinelli, the home plate umpire, calling the final strike.

The First Subway Series

The 1947 World Series between the Yankees and Dodgers was the opening act in New York's postwar baseball spectacular. It was in fact a Series that featured a number of firsts. In the first of six postwar "Subway Series" between the interborough rivals, Jackie Robinson capped his historic rookie season by becoming the first African American to appear in a World Series. It also marked the first time a pinch-hit home run was hit in a World Series game and the first time the Series was televised. And Game 1 established a new Series attendance record, which was quickly broken in Game 6.

Both lineups included several players of Italian descent, most of whom already were or soon would be among the biggest stars of the postwar era. The Italian language daily, *Il Progresso Italo-Americano*, proudly announced on the day of the opener that "ten Italian Americans will play in the World Series." A large photo of

Branca, the starter in Game 1, together with smaller photos of Rizzuto, DiMaggio, Lavagetto, and Furillo appeared alongside the story. The paper then provided daily front-page coverage of the Series.[2] The biggest name in the Yankee lineup, and in all of baseball, was of course DiMaggio. After a disappointing '46 season, he had won his third MVP Award in '47. Phil Rizzuto, now in his fourth year, was recognized as one of the best-fielding shortstops in the Majors. Yogi Berra, in his first full year in the Majors, caught and played in the outfield. And there was Vic Raschi, a second-year righthander with a 7-2 record in '47 who would emerge as one of the best pitchers in the Majors in the coming years.[3]

The ace of the Dodgers staff was Ralph Branca, a twenty-one-year-old phenom who was already in his fourth big league season. In 1947 he had won twenty-one games while still a student at New York University. Carl Furillo, the young outfielder known as the "Reading Rifle" for his outstanding arm, had hit .295 and driven in eighty-eight runs in his second big league season. The Dodgers also had Vic Lombardi, a lefthander who became a late-season stalwart and posted a 12-11 record. But by the end of the 1947 World Series all of them would be overshadowed by two other players of Italian descent, one an unheralded veteran at the end of a ten-year career and the other an obscure, seldom-used outfielder.

On September 30, 73,365 fans crowded into Yankee Stadium for the opener. Among the spectators were former president Herbert Hoover and more than forty former Major Leaguers, including Babe Ruth, Ty Cobb, and Cy Young. (Ten days earlier, on September 20, Fiorello La Guardia, the Italian American mayor of New York since 1934, had died of pancreatic cancer.) But Series fever spread far beyond the House that Ruth built. In Kings County Court Judge Samuel

Liebowitz, a diehard Dodgers fan, was presiding over a rape trial the day the Series opened. When he realized that several jurors were becoming fidgety as game time approached, he called a two-hour recess and invited the jurors to watch the game on television in the court's library. The defendant had to be content listening to the game on a portable radio in the detention pen.[4]

When the Dodgers and Yankees faced each other, it was more than a World Series, at least to fans in and around New York. In their minds it was an intercity conflict on the magnitude of Sparta versus Athens. The Bronx and Flatbush were separated by only a few miles geographically, but in terms of public perception the two teams were on separate continents. The rivalry was seen by many as a clash of cultures: the cold corporate efficiency of the Bronx Bombers, who had already won ten Series titles, against the gritty blue-collar work ethic of the Brooklyn Bums, who had yet to win a Series in three tries.

Before that huge crowd and just ten miles from his hometown of Mount Vernon, Ralph Branca retired the first twelve Yankees he faced. Then an infield single by Joe DiMaggio to lead off the fifth led to a quick meltdown by the young righthander. Before a single out was recorded, the Yanks had scored two runs, and when Branca walked Phil Rizzuto to load the bases and fell behind 2-0 on Bobby Brown, Brooklyn manager Burt Shotton removed his young ace. The Yankees scored five runs in the inning (all charged to Branca) and won the game, 5–3. After the game Branca told reporters that he was confident he could come back strong in his next start, but Shotton obviously didn't agree. Because of that one inning, he decided that Branca was a bad risk and limited him to two brief relief appearances in the rest of the Series.

Vic Lombardi started Game 2 for the Dodgers. A native of Reedley,

California, the five-foot-seven, 158-pound lefty (dubbed "the vest pocket southpaw" by one writer), then in his third year, had won twelve and lost eleven but had been the anchor of the staff during the second half of the season. What he lacked in size and speed he made up for in guile and grit, but neither sufficed that day. In four innings he gave up five runs on nine hits, and the Yankees cruised to a 10–3 win behind the complete-game pitching of Allie Reynolds.

Game 3 moved to Ebbets Field, which held half as many spectators as Yankee Stadium. But according to a *New York Times* story, it seemed that the enthusiasm of the smaller crowd was "obviously more feverish than it had been in the Bronx," and their cheers "seemed louder and longer" than those at Yankee Stadium, where the "snob set" was "more interested in being seen than seeing."[5]

The Dodgers bounced back in the third game, taking a 6–0 lead in the second inning. They added three more runs, but the Yanks closed the gap to 9–6 when DiMaggio hit a two-run homer in the fifth. Then in the seventh, Yankee manager Bucky Harris sent Yogi Berra up to pinch-hit for catcher Sherm Lollar.(Berra had been the starting catcher in the first two games but was benched because of his inability to throw out Dodger runners.) Berra cut the lead to 9–8 when he hit the first pinch-hit home run in World Series history with a solo shot off of Branca. Following Berra's home run, Branca gave way to Hugh Casey, who shut down the Yanks to preserve the 9–8 win. Now the stage was set for one of the most dramatic games in Series history.

The Yankees' starter in Game 4 was Bill Bevens, a thirty-year-old righty who, after three winning seasons, had posted a record of 7-13 in '47. But on October 3 he pitched the game of his life. Going into the ninth inning, he had walked nine batters—the Dodgers had scored their lone run in the fifth on two walks and a groundout—but had given up no hits. With the Yanks leading 2–1, Bevens was poised to pitch the first no-hitter in World Series history. He retired the first batter in the ninth, then walked Carl Furillo, who was replaced by pinch runner Al Gionfriddo. After Bevens got the second out on a pop foul, Gionfriddo broke for second in a steal attempt. Berra fired the ball to shortstop Rizzuto, who snared the high throw and came down with the tag, but Gionfriddo was called safe by Babe Pinelli. For years after, Rizzuto insisted that Gionfriddo was out.

Ironically, Pinelli, whose call on Gionfriddo prevented Bevens from closing out his no-hitter, would be the umpire who made the called third strike for the final out of Don Larsen's perfect game in the 1956 World Series. As for Rizzuto, he almost missed the game. In a sidebar following the game story the *New York Times* reported that the diminutive shortstop had trouble getting into Ebbets Field before the game when a policeman refused to believe he was a ballplayer. "Don't give me that stuff," said the cop. "You can't even play first for a midget team."[6]

Gionfriddo's steal proved to be pivotal. With the count now 3-1 on Pete Reiser, Yankee manager Bucky Harris broke one of the cardinal rules of baseball by signaling Berra to walk Reiser, putting the winning run on base. Eddie Miksis then ran for the injured Reiser. Eddie Stanky was due up, but Shotton called on Cookie Lavagetto to pinch hit, a move that left Dodger fans shaking their heads. A fan favorite since his arrival in Brooklyn in 1937, Lavagetto had enjoyed five solid seasons with the Dodgers before entering the service in 1942. But now, almost thirty-five years old and having lost four years to the war, he was a seldom-used backup outfielder in the final season of his ten-year career. During the regular season, in fact, he had been to bat only sixty-nine times, and in the Series he had gone hitless in five at bats.

15. Cookie Lavagetto. National Baseball Hall of Fame Library, Cooperstown NY.

Fans became even more skeptical when Lavagetto swung and missed on the first pitch. But then came redemption and immortality for Cookie. He laced Bevens's next pitch—a high, outside fast ball—to the opposite field, a line drive that went over the head of right fielder Tommy Henrich and caromed off the tricky Ebbets Field wall. The ball eluded Henrich momentarily, and by the time he retrieved it and threw it in, Gionfriddo and Miksis had scored, Lavagetto was on second, and the Dodgers had won the game, 3–2.

Delirious Dodger fans stormed the field and raced toward their unlikely savior. Lavagetto, who was being pummeled by both fans and teammates, had to be escorted off the field by police. This is how Dodgers radio broadcaster Red Barber called the scene as it unfolded: "Friends, they're killing Lavagetto, his own teammates. They're tearing him to pieces and it's taking a police escort to get him away from the Dodgers." Barber later called it "the most exciting individual moment I was ever around in baseball." In the clubhouse Lavagetto said it was "the top thrill of my life."[7] Meanwhile, legendary Ebbets Field organist Gladys Goodding was celebrating Harry "Cookie" Lavagetto's instantaneously legendary feat by serenading the fans with two tunes: "Lookie, Lookie, Lookie, Here Comes Cookie" and "I'm Just Wild About Harry."

That double would prove to be Lavagetto's last hit in the Majors. The next day he came to bat as a pinch hitter in the ninth with the Dodgers trailing by one run and the tying run on base, but there was no magic this time as he struck out. He pinch-hit again in each of the final two games, driving in a run with a sacrifice fly in Game 6 and popping out in Game 7. When the season ended, his moment of glory couldn't buy him any more time with the Dodgers, who released their momentary hero. But that one swing of the bat was enough to enshrine Cookie in the hearts of Dodgers fans as long as they lived.

In Game 5, Yankee pitcher Spec Shea threw a complete-game four-hitter, DiMaggio accounted for the winning run with a fifth-inning homer, and the Bronx Bombers won 2–1. With the Dodgers now trailing three games to two, it was another seldom-used Italian player who stole the spotlight in Game 6. Al Gionfriddo, the guy who stole second and scored on Lavagetto's game-winning hit in Game 4, was a twenty-five-year-old, five-foot-six left-handed-hitting outfielder, one of thirteen children of an immigrant Italian father who worked in the coal mines of Pennsylvania. Now in the fourth and final year of his brief career, his one shot as a starter had come in 1945, when he hit .284 as a wartime replacement player with the Pirates. When in June 1947 Gionfriddo had come to Brooklyn in a trade with Pittsburgh, the joke was that his role was to carry the satchelful of money that went to the Dodgers as part of the deal. Going into the World Series, he had seen even less action than Lavagetto, with eleven hits in sixty-three times at bat.

Roger Kahn, in *The Era*, recounts a story told to him by Gionfriddo in a 1991 interview. When Gionfriddo came to the Dodgers from Pittsburgh in May, he was given the locker next to Jackie Robinson. He noticed that Robinson didn't shower with the other players, always waiting to shower last. Gionfriddo knew what it was like to feel like he didn't belong, having been ignored by the older players when he came to the Dodgers. One day he said to Robinson, "Jackie, let's go in the shower together. If those southern guys don't want to shower with you—with you and me, Jackie—let 'em get the hell out." When they went into the shower together, reported Gionfriddo, no one got out. "Another barrier, that shouldn't have existed in the first place," wrote Kahn, "came tumbling down."[8]

Game 6 was played before a new Series record crowd of 74,065 at Yankee Stadium. Vic Lombardi, the losing pitcher in Game 2, started for the Dodgers and left with two out in the third after giving up four runs. Branca came on in relief and held the Yankees to one run in 2⅓ innings. After the Dodgers scored four in the sixth to take an 8–5 lead, Shotton, calling him by his nickname of "GI," told Gionfriddo to take over in left field. "The players called me 'GI' or 'Friddo' or 'the Little Italian,'" said Gionfriddo. "Shotton never could remember my name. He used to say, 'What's that Little Italian's name?'" Fans and some players had other names for him, such as wop, guinea, and spaghetti bender, but he said, "It was hard to figure out if they were directed angrily because you tried not to hear them."[9] With Gionfriddo in left, the stage was set for the play that would put him alongside Lavagetto in the Dodgers' shrine.

In the sixth, with Joe Hatten in for Branca, the Yankees put two men on with two out, bringing DiMaggio to the plate as the tying run. When the Yankee slugger launched a long drive toward the visitors' bullpen in deep left, Gionfriddo, who was playing shallow, took off in a pursuit that, as one writer put it, "seemed as fruitless as a greyhound chasing a mechanical rabbit."[10] Gionfriddo's apparently futile pursuit took him closer and closer to the bullpen. With his back to the plate, he looked over his left shoulder to find the ball. Then just short of the bullpen, he reached across his body with his gloved right hand, jumped, and snared the ball near the 415-foot sign just before crashing into the waist-high gate with his right hip. Dodger announcer Red Barber called it this way: "Back goes Gionfriddo, back, back, back, back, back. He makes a one-handed catch against the bullpen. . . . Oh, doctor!"[11]

Although many accounts say Gionfriddo robbed DiMaggio of a home run, others claim—and the film evidence seems to support this—that Gionfriddo caught the ball just short of the fence. Even so, two runs would have scored, and DiMaggio would have been on second with the tying run. In any case it was immediately hailed as one of the greatest catches in World Series history. The magnitude of the catch was immediately confirmed by DiMaggio himself, who, in a rare display of emotion, kicked at the dirt near second base when he saw that he had been robbed by the little left fielder.

The Yankees scored a run in the ninth, but the Dodgers held on, 8–6, with Branca getting credit for the win. A Hollywood ending would have the Dodgers winning the seventh game and the Series, as a fitting conclusion to the Lavagetto/Gionfriddo heroics. But the script wasn't written by a Brooklyn fan. The Dodgers lost the anticlimactic last game, 5–2. Lavagetto popped out in the seventh, and Gionfriddo never even got into the game. In fact he never again played in the Majors and spent the next several years in the Minors, ending his career in 1956 with the Channel Island Oilers of the California League.

A total of nine Italian American ballplayers took part in the '47 Series, as well as umpire Babe Pinelli. Lavagetto and Gionfriddo may have stolen the spotlight with their respective moments of brilliance, but most of the others were key players on their respective teams and would continue as such in future years. Three of them (DiMaggio, Rizzuto, and Berra) would win a total of seven MVP Awards in their careers. Raschi would go on to win nineteen games the next year, then twenty-one games in each of the next three seasons. Furillo, then in his second year, went on to hit .299 over a fifteen-year career (all with the Dodgers) and win a batting title in 1953.

Of those who appeared in the '47 Series, only DiMaggio, Rizzuto, and Lavagetto had played in the big leagues before the war. Berra, Raschi, and Furillo had made their debuts in '46, Branca in '44. Soon would follow Roy Campanella, Johnny Antonelli, Billy Martin, and Sal Maglie. They would all play significant roles in the era of New York domination, and four of them (DiMaggio, Rizzuto, Berra, and Campanella) would win MVP Awards and end up in the Hall of Fame.

10

The DiMaggio Brothers
Realizing the American Dream

When Joe DiMaggio died on March 8, 1999, the story was front-page news in every major newspaper, and all three major television networks gave the story extensive coverage on their evening newscasts. The *New York Times* ran an uncustomarily large photo of DiMaggio on the front page, and the following week his picture was on the cover of *Newsweek*. On March 16 the House of Representatives passed a resolution honoring DiMaggio "for his storied baseball career, for his many contributions to the nation throughout his lifetime, and for transcending baseball and becoming a symbol for the ages of talent, commitment and achievement." More than fifty years after his final baseball game, Joe DiMaggio was still a cultural icon.

So large does the figure of Joe DiMaggio loom in the history of baseball, and of American popular culture, that many may not even be aware that he had two brothers, Vince and Dom, who also played Major League Baseball. Yet few if any of the more than 350 brother combinations that have played in the big leagues have matched the combined achievements of these three sons of Sicilian immigrants.[1] Joe, a three-time MVP Hall of Famer, was widely considered the best all-around player of his era. Dom, an All-Star in seven of his ten years in the Majors, was the equal of Joe as a center fielder and had a lifetime .298 average. Though less successful than his brothers as a hitter, Vince was a two-time All-Star and was among the top ten home run hitters in the league six times in his ten-year career.

The saga of the DiMaggio brothers has often been cited as a classic example of the American Dream realized: the sons of poor immigrants achieving fame and fortune by playing the national pastime. But while their ability to play the game at the highest level opened up doors that were unavailable to their parents, their dramatically different post-baseball lives also reveal the variety of ways in which many second-generation Italian Americans broke away from the Old World way of life, with varying consequences.

Just as Archangelo Abbaticchio could never have imagined, when he arrived in America in 1873, that one of his sons would earn a living playing a game he had never heard of, neither could Giuseppe DiMaggio have imagined, when he arrived in 1898, that three of his sons would play in the Major Leagues, much less that one of them would become one of the great American heroes of the twentieth century. Giuseppe had been a fisherman in Isola delle Femmine, located ten miles west of Palermo, but like others from his small town he immigrated to California, settling initially in Martinez, just northeast of San Francisco, where he continued to earn a living as a fisherman.

By 1902 Giuseppe had saved enough money to send for his wife, Rosalia, and their daughter, Nellie. Once reunited in Martinez, the DiMaggios had seven more children, three daughters and four sons, including Vincent, born in 1912, and Joseph, born in 1914. Soon after, they moved to the North Beach area of San Francisco, where Dominic was born in 1917. "Everyone in the family spoke Italian with mother and dad," Dom told me. "Dad spoke some broken English. Mom

16. This photo of the DiMaggio family was taken on October 13, 1936, soon after Joe (seated in center) completed his rookie year. Giuseppe (father) is standing at far left and Rosalia (mother) is standing at far right, with Dom to her right. Vince is not pictured. Hulton Archive/Getty Images.

spent most of her days raising the family, so she didn't get involved with Americans all that much."[2]

As we saw in chapter 2, the fishing industry in San Francisco was controlled by earlier immigrants from Genoa, making it difficult for southerners like Giuseppe DiMaggio to gain a foothold. As soon as they were old enough, the sons were expected to help their father on his fishing boat when they weren't in school. But like most sons of immigrants, the DiMaggio boys were drawn to baseball. "We spent a good deal of our time at North Beach Playground," said Dom, referring to the playground located a few blocks from their home, where local kids played basketball, soccer, and baseball. There was never any problem finding a place to play baseball, given the city's rich baseball tradition. In time their passion for baseball would bring the DiMaggio boys into conflict with their father.

Vince

Although he would ultimately be overshadowed by his two younger brothers, it was Vince who convinced a reluctant Giuseppe that there was another way to earn a living than by spending endless hours on a fishing boat. That was no easy task. The concept of ambition and change was alien to Giuseppe DiMaggio, who brought with him to America his Sicilian sense of fatality, the conviction that tomorrow would be the same as today, with nothing to look forward to but more hard work to stave off hunger. As one Sicilian saying has it, "I was born with a hoe in my hand, and I will die with a hoe in my hand."

Like his father before him, Giuseppe was born to be a fisherman, and he assumed his sons would follow the family tradition. Had the DiMaggio family remained in Isola delle Femmine, Vince and his brothers likely would have had little choice but to be fishermen, like their father and grandfather.

Even in America the DiMaggio family initially embodied the basic principles of Italian immigrant life: the family came first, and if the family was to survive in the New World, everyone had to contribute to its well-being. Giuseppe was Old World to the core. In his blood was the innate Sicilian distrust of anyone outside the family, a lesson learned from centuries of invasion and conquest of the island.

Some of the children had other ideas, however, especially once the family moved to San Francisco. While the oldest sons, Tom and Mike, did follow in their father's footsteps, Vince discovered that more than fishing, he loved baseball and singing; his dream was to become an operatic tenor. Dom recalled that his father was unhappy

17. Vince, Joe, and Dom DiMaggio, 1940. Courtesy of Boston Red Sox.

about the time Vince spent playing sandlot baseball. "Dad thought he was wasting his childhood," he said. "The Italian families always had the work ethic uppermost in their minds, and they thought you should be working."

When Vince's success on the local sandlots brought an offer from the San Francisco Seals to play professionally, his father refused to sign the contract. Defying his father—not to mention the entire code of family unity—Vince left home to pursue his dream. In 1932 he spent most of the summer playing for the Seals' Tucson affiliate in the Arizona State League, and by the time the season was over, he had saved $1,500. When he returned home, he wanted to show his father that there was more money to be made playing ball than fishing. He placed the money, in cash, on the kitchen table for his father to see. As so often happened with Depression-era fathers, Giuseppe's skepticism about baseball evaporated when he saw how much money his son was making. The door was now open for Joe and later for Dom.

Vince would spend the next four years in the Pacific Coast League before making his Major League debut with the Boston Bees in 1937. In his first two years in the Majors the five-foot-eleven, 180-pound outfielder was a defensive standout, but he hit only .256 and .228. He distinguished himself primarily by leading the National League in strikeouts both seasons, including a then Major League record 134 in 1938.

Traded to the Yankees in 1939, Vince spent most of the season with their Kansas City farm team before being traded to the Reds in August. In May 1940 he was traded to Pittsburgh, where he would be the starting center fielder for the next five years. He made the All-Star team in 1943 and 1944 and also led the National League in strikeouts four straight years, from 1942 to 1945. His career came to an end in 1946, when he appeared in twenty-one games for the Phillies and the Giants. In his ten seasons he hit .249 with 125 home runs (ranking in the league's top ten in six seasons) and 584 RBIs. Though no match for his brothers as a hitter, Vince was, like them, an outstanding center fielder, leading the league in outfield assists three times.

A Myth Is Born

It was during his first year as a professional that Vince, who was called up to the San Francisco Seals when the Tucson season ended, helped introduce Joe to pro ball. With a few days left in the long PCL season, Seals shortstop Augie Galan asked to leave early to play in Hawaii. When Vince heard manager Ike Caveney protest that the team would be left without a shortstop, he told Caveney that his brother could do the job. At the time seventeen-year-old Joe, who had no interest in fishing with his father and had left school when he was sixteen, had established a solid reputation playing for several of the amateur and semi-pro teams that were a hallmark of the city's fascination with baseball. With the Seals he played at shortstop in their final three games, then signed a contract for the 1933 season at $225 a month. Suddenly Joe was getting paid to play ball at one level below the Major Leagues.

After a slow start in 1933 DiMaggio (moved to the outfield because of his strong, if erratic, arm) began the kind of hitting that would propel him to the Majors within two years. Starting on May 28, he hit in sixty-one straight games. (When Joe's streak reached fifty games, setting a new PCL record, San Francisco mayor Angelo Rossi presented him with a gold watch.) Even though he became the biggest story in the league, young Joe was too shy to correct the spelling of his name, which routinely appeared as DeMaggio (and even De Maggio), as it did on his PCL baseball card.

Joe continued to hit well at the start of the 1934 season, and scouts were paying close attention to the West Coast sensation. But by August a knee injury sustained in May forced him to miss the remainder of the season, leading Major League teams to wonder if the young star was now damaged goods. While many clubs were reluctant to sign DiMaggio, when Yankee scout Bill Essick assured General Manager Ed Barrow that in spite of the injury DiMaggio was worth the chance, the Yankees purchased his contract for $25,000. But the offer had a contingency: DiMaggio would stay with the Seals through the 1935 season and the deal would go through only if he proved he was healthy. Not only did he stay healthy, he also hit .398 with thirty-four homers and 154 RBIs and played outstanding defense.

The Yankee Clipper

When he made his Major League debut in 1936, DiMaggio, heralded as the most promising rookie since Ty Cobb and the "embryo Babe Ruth," received extensive media coverage, much of it focusing on his background as the son of poor Italian immigrants.[3] In spite of the attention he had received as a Minor League star, some in the media still found the DiMaggio name to be problematic. It wasn't long, however, before everyone was familiar with the name. Only three months into his rookie season, when he was hitting around .350 and had been selected to the All-Star team, Joe was on the cover of *Time* magazine. The story noted that his fan mail was "as large as [Babe] Ruth's" and that most of it "comes from Italian well-wishers." The *Time* story also helped to establish the national image of DiMaggio as an example of the poor kid from a large immigrant family finding success in America thanks to baseball. The family was now living more comfortably because the same youngster who had once sold newspapers on the street to help support the family not only "sends home almost his whole salary from the Yankees," but he also bought a fishing boat for his brother Mike.[4] DiMaggio's arrival also elicited greater interest in baseball from *Il Progresso Italo-Americano*, which provided frequent, though not daily, coverage of the rookie's progress.

Of course it wasn't just the media that took note of DiMaggio's ethnicity. Before Ted Williams arrived in 1939, DiMaggio's main rival for the title of greatest power hitter was Tiger outfielder Hank Greenberg, who, as the first great Jewish ballplayer, was also an "ethnic" hero and subject to verbal abuse. "I was young and I was sensitive when they called me 'Hey, Heeb' or 'Jewboy' or 'Sheeny Jew' or something like that," said Greenberg, who made his debut in 1930. "I realized after a while that that was the way it was. They talked like that to everybody. Guys on our club would yell at DiMaggio, 'Hey, Dago,' 'Hey, Wop,' 'Hey, you big Guinea,' and things like that."[5]

Welcomed and supported by his fellow San Francisco teammates, Lazzeri and Crosetti, the rookie exceeded expectations. Not only did he hit .323 with twenty-nine homers and 125 RBIs, but he also displayed an all-around ability that had rarely been seen in the Major Leagues. He could hit—for average and with power—was a fast and smart base runner, had a strong and accurate arm, and glided across the outfield, making tough plays look easy. Even more important to Yankee fans, he helped lead the team to its first pennant and World Series title since 1932. Following the Series, DiMaggio returned to a hero's welcome in San Francisco. From the train station he was driven to City Hall in the mayor's car, then carried inside on the shoulders of fans and presented with a key to the city by Mayor Rossi. He had also become an inspiration to the city's aspiring ballplayers; the *Sporting News* reported that DiMaggio's success "has fired the imagination of many of the Italian boys and they are hustling hard for jobs" in the San Francisco winter leagues.[6]

There was no sophomore jinx awaiting DiMaggio in 1937. The twenty-two-year-old, whose six-foot-two frame had bulked up to 190 pounds, hit .346 with forty-six home runs and 167 RBIs, finished second in the MVP voting, and led his team to its second straight World Series win. Playing as he did in his first two seasons, leading the Yankees back to the promised land in the nation's media capital, DiMaggio was a bona fide hero. In addition to him and Lazzeri, the Yankee lineup featured four other future Hall of Famers: Lou Gehrig, Bill Dickey, Lefty Gomez, and Red Ruffing. But there was no doubt who was the star of the team. The young sensation had indeed become what the Yankees had hoped for; Joe DiMaggio was the successor to Babe Ruth, who had left the Yankees after the '34 season.

By the end of the 1937 season, DiMaggio had made enough money to buy a home for his parents in the more upscale Marina district of San Francisco and to open a restaurant, Joe DiMaggio's Grotto, right on Fisherman's Wharf, a visible reminder to both fishermen and tourists that the immigrant's son had arrived.

In 1939 DiMaggio won his first batting title, hitting .381, and the first of three MVP Awards, becoming just the second Italian American, after Ernie Lombardi, to win either title. The Yankees won their fourth straight Series, sweeping the Reds. Then on November 19 DiMaggio and twenty-one-year-old Dorothy Arnold, a singer/actress he had met while filming a bit part in *Manhattan Merry-Go-Round*, were married in Sts. Peter and Paul Church near the North Beach home where he had grown up.

Even as he was being widely recognized as the best player in baseball, the new Bambino was not immune to stereotypical depiction. He may have been the leader of the best team in baseball, but he was routinely identified as an *Italian* ballplayer. DiMaggio's picture appeared on the cover of the May 1, 1939, issue of *Life*, at the time one of the most widely read magazines in the country. While praising DiMaggio as "baseball's No. 1 contemporary player," writer Noel Busch immediately identified him as a "tall, thin Italian youth equipped with slick black hair" and "squirrel teeth." The entire article is suffused with stereotypes. "Italians, bad at war, are well-suited for milder competitions," wrote Busch. As a youngster DiMaggio was so lazy that his father "decided Joe was incorrigible and soon gave up on all hope of making him amount to anything." Based apparently on his perception of Italian Americans as greasy garlic eaters, Busch seemed surprised by DiMaggio's level of assimilation. "Although he learned Italian first, Joe, now 24, speaks English without an accent and is otherwise well adapted to most U.S. mores. Instead of olive oil or smelly bear grease he keeps his hair slick with water. He never reeks of garlic and prefers chicken chow mein to spaghetti."[7]

While such a blatantly biased portrayal was not common, the appearance of Busch's story in a major publication suggests that such sentiments were, if not openly advocated, at least tolerated by the American public. *Life*'s ambiguous portrait of DiMaggio was a poignant reminder that at a time when Mussolini had become a more ominous figure and Fascist Italy was aligning with Nazi Germany, Italian Americans were still well outside the mainstream and perceived by many with suspicion as the world edged closer to war. Nor did it help that organized crime figures such as Lucky Luciano, Vito Genovese, and Frank Costello were among the most widely publicized Italian Americans at the time.

A few weeks after Joe Jr. was born on October 23, 1941, it was announced that DiMaggio had won his second MVP Award. But it was his fifty-six-game hitting streak that year that cemented his place in baseball history. By now there were few people in America who were not familiar with the fisherman's son from San Francisco, the biggest star on the best team in the nation's most important sport.

Following the 1942 season, DiMaggio joined the many other Major Leaguers who enlisted in the service. He spent the remainder of the war years in the Army Air Force, primarily in a morale-boosting role, serving as a physical education instructor playing on service baseball squads. It was while he was in the service, on May 12, 1944, that Dorothy Arnold was granted a divorce and awarded custody of their son.

DiMaggio's military service divided his career into two almost equal parts, seven years before (1936–42) and six years after (1946–51). While he continued to be the biggest star in the game and to provide any number of memorable performances, his skills gradually eroded due to age and injury. The start of his 1947 season was delayed by surgery to remove a bone spur in his left heel, one of the many injuries that plagued him throughout his career. But at the end of the year his .315 average, twenty home runs, and ninety-seven RBIs were enough to earn him his third MVP Award as he edged out archrival Ted Williams, the 1946 MVP, by a single point.

After finishing second in the MVP vote in 1948, DiMaggio entered the 1949 season with the first $100,000 salary in baseball. John Drebinger wrote the following in the *New York Times*: "Thus, the 34-year-old son of an Italian immigrant fisherman, who used to sell newspapers for a dollar and a half a day on the streets of San Francisco, becomes the highest salaried player in Yankee history and perhaps in all baseball."[8]

Another bone spur limited DiMaggio to seventy-six games in that 1949 season, but two remarkable performances helped cement his reputation as a winner and leader. After sitting out the first sixty-five games of the season, he decided to play in a crucial June series against the Red Sox, who were trailing New York by five games. In his first regular-season series since the previous September, DiMaggio hit four homers and drove in nine runs in a three-game sweep that put the Yanks eight games ahead of the Sox. Then in mid-September a case of pneumonia put him in the hospital. Going into the final two games of the season, the resurgent Red Sox held a one-game lead over the Yanks with two games left. By the time the Sox series began on October 1, DiMaggio had lost eighteen pounds, but he insisted on playing. In the first game, DiMaggio had a single and double as the Yankees won 5–4, leaving the teams tied with one game to go. In the final game Vic Raschi shut out the Sox through eight innings.

Then in the ninth inning, DiMaggio took himself out of the game after stumbling as he failed to catch a Bobby Doerr drive that went for a triple as two runs scored. The Sox scored one more run, but the Yankees held on for a 5–3 win and the pennant. His performance in these final two games did not match what he had done in the June series, but his very presence in the lineup, his insistence on playing, gave a psychological boost to the entire team. The Yankees went on to beat the Dodgers for the first of their five consecutive World Series titles under Casey Stengel.

Limited to 116 games by injury and age in 1951, DiMaggio hit only twelve home runs and compiled the lowest average of his career at .263. The end had come and he knew it; if he couldn't play like Joe DiMaggio, he wouldn't play. On December 11, 1951, citing injuries as the decisive factor, he officially announced his retirement, saying, "If I can't do it right, I don't want to play any longer."[9]

Sprezzatura *in Pin Stripes*

In DiMaggio's thirteen years in New York the Yankees won ten pennants and nine World Series. Named to the All-Star team each year, he compiled a lifetime average of .325 with 361 home runs and 1,537 RBIS.[10] Perhaps the single most impressive statistic is this: in 6,821 times at bat he struck out 369 times. That comes out to an average of 36 times a year, or once every 18.5 times at bat, and his total number of strikeouts was only eight more than his total number of home runs. By comparison, his predecessor, Babe Ruth, struck out once every 6.3 times at bat, and his successor, Mickey Mantle, struck out once every 4.7 times at bat.

Given the relative brevity of his career, DiMaggio's totals don't measure up to those of many other major stars, leaving open to question his all-time ranking. In DiMaggio's case the statistics tell only part of the story. He was the undisputed leader of the Yankee dynasty; in the words of teammate Jerry Coleman, when the game was on the line, "he was the guy we all looked to."[11] In 1969, on the occasion of baseball's centennial celebration, sportswriters selected him as "the greatest living ballplayer." Moreover, among teammates and opponents alike, it became a veritable mantra that DiMaggio was the best player they had ever seen. None other than his archrival, Ted Williams, with whom DiMaggio was always compared, said, "I have always felt I was a better hitter than Joe, but I have to say that he was the greatest baseball player of our time. He could do it all."[12]

What set DiMaggio apart from his peers, other than his exceptional athletic skill, was the graceful elegance he displayed in everything he did on the diamond. It wasn't just what he did, but how he did it, how he *looked* doing it. At the plate he was a stoic figure, waiting quietly, patiently, in his wide stance, then unleashing that long, fluid swing with its long follow-through, his right arm fully extended and parallel to the ground, his whole body showing perfect balance. In the field DiMaggio was the Yankee Clipper, gliding smoothly and effortlessly across the expanse of the Yankee Stadium outfield and making even the tough catches look routine. He had the uncanny ability to see the ball coming off the bat, turn and run to the spot where it came down, and let the ball fall quietly into his glove. One writer said of his style, "There is something about it, at bat and in the field, that suggests some of the great sculptures of the Italian Renaissance." According to teammate Jerry Coleman, "He was the only professional athlete I've ever seen who had an imperial presence."[13]

DiMaggio made everything look easy, and he did it all with a coolness that a jazz artist could envy. The Italians have a word for it: *sprezzatura*—the art of making the difficult look easy. But *sprezzatura* defines the *appearance* of ease and simplicity. In reality it is a mask concealing all the preparation and effort that precede excellence. DiMaggio may have looked like the coolest guy on the diamond, but the calm exterior concealed the inner turmoil that drove him to always be at his best, to live up to his reputation and the expectations that everyone, including himself, had of him. Whatever emotions he stuffed inside and hid from the paying customers manifested themselves in the ulcers that chewed away at his guts as he sat on the bench, drinking coffee and chain-smoking cigarettes.

The Little Professor

The youngest and, at five-foot-nine, the smallest of the brothers, Dom did not play high school baseball until his senior year. But he wanted to prove that he too, like Vince and Joe, could play professionally. By then there was no longer any opposition at home. But there was another obstacle to overcome if he were to follow his brothers to the big leagues: he wore glasses. "Prior to wearing glasses, I couldn't hit a thing," he said. "One day I decided to wear glasses, even though there was a danger of getting hurt. The first time I wore glasses, I hit the baseball like never before, so I wore the glasses." After playing well at a local tryout camp in 1937, he was signed by the Seals, becoming the third DiMaggio brother to play professionally.

Under the tutelage of Seals manager Lefty O'Doul, DiMaggio improved so dramatically that in 1939 he hit .360 and was the MVP of the Pacific Coast League. In spite of his record some teams shied away because of the glasses. The Red Sox, however, were not deterred, and in 1940, at the age of twenty-three, Dom joined his brothers in the Majors, playing the outfield in Fenway Park, glasses and all.

Dom's eyeglasses were not the only uncommon thing about this rookie. He played the outfield unlike anyone else. When taking his position, rather than face the batter, he turned his body so that he

18. Dom DiMaggio, "the Little Professor," 1942. Courtesy of Boston Red Sox.

was facing the left field foul line. "I felt I would get a better break coming in for line drives or ground balls, and going back on the ball I'd get a jump," he said. "The only question was, if I was standing facing left field, could I go to my left going to right field. I had no problem with that whatsoever."

In fact the bespectacled outfielder, nicknamed "the Little Professor" because of his size and his wire-rimmed glasses, had no problem with any aspect of his position. He was the best Red Sox center fielder since Tris Speaker and was generally considered the equal of his brother Joe with the glove if not with the bat. He led the American League in outfield assists three times and twice in both putouts and double plays, and his 503 putouts in 1948 stood as the American League record until 1977.

Offensively Dom excelled as the Boston leadoff hitter, scoring more than one hundred runs in both 1941 and '42. After missing three years to military duty, he bounced right back in 1946, hitting .316, fifth best in the league, and finishing ninth in the MVP vote. In 1949 Dom proved that Joe was not the only DiMaggio who could put together a hitting streak when he hit in thirty-four straight games, still the Red Sox record. When he retired in 1953, DiMaggio had compiled a lifetime average of .298, hitting over .300 four times, and in the ten full seasons he played (1940–42, 1946–52), no one in the Major Leagues had more hits.

As good as he was, Dom DiMaggio has always been considered by some, implicitly or explicitly, as the other guy. As Joe DiMaggio's younger brother and as Ted Williams's teammate and outfield partner, he had a hard time crawling out from under such large shadows. Playing not only in the same league as his brother but for the Yankees' archenemy, Dom inevitably faced continual comparisons to Joe.

When I asked him if he felt like he was competing with his brother, he replied, "I may have, but I think I was competing against the New York Yankees. I had a great desire to beat the Yankees, and Joe was part of the Yankees, so I guess in that respect you might say I was. But I knew there was a big difference. Joe was much bigger than I was, and he hit the ball harder than I did." When asked if he thought he didn't get the recognition he deserved because of being compared to Joe, he said, "Well, not only Joe, but because of Ted [Williams]. I've got Ted on one side of me, and Joe's my brother. I don't think there's a doubt that people have been saying for some years that I have been grossly underrated."

One of the people who believed Dom was underrated was Williams himself, who, as a member of the Hall of Fame Veterans Committee, lobbied unsuccessfully for DiMaggio's election. Teammate Johnny Pesky was another admirer of the Little Professor. "To me Dominic DiMaggio was the perfect player," he said. "He never made any mistakes, threw to the right base, was a good hitter, could run, catch the ball. That's what they always say about his brother of course. Well, he was every bit as good a fielder as Joe."[14]

Post-Baseball Lives

The 1981 film *Tre fratelli* (Three Brothers), by Italian director Francesco Rosi, depicts the lives of the sons of a poor southern Italian farming family, each of whom leaves home to pursue vastly differing lifestyles. One is a prominent judge in Rome, another a teacher in a school for delinquent boys in Naples, and the third a militant factory worker in Turin. The film is ultimately an examination of the consequences of leaving behind the traditions of the past in search of a new life. The saga of the three DiMaggio brothers is an Italian American version of Rosi's film.

Vince

Joe was "the Yankee Clipper" and Dominic "the Little Professor," but Vince was just Vince, more than a journeyman ballplayer but never approaching the status of his younger siblings. Even in retirement, Vince maintained a lower profile. Unlike Joe, he had no lucrative endorsement deals or pitchman opportunities waiting when he retired, and unlike Dom, he had no inclination to enter the business world. Like many former Major Leaguers, he returned to his roots in the Pacific Coast League, appearing in forty-three games with the Seals in 1946. He spent the 1947 season with the Oakland Oaks, then four years as a player/manager for the Stockton Ports of the California League (1948) and the Pittsburg (California) Diamonds of the Far West League (1949–51) before ending his career with the Tacoma Tigers in the Western International League in 1951.

The only one of the three brothers to settle permanently in California, Vince then took on a number of jobs: bartender, liquor salesman, carpenter, and, finally, Fuller Brush salesman. In a 1983 interview the seventy-one-year-old door-to-door salesman said that he spent his spare time fishing, tending his garden, and studying the Bible, "in pursuit of 'that higher league.'" He had found inner peace, he said, and his only disappointment was that except for an occasional phone call, he had lost touch with Joe. (The three brothers would make their last public appearance together on May 17, 1986, at an Old-Timers' game at Fenway Park.) "Joe's always been a loner," said Vince, "and he always will be. When the folks were alive we were a lot closer. It's only a shame that we have gone such different ways. That's real sad. Family should stick together."[15] He died at his home in North Hollywood on October 3, 1986, survived by his wife of more than fifty years, Madelaine, and two children.

Dom

When his playing days ended in 1953, Dom immediately entered the business world. With two partners he formed the American Latex Fiber Corporation, which produced padding for items such as furniture, mattresses, and automobile seats at its plant in Lawrence, Massachusetts, then purchased another automotive supply firm and combined the two companies into the Delaware Valley Corporation. His business acumen made him wealthy enough to be one of the ten original owners of the New England Patriots franchise in the NFL. (Later he was part of a group that made an unsuccessful bid to buy the Red Sox.) However, neither his wealth nor his fame prevented Dom from being blackballed when he applied for membership in the Kittansett Country Club in Marion, Massachusetts. "I was a jock, an Italian, and Catholic," he said. He was later admitted after the club, embarrassed by the situation, asked him to reapply. DiMaggio was no less successful in his personal life than he had been in business. He and Emily Frederick (a native of Wellesley, Massachusetts, whose family name was originally Federico) had been married for fifty-three years at the time of my interview with him, and their three children were all college graduates.

When I first met Dom DiMaggio, during the All-Star Game festivities in Milwaukee in 2002, he didn't look like the other ex-Major Leaguers in attendance. He was small in comparison to former stars such as Bob Feller, Harmon Killebrew, and Bill Mazeroski. What's more, the Paget's disease that afflicted him had bent him at the waist, making him appear smaller than his listed height of five feet, nine inches. Even though illness and age—he was eighty-five at the time— had slowed him physically, Dom was still razor-sharp mentally, and it was easy to see how he had been so successful in his business ventures. Unlike his brother Joe, who by all accounts was reserved and shy, Dom was articulate and self-assured, but with no trace of arrogance.

When asked in a 1949 interview how it was that so much baseball skill was concentrated in one family, Dom replied, "I suppose it's the love of the game." But then he added, "Ambition is in there, too. We saw men rise out of our neighborhood. Men like Tony Lazzeri. Men had gone from San Francisco's Little Italy into the Major Leagues. In that direction lay fame and a good living."[16] "That direction" had taken those California ballplayers east, away from their families and, to some extent at least, away from the Old World traditions in which they had been raised. Their ambition motivated them to seek something more, to take advantage of the opportunities that their parents' journey to the New World had made possible. In their case the opportunity came in the form of baseball.

Joe

As a ballplayer, Joe DiMaggio had become the best-known and the most popular man in America. Unlike most athletes whose star power begins to diminish soon after retirement, he reached a new level of celebrity when in January 1954 this olive-skinned, slick-haired son of immigrants married Marilyn Monroe, the golden goddess of postwar America who was perceived by many as the feminine manifestation of the American Dream. But not even Marilyn Monroe could match DiMaggio's celebrity. When she returned from entertaining the troops during the Korean War, she told her husband, "Joe, you never heard such cheering," to which he simply replied, "Yes, I have."[17]

The merger of two icons was a match destined to fail; the movie star eager for fame could never live the life of devoted housewife that DiMaggio expected of her. According to Dom, "Her career was first.

19. Joe DiMaggio and Marilyn Monroe, 1954. Transcendental Graphics.

Joe could not condone the things that Marilyn had to do. Joe wanted a wife he could raise children with. She could not do that." The marriage lasted nine months, but DiMaggio remained devoted to Monroe and even held out hope that they would remarry. "Joe had wanted that relationship to work," said Dom. "He held on to it for the rest of his life."[18] When Monroe died in 1962, DiMaggio took charge of her funeral and kept away most of the Hollywood and Washington crowd who, in his mind, had abandoned her when she most needed help. He then ordered that roses be placed at her grave twice a week.

DiMaggio had the good fortune to age well. A full head of silver hair atop his still trim physique made him look distinguished rather than elderly. His good looks and his baseball fame opened the door to a lucrative second career as a television spokesman in the 1970s, first locally for the Bowery Bank in New York, then nationally for the "Mr. Coffee" coffee maker. He became a television celebrity to an entire generation that had never seen him play baseball. He remained visible through most of the remainder of his life, appearing at celebrity golf outings, card shows, and Old-Timers' games. But he was always careful to maintain his mystique by limiting his personal appearances and rigidly protecting his privacy.

DiMaggio was a malleable hero; he represented different things to different generations. In his early years as a baseball star he resonated with the American public, not just because he was the best ballplayer in the land, nor because he played in the media capital, though both were factors. I suspect it was also because he was a sober, serious young man doing his job very well. He was an ideal hero for a nation that was rolling up its sleeves, first to survive the worst economic crisis in American history and then, both at home and on the front lines, to win a war. Like other citizens, DiMaggio did his job quietly and efficiently, with dignity and a total dedication to winning. As noted in chapter 8, "We want you on our side" was the refrain to the 1941 hit song "Joltin' Joe DiMaggio." On *our* side; never before had the American public so embraced an "ethnic" hero, someone who, the media routinely reminded the public, was of Italian heritage, the son of an immigrant fisherman.

In the postwar era DiMaggio's ethnicity, like that of other players of European origin, became less and less a topic of discussion as he morphed into a national hero celebrated in music and literature.[19] Ernest Hemingway, in his 1952 novel *The Old Man and the Sea*, honored "the great DiMaggio" as the hero of the working class. In his 1968 hit song "Mrs. Robinson," Paul Simon asked, "Where have you gone, Joe DiMaggio? / A nation turns its lonely eyes to you." And in 1998, in the midst of a presidential scandal, Garry Trudeau, in one of his *Doonesbury* cartoons, cited DiMaggio as an example of someone with enough moral authority to rebuild traditional American institutions. It was as if DiMaggio was always lurking in the national psyche, waiting to be invoked whenever a heroic icon was needed.

Paul Simon's question, posed at a time when the country was going through social and political upheaval, captured the essence of DiMaggio's post-baseball celebrity. No matter that Simon himself said he used the DiMaggio name because that of his boyhood hero, Mickey Mantle, didn't fit the rhythm. It was DiMaggio, not Mantle, who had become a nostalgic touchstone; he represented an earlier time, when America was, or at least thought itself to be, a simpler and more innocent place. The era he evoked in the American memory was of course mid-century New York, when the nation seemed young again and baseball mattered a great deal.

Joe DiMaggio epitomized New York glamour of the postwar period. In his elegant tailored suits he seemed to step out of one of those fifties movies that fixed in our young minds the image of Manhattan as the capital of the world: large, well-furnished apartments and offices, all with panoramic views of the city; large, luxurious cars and sleek women in the latest fashions. Not only was he a part of that world, but he also seemed to rule it from his table in Toots Shor's Restaurant. The shy youngster had been transformed into the most admired man in America, hanging with, and being fawned over by, the city's glamorous elite.

It is important to remember that before he became a national treasure, before he was sanctified as a genuine American hero, Joe was first an ethnic hero. Yankee pitcher and close friend Lefty Gomez said, "All the Italians in America adopted him. Just about every day at home and on the road there would be an invitation from some Italian-American club." In his history of the Yankees, Frank Graham wrote, "DiMaggio's popularity was tremendous. As they had done when Lazzeri had first worn a Yankee uniform nine years before, Italian fans poured into the ball parks all over the circuit to see the new hero."[20]

Joe DiMaggio may not have been my childhood hero—as a Red Sox fan, I favored Ted Williams—but I have come to understand why he meant so much to my parents' generation. To those who lived through the Depression and World War II, this son of immigrants who excelled at the quintessential American game became a symbol of their own hopes of finding a place in a new land that was not always welcoming. And no one, before or since, gave them a greater sense of pride; here was one of their own not only countering the common stereotypical perceptions of Italian Americans, but also being idolized by millions of Americans. It was not a role DiMaggio sought, and given his innate shyness, he was probably somewhat uncomfortable bearing that mantle. But he had no choice; the time and the place were right.

For former New York governor Mario Cuomo, "[DiMaggio's] life demonstrated to all the strivers and seekers—like me—that America would make a place for true excellence whatever its color or accent or origin." *New York Daily News* sports columnist Mike Lupica recognized what DiMaggio meant to his father and grandfather: "There was only one ballplayer for them, an Italian American ballplayer of such talent and fierce pride it made them fiercely proud, fiercely biased toward their man even after he had left the playing field for good."[21]

Tommy Lasorda said, "I knew every big leaguer when I was growing up, but Joe DiMaggio was my hero. He was our hero; he was everything we wanted to be." Tony Machi, a Milwaukee native whose parents emigrated from Sicily, first saw DiMaggio play in 1939, at Comiskey Park in Chicago. "He became our hero," he said. "We all related to him; we lived through him. He was a hero like Sinatra was later on."[22]

DiMaggio and Sinatra were indeed the two most popular Italian American celebrities of the mid-twentieth century. But DiMaggio was a hero well before Sinatra appeared on the national scene in the early 1940s. It was DiMaggio who lifted the nation from the doldrums of the Depression when he burst on the scene as the biggest star since Babe Ruth. And it was DiMaggio who, with his fifty-six-game hitting streak in 1941, captivated a nation preoccupied with the specter of a looming war. Unlike Sinatra, DiMaggio did not bristle at ethnic slurs, nor was he an outspoken advocate on behalf of Italian Americans. Nevertheless, in my opinion, DiMaggio had a greater impact in changing the public's perception of Italian Americans, primarily because he better embodied the qualities Americans most valued at the time. Both were the best at what they did, but what DiMaggio did as an athlete was more important to more Americans than what Sinatra did as a singer. He excelled in physical competition and was acclaimed as a leader of men, qualities that tapped into America's sense of the frontier spirit and had particular resonance just before and after the war. Before the concept of celebrity was tarnished by ubiquitous television talk shows and before the image of baseball was tinged by agents, bloated salaries, strikes, and steroids, Joe DiMaggio was a genuine hero, the biggest star in America's national pastime since Babe Ruth. As one Brooklyn native said on the occasion of DiMaggio's death, he "epitomized an era when, for a lot of us, baseball was the most important thing in life."[23]

Sinatra may have been the coolest cat around, but he didn't lead a team into athletic competition, and he didn't combine raw power with physical grace. Moreover, DiMaggio's reserve and stoic approach to his craft gave him, in the public mind, an aura of dignity and class, whereas the public perception of Sinatra was tainted to some degree by both his open association with known mob bosses and his hard-drinking Vegas lifestyle.[24]

Like Tony Lazzeri before him, Joe DiMaggio undermined the stereotypical image of the "colorful," "fiery" Italian that the media had for so long perpetuated. But Lazzeri, who had neither the extraordinary skill nor the glamour of DiMaggio, played in the shadow of Ruth and Gehrig, whereas it was DiMaggio who cast the big shadow on his Yankee teams. In any case Lazzeri came along about ten years too early. America was not ready, in the immediate aftermath of anti-immigration laws and the Sacco and Vanzetti case, to embrace an Italian American hero as it would DiMaggio. By doing what he did without displaying what most Americans would have considered "typical" Italian behavior, DiMaggio became an acceptable hero to those same people who were accustomed to movie images of fruit peddlers, Latin lovers, and gangsters. That was the bargain required of all transitional ethnic Americans who hoped to be accepted by the mainstream: forfeit, either consciously or unconsciously, the part of your heritage that made others perceive you as different.

DiMaggio was deified by both the media and his fans. "He was our god, the god of all Italian Americans," said famed actor Ben Gazzara.[25]

Of course he was not a god, nor even a saint. Inevitably DiMaggio (like most heroes in the postmodern age) has been subject to revisionist history. Gay Talese, in his famous 1966 *Esquire* essay "The Silent Season of a Hero," portrayed a more suspicious and testy DiMaggio than the one depicted by the friendly media of an earlier generation. Later Richard Ben Cramer, in his thoroughly researched and controversial biography *Joe DiMaggio: The Hero's Life*, painted a portrait of a fiercely private, somewhat unsavory, character who was self-absorbed and obsessed with money. But the ultimate significance of Joe DiMaggio lies less in the facts of his personal life than in the legend that was created around him and which he himself helped to perpetuate. It was the public's perception of him that made him the hero he was.

Joe DiMaggio traveled a much different road from those followed by Vince and Dom, both of whom remained married to one woman. It seemed to some that DiMaggio had realized the American Dream for a second time when he married Marilyn Monroe, but that dream was short-lived. In fact both his marriages reflected the distance he had moved from his close-knit, tradition-bound family. Though he may have wanted his actress wives to at least approach his mother's role as dutiful homemaker, he chose two women from the glitzy world of show business, neither of whom was interested in staying in the kitchen.

The celebrity-centered world Joe inhabited by hanging out at Toots Shor's was far removed from either Isola delle Femmine or the family home in North Beach. Ultimately it was a world that left him isolated and increasingly reclusive. Dom was quoted as saying, "At his funeral my daughter said, 'My uncle was a lonesome hero.' She hit it right on the button."[26] In his eulogy Dom noted that Joe had lacked a constant companion in his life, for which he compensated by devoting much of his time to children and funding the children's wing at the Hollywood, Florida, hospital where he died. The standard-bearer of the Italian American success story was destined to live a life that differed radically not only from that of his immigrant parents, but that of his siblings as well. But whatever the personal consequences of his choices, the DiMaggio mystique remains intact and the myth endures.

11

Italian Yankees
Paesans in Pinstripes

An Italian presence in New York City dates all the way back to the early sixteenth century, when the Florentine explorer and navigator Giovanni da Verrazano became the first European to sail into New York Bay. Not many followed Verrazano's lead; by 1850 there were fewer than four thousand Italians living in the United States. But ever since the wave of immigration that began in the 1880s, New York City has always been home to the largest contingent of Italian Americans in the United States. It was the main port of entry, and for many it was as far as they needed to go.

By the 1940s, when an estimated 1 million New Yorkers were of Italian descent, Italian American culture had become part of the personality of the city, in no small part due to the popularity and impact of Mayor Fiorello La Guardia, the "Little Flower." After serving as a U.S. congressman, La Guardia, the son of Italian immigrants—his father was Catholic, his mother Jewish—was elected mayor in 1933. As mayor, La Guardia, who spoke Italian, openly displayed pride in his heritage and gave a face and voice to the city's Italian American population. Elected as a reform candidate, he managed to secure funding for many public works projects and root out corruption. A colorful and unconventional politician, he was a dominant figure on the city scene during his twelve years in office. Both for his accomplishments and his energetic personality, the five-foot-two dynamo became one of the most popular mayors in the city's history and thereby a goodwill ambassador for Italian Americans, not only in New York but throughout the country.

The large Italian population in New York spurred the Yankees to bring Tony Lazzeri from the West Coast in 1926, to be followed by Frank Crosetti in 1932 and Joe DiMaggio in 1936. Throughout almost all of the Yankees' incomparable run as a sports dynasty, players of Italian descent played key roles. With the exception of 1943, when the frontline players had gone into the service, once Crosetti teamed up with Lazzeri, every one of the Yankee squads that won fourteen pennants and thirteen World Series from 1932 until 1953 had at least two Italian Americans in the starting lineup. In the Yankees' run of five straight Series wins from 1949 to 1953 there were three position players in the starting lineup (Berra, Rizzuto, and DiMaggio until 1951; then Berra, Rizzuto, and Martin), plus Vic Raschi in the starting rotation. Given the large number of New Yorkers of Italian descent and the legacy of Lazzeri, Crosetti, and DiMaggio, it is not surprising that the Yankees featured more outstanding Italian ballplayers than any other franchise in the postwar era. Never before had so many prominent Italian players been in the spotlight, and nowhere did the spotlight shine more brightly—and relentlessly—than it did in New York.

No wonder New York native Neil Simon felt frustrated. He would grow up to be the most prolific and successful playwright of his era, but as a youngster he dreamed of playing for the Yankees. In *Brighton Beach Memoirs*, set in 1937, Simon, through his fifteen-year-old alter-ego protagonist, acknowledged the obstacles that threatened to thwart the dreams of a Jewish boy from Brooklyn: "I hate my name: Eugene Morris Jerome. How am I going to play for the Yankees with a name like that? You have to be a Joe [DiMaggio] or a Tony [Lazzeri] or a Frankie [Crosetti]. If only I was born Italian. All the best Yankees are Italian."[1]

In fact three Italian Americans won seven of the first ten MVP Awards garnered by Yankee players: DiMaggio ('39, '41, '47), Rizzuto ('50), and Berra ('51, '54, '55). In 1950, the year Phil Rizzuto won the American League MVP Award, three other Italian Yankees finished in the top ten: Berra (third), Raschi (seventh), and DiMaggio (tenth). In both 1950 and 1952 three of the nine starters for the American League All-Stars were Italian Yankees: Berra, Raschi, and Rizzuto. Jerry Coleman, a Yankee infielder from 1949 to 1957 and longtime broadcaster for the San Diego Padres, is acknowledged as one of the true gentlemen of the game. But when I asked him what the Italian American players meant to the Yankees in the postwar years, he offered, with no hint of irony, this politically incorrect assessment: "If we didn't have the wops and dagos—Raschi, Rizzuto, Berra, DiMaggio—we never would have won."[2] Indeed, in addition to DiMaggio, the Scooter (Rizzuto), Yogi, and the Springfield Rifle (Raschi) were all mainstays of that Yankee dynasty of the forties and fifties.

The Scooter

Joe DiMaggio was a constant in the long run of Yankee stars of Italian descent. Playing between 1936 and 1951, he was the link between the generation of Lazzeri and that of the young players who would carry on the tradition initiated by the San Francisco transplants of the twenties and thirties. No less of a constant was Frank Crosetti, the shortstop who came to New York in 1932, six years after Lazzeri arrived, and remained with the Yanks as a coach until 1968. He had

been the starting shortstop for nine years when his unlikely replacement came on the scene in 1941.

At five-foot-six and 160 pounds, Phil Rizzuto had been dismissed
by other teams as too small to play in the Majors. At his first tryout, in
1936, a Dodgers coach told him, "Hey, kid, listen. You go out and get
a shoeshine box—that's the only way you're going to make a living.
You'll never make it in the big leagues."[3] Not only did Rizzuto make
it to the big leagues, but he also became the anchor of the infield
for Yankee teams that won nine pennants and seven World Series in
his thirteen-year career, won an MVP Award, and was voted into the
Hall of Fame. He and Crosetti in fact were the starting shortstops for
every one of the fourteen pennant-winning Yankee teams between
1932 and 1953.

Rizzuto was the first of the Italian Yankee stars who was not a
San Francisco native. He was born in Brooklyn on September 25,
1917, to Fiore and Rose (Angotti) Rizzuto, both of whose families
were from the province of Cosenza, in the southern Italian region of
Calabria, at the toe of the peninsula. (His mother was born in Italy,
his father in the United States.) Their families had come to New York
City because other relatives had preceded them and because that's
where the jobs were.

Sitting in the visitors' broadcast booth at County Stadium in
Milwaukee in 1993, Rizzuto spoke animatedly of his family and his
childhood in Brooklyn. (Then seventy-six years old, he retained the
boyish enthusiasm and childlike innocence that had endeared him
to fans and teammates.) "They were laborers," he said. "They built
homes, they built sidewalks, they built garages, in New York City and
out in Long Island." Eventually his father got a job as a motorman
on a trolley car and later as a watchman on the docks.

It was a hard life but one made more bearable by the closeness of the family. "They all moved into these three family houses that were connected to each other with a little alleyway and a backyard," Rizzuto recalled. "It was one of the greatest times of my life because they all played musical instruments; they'd sing, they'd tell stories in Italian, they'd make wine. As long as there was food on the table, everyone was happy."

The Rizzutos baptized their son Fiero, a name that didn't suit a kid growing up in Brooklyn, much less a big league ballplayer. So Rizzuto chose to call himself Phil. "I just took Phil because it sounded more American," he once said. "A ballplayer has to be as American as the Statue of Liberty, is the way I figure."[4]

Rizzuto personified the cliché of the "scrappy" ballplayer. From the time he was a kid he had to prove that he could play the game in spite of his size. "More than 50 percent of the time nobody would pick me because I was so small," he said. He began to prove himself in earnest while playing for Richmond Hill High School in Queens, and he was good enough to play for a semi-pro team (under an assumed name) during the summer before his final year of school. "That was better than any Minor League experience," he said. "I batted against Satchel Paige, the House of David, the Black Yankees. These guys, they knew how to play the game. So many of them could have been in the big leagues, but because of the color line, you know. . . ."

Like so many Italian fathers, Signor Rizzuto had never wanted his son to play baseball. "He wanted me to get a job, to follow in his footsteps," recalled Rizzuto. "He said, 'You can't make a living playing baseball.'" When Mrs. Rizzuto supported her son's desire to play ball, his father finally relented. Signed by the Yankees in 1937, Rizzuto was assigned to their farm team in Bassett, Virginia. Like his mother, who had come from Calabria to New York, the young ballplayer was setting out on his own, though much more modest, voyage of emigration, one that reversed the rural-to-urban journey of his mother. In Virginia her city-reared son found himself in a place that seemed to him almost as foreign as New York must have first seemed to Rose Angotti. "I get off the train, and there's nothing there. I said, 'Where the hell is the town?' Then the train pulled away, and there was the town. There was a drugstore, a post office, and a diner. They had only thirteen hundred people in the whole town. The people were so nice, but they couldn't understand me with my Brooklyn accent, and I couldn't understand them with their Southern accent."

Rizzuto moved quickly through the Yankee farm system. After hitting .336 at Norfolk in the Piedmont League in 1938, he was sent to Kansas City, the Yankees' Double A affiliate in the American Association. (It was while he was playing for Kansas City that teammate Billy Hitchcock gave the quick-footed shortstop his trademark nickname of "Scooter.") He continued to excel in his two years at Kansas City; in 1940 Rizzuto was the MVP of the American Association and was named Minor League Player of the Year by the *Sporting News*.

The following year Rizzuto was slated to be the Yankees' starting shortstop. In spite of his credentials he was not initially welcomed with open arms by the Yankee veterans; they resented the rookie who was slated to depose Frank Crosetti, the popular veteran shortstop who had hit only .194 in 1940. Players tried to keep him out of the batting cage until Joe DiMaggio intervened and told them to let the kid hit. "I had a rough time," Rizzuto admitted. "Crosetti was one of their big favorites and a great guy, and here I was a fresh rookie trying to take his job."

Crosetti himself was much more supportive of his potential replacement than were the other veterans. Rizzuto recalled how Crosetti helped position him in his very first series, against the Washington

Senators. "If it hadn't been for Crosetti, I'd have looked like a bum in that series. He made me look great. Here's a guy whose job I'm trying to take." Rizzuto, the little guy who always had to prove himself, did replace Crosetti in the starting lineup when the season began, and once again, given the chance, he showed that he belonged. In his rookie year he hit .307, second only to DiMaggio's .357 among Yankee players, and in 1942 he hit .284 and led American League shortstops in double plays and putouts.

Rizzuto then spent the next three years in the navy, initially playing baseball at the Naval Training Station in Norfolk, Virginia. In 1944 he was sent to New Guinea and assigned to lead a gun crew on a ship, but his naval combat duty was hampered both by malaria and chronic seasickness. He was then mercifully assigned to organize sports programs in Australia and the Philippines.

The Mexican League

When he returned from the war, Rizzuto briefly got caught up in the bizarre world of the Mexican League, which was making a strong attempt to lure ballplayers away from the Major Leagues with the promise of big money. Jorge Pasquel, a wealthy industrialist who was the president of the league, which had been in existence since 1924, sought to tap into the surplus of Major Leaguers created by the return of war veterans. But it wasn't just marginal players that he pursued. Early in May 1946 he and his brother Bernardo offered Rizzuto $12,000 a year for a five-year contract, plus a $15,000 signing bonus.[5] "Right after the war," said Rizzuto, "you couldn't get a car, you couldn't get tires, you couldn't get butter, you couldn't get anything. They had *everything*. I was ready to go, and so was George [Sternweiss]." But the Yankees filed a law suit to enjoin the Mexican League from inducing their players to jump their contracts.

In spite of Commissioner A. B. "Happy" Chandler's decree that anyone who jumped his contract would be barred from Organized Baseball for five years—the so-called reserve clause denied a player the right to sign with any other team, even after his contract expired, unless he was given an unconditional release—several players were lured away by the promise of more money than they were offered by their Major League teams. Among them was an Italian American outfielder for the Giants named Danny Gardella. A wartime replacement player, Gardella jumped to the Mexican League in 1946. But like many of the other Major Leaguers, Gardella soon became disillusioned with the poor facilities and questionable financial future of the league and left. What he did when he returned to the United States was much more interesting, and consequential, than anything he did in a baseball uniform.[6]

As one of the players suspended by Chandler for violating the reserve clause and thus unable to play baseball in the United States, in October 1947 Gardella filed a $300,000 suit against Major League Baseball for violating antitrust laws. A federal judge dismissed the suit in July 1948 on jurisdictional grounds, but when in February 1949 the Second Circuit Court of Appeals reversed that decision, Gardella and his attorney prepared to take the case to trial. In the face of impending litigation by other players seeking reinstatement, Chandler rescinded his ban on June 5, 1949, enabling the jumpers to return to the Major Leagues.

Initially Gardella maintained his resolve to go to trial, but in October 1949 he settled for $60,000 in return for dropping his suit, thus ending the immediate challenge to the reserve clause. Gardella attempted to return to baseball, but his Major League career ended after one time at bat with the Cardinals in 1950, when he was sent to the Minors. Although he did not pursue his legal battle to conclusion,

Gardella was the first to openly challenge the reserve system. In that sense he opened the door for subsequent legal action, which ultimately led to free agency when in 1976 an arbitrator ruled in favor of Andy Messersmith and Dave McNally, giving players the right to leave their teams and become free agents when their contracts expired. The economics of baseball have not been the same since.

Gardella later achieved another level of notoriety when his name was among those listed in "Van Lingle Mungo," the 1969 song by the jazz pianist and songwriter David Frishberg that, except for two words, consists entirely of the names of baseball players and one umpire. Seven of the thirty-seven names are those of Italian Americans: Gardella, Ernie Lombardi, Roy Campanella, Phil Cavarretta, Frankie Crosetti, John Antonelli, and Augie Bergamo.[7]

Career Years

After three solid but unspectacular postwar seasons Rizzuto had the two best years of his career. In 1949 he hit .275, scored 110 runs, and finished second to Ted Williams in the MVP vote. He followed that performance with his single best season, with career highs in hits, average, slugging average, runs, doubles, and walks. He also led the American League in fielding percentage for the second consecutive year, at one point handling 238 consecutive chances without an error, a Major League record at that time. He was named the American League MVP, easily outdistancing Billy Goodman, 284 votes to 180.

Following his MVP season, Rizzuto signed for a reported $50,000, making him the third-highest-paid Yankee to that time, trailing only Ruth and DiMaggio. Beginning in that MVP year of 1950, Rizzuto was named to four consecutive All-Star teams, starting at short in '50 and '52. But in '54 he hit only .195, and in '55, now thirty-seven years old, he played only seventy-nine games at short.

20. Phil "the Scooter" Rizzuto. National Baseball Hall of Fame Library, Cooperstown NY.

The unprecedented and relentless postwar Yankee dynasty fostered among the team's detractors the image of a cold, efficient corporation without a soul; it became the team America loved to hate. Nothing was done to soften that image when on August 25, 1956, Rizzuto was summoned to Casey Stengel's office and told by General Manager George Weiss that he was being released. It was an abrupt and unceremonious end to the thirteen-year career of a player who had become synonymous with the Yankees. The news came as a shock to Rizzuto, the consummate company man. "I couldn't believe it," he told me. "The pinstripes meant so much then. It was something to live up to and live for." He had defied the odds and the cynics who dismissed him because of his stature. The man known even in his prime as "L'il Phil" and the "Mighty Mite" had become (along with Pee Wee Reese) one of the two best shortstops of his era and played in five All-Star games and nine World Series for one of the greatest teams of all time.

Suddenly it was over, and it was time for the thirty-nine-year-old Scooter, the last of the prewar Yankees, to move on. Whatever resentment he may have felt over his dismissal, he soon accepted the Yankees' offer to become a broadcaster. With his rambling, stream-of-consciousness style, featuring his trademark call of "Holy Cow," he entertained Yankee fans for forty years and endeared himself to a new generation. In 1993 Rizzuto's broadcast musings were transcribed into free verse in *O Holy Cow: The Selected Verse of Phil Rizzuto*. In his review of the book, poet Robert Pinsky, alluding to the equally idiosyncratic linguistic stylings of Yogi Berra and Yankee manager Casey Stengel, wrote, "Mr. Rizzuto now joins Mr. Berra and the creator of Stengelese in a New York School of diamond-oriented language manipulators."[8]

Cooperstown, Finally

When Pee Wee Reese, Rizzuto's alter ego with the crosstown rival Dodgers, was elected to the Hall of Fame by the Veterans Committee in 1984, there were many who thought that if one deserved admission to Cooperstown, so did the other. While their career batting averages were nearly identical (.273 for Rizzuto, .269 for Reese), overall Reese had more impressive offensive numbers, but both were best known for their great defensive skills. Finally, on February 25, 1994, Rizzuto got the call from Yogi Berra, a member of the Veterans Committee, telling him he was in. Rizzuto's response? "Holy Cow!"

Rizzuto's selection was somewhat controversial. Notwithstanding his remarkable performance in his MVP season, questions about Rizzuto's qualifications always centered around his modest hitting statistics. In his defense supporters pointed to his ability to hit behind runners, his intangible value as the sparkplug of teams that won ten pennants and eight World Series in his thirteen-year career, and his remarkable skill as a bunter. There was never any controversy over his defensive skills. He had great range, was exceptionally skillful at going back on popups, and was a fearless and agile pivot man on double plays. Jerry Coleman, who played alongside Rizzuto for eight years, had this to say: "He didn't have a great arm, but he had a great pair of hands, and he never made a mistake. You can look at the numbers and Reese looks better, but you don't win ten titles with a shitty shortstop. I always thought he exceeded Reese defensively but not with the bat. The only other shortstops I'd put in his class were Ozzie Smith and Luis Aparicio." Casey Stengel, with whom Rizzuto had an increasingly uneasy relationship because of what he perceived as the manager's preference for younger players, called him "the greatest shortstop I ever saw. He can't hit with Honus Wagner, but I've seen him make plays the old Dutchman couldn't."[9]

Whatever the controversy over Rizzuto's selection to the Hall of Fame, there was no question about his popularity, both with fans and his fellow players. For all the resentment he faced at the start of his rookie year, Rizzuto soon won over his teammates with his boyish enthusiasm and willingness to be the butt of their pranks. As scrappy as he was on the field, Rizzuto had an almost manic fear of creepy-crawly things, which only served to make him a more inviting target. "They were always playing tricks on him," said Coleman. "Once [outfielder] Johnny Lindell put a dead mouse in his glove (when infielders still left their gloves on the outfield grass between innings). He put the glove on, then threw it in the air and ran into center field screaming."

When he retired in 1996, at the age of seventy-nine, the Scooter had logged fifty-three year of service to the Yankees, more than anyone in the history of the franchise. In 1985 the Yankees retired his number 10 and added his plaque to those in Yankee Stadium's Monument Park. In his characteristically rambling but hilarious Hall of Fame acceptance speech in 1994, Rizzuto said, "I've had the most wonderful lifetime that one man could possibly have." The Scooter died on August 13, 2007, survived by his widow, Cora, and their four children.

Yogi

Rizzuto was in his third year as a Yankee when a twenty-one-year-old catcher-outfielder named Larry "Yogi" Berra joined the team near the end of the 1946 season. They became close friends, roomed together on the road, and eventually became business partners. In addition to sharing the same ethnic background and being teammates, they had something else in common. Like Rizzuto, Berra had to prove wrong the skeptics who said he would never make it to the Major Leagues. At five-foot-eight, he was considered too small, and his square body made him look even shorter. Not only that, but he was also awkward and kind of funny looking; he just didn't fit the mold of a big leaguer. He looked like he should be carrying a lunch bucket, not a baseball bat.

Berra of course would confound his critics by becoming a Hall of Fame player. And like Rizzuto, he would become beloved by teammates and fans. In fact Hall of Fame pitcher and Atlanta Braves broadcaster Don Sutton said of Berra during a 2005 telecast, "He is without a doubt the most beloved baseball figure I've ever seen."[10] He is certainly one of the most recognizable. For a half century he has been a highly visible part of American popular culture, as a spokesperson for products ranging from Yoo-Hoo chocolate drink to Rheingold Beer to AFLAC Insurance; as a film critic; even as the inspiration for a popular cartoon character. Though he never got beyond the eighth grade, he is one of the most frequently quoted men in America. He has a museum and learning center named for him on the campus of Montclair State University and was portrayed by renowned actor Ben Gazzara in a one-man play entitled *Nobody Don't Like Yogi*.

Like Joe DiMaggio, Berra transcended his fame as a ballplayer to become an American cultural icon. And like DiMaggio, to a younger generation who never saw him play ball he became known as a commercial spokesman. But whereas DiMaggio, the cool perfectionist, evoked reverence, Berra, the homely, folksy guy-next-door with the awkward syntax and broad grin, is as cuddly and lovable as his cartoon namesake, Yogi Bear. Of course Berra would never have attracted nationwide attention if he hadn't first been one of the great players in the history of the game. He won three MVP Awards, was an All-Star for fifteen consecutive years, played on fourteen pennant and ten World Series winners, holds numerous Series batting records, and was considered the most dangerous clutch hitter of his time and one of the best defensive catchers ever.

It was an unlikely outcome for the kid who grew up in the "Dago Hill" section of St. Louis. In front of St. Ambrose Church, which sits in the heart of that Italian neighborhood, there is a life-size sculpture entitled "The Italian Immigrants." The statue depicts a man carrying a small suitcase in his right hand, with a destination tag reading "St. Louis" dangling from his lapel. To his left his wife holds their young child in her arms. The Berra family saga exemplifies the Italian immigrant experience portrayed in that statue. Not long before World War I, Pietro and Paolina Berra found their way to St. Louis, emigrating from Malvaglio, a small town near Milan. Pietro, who had been a tenant farmer in Italy, found work in the local brickyard. A few blocks away from St. Ambrose, at 5447 Elizabeth Avenue, they struggled to raise four sons and a daughter. (Lawrence Peter, their fourth son, was born May 12, 1925.) In his 1961 autobiography, *Yogi*, Berra described the Hill as "a poor but very respectable neighborhood where all the people own their own homes, which are really taken care of. . . . When you see the stained glass windows on the front doors and the statues of the Virgin Mary and other religious shrines in the yards, you know it's an Italian neighborhood."[11]

The kids from the Hill played all kinds of sports: soccer, football, even hockey on roller skates, right on Elizabeth Avenue. And of course baseball. Like so many second-generation Italian American boys, Larry Berra (known as "Lawdie" because that's how his mother pronounced his name in her heavy accent) loved to play baseball, as did his three brothers. "We had our own clubs on the Hill, and we used to play each other," said Berra in a telephone interview. "We formed them ourselves. They were all Italian. I played with the Stags AC." But like so many immigrant parents, Pietro thought the game was a waste of time. "He liked soccer," said Berra, "but he didn't know anything about baseball. He wanted me to go to work, get a job."[12] It was the Depression, and the family needed every penny the boys could bring in.

Yogi never made any pretense to be a scholar, and when he completed the eighth grade, his parents agreed that it would be best if he
were to go to work full time. But he had trouble keeping jobs since he
found it hard to resist the urge to leave work and join his friends who
were out of school and playing ball by 3:30. Not surprisingly, this did
not please his several employers, and it pleased his father even less.
Yogi, who by now knew he wanted to play ball professionally, pleaded
with his father to give him a chance to pursue his dream. Pietro finally
relented and said Yogi could try to make it in baseball so long as he
worked odd jobs to bring in some money for the family.

By now Yogi was playing for the Stockham Post American Legion
team, whose coach, Jack Maguire, was a scout for the Cardinals.
Yogi recalled that it was the coach's son, Jack Jr., a teammate on the
Legion team, who gave him the nickname that would stick with him
the rest of his life. One day Maguire saw a travelogue about India
that included a Hindu yogi who sat with his arms and legs crossed,
the same way his friend sat on the ground during ball games. From
then on "Lawdie" Berra would be known as Yogi.[13]

Another teammate on that Legion team was Joe Garagiola, who
lived directly across Elizabeth Avenue and was Yogi's best friend.[14] In
1942, following a baseball school sponsored by the Works Progress
Administration (wpa) in which both boys participated, Cardinals
general manager Branch Rickey authorized a bonus of $500 for Ga-
ragiola. Rickey, who didn't believe that Berra, with his squat body
and lack of discipline at the plate, could ever make it past the Minor
Leagues, would offer him no more than $250. Believing he was just
as good a player as his buddy, Berra refused the offer and went back
to work at a local shoe company but continued to play baseball. Leo
Browne, who had been commander of the Stockham Legion post
that sponsored Berra's team, recommended Yogi to John Schulte, the

Yankee bullpen coach who lived in St. Louis. After scouting Berra, Schulte was authorized to offer him his requisite bonus of $500, plus $90 a month to play for Norfolk in the Piedmont League. It was 1943, Yogi was eighteen, and he was a professional ballplayer.

World War II quickly put his career on hold; having received his draft notice, he enlisted in the navy following the season with Norfolk. Unlike the majority of Major League ballplayers, Berra went into combat. After volunteering to serve on a rocket launcher, on June 6, 1944, he found himself in the middle of the Normandy invasion, firing a machine gun to provide cover for the troops landing on the beach.

Following his discharge in May 1946, Berra was assigned to the Yankees' top Minor League team, the Newark Bears, then was called up to the Yankees for the final week of the season. After less than two full seasons in the Minors, Yogi Berra's nineteen-year Major League career had begun at the age of twenty-one. In 1947, his first full season, he appeared in eighty-three games (as a catcher and outfielder), hitting .280 with eleven homers and fifty-four RBIs.

Berra improved as a hitter in 1948—he hit .305 and drove in ninety-eight runs—but he struggled behind the plate. By the time he reported to spring training in 1949, the Yankee bosses had decided to replace Bucky Harris with Casey Stengel, a move that surprised many, given Stengel's less than impressive track record as a Major League manager—in nine years with the Brooklyn Dodgers and Boston Bees, he had never finished higher than fifth—and his reputation as a baseball clown. Stengel announced early on that Berra was to be his regular catcher, and he brought in as one of his coaches Bill Dickey, the great Yankee catcher from 1928 to 1946, one of whose duties was to turn Yogi into a dependable receiver.

The criticism had been relentless since Berra's rookie year, and the media questioned whether Berra could ever be a big league receiver. Under Dickey's patient and encouraging tutelage Berra learned how to be a good catcher and in time was acknowledged as one of the best ever at his position. Looking back on Dickey's influence, Berra later said, "He opened my mind to the position, got me to think behind the plate. . . . I always say I owe everything I did in baseball to Dickey."[15]

The proof of Berra's transformation behind the plate lies in the numbers. After catching 109 games in '49, he caught an average of 139 games from 1950 to 1957, leading the league in games caught in each of those years. In one stretch, between July 28, 1957, and May 10, 1959, he set a Major League record by handling 950 chances without an error. But the numbers tell only part of the story. Berra became a master of the intangible aspects of catching. He knew the strengths and weaknesses of opposing hitters and was an excellent handler of pitchers, learning which ones needed praise and which needed a kick in the butt.

Berra also liked to break a hitter's concentration at the plate by talking to him. Former Indian and Tiger star Rocky Colavito said, "Yogi was always talking behind the plate. One day, I said, 'Hey, Yog, we're both Italian. Give it a rest. Give me a break. I'm trying to make a living.'" Jim Fregosi, an eighteen-year Major Leaguer, echoed Colavito's remarks. "I used to have to tell him to shut up because whenever I was hitting, he'd be talking to me," he said. "I couldn't concentrate on what I was doing. He was quite a character."[16]

Berra more than justified Casey Stengel's faith in his initially un-promising catcher. They were an odd couple, these two ugly ducklings with the craggy faces and big ears. They both spoke in gnarled syntax, though Berra specialized in unwittingly cryptic aphorisms, while

21. Lawrence Peter "Yogi" Berra. Transcendental Graphics.

Stengel's forte was a rambling stream-of-consciousness monologue that left his listeners baffled but amused. Though neither had extensive formal education (Stengel did finish high school), both had a seemingly intuitive knowledge of baseball. But theirs was an intuition rooted in extensive experience and astute observation. Stengel could ride Berra mercilessly at times (as he did with several players), but he came to have great respect for his ability, often referring to him as "my assistant manager."

Berra's offensive contributions to the Yankees' postwar dynasty were no less important. Under their new manager the Yankees set an unprecedented, and still unmatched, mark of five straight World Series titles from 1949 to 1953. In each of those five years Berra led the team in RBIs, averaging 102 per year. What impressed people was not just how many runs he drove in, but also when he drove them in. He is generally acknowledged as one of the best clutch hitters in the history of baseball. I know that as a young Red Sox fan, I always worried when Berra came to the plate with the game on the line; he always seemed to deliver when the Yankees needed a hit. Jerry Coleman confirmed my recollection: "In the seventh, eighth, and ninth innings he was as tough as they get."[17]

What was even more frustrating to opposing pitchers and opposing fans alike was Berra's ability to hit pitches most hitters would never swing at. Never one to adhere to Ted Williams's first rule of hitting—"Get a good pitch to hit"—Yogi was more a devotee of Will Rogers: he never met a bad pitch he didn't like. Any ball he could see and reach was a good ball to hit. Virgil "Fire" Trucks, who pitched in the big leagues for seventeen years, told me that the two toughest hitters he faced were Ted Williams and Yogi Berra. "Once I threw him the best curve ball I ever threw in my life; it ended up about six inches off the ground," he said. "He swung, and I never saw the ball, he hit it so hard. I turned and saw my center fielder chasing it down."[18]

Even swinging at bad pitches Berra generated enough power to never finish lower than second in home runs among Yankee hitters from 1949 to 1959, leading the team for three consecutive years from 1951 to 1953. Yet for a power hitter, especially an undisciplined one with a love of the out-of-the-strike-zone pitch, Berra had a remarkably low strikeout ratio, attesting to his exceptional hand-eye coordination. Over his nineteen-year career he struck out only 414 times in 7,555 times at bat, or once in every 18.2 times at bat, which almost matches Joe DiMaggio's rate of 18.5. In 1951 Berra was selected as the American League's MVP, becoming the third Yankee of Italian descent to win the award in the past five years. Berra won the MVP Award again in both 1954 and 1955, joining DiMaggio, Jimmy Foxx,

Stan Musial, and Roy Campanella as the only three-time winners at that time.

In 1963, now thirty-eight years old, Berra served as a player/coach, then was named manager in October. In 1964, his very first year at the helm, he became the first Italian American manager to win a pennant, only to be fired the day after the Yankees lost the World Series to the Cardinals. He would then manage the expansion Mets for three-plus years, winning another pennant in 1973, then return to the Yankees in 1984. His managerial career ended after sixteen games into the 1985 season when he was fired by volatile owner George Steinbrenner.

After four years as a coach with the Houston Astros, from 1986 to 1989, Berra retired from baseball, his legacy firmly established. In his nineteen-year career he hit 358 home runs—his 306 homers as a catcher remained the career record until 1980, when Johnny Bench passed him—drove in 1,430 runs (most ever by a catcher), and had a lifetime average of .285. Selected to fifteen consecutive All-Star teams, he also played on a record ten World Series champions and holds the Series record for most games, at bats, hits, and doubles. According to baseball historian Bill James, "Yogi's record of sustained excellence over a period of a decade [1948–59] is without parallel by any catcher in the history of baseball."[19]

Eventually Yogi Berra convinced the skeptics who doubted his ability and was recognized as one of the great catchers in baseball history. He also became one of the most recognizable and beloved figures ever to play the game. But along the way Berra was much maligned. As was true of Ernie Lombardi, his looks and awkwardness—in his case linguistic as well as physical—made him a target of ridicule, some of it good-natured, some less benign. Berra's build evoked memories, in those old enough to remember, of an earlier Italian Yankee, Ping Bodie. In a front page story in the *Sporting News* J. G. Taylor Spink compared the young Berra to Bodie, "a baseball oddity" who was "almost as broad as he was long" and who "spaghettied himself out of the majors." While Spink did not think Berra would suffer the same fate, he did add, "No photogenic bird is this new Bodie, any more than the original Ping was a thing of beauty."[20]

Over the years Berra's syntax was lampooned as much as his looks. His sayings, which became known as Yogi-isms, have become better known than his statistics and help define his public persona. They cannot be ignored, obviously, because they have become so much a part of the legend, and I confess to having my own favorites, but they will receive relatively little attention here, both because they are so widely known and readily accessible and because, in my opinion, they contribute to an incomplete and ultimately unfair caricature of the man.

It is perhaps both a blessing and a curse that today Yogi Berra is best known for his unintentionally witty aphorisms. On the one hand, they capture the essence of his lovable innocence. At the same time, his malapropisms unfairly perpetuate the image of a man of limited intelligence and obscure his status as one of the great players in baseball history. His squat, ungainly physique; his less than matinee-idol looks; his amusing Yogi-isms; his undisciplined approach at the plate—all added up to a perception of Berra as something of a primitive with a dull mind. But to those inside the game Yogi Berra had an exceptionally keen baseball mind.

Craig Biggio of the Houston Astros, who began his Major League career as a catcher before becoming a second baseman and a center fielder, got to know Berra when Berra was a coach with the Astros. "He's the smartest baseball man I've ever been around," said Biggio.

"Everybody gets on him for his Yogi-isms, and he does have them, but as far as his knowledge of the game, he's a very, very smart man." Phil Garner, another former Astro player, added, "He doesn't have a look or demeanor about him that suggests brilliance, but the man is very, very bright. With all the stuff that's going on, he'll say the one thing that makes everything make sense. I've never been around anyone quite like him. When it comes to baseball, he has a computer-like mind."[21]

Late in 1959 Berra and his wife Carmen visited his parents' hometown of Malvoglia, forty miles from Milan. There he met five of his mother's sisters and one of her brothers and discovered that he could converse easily with them since they spoke the dialect he had spoken with his parents. "I was right at home," he wrote in his autobiography. "It was just the same as talking to Mom and Pop." His return to his parents' birthplace touched him deeply: "I felt as though I had done one of the best things of my life." At the end of his autobiography, Berra's thoughts turned to his father, now a widower who continued to live in the family home. "I know one thing," he wrote. "He would never leave the Hill, and I don't blame him. . . . It's Pop's own world, and it's the world in which he has his own identity."[22]

Berra had made his own life far from the Hill, and there is a touch of nostalgia in his description of his father's sense of belonging and of the world of stability and tradition that he, like so many second-generation Italian Americans, gave up to make his own way in the world. He had taken advantage of the opportunity for a better life that had motivated his parents to leave their home in Italy. Like them and like the couple in the statue outside St. Ambrose Church, Berra and his wife had ventured into their own new world, leaving behind one home to find a new one, not across an ocean but halfway across the continent.

Berra's nostalgic look back at the stability of life on the Hill only underscores the break between that life and the new life he made for himself; it is an acknowledgment that he has given up a part of what made him who he was, but it was a price he was willing to pay. For him baseball provided the means to prosperity and even fame as an American. For others the opportunity would come through business, academia, the professions, but the result would be the same: success, and acceptance as an American, would require at least a partial break with the past.

Even for someone of Berra's stature acceptance was not always simple. In spite of the ridicule to which he had been subjected, Berra denied that he had encountered any ethnic prejudice during all his years in baseball. He didn't recall hearing anyone calling him a dago, adding, "If they did holler that, I didn't hear it." He did say, however, that around 1950 or '51—in the prime of his career—he was denied membership in a New Jersey country club. "They didn't like Italians then," he said, then added, "I went to an Italian club; I got in there real quick."[23]

The Springfield Rifle

With a lineup featuring sluggers like DiMaggio, Berra, Hank Bauer, Moose Skowron, Johnny Mize, and Mickey Mantle, the postwar Yankees—the Bronx Bombers—have always been synonymous with power. But power without pitching is a formula for failure in the big leagues. The key to the Yankees' five-year streak between 1949 and 1953 was their trio of starters: Vic Raschi, Allie Reynolds, and Ed Lopat. In those five years they won a combined total of 255 games, an average of 17 wins each per year. Of the three none was better than Raschi, who won 21 games each year from 1949 to 1951 and was considered by Stengel to be his best starter.

Victor John Angelo Raschi, the son of Italian immigrants, was born in 1919 in West Springfield, Massachusetts, the birthplace of Hall of Famer Leo Durocher. (His classic nickname of "the Springfield Rifle" combined the speed of his fastball and the name of his hometown, the site of the U.S. Armory, which had been producing army rifles since 1794.) A star in baseball, football, and basketball at Springfield Tech High School, he was scouted by the Yankees while still a freshman. In 1936 Raschi signed an agreement that provided for covering the cost of his college education in return for giving the Yankees the first chance to sign him when he graduated. He enrolled at the College of William and Mary—one of the schools to which the Yankees sent potential players—but his education was interrupted by the war. After spending three years in the Army Air Force, he returned to school part time while pitching for the Yankees, earning a degree in physical education in 1949.

In his 1936 article on the upsurge of Italians in the Major Leagues, Dan Daniel had wondered whether the absence of Italian pitchers may have been due to "a coincidence, or a quirk of Fortune or race." Beginning in 1948, Raschi went on a four-year spree of pitching magnificence that put the lie to Daniel's inference that because of their "race," Italian pitchers lacked the ability, or intellect, to succeed in the Majors.[24]

From 1948 to 1951 the six-foot-one, 205-pound righthander posted records of 19-8, 21-10, 21-8, and 21-10. During the Yankees' five-year title run from 1949 to 1953 he went 92-40 while completing 73 of the 160 games he started. He pitched more innings than Reynolds or Lopat in each of those years except 1952, when Lopat edged him by twenty-one innings. What makes this stretch of endurance even more impressive is that a collision at home plate with Indians catcher Jim Hegan in August 1950 resulted in torn cartilage in Raschi's right knee.

From then on Raschi played in pain; it was difficult for him to run or to put all his weight on his right leg when he pushed off the pitching rubber. But he and the Yankees kept the injury to themselves to prevent other teams from taking advantage of his injury by bunting on him. It wasn't until November 1951, after he had won 21 games for the third straight year, that he underwent surgery to remove the cartilage. His winning percentage of .724 in 1950 led the American League, and in his eight years with the Yankees, his record of 120-50 translates into a .706 winning percentage.

Big win totals are impressive, but some pitchers who pile up the numbers during the course of the season prove to be less effective in decisive games. Raschi, however, was at his best in the big games. Tommy Henrich said, "If there was only one game I had to win, the man I'd want out there on the mound for me would be Vic Raschi." Jerry Coleman told me, "He was our bread-and-butter guy. Reynolds had a better arm, but Raschi was a great competitor. Off the field he was shy and unassuming, nothing like he was on the mound. There he was a beast. Casey considered him our best starter." Stengel was quoted as saying, "I thought Raschi was the best pitcher I had on the team for nine innings. . . . Boy, he was the best on the club in the eighth and ninth inning."[25]

Raschi was an intimidating pitcher, and not just because of his fastball. With his hazel eyes peering out from beneath his dark eyebrows, he stared down batters in an attempt to unsettle them and gain a psychological edge. "I figured if I could break their concentration when they came up to the plate I had them beat, or at least gained an advantage," he said. "Once you had made them turn their eyes away you had a slight psychological edge." Yogi Berra said, "He'd keep his eyes on their eyes, like a boxer before a fight."[26]

Raschi won five World Series games, including a two-hit shutout of the Phillies in the 1950 opener and two wins against the Dodgers in the '52 Series, but the game for which he is best remembered came on the final day of the 1949 season, when the Yankees hosted the Red Sox with the pennant at stake. The Sox, who had trailed the Yankees by twelve games early in July but stormed back to take a one-game lead with two games left, needed only to win one of the two to take the flag. But the Yanks won the first game 5–4 to force the Sox into a do-or-die finale. Raschi, with a 20-10 record, was matched up against Ellis Kinder, the talented, heavy-drinking farm boy from Arkansas who had won twenty-three (four against the Yankees) and lost five going into that final game.

With 68,055 fans on hand Raschi, given a 1–0 lead in the first, shut down the power-laden Sox on two hits over the first eight innings, with the Yankees taking a 5–0 lead after scoring four in the eighth. But the Sox, who had been favored to win the pennant, wouldn't go quietly, scoring three in the ninth with the tying run at the plate in Birdie Tebbetts. First baseman Tommy Henrich approached Raschi to offer some encouragement. But the glowering Raschi was in no mood for chitchat, and before Henrich could say a word, he told him, "Give me the goddamned ball and get the hell out of here."[27] He then got Tebbetts to hit a foul pop, which Henrich squeezed for the final out and the pennant.

As was true of many Yankees, Raschi's contract talks with General Manager George Weiss were often contentious. He knew he had given everything he had each season, even playing through the pain caused by the torn cartilage in his knee, but Weiss tried to make his players feel as if they hadn't done enough to merit more money. "Talking to him," said Raschi, "you felt your own contribution getting smaller and smaller." In 1952 Raschi signed for a reported $40,000, making him the highest paid pitcher in Yankee history. But the signing came with a stern warning from Weiss: "Don't you ever have a bad year."[28]

The next year Raschi did have what Weiss considered a bad year, winning thirteen and losing six, leading the general manager to offer a contract calling for a 25 percent cut in 1954. Raschi refused to sign and again held out until spring training, one of twelve Yankee holdouts. Once he got to St. Petersburg, he was informed by newspaper reporters, not by Weiss, that he had been sold to the Cardinals. Raschi was understandably disappointed, but his mother, Jesse, in Springfield, was not. (According to Raschi's sister Santina, it was his mother who had first nurtured Raschi's love for baseball, playing with him in their backyard when he was very young. When he became a Major Leaguer, she would say the rosary, praying that he wouldn't get hurt.)[29] Admitting she had never liked the Yankees, she told her son, "I always wished you could be a Boston Red Socker."[30]

Raschi spent his final two seasons with the Cardinals and Kansas City Athletics before retiring in October 1955. In his ten-year career he won 132 while losing only 66, with an ERA of 3.72. As of 2008 his win-loss percentage of .667 was tied for thirteenth best for any pitcher with at least one hundred decisions. He finished seventh and eighth in the MVP voting in 1950 and 1951 respectively, and he pitched in four All-Star games, starting in both 1950 and 1952.

Raschi spent his retirement years in rural upstate New York, living in Groveland, on the shores of Lake Conesus, and operating the Green Valley Liquor Store in nearby Geneseo. He also coached high school basketball and taught physical education at Geneseo State Teacher's College (now the State University at Geneseo), where the baseball field was named in his honor. Beginning in 1969, at the age of fifty, he even taught elementary school. Raschi died in 1988 at the age of sixty-nine, survived by his wife and three children.

22. Billy Martin (left) and Vic Raschi, "the Springfield Rifle," 1952. National Baseball Hall of Fame Library, Cooperstown NY.

Billy The Kid

Billy Martin is now best remembered for his mercurial managerial career and his legendary boozing and brawling, all of which make it easy to forget that he had an eleven-year Major League career as an infielder and, for a few of those years, contributed to the success of the postwar Yankee dynasty, especially during the World Series. But with big ears and a big nose atop his thin, 165-pound body, he hardly looked like a prototypical Yankee. Possessing limited natural ability and haunted by insecurities, Martin was driven by an obsessive need to prove himself. A classic overachiever, he approached the game as a war, with a win-at-all-costs attitude. It was a combustible combination that, especially when fueled by alcohol, occasionally flared into uncontrollable rage. Both as player and manager, he was a fighter, in every sense of the word; in spite of his size he backed down from no one, either with his mouth or with his fists.

Martin's fiery temperament was forged by both blood and environment. Like Tony Lazzeri, he grew up in a tough neighborhood of the San Francisco Bay Area, in his case West Berkeley. And like Lazzeri, Martin claimed he never got licked. But his disposition was first established at home, where he was raised by his mother and grandmother. In his autobiography, *Number 1*, Martin portrayed his mother, Joan ("Jenny") Salvini, as being just as tough and combative as he was, always willing to stand up to any man to protect her son. She in turn had learned from her Italian-born mother. "My mother never took shit from nobody," wrote Martin. "It was her motto, something her mother had taught her."[31]

Martin's mother left her first husband (from an arranged marriage to an Italian man named Pesano) when she met Alfred Manuel Martin, a Portuguese musician raised in Hawaii. Even though she threw Martin out of the house for cheating on her while she was pregnant, she named their son Alfred Manuel Martin Jr. But the son would always be known as Billy because of his grandmother's nickname for him; she called him "Belliss," short for *bellissimo*, Italian for "most beautiful one." His friends thought she was calling him Billy, and that's the name that stuck.

Given the absence of his father and the strong influence of his mother and grandmother, it is not surprising that Martin identified more with his Italian heritage. On one of his two Hall of Fame questionnaires he listed his nationality as "½ Italian, ½ Portuguese" and on the other, "Italian." Martin would refer to himself as a "dago," and several Italian American Major Leaguers, including Frank and Joe Torre and Rocky Colavito, have said that Martin referred to them affectionately as "daig."

In 1947, his first full season as a professional, Martin was named MVP of the Texas-Arizona League after hitting .392 with 174 RBIs for Phoenix. His big break came in 1948, when he played for the Oakland Oaks, the "Nine Old Men" who won the Pacific Coast League title under manager Casey Stengel. At age twenty Martin was the youngest player on the team, earning him his nickname of "Billy the Kid." He benefitted by being tutored by two former Major Leaguers: Ernie Lombardi gave him tips on hitting, and Cookie Lavagetto taught him the fine art of turning the double play. Martin hit .277 for the Oaks, but it was his hustle and competitive drive that most appealed to Stengel, who became something of a father figure to his young protégé. The following year Stengel became the Yankees' manager, and in 1950 he convinced the team brass to bring Martin to New York.

With Jerry Coleman playing well at second base, Martin played little in his first two years with the Yankees. (When he was in the lineup at second, the Yankees were all-Italian up the middle in 1950 and '51, with Berra behind the plate, Rizzuto and Martin at short and second, and DiMaggio in center.) He finally convinced Stengel to start him in 1952, and while he hit only .267, he did the little things that help a team win games. It was in the World Series against the Dodgers, the closest ever between the intercity rivals, that he made his mark. In Game 2 he hit a three-run homer to spark a 7–1 win in which Vic Raschi pitched a complete-game three-hitter. In Game 7 the Yankees led 4–2 when the Dodgers loaded the bases with one out in the bottom of the seventh. Duke Snider popped up for the second out, then Jackie Robinson hit what looked like a routine pop-up between the mound and first base. When Martin realized that first baseman Joe Collins had lost the ball in the sun, he came rushing in and made a lunging shoestring catch to end the rally and ensure the Yankees' fourth straight title under Stengel.

The next year, in a Series rematch with the Dodgers, Martin did it with his bat. He hit .500—his twelve hits set a new record for a six-game Series—with two home runs and eight RBIs, but he saved the best for last. In the sixth and deciding game, with the score tied at 3–3 in the bottom of the ninth, Martin lived every kid's fantasy by hitting a single to drive in the winning run, giving the Yankees their fifth straight title. He was voted the Series MVP and later won the Hickock Award as the top professional athlete in the country.

After missing all of the 1954 season and most of '55 due to military service, Martin returned to his starting job in 1956 and made the All-Star team. But his career with the Yankees came to a sudden end in 1957 following a brawl in mid-May at the Copacabana night club in New York. Martin was there to celebrate his birthday along with several teammates when an argument with another group escalated into a fight. It was of course front-page news the next day and an embarrassment to the Yankee organization. Fights with opponents Clint Courtney and Jimmy Piersall early in his career had established Martin's reputation as a brawler, and General Manager George Weiss, who had never cared for the volatile infielder, saw this as his opportunity to get rid of him. He blamed Martin for starting the fight and one month later traded him to Kansas City. The irony is that by all accounts Martin was not involved in the nightclub brawl.

Devastated by the trade, Martin was never the same player again; in his final six years in the Majors he played for six different clubs. It was as if the competitive fire had been drained from him once he left the Yankees. "I tried and tried," he wrote, "but I couldn't get my heart into it."[32] Eight years after his playing career ended in 1961, he began his managerial career, which was to bring him greater fame but no less controversy.

12

Interborough Warfare
Dodgers versus Giants

The seven "Subway Series" that matched the Yankees against the Dodgers (six times) and the Giants (once) between 1947 and 1957 confirmed both the postwar supremacy of the three New York franchises and the intensity of their interborough rivalry. But in terms of ferocity and passion, those brief scuffles, as dramatic as some of them were, paled in comparison to the annual six-month fist fight that was the Dodgers-Giants rivalry. Fans and players alike were caught up in the conflict, sometimes with violent consequences, both on and off the field. Giants pitcher Sal "the Barber" Maglie routinely knocked down Dodgers stars Carl Furillo and Roy Campanella, and Furillo once vented his frustration by charging the Giants dugout to get at manager Leo "the Lip" Durocher. Dodger fans in particular were renowned for their exuberance, to put it politely. In her memoir *Wait 'Til Next Year*, historian Doris Kearns Goodwin, a Dodger fan as a child, wrote that "every meeting was regarded as a separate war, to be fought with implacable hostility."[1]

The oldest of the three New York franchises, dating from 1883, the Giants had the greater legacy, going back to the glory days of John McGraw, who, as manager from 1902 to 1932, led the team to

23. Brooklyn Dodgers "Sym-Phony." National Baseball Hall of Fame Library,
Cooperstown NY.

ten pennants and three World Series titles. But after winning the
pennant in 1937, the Giants would not win another until 1951. The
Dodgers, on the other hand, had a less impressive legacy but a more
promising future as America entered World War II. With the exception of 1941 they had not won a pennant since 1920. Their identity
as lovable losers was certified by the memorable cast of characters
who populated cozy Ebbets Field, including super fan Hilda Chester,
who clanged her cow bell often and loudly, and the five-member
all-Italian "Sym-Phony" band, whose music was about as melodious
as Hilda's cow bell.

In the postwar era, however, it was the Dodgers who dominated;
between 1947 and 1957 they won six pennants to the Giants' two and
eight of the eleven season series. With a nucleus that featured Pee

Wee Reese, Jackie Robinson, Duke Snider, Roy Campanella, Carl Furillo, Don Newcombe, and Carl Erskine, the Dodgers were rivaled only by the Yankees. These were the Dodgers who would be rendered mythical by Roger Kahn's celebrated book *The Boys of Summer.*

Among the actors in the postwar interborough drama were several Italian American players, though there were fewer of them on the Giants' roster. In lead roles were Furillo, Campanella, Ralph Branca, Sal Maglie, and Johnny Antonelli, with supporting roles going to such players as Cookie Lavagetto, Al Gionfriddo, Herman Franks, Joe Garagiola, Gino Cimoli, and Joe Amalfitano. Even future Hall of Famer Ernie Lombardi was a bit player with the Giants, appearing in eighty-eight and forty-eight games respectively in '47 and '48, his final two seasons in the big leagues.

Unlucky 13

Of all the Italian Americans who played major roles in postwar New York baseball, none was involved in a more memorable moment than Ralph Branca. The home run he surrendered to Bobby Thomson to end the 1951 Dodgers-Giants playoff—the iconic "shot heard 'round the world"—is considered by many to be the single most dramatic event in baseball history. Unfortunately for Branca, that one pitch branded him as one of the all-time goats. Years later Branca would say that Thomson's home run was one of the best things to happen to him, but at the moment that ball flew over the left field wall of the Polo Grounds, he wondered why God had chosen him to bear such a cross.

It is a cruel irony that Branca is remembered for one infamous pitch since he showed so much promise at the start of his career. When he won twenty-one games in 1947 as a twenty-one-year-old college student, he seemed destined to become the first great pitcher of Italian descent. Nicknamed "Hawk" because of his prominent nose, the six-foot-three, 230-pound righty threw hard, and in the words of Roger Kahn, "his curve ball snapped like a flag in March."[2] But that 1947 season would prove to be the high point of his career. He would pitch in the Majors for another seven years and three times win thirteen or more games, but a succession of injuries limited his success. Three others—Vic Raschi, Sal Maglie, and Johnny Antonelli—would steal the New York spotlight and emerge as the finest Italian pitchers of their generation.

Unlike most Italian American ballplayers of his era, Ralph Theodore Branca was the child of a mixed marriage. He was born in Mount Vernon, New York, on January 6, 1926, the fifteenth of seventeen children of John Branca, the son of an immigrant from Lapana (a small town in the Calabria region) and Katherine Berger, a native of Hungary. Branca identified more with his father's ethnic heritage. "I've always thought of myself as Italian," he told me. "I took [Italian] in high school for two years, but I had no one to communicate with. My father and mother spoke English." Branca was also very much aware of those Italian American players who had paved the way for him. "There were so many good Italian ballplayers," he said. "Lodigiani, Lavagetto, Lombardi, Cavarretta. I remember, as a kid, the Yankees up the middle were Lazzeri, Crosetti, DiMaggio, Berra. They had a lot of *paesans* up the middle."[3]

An excellent student and athlete in high school, Branca was awarded a full scholarship to New York University, where he became the starting center on the basketball team as a freshman. Then after posting a 9-3 record for NYU in the spring, he was signed to a Major League contract by the Dodgers on June 6, 1944, D-Day. (Branca had tried to enlist in the service when he turned eighteen, but a punctured eardrum and asthma earned him a 4-F classification.) Six days later, wearing number 13—the same number he would be wearing five years later when he surrendered the Thomson home run—Branca made his Major League debut at the age of eighteen years, five months.

In 1946 in the first-ever playoff in Major League history, Manager Leo Durocher chose Branca to start the first of the three-game series with St. Louis. The Cardinals got to him for six hits and three runs in 2⅔ innings and won the game 4–2. No fewer than five Italian Americans played for the Dodgers in that opening game, but they provided little help. Lavagetto, Furillo, and pinch hitter Bob Ramazzotti went a combined 0 for 8 at the plate, while Branca and reliever Vic Lombardi yielded all four runs in their combined three innings. On the other hand, the Cardinals' lone Italian—twenty-year-old rookie catcher Joe Garagiola—played a key role in the game, going 3 for 4 and driving in two of the Cards' four runs. Garagiola irritated home plate umpire Beans Reardon by repeatedly questioning his calls. Fed up, Reardon finally said to Garagiola, "Shut up, dago! You're lucky you're not pushing a damn wheelbarrow selling bananas!"[4]

It was in 1947 that Branca, now twenty-one years old and still a student at NYU, came into his own. He won twenty-one games and lost twelve, becoming the youngest National League pitcher to win twenty games, a record that stood until 1985, and he was named to the All-Star team. He was an All-Star again in '48 and '49, but all of that would prove to be prologue to the defining moment of his and Thomson's careers.

With a 13½-game lead over the second-place Giants on August 12, the Dodgers looked like a sure bet to win the National League title in 1951. But a remarkable streak in which the Giants won sixteen straight and thirty-seven of their final forty-four games forced a three-game playoff with Brooklyn. What had been a runaway turned into, in the words of novelist Don Delillo, the pennant race that "brought the city to a strangulated rapture."[5] Branca started the opening game in Brooklyn, limiting the Giants to five hits in eight innings, but two of those were home runs, one a two-run shot by Thomson, and the Dodgers lost, 3–1. The next day Clem Labine pitched a six-hitter for the Dodgers to even the series.

On Wednesday, October 3, 34,320 fans gathered in the Polo Grounds, the elongated ballpark with the cavernous center field, above which rose the uniquely situated clubhouse. The deciding game featured a matchup between Giants ace Sal Maglie, who entered the game with a career-best 23-6 record, and Don Newcombe (20-9). The Dodgers could manage only a single run through seven innings, but then they stung Maglie for three in the eighth to take a 4–1 lead into the last inning. Newcombe had been just as stingy as Maglie, but Al Dark and Don Mueller singled to lead off the ninth. Then with one out, Whitey Lockman drove a double to left, scoring Dark and sending Mueller to third. Manager Charlie Dressen signaled for Branca to come in from the bullpen to face Thomson, the twenty-seven-year-old two-time All-Star third baseman who had hit thirty-two home runs that year. So it all came down to a duel between two local boys: Thomson, the "Staten Island Scot" who had come to America at age two, and Branca, born, raised, and still living at the time in Mount Vernon.

After getting ahead 0-1 on a fastball, Branca threw another fastball, up and in. When the ball left Branca's hand, it was just another in the thousands of pitches he had thrown in his career. Then, just like that, at 3:58 p.m., it turned into the most infamous pitch in baseball history. Jumping on the fastball, Thomson lashed a line drive to straightaway left. Branca spun around, hoping the ball would dive before it reached the fence. It didn't. As left fielder Andy Pafko looked

24. Ralph Branca and his wife, Ann. National Baseball Hall of Fame Library, Cooperstown NY.

on helplessly, the ball flew over his head and fell into the stands, barely making it into the first rows beyond the 315 foot sign. Not far, but just far enough to snatch a pennant and break the hearts of Dodger fans. As Thomson danced around the bases and his team-mates gathered at home plate to welcome him, Giants announcer

Russ Hodges shouted into the microphone his now legendary call: "The Giants win the pennant, the Giants win the pennant." Four times he repeated the refrain, tossed in another phrase, then said it one more time for good measure.

Branca, meanwhile, picked up the rosin bag, slammed it to the dirt, and began the long, torturous walk to the center field clubhouse. When Branca went to his car—license plate RB-13—Ann Mulvey, his fiancée, and Reverend Pat Rowley, her father's cousin, were waiting for him. "Why me?" Branca asked the priest, who answered, "God chose you because he knew your faith would be strong enough to bear this cross."[6]

Branca and Thomson would both capitalize on their shared moment of history, appearing together for years at baseball dinners, card shows, and corporate events and becoming friends in the process. Their road show not only kept them in the public eye, it probably earned them more money than they ever made playing ball. In a 1969 interview Branca called the home run "one of the best things to happen to me . . . a blessing in disguise."[7]

The drama of the '51 season was given a new twist fifty years later, when a story by Joshua Prager appeared in the *Wall Street Journal* claiming that the Giants had been stealing the opposing catcher's signs and relaying them to the batter in the final ten weeks of the season.[8] According to Prager, one of the key figures in the conspiracy was Herman Franks, a Giants coach since 1949. Beginning on July 20, Franks, along with reserve infielder Hank Schenz, was stationed in Durocher's office in the center field clubhouse of the Polo Grounds, 483 feet from home plate. There, using the Wollensak telescope provided by Schenz, they intercepted the opposing catcher's signals and relayed them, by means of a buzzer system, to backup catcher Sal

Yvars in the bullpen. In turn Yvars would toss a baseball in the air to signal a breaking ball or hold it to signal a fast ball. For the record Franks never publicly admitted playing a role in the conspiracy. Yvars, on the other hand, was the first of the Giants to admit to the scheme publicly and remained the most vocal whistle-blower.[9]

In 1954, when he was playing for the Tigers, Branca himself learned of the sign stealing from his roommate, Ted Gray. Many years later he would call the Giants' tactics "one of the most despicable acts in the history of the game," but at the time he maintained his silence. "I didn't want to cry over spilled milk," he said. "I didn't want to diminish a legendary moment in baseball. And even if Bobby knew what was coming, he had to hit it."[10] Thomson admitted to taking the signs from Yvars on occasion but denied that he took it before hitting the home run off Branca.

In his remaining four seasons Branca would never again come close to being the dominating pitcher he had once been, compiling a modest record of 12-12, never winning more than four games in a season. Five months after his thirtieth birthday his once promising career came to an end, and Branca went to work as an insurance salesman. In twelve years he won eighty-eight games, was a three-time All-Star, and won a World Series game. Yet given his prodigious start (winning twenty-one games at age twenty-one), more was expected of him.

A genial and intelligent man, Branca was well liked by his teammates, who trusted him to serve as their player representative beginning in 1946. In 1986 he became the first president of the Baseball Alumni Team (BAT), later renamed the Baseball Assistance Team), the charitable organization established by the commissioner's office to assist retired ballplayers in need, and he later served as its chairman for many years.

For all that Branca endured because of the "shot heard 'round the world," the effects of his darkest moment in baseball did not sour him on the game that brought him early fame and ultimate infamy. At the All-Star Game festivities in Milwaukee in 2002, I asked Branca, still fit and engaging at age seventy-five, what baseball meant to him. "I played football in high school, I played basketball in college," he said, "but baseball was always my first love. It's still the greatest game ever."[11]

Joe Garagiola

For Joe Garagiola, the twenty-year-old rookie who drove in two of the four runs off Branca in the opener of the 1946 playoff, that first of his nine years in the Majors would prove to be the most memorable. Over the next eight years he was primarily a backup catcher with the Cardinals, Pirates, Cubs, and Giants, appearing in an average of seventy games a year and compiling a modest lifetime average of .257. But his baseball career proved to be a prelude to greater acclaim as a popular television celebrity known for his humorous anecdotes, many of which focused on his childhood neighbor and best friend, Yogi Berra. Soon after retiring as a player in 1954, Garagiola became a broadcaster, first for the Cardinals, then for the Yankees. From 1961 to 1988 he was part of NBC Television's *Game of the Week* team. In 1967 he gained a much wider audience as co-host of the *Today* show, all of which made him one of the best-known televison celebrities of the time. In 1973 he won a Peabody Award for excellence in broadcasting and in 1991, the Ford Frick Award, presented annually at the Baseball Hall of Fame induction ceremony to a broadcaster "for major contributions to baseball."

In addition to his work as a broadcaster, Garagiola became involved in charity work. In 1986, the same year Branca was elected the first president of BAT, Garagiola was elected vice president. When he later succeeded Branca as president, he capitalized on his television fame to raise money for indigent former ballplayers. He also became an outspoken critic of the use of chewing tobacco by ballplayers, visiting Major League camps during spring training to warn of its cancer-causing potential. Roland Hemond, a former general manager and one of the most highly respected men in baseball, said of Garagiola, "He's one of the finest people in the game in terms of taking care of his fellow man. I don't know of anyone in the game who's been so involved in charitable activities."[12] But for all the adulation Garagiola has received over the years, there remains the still unsettled controversy over his role in the Cardinals' harsh treatment of Jackie Robinson in his rookie year of 1947.

Baseball in the forties was still a rough and tumble game, with no quarter given and none asked. Rivalries were often intense, even bitter, and players policed the game themselves, with the knockdown pitch the accepted means of enforcement. Fierce bench jockeying was also part of the code; anything and everything about a rival player was fair game, with little if any regard for political correctness.

When Jackie Robinson made his historic debut in 1947, he was subjected to a barrage of taunts and slurs that were unprecedented, both in number and viciousness. When hurled by those unwilling to accept the presence of a black man in the Major Leagues, their object was not simply to unsettle an opposing ballplayer, but also to drive him out of the game entirely. The assault on Robinson appeared to reach a new level during an August series against the Cardinals in New York. When Robinson, playing first, stepped on the bag after fielding a routine grounder, St. Louis outfielder Enos Slaughter spiked him above the right heel. "The only real question," wrote Jonathan Eig in his book on Robinson's rookie year, "was whether he'd done it out of racial bias or pure competitive passion."[13]

Garagiola became a part of the story when the two teams met the following month in St. Louis for a crucial series. In the second inning of the series opener on September 11, as Garagiola ran to first trying to beat out a double play, he stepped on Robinson's foot; the first baseman's shoe was torn, but there was no injury. In the next inning Robinson came up to bat. The rookie, who had restrained himself all season from reacting to the abuse he had taken, said something to Garagiola. The brash and vocal twenty-one-year-old catcher rose from his crouch and replied in kind. The tension mounted as the two of them stood face to face, exchanging further pleasantries. But order was soon restored and the game continued without further incident.

Contemporary game stories did not suggest that Garagiola had spiked Robinson on purpose, and Robinson himself was quoted as saying, "I don't think Garagiola did it intentionally," then adding, "but this makes three times in two games with the Cardinals that it's happened." In his autobiography Robinson cites the Slaughter spiking incident but makes no mention of Garagiola. In fact earlier in the season, Wendell Smith, the ghostwriter for Robinson's newspaper column, had identified Garagiola as one of several Cardinal players who were nice to Robinson: "The St. Louis Cardinals aren't only good ballplayers, but they're good guys as well."[14]

Why then, if there was no contemporary outcry against Garagiola, did his name continue to be linked to the controversy surrounding the Cardinals and Robinson? Jonathan Eig attributes the rebirth of the issue to a 1984 book for young readers by Bette Bao Lord, *In the Year of the Boar and Jackie Robinson*, which was widely read in elementary schools: "The book, which singles out Garagiola for his attack on Robinson, has haunted the former ballplayer since its first publication, establishing him as a bigot in the minds of a generation that never saw him play."[15]

Set in 1947, *The Year of the Boar and Jackie Robinson* is the semi-autobiographical story of Shirley Temple Wong, an immigrant girl from China who lives in Brooklyn and begins to become American by playing baseball, "our national pastime." Jackie Robinson is portrayed as a role model, someone who "is making a better America." For whatever reason, Lord chose to use Garagiola (rather than Enos Slaughter) as the villainous antithesis of Robinson. Shirley hears on a radio broadcast that "Joe Garagiola hadn't beaten the throw but had spiked Jackie Robinson's foot instead and given all Dodger fans one more reason to hate the Cardinals."[16]

Whether or not Lord's book was the source, Garagiola's guilt was well enough established—if not in the public consciousness, at least in the minds of some baseball historians—that occasionally he has been paired with Enos Slaughter as one of the two Cardinals most hostile to Robinson. While most scholars acknowledge the complexity of the issue and maintain an open mind, others are blatantly unequivocal. Historian Carl Prince, for example, tabbed Garagiola as "sadistic": "He and Slaughter were the racist leaders of the Cardinals; both were guilty of deliberately spiking Robinson as he played first base." And a 2006 story on Curt Flood in the *New York Times* stated that "two Cardinals, Enos Slaughter and Joe Garagiola, had harassed Jackie Robinson."[17]

Garagiola vehemently denied any guilt in the matter, but at times he clouded the issue by avoiding discussion about the 1947 incident. When I interviewed him in 1999, he himself brought up the Robinson question. "Nothing happened," he insisted. "They talk about spiking. There was no spiking incident." He then gave his version of the story. "I avoided stepping on Jackie Robinson. I was hitting .348. I landed on my shoulder. I went to the hospital; Jackie went back to the hotel." This was an accurate description of what happened, but it happened on June 1, 1950, not in 1947. Garagiola, bunting into a double play, tripped over Robinson, who was taking the throw at first base. Taken to the hospital, Garagiola underwent surgery for a separated shoulder.[18]

Is Garagiola's recollection of his encounters with Robinson a case of faulty memory or conscious evasion? Did he step on Robinson's foot intentionally or accidentally? The evidence is at best inconclusive. At the least, there is enough doubt to preclude any definitive statement about Garagiola's intent or about his attitude toward Robinson. Garagiola himself attributed the lingering controversy to his celebrity status. "It may be the price of being recognizable," he said. "This happened later, after I became well known, because I was an easy target."[19]

It is worth noting that before either Garagiola or Robinson came on the scene, New York mayor Fiorello La Guardia played a minor role in paving the way for the desegregation of baseball. In 1945 La Guardia, who, according to historian Thomas Kessner, "stood well ahead of contemporary American society" with regard to civil rights for blacks, created the Mayor's Committee on Unity "to study the root causes of prejudice, discrimination, and exploitation."[20] That same year he established a committee charged with studying the question of segregation in baseball and making recommendations to the Major Leagues. The committee's report concluded that no one should be excluded from the Majors "because of color," and that blacks should be given a chance "to compete on an equal basis."[21]

Campy

Another step forward in the integration of baseball came in 1948, when Roy Campanella joined Jackie Robinson in the Dodger lineup. That statement obviously identifies Campanella as an African American

276

ballplayer. Yet genetically at least he was no less Italian than his team-mate Ralph Branca, whose mother was Hungarian. Born on November 19, 1921, in Philadelphia, he was the son of John Campanella, an Italian American whose parents were from Sicily, and Ida Mercer, an African American from Maryland. Because of the racial climate of the time, pigment trumped blood; Campanella's public identity was determined not by the vowel at the end of his name but by the color of his skin. To the baseball establishment—and to most of America for that matter—his Italian bloodline was irrelevant. On his Hall of Fame questionnaire under "nationality" he listed "American Negro (mother), Italian (father)," but in the eyes of his fellow Americans he was a black man. And he identified himself as a black man, as the world dictated that he must. "I've had a struggle all my life," he wrote in his autobiography. "I'm a colored man."[22]

The ban on black players meant that Campanella got a relatively late start in the Major Leagues, making his debut at the age of twenty-six. He made up for lost time by establishing himself as one of the two greatest catchers of his time (along with Yogi Berra); he was named to eight All-Star teams, played in five World Series, and won three MVP Awards. And he did it all in only ten seasons, his career being cut short by an automobile accident that left him paralyzed at the age of thirty-six.

While racial discrimination delayed his entry in the Majors, Campanella's great talent earned him an early start as a professional in the only place open to him. He was so gifted as a youngster that in 1936 he was signed by the Baltimore Elite Giants of the Negro National League at the age of fifteen. Except for part of 1942 and all of '43, when he jumped to the renegade Mexican League, Campanella was with the Elite Giants from 1936 to 1945. Beginning in 1939 he played winter ball in the Carribean and South America, which meant that he played baseball for fifty weeks a year. (Also in 1939 he married fellow Philadelphian Bernice Ray, with whom he had two children. But Campanella's baseball schedule took its toll and the marriage dissolved.) A natural leader with good baseball instincts, he also managed in winter league ball, having learned enough Spanish to communicate with the Latin players.

Campanella's performance over those years caught the attention of Branch Rickey, the Dodgers' general manager who was secretly planning to integrate the Major Leagues. In March 1946, only five months after Jackie Robinson had been signed, Campanella signed with the Dodgers and was assigned to their affiliate in Nashua, New Hampshire, in the Class B New England League. (Buzzie Bavasi, Nashua's young Italian American general manager, agreed to take Campanella after another Dodger farm team had refused.) The twenty-four-year-old catcher wasted no time taking advantage of his opportunity, winning the MVP Award of the New England League in 1946. The next year he was again named league MVP, this time with the Dodgers' top farm team, the Montreal Royals of the International League. After spending the first half of the 1948 season with the Saint Paul Saints to carry out Rickey's desire to integrate the American Association, on July 2 Campanella was in the Dodgers' starting lineup, where he would stay for the next nine and a half seasons.

In the same way that the ethnicity of Italian ballplayers was noted when they first made inroads in the big leagues, at the start of his career Campanella was routinely identified in the press as a "Negro" or as a "Negro catcher." Rarely did stories about him even refer to his Italian heritage. Ironically on the occasion of his debut with the Dodgers in April 1948, it was an African American paper, the *Chicago Defender*, that acknowledged his mixed heritage: "His father is an Italian and his mother a Negro."[23] Though not as virulent or

25. Roy Campanella in action. National Baseball Hall of Fame Library, Cooperstown NY.

persistent as the attacks on Jackie Robinson had been in 1947, racial slurs did find their way to Campanella's ears. But his hearing, and his sensibility, were not as acute as Robinson's. "Campy" was as placid as Robinson was intense, as congenial as Robinson was confrontational. This is not to say that Campanella was accepting of prejudice or mistreatment, only that his approach was different. Unlike Robinson, Campanella preferred pacifism to activism as a means of confronting racial prejudice. "I tried not to notice the things that bothered Jackie," he wrote.[24]

After appearing in 83 games in his shortened rookie season of 1948, over the next nine seasons Campanella played in an average of 126 games, in spite of a series of nagging injuries. Beginning in 1949, his first full season, Campanella was named to the All-Star team eight consecutive years. He played on a great Dodger team that featured future Hall of Famers Robinson, Duke Snider, and Pee Wee Reese,

279

but it was Campanella who was selected as the National League MVP three times, in 1951, '53 and '55. In each of those seasons he hit over .300, with more than thirty home runs and one hundred RBIs.

By 1957 the combination of twenty-one years of pro ball and various injuries had taken its toll on the thirty-four-year-old catcher, who appeared in only 103 games. Nevertheless, Campanella was preparing to make the move to California with the Dodgers in 1958. But just as his career had been delayed at the start by discrimination, it was now cut short by a life-altering injury. In the early morning hours of January 28, 1958, after closing the liquor store he owned in Harlem, Campanella was driving home when his car hit a patch of ice, skidded off the road, hit a telephone pole, and flipped over. Campanella was pinned under the dashboard, unable to move. Four hours of surgery saved his life, but his career was over; he would remain paralyzed from the chest down for the rest of his life.

In his ten years with the Dodgers, Campanella hit .276 with 242 home runs and 856 RBIs. Like Yogi Berra, Campanella did not look like a ballplayer. Given his five-foot-nine, 200-pound frame, "stocky" was a generous description. But he was a gifted athlete with a strong and accurate arm, surprising agility behind the plate, and speed on the base paths. Also like Berra, Campanella excelled at the more intangible aspects of a catcher's job; he was a master at handling his pitching staff, knowing which ones responded best to gentle encouragement and which required a stern reprimand. That he was the first black catcher to handle a predominantly white Major League staff makes his accomplishments all the more impressive.

Following his accident, Campanella initially struggled emotionally to cope with his paralysis. "Those first hundred days after the accident were the worst in my life," he later wrote.[25] Gradually he dedicated himself to therapy, and in time he regained some use of his arms and hands. And as the title of his autobiography, *It's Good to Be Alive*, suggests, he also recovered his enthusiasm for life. In 1978 he finally made the long-delayed move to California after accepting a position as assistant director of community relations for the Dodgers.

It was not his first trip to California. On May 7, 1959, the Dodgers honored their former catcher with Roy Campanella Night, featuring an exhibition game at Los Angeles Coliseum against the Yankees. Between the fifth and sixth innings the stadium lights were dimmed and the 93,109 people in attendance—at that time the largest number ever to attend a big league game—lit matches as a tribute to Campanella, who watched, in tears, from his wheelchair.

Roy Campanella not only overcame great odds to become one of the first black players in the Major Leagues, but he also established a reputation as one of the great catchers in the history of the game. He was elected to the Hall of Fame in 1969, and on June 4, 1972, the Dodgers retired his number 39 along with those of Jackie Robinson and Sandy Koufax. But his most important contribution came after his career-ending injury, when he showed great courage by enduring his hardship with characteristic grace and good humor. While Campanella was undergoing physical therapy, his doctor said, "The way he has been able to combat this misfortune has given hope to so many, many thousands of disabled persons, not only in this country, but all over the world."[26]

Steel and Velvet

Two years before Campy brought his cheerful disposition and portly physique to Brooklyn, a more taciturn twenty-four-year-old rookie named Carl Furillo broke into the Dodgers lineup. Furillo had just served three years in the army, seeing action in the Pacific theater, but his was a less dramatic debut, with none of the sociological implications of Campanella's arrival. Furillo, however, would soon establish himself as a key component of the Dodgers' postwar dynasty.

A decade after Furillo's career ended in 1960, Roger Kahn, who was doing research for *The Boys of Summer*, went in search of the retired outfielder. He finally tracked him down at the construction site of the World Trade Center, where Furillo was working as a laborer, installing elevator doors. At first glance that might seem like a fall from grace for someone who had been a Major League batting champion and a star on one of the great teams of his era. But Furillo had always been a lunch bucket kind of guy, even in his glory days, a working stiff who played hard all the time. It was how he made a living. There was nothing glamorous about him. He approached life with the hard-nosed realism of a child of the Depression and never made any pretense of being more than what he was, which was, in Kahn's words, "a man of uncomplicated virtues."[27]

Born on March 8, 1922, in Stony Creek Mills, a small town near Reading, Pennsylvania, Carl Anthony Furillo was the youngest of six children whose parents were immigrants from Naples. He never forgot the Italian he learned at home and would speak the language with siblings and friends when, as his son, Carl Jr., said, "they didn't want us to know what they were talking about."[28] For someone who dropped out of school after the eighth grade, a career as a professional ballplayer looked more promising than the other available options. In 1942 Furillo hit .281 with the Montreal Royals, the Dodgers' top affiliate, but his career was then interrupted by the three years of military service.

Upon returning in 1946, Furillo made the jump to the Dodgers. In his fifteen-year career he hit above .290 or above eleven times, five times above .300, with a career-high and league-leading .344 in

1953, and he hit 192 home runs with 1,058 RBIs. On a team loaded with stars, including three destined for the Hall of Fame, Furillo was somewhat overshadowed. Nevertheless, of the "boys of summer," only Jackie Robinson, at .311, had a higher career average than Furillo's .299. Had he come up with one more than his total of 1,910 hits, he would have been a lifetime .300 hitter.

As productive as Furillo was as a hitter, it was his powerful arm that made him an Ebbets Field legend, inspiring wonder in both fans and writers. After playing center field his first three years, in 1949 Furillo moved to right, the proper place for someone blessed with such a lethal arm. He led the league in outfield assists in 1950 and '51, before intimidated runners hesitated to test his arm. "Right field in Brooklyn was his destiny," wrote Kahn, who covered the Dodgers for the *New York Herald Tribune* in 1952 and '53. "People came early just to watch Furillo unlimber his arm. The throws whined homeward, hurtled off a bounce and exploded against Roy Campanella's glove—pom, pom, pom, pom—knee-high fast balls thrown from three hundred feet."[29]

What made the speed and accuracy of Furillo's throws even more effective was his uncanny ability to "read" the mysterious caroms off the odd right field wall of Ebbets Field with the interpretive acumen of a biblical scholar. The nineteen-foot concrete wall was concave, slanting away from the field at the bottom, then becoming vertical at its midpoint. Above it was a nineteen-foot screen made of wire mesh. If the ball hit the screen above the cement wall, it would drop straight to the ground, but if it hit the cement, it would carom back toward the infield at different angles, depending on where it hit. Furillo, who stood six feet tall, weighed 190 pounds, had thick black hair, and was rock hard, reminded writers of a Roman centurion, an appropriate title for someone who guarded that right field wall

26. Carl Furillo, "the Reading Rifle," 1953. Transcendental Graphics.

so zealously. He learned how to judge the flight of a fly ball so that he would know where to position himself to grab the carom, wheel, and make the throw. The way he learned how to play the wall sums up his workmanlike approach to the game as a whole. "I'd be out early and study it," he said. "The angles were crazy. I worked, that's how I learned it."[30]

Furillo's arm and his home town earned him the nickname of "the Reading Rifle." But he had another, less flattering nickname: "Skoonj," a corruption of *scungilli*, the Italian word for conch. While writers commonly attributed the nickname to Furillo's love of the dish, his son Jon dismissed the notion. "People thought it was because he liked *scungilli*, but that's not true," he said. "He didn't like them. It was because he wasn't the fastest runner in the world. He had a big frame and short legs."[31]

An intense competitor, Furillo was caught up in the bitter rivalry with the Giants. "You had that Giants uniform on, you were out to get us," he said. "And we were out to get you." And the person he was convinced was most out to get him was Leo Durocher. "Leo the Lip" had been Furillo's manager with the Dodgers since his rookie year of 1946, and like many players, Furillo was not fond of him. "Durocher was a dirty manager. He was a dirty ballplayer. . . . I hated his guts."[32]

The animosity intensified when Durocher left the Dodgers in the middle of the '48 season to manage the Giants. Several Giants pitchers seemed to have sudden bouts of control problems when they faced the Dodgers; they had trouble keeping the ball out of close proximity to the bodies of Brooklyn batters. Furillo, who was hospitalized after being beaned by Sheldon Jones in 1949, was convinced that Jones and others were ordered to throw at him by Durocher, who, from his perch in the dugout, enjoyed encouraging his pitchers to "stick it in his ear." In fact before the game in which Furillo was hit by Jones, Durocher reportedly stopped by the Dodgers' clubhouse to tell him to be ready to duck that night. Then Giants coach Herman Franks, a fellow Italian, came by to say, "Tonight, we get you, dago."[33]

One of the Giants' pitchers who zeroed in on Furillo with some regularity was fellow Italian American Sal "the Barber" Maglie. In the April 25, 1953, game Maglie threw a pitch that sailed over Furillo's head. On the next pitch, as Furillo swung and missed, the bat slipped out of his hands. The bat twirled, end over end, straight toward Maglie, who deftly jumped over it, looking like some movie cowboy dancing to avoid the gunslinger's bullets aimed at his feet. Furillo headed toward the mound (just to retrieve his bat, he later claimed), and both benches emptied, but the umpires quickly restored order. Furillo then struck out, this time holding onto the bat.

Furillo's feud with Durocher came to a head later that season. By September 6, when the teams met in their season finale, the Dodgers had beaten the Giants nine times in a row. In the second inning, after Campanella hit a two-run homer, Ruben Gomez hit Furillo on the left wrist. After being stopped by umpires from going after Gomez, Furillo went to first base. Giants coach Herman Franks, who was standing near Durocher in the dugout, offered this firsthand account of what happened next: "He gets to first base and he's pointing at the dugout and yelling, and I said to Leo, 'He's hollering at you.' With that Leo starts hollering back, and Carl left first base and was running to the dugout. Leo went out of the dugout and met him head on. All the players jumped in, but I think they traded punches. Durocher could get most anyone mad. He was tough."[34]

Other accounts have Furillo clamping Durocher in a headlock as they grappled on the ground while others tried to separate them.

One observer who did not try to break up the fight, according to Duke Snider, was umpire Babe Pinelli, who reportedly yelled, "Kill him, Carl, kill him."[35] Fifty-three years later Dodger pitcher Carl Erskine—known as "Oisk" to the Brooklyn faithful—confirmed Snider's assertion. "Furillo had Leo on the ground and was choking him," he told me. "I was on the perimeter, as was Babe Pinelli. He was exclaiming, 'Kill that SOB, kill him.' He then saw that I had heard him, so he went on, 'I mean it. That no good low life. I mean it.'"[36] Before the combatants could be pried apart, someone stepped on Furillo's left hand, breaking the metacarpal bone in his little finger. Forced to sit out the remainder of the regular season, Furillo, who was hitting .344 at the time, ended up winning the batting title by two points over Red Schoendienst.

In his second year in the Majors Furillo was implicated in the 1947 protest among Dodger players against playing with Jackie Robinson. While there is a difference of opinion as to whether Dixie Walker, the Southerner who spearheaded the protest, marshaled support for his position by means of a petition or word of mouth, several writers have indicated that Furillo signed the petition, though they are not always precise in identifying their sources.[37] While Jonathan Eig lists Furillo as one who joined the protest, he also points out that when Branch Rickey asked the protesters, one by one, if they were willing to play with Robinson, "Furillo gave in at once and apologized, saying he'd made a mistake." In 1989 Roger Kahn would write, "Early on he had a hard time accepting the integration of baseball. But Furillo changed and grew, a quiet man learning from the times."[38]

Furillo, on the other hand, swore that he never signed any petition. In an interview with this writer, his son Jon took exception to the portrayal of his father as a bigot. "My father's been getting a bad rap about being prejudiced," he said. "I was never brought up with that. As a kid, I remember going to Campy's house all the time. If there was any truth to it, my father wouldn't have shown up at his door." Campanella, who loved fish, recalled that when the Dodgers trained in Vero Beach, Florida, every morning Furillo would "slip away from camp and go catch me a fish or two. I never asked him; he just went and did it. Things like that you don't forget."[39]

It is rarely, if ever, easy for a Major League ballplayer to walk away from the only job he has ever had or wanted. But the way Furillo's career ended left him bitter and resentful. When the Dodgers were lured west in 1958, the thirty-six-year-old veteran reluctantly made the move to Los Angeles. Roger Kahn found Furillo to be out of place in the cavernous Los Angeles Coliseum; without the familiar backdrop of the Ebbets Field wall he was "a gladiator in a cardboard coliseum."[40]

The end came quickly in 1960. On May 7, in only his tenth time at bat, Furillo tore the calf muscle in his left leg while running the bases. The Dodgers responded by giving him an unconditional release. An irate Furillo turned his anger into litigation and sued the Dodgers, claiming that according to contract provisions, a player could not be released when unable to play due to a baseball-related injury. The court agreed and awarded him back pay for the $21,000 balance due him for 1960. The Dodgers got their revenge, according to Furillo, by blackballing him from any further jobs in baseball. While it is unlikely that there was any orchestrated conspiracy among owners—Furillo, after all, was a thirty-eight-year-old veteran coming off an injury—he had branded himself as something of a rebel by going outside the baseball fraternity and seeking legal counsel. He won his suit, but by breaking one of the unwritten rules of the game, he probably cost himself any chance of getting back into uniform or of getting any baseball job.

Furillo was forced to find other ways to make a living. He was an iron worker and for seven years co-owner of a delicatessen in Queens. Then he moved his family—wife Fern and sons Carl Jr. and Jon—back to Stony Creek Mills and took the job with Otis Elevators. When that job ended, he returned to his home town, semi-retired, working briefly as a sheriff's deputy, then as a security guard. On January 21, 1989, Furillo suffered a heart attack and died at his home at the age of sixty-six.

By all accounts Carl Furillo was a very private person. He didn't hang out with the guys in the clubhouse, some of whom he felt looked down on him because of his limited education. But he did have a few close friends on the team, Campanella and Erskine among them. "He and I were good friends, on and off the field," Erskine told me. "I often went with him to his Italian friends' functions, and I fished with him a lot. Carl was a no-nonsense person. He was intolerant of players who were half-hearted or didn't take their job seriously. He had a temper but only when provoked. I saw him in two fights; he started neither but handled them both."[41]

His sons remembered Furillo not as the tough ballplayer but as a devoted family man. "My dad had a great heart," said Carl Jr. "He and my mom had a great relationship. He believed very much in the family. He took me and my brother fishing and hunting a lot." Said Jon, "He grew up in the Depression, in the hard times. He didn't care what type of work he had to do to put food on the table. There were always people at our house. The old Italian family: you visit, you eat, you talk, you play cards. My parents were always there for us, regardless of what it was. I have very fond memories of both of them."[42]

In his eulogy at Furillo's funeral Carl Erskine summed up the two sides of his friend. "I remember how tough he was, how strong he was,

27. Sal "the Barber" Maglie. Transcendental Graphics.

how consistent he was as a player. But he also had great sensitivity and tenderness. Carl Furillo was like steel and velvet."[43]

The Barber

In the glory days of New York baseball no pitcher was more feared, or reviled, by opponents than Sal Maglie. In the perpetual battle for control of home plate he intimidated batters, first with his ominous scowl, enhanced by his shadowy stubble—he chose not to shave before games—and gaunt appearance, then with his habit of "shaving" hitters with his high, hard one, earning him the renowned nickname of "the Barber." No one better personified the bitter rivalry between the Giants and Dodgers, and no Giant pitcher had more success against the powerful Brooklyn lineup; his overall record was 32-11. "Sal Maglie," wrote Roger Kahn, "was a name used by mothers in Brooklyn to frighten disobedient small boys."[44]

Unlike Branca, who was a star at age twenty-one, Maglie achieved his fame—or infamy, depending on your point of view—relatively late. He was thirty-three years old before he established himself as a solid Major League pitcher. Before that he underwent an uncommon apprenticeship that included five years in the Minors, two years away from the game during the war, winter ball in Cuba, two years as an "outlaw" player in Mexico, a season in Canada, and a ban from playing organized ball in the United States.

The son of Giuseppe and Maria (Bleve) Maglie, immigrants from the Puglia region of Italy, Salvatore Anthony was born on April 26, 1917, in Niagara Falls, New York, one of the many eastern industrial towns that attracted European immigrant laborers. In order to help out the family during the Depression, upon graduating, Sal turned down a basketball scholarship to Niagara University and went to work at the local Union Carbide plant, earning additional money pitching for the company team and local semi-pro nines.

Maglie's pro career began in 1938, when he was signed by the Buffalo Bisons of the AA International League. Drafted by the Giants
in 1942, he appeared to be on the verge of making it to the Majors
after five years in the Minors, but the outbreak of the war meant
more delays. Though he was deferred from service because of a
sinus condition, Maglie chose to do defense work in a Niagara Falls
factory rather than play ball in 1943 and '44. It was not until June
1945 that he resumed his career with the Giants' farm team in Jersey
City, and on August 9 he made his Major League debut at the age
of twenty-eight. By the end of the season Maglie, with a 5-4 record
in ten starts and a 2.35 ERA, seemed to have secured a place with the
Giants, but the drama was just beginning.

At the suggestion of Giants pitching coach Dolf Luque, Maglie
played winter ball in Cuba following the '45 season. Then when
Giants manager Mel Ott gave him little chance to pitch in spring
training in 1946, Maglie, like Danny Gardella and six other Giants,
made the jump to the outlaw Mexican League. There he was reunited
with Luque, who had left the Giants to manage the Puebla Parrots,
the team to which Maglie was assigned.

While his salary was higher than what the Giants had been paying
him, Maglie, like other American "jumpers," found the conditions in
Mexico, both on and off the field, well below what he was accustomed
to in the United States. He endured for two seasons, winning twenty-
one and twenty games respectively, but the deteriorating financial
condition of the Mexican League convinced him to return home. The
most important benefits he took with him were the lessons he learned
from Luque, who had pitched in the Majors for all or part of twenty
seasons. An article in the *Sporting News* gave the following version
of Luque's innovative training methods. One day Luque "pulled out
a pistol and shot at Maglie's feet every time he missed throwing the

ball over the plate during bullpen warmup sessions."[45] (If this story seems implausible, remember that this was the same Dolf Luque who had challenged Babe Pinelli to a gun duel when both played for the Reds in the twenties.) Whatever tactics Luque employed, according to Maglie's biographer Judith Testa, Maglie returned from his Mexican experience "a grim, tough, ruthless competitor unfazed by weather, taunts, or pressure, a pitcher who could bend a curve three different ways at three different speeds from a variety of arm slots or send a batter sprawling with a fastball that grazed his chin."[46]

Maglie may have emerged from his southern sojourn a better and tougher pitcher, but it would be another two years before he could prove himself in the big leagues. Ineligible to play organized ball in the United States until 1951 under the ban imposed by Commissioner Chandler, Maglie spent the 1948 season barnstorming with a team led by Max Lanier, another Major League "jumper." Then in 1949 he continued his transcontinental career, this time going north of the border to play for the Drummondville Cubs in the Quebec Provincial League. It was while he was in Drummondville that he learned that the ban on Mexican League players had been rescinded, but Maglie chose to finish the season in Canada rather than return immediately to the Giants. He won eighteen games in the regular season and another five in the playoffs to lead the Cubs to the championship.

When Maglie reported to the Giants' spring training camp in 1950, just shy of his thirty-third birthday, Mel Ott, the manager who had snubbed him in 1945, was gone, replaced by Leo Durocher. Unlike Ott, Durocher paid attention to Maglie and gave him a chance to pitch. By the end of the season he had won eighteen while losing only four, with a Major League–leading five shutouts and an ERA of 2.71.

It was during the 1950 season that Maglie was given his nickname of "the Barber." There are several versions of its origin, but the first to use it in print was Jim McCulley of the *New York Daily News*. According to one version, McCulley got the idea from a comment by Durocher, who reportedly said that Maglie "looks like the guy in the third chair in the barber shop."[47] Roger Kahn, who found Furillo's nickname of "Skoonj" to be derogatory, saw in "the Barber" an implicit ethnic slur, "a racial comment on Italian barbers." Another comment by Durocher, as reported by Kahn, supports the notion that his "barber" allusion was ethnically motivated: "Now the dago pitcher is a different kettle of fish. . . . I say, 'Whatsa matter, you stupid wop, you choking?' He gets so mad he wants to kill me, but he don't. He takes his dago temper out on the fucking hitters."[48] Whatever the origins of the nickname or its original inference, in time it came to be associated with Maglie's penchant for throwing high and inside to back hitters away from the plate, and Maglie himself realized that it gave him a psychological edge as a pitcher.

As impressive as it was, Maglie's 1950 breakthrough performance proved to be a prelude to 1951, the high point of his career. In thirty-seven starts he won twenty-three games while losing only six, tying him for the league lead in wins with teammate Larry Jansen. His ERA of 2.93 and twenty-two complete games were both second-best in the league, and he finished fourth in the MVP vote. Then with the Giants leading the Yankees two games to one in the World Series, Maglie gave up four runs in five innings in a 6–2 loss in the fourth game. He later attributed his poor performance to overindulging in spaghetti and macaroni at an Italian restaurant the night before, which left him feeling heavy. "I hate to admit it," he said, "but to this day I believe I ate us out of that Series."[49]

Maglie got some measure of redemption in the opening game of the 1954 World Series. In seven-plus innings he limited the heavily favored Indians to two runs in a 5–2 win, opening the door to a four-game sweep by the Giants. His hometown of Niagara Falls honored him with Sal Maglie Day on December 1, but soon it would appear as if that would be the last hurrah for the veteran who would turn thirty-eight early the next season.

Even though Maglie had a 9-5 record, at the end of July the Giants released their former ace, who was claimed off waivers by the Indians. Then in mid-May 1956 the unthinkable happened: he was sold to the Dodgers. But even before he threw a single pitch for his new team, the move to Brooklyn provided one highly anticipated sidelight: the first meeting between Maglie and archenemy Carl Furillo, one of the favorite targets of the Barber's close shaves. It was Furillo, after all, who had reportedly said, "If that son of a bitch Maglie throws at my head again, I break my bat across his fucking dago head."[50] Several versions of the encounter have been reported, but the most colorful (and, according to Testa, probably the most accurate) was provided by Tom Villante, the man in charge of Dodgers broadcasting. He happened to be in the locker room on the day of the dreaded meeting. The only other people there were Furillo, who had just come in from practice, and Charlie DiGiovanna, the assistant locker room attendant. Then in walked Maglie, making his initial appearance in the clubhouse. According to Villante, Furillo and Maglie stared each other down until DiGiovanna finally said, "Don't do it! We're all dagos in here!" With that the ice was broken, and Furillo extended his hand to welcome his new teammate.[51] In time the two became good friends.

Peddled twice in less than a year, Maglie seemed destined for a sad end to a stellar career. However, 1956 would prove to be something of a reprise of his 1950 season. After getting off to a slow start, he won eleven of his last thirteen starts, including a no-hitter against the Phillies. His record with the Dodgers that year was 13-5, with an ERA of 2.87, his lowest mark since 1950. His strong performance earned him a second-place finish (behind teammate Don Newcombe) in both the MVP vote and the first-ever Cy Young Award vote.

Maglie continued to excel in the World Series. In Game 1, he beat the Yanks 6–3. By the time he started Game 5, the Series was tied at 2–2. In eight innings he allowed only five hits and two runs. It was a brilliant performance by the thirty-nine-year-old veteran, but it was also his bad luck to be facing Don Larsen, who that day pitched the only perfect game in World Series history. The discarded Giant would later say of his sale to Brooklyn: "That was the biggest and nicest break of my big-league career. I wouldn't have believed it—me the old Dodger hater—but I was made for Brooklyn and Brooklyn for me."[52]

The next year Maglie was placed on waivers by Brooklyn and signed by the Yankees on September 1, making him the fourteenth—and last—person to play for all three New York teams. In June 1958 he was sold to the Cardinals, who released him on April 10, 1959, sixteen days before his forty-second birthday. Sal Maglie stayed in baseball for a time, first as a roving Minor League coach for the Cardinals in 1959, then as a Major League pitching coach for the Red Sox (1960–62, 1966–67) and the expansion Seattle Pilots (1969). He died on December 28, 1992.

Given his reputation as an intimidating pitcher, it is ironic that Maglie, who stood six-foot-two and weighed 180 pounds, was a curve ball specialist with pinpoint control and not a big strikeout pitcher. Roy Campanella said that Maglie "threw the best curve ball I ever caught." His high, inside fastball was used for effect; it was the location, not the velocity, that made it effective. "Sometimes I'd throw over the hitter's head, but most of the time I'd pick a target just beneath the chin," he said. "I wasn't trying to hit him in the chin.... I just wanted to move him back from the plate, shake him up. When I was on the mound I was in business. I didn't give a damn if my grandmother was in there."[53] Not surprisingly, the image of Sal Maglie that endures is that of the dark, sinister figure peering in to home plate, his dark beard, long, thin face, and doleful eyes giving him an expression that hovered between menacing and morbid as he prepared to fire another fastball under the batter's chin. It is an image that Maglie himself exploited as a way to gain an edge over his opponent.

But that was Maglie's business persona. By all accounts once he took off the uniform, he was a different person. Johnny Antonelli, a teammate from 1950 to 1955, acknowledged Maglie's approach to pitching: "On the field he was "the Barber." He taught me to be aggressive out there. He only knew one way—shave 'em back, then throw that curve ball low and away. He didn't wait until somebody hit a home run off him; he did it because that's how he pitched." But then he added, "You wouldn't meet a nicer person than Sal Maglie." Herman Franks, a Giants coach from 1949 to 1955, offered this assessment: "He was a tough competitor, but a nice guy, a real nice guy."[54] In her biography Judith Testa acknowledged Maglie's foibles (as a heavy drinker and occasional womanizer) while emphasizing his positive attributes. Away from the field he was "relaxed and affable," a man "without prejudices," remembered for his "extraordinary warmth, gentleness, and generosity."[55]

Bonus Baby

While Sal Maglie was barnstorming across the country in 1948, scraping to make a living, an eighteen-year-old phenom from Rochester,

New York, was being signed by the Boston Braves for a bonus estimated to be between \$65,000 and \$75,000, twice what Maglie would earn even in his peak seasons. Long before agents had become a fixture in the baseball business, Johnny Antonelli had his own self-appointed representative: his father.[56] Agostino Antonelli had emigrated from Casalbordino, a small town in the province of Chieti, Abruzzo, along with his father, in 1913. After working as a foreman for the New York Central Railroad, he became a railroad construction contractor and a baseball fan.

When I met him in March 2002, Johnny Antonelli (a distinguished looking man who appeared much younger than seventy-one) recalled his father's role in his baseball career. "My father would go to spring training every year," he said. "When I was playing in Rochester, he started bringing my writeups to Florida. He really went out and pushed me. I became a Major League ballplayer primarily because of my father."[57] Nine teams sent scouts to confirm Mr. Antonelli's glowing reports on his son, and several made offers to the young lefthander, but in the end the Braves won the bidding war with what was reported to be the biggest bonus ever paid. Owner Lou Perini personally went to Rochester to sign Antonelli on June 29, 1948, then flew Johnny and his father to Boston on his private plane.

"It was exciting," recalled Antonelli. "The first night we went right to the ballpark, and I saw thirty thousand people in the stands. I thought that was all the people in the world. I'd never really been out of Rochester, so I was very impressed." Five days later, on July 4, Antonelli, who had turned eighteen on April 12, made his big league debut, giving up one run in one inning of relief. But the excitement of his big league arrival soon turned into disappointment. That would be one of only four appearances the youngster made that season. The pennant-winning Braves, with a strong pitching staff led by the tandem of Warren Spahn and Johnny Sain, had little need for the untested teenager, who was with the Braves because of a clause in his contract, inserted at his father's insistence, stipulating that he could not be sent to the Minors.

Over the next two seasons Antonelli continued to be used sparingly, appearing in a total of forty-two games. Looking back on those years, he later said, "I wasn't a ballplayer—I was a tourist." In 1951 he was drafted into the army but was able to maintain his skills by pitching every fourth day for the Fort Meyer (Virginia) post team. "I got my Minor League experience pitching in the Army," he said. "In those two years, I learned how to pitch."[58] In 1953 he returned to the Braves (now in Milwaukee), going 12-12 in twenty-six starts.

Antonelli's big break came when he was traded to the Giants prior to the 1954 season, joining Sal Maglie, who became a close friend. The trade, which sent 1951 hero Bobby Thomson to the Braves, upset a lot of Giants fans, but it wasn't long before Antonelli won them over. He won twenty-one games, lost seven, and led the National League in ERA (2.30), shutouts (six) and won-lost percentage (.750). He also won one game and saved another as the Giants swept the Indians in the World Series. Not surprisingly, he acknowledged that the '54 season was the highlight of his career. "When you're growing up, you want to be on an All-Star team," he said. "I was chosen that year. You want to win twenty; I won twenty. You want to win a World Series; I won a World Series. Before the Cy Young Award, they had the *Sporting News* Pitcher of the Year Award, and I won that. I did everything that a lot of pitchers, even Bob Feller, never accomplished in one year. I was thrilled with that."

Antonelli never matched that 1954 performance, but he did win twenty in 1956 and nineteen in 1959. Following the 1960 season he was traded to Cleveland, then returned to Milwaukee in July 1961.

28. Johnny Antonelli. Transcendental Graphics.

When his contract was purchased by the expansion New York Mets in October 1961, Antonelli, who had been hampered by arm trouble, chose to retire at the age of thirty-one. In his twelve-year career the five-time All-Star won 126, lost 110, and compiled a 3.34 ERA.

Antonelli had been planning for the future long before he left the game. In 1954 he capitalized on his successful season by opening a tire store in the Rochester area, a venture that eventually led to a chain of twenty-eight Firestone outlets in upstate New York. In fact he credited baseball with everything good in his life. "Baseball meant everything to me," he said. "I met my wife (Rosemarie Carbone, whom he met in Boston while playing for the Braves). We've been married fifty years, and we have four children and ten grandchildren. I got in the [tire] business because of baseball. Without baseball I don't know what I would have achieved in life."

Manifest Destiny

In his book *The Era*, Roger Kahn calls the postwar period of New York dominance "the greatest age in baseball history."[59] For those outside New York "the era" may have been an unpleasant but undeniable reality, as if America's game had been highjacked by one city, but for fans in Gotham it was indeed a golden age. Like every golden age, however, this one came to an end. Within two years of winning the World Series, the Giants were fading, dropping to sixth place in both '56 and '57. Attendance, which had been 1.6 million in 1947, was down to 629,000 by 1956. The Dodgers were growing old. They won the Series in '55 and the pennant in '56, but with their core of stars all past their prime, they fell to third in '57. Their drop in attendance was less dramatic than that of the Giants, but from a high of 1.8 million in 1947 they had fallen to just over 1 million by 1954. In the meantime other changes were taking place that would further motivate both franchises to consider what to their fans was unimaginable: leaving New York.

For a half-century the landscape of Major League Baseball had remained constant, the same sixteen teams housed in the same ten cities, none west of St. Louis, none south of Washington DC. But in 1953, with attendance plummeting to 281,000 the previous season, Lou Perini, enticed by a brand new stadium and a large parking lot, moved his Boston Braves to Milwaukee, where attendance soared to 1.8 million that year and 2 million the next. Others soon left for what they hoped would be greener pastures, the St. Louis Browns becoming the Baltimore Orioles in 1954 and the Philadelphia A's moving to Kansas City in 1955.

Dodger owner Walter O'Malley, stuck with an aging ballpark, 750 parking spaces, and declining attendance, was envious of Perini's sudden success (even though the Dodgers reportedly were making more money than any other National League team).[60] After a fruitless flurry of negotiations with city and state officials over the possibility of building a new stadium, O'Malley became a latter-day disciple of Horace Greeley and decided to go west, taking his team to the new baseball frontier of Los Angeles in 1958. The move would forever brand him in the minds of Dodger fans as a heartless villain who deprived them of their beloved team, while others regarded him as a businessman more concerned with the bottom line than with nostalgia, one who was stonewalled by public officials unwilling to provide what he needed to keep the team in New York. Whatever the motives and maneuvering may have been, the outcome was that Giants owner Horace Stoneham chose to transfer the rivalry to California by moving his team to San Francisco.

On a warm, sunny afternoon on September 29, 1957, Johnny Antonelli took the mound—the same mound where Christy Mathewson had become a legend half a century earlier—in the final game played at the Polo Grounds. The 11,606 fans who turned out to bid farewell to the sixth-place Giants saw Antonelli give up four runs in two innings to take the loss as the Pirates cruised to a 9–1 win. Five days earlier the Pirates had also been involved in the final game at Ebbets Field. The Brooklyn lineup that day included Gino Cimoli in center, Roy Campanella behind the plate (replaced by Joe Pignatano in the fifth), and Jim Gentile at first, with Augie Donatelli the home plate umpire. During the game (won by "the Bums," 3–2), organist Gladys Goodding serenaded the 6,202 fans with such songs as "Thanks for the Memories," "How Can You Say We're Through," and, after the final out, "Auld Lang Syne."[61] For all the anguish associated with the departure of the Dodgers and Giants, with the end of the color line in 1947 and the move to the West Coast in 1958 by two of the game's most storied franchises, baseball was moving closer to truly being the national pastime.

Four

TRANSITIONAL ITALIANS

13

The Last "Italians"

By the time Joe DiMaggio retired in 1951, media references to his Italian background had all but disappeared. The player once routinely referred to as Giuseppe, or as the son of an Italian immigrant, had become simply Joe DiMaggio, the Yankee Clipper. His ethnicity was no longer remarkable. This was due in part to his performance on the field, but the decisive event came when he signed up on the side of Uncle Sam and against the native country of his own parents (who were identified by the U.S. government as "enemy aliens"). By proving his patriotism during the war, he had firmly established his credentials as a bona fide American.

Proof of patriotism became important when suspicion of Italians in America, which had subsided as the number of immigrants dropped significantly following the restrictive 1924 immigration law, reappeared when Mussolini allied himself with Hitler, making Italy the enemy. Ultimately World War II proved to be a watershed event in the history of Italian Americans. The war itself provided some stimulus for assimilation. Especially for those who lived outside the ethnic enclaves of large cities, in order to avoid any hint of disloyalty it was better not to speak Italian or to behave in ways that called attention to one's "Italianness." Better to blend in than to stand out. And in addition to those who worked in defense plants and otherwise served on the home front, as many as 1 million Italian Americans served in the armed forces, more than from any other ethnic group.

Widespread participation in the military by Italian Americans served both to demonstrate their loyalty and to expose them to other ethnic and racial groups. More than ever before people of various ethnic backgrounds were working and fighting together, and a sense of solidarity was established as "Americans" were allied against a common enemy. As a result ethnic tensions diminished somewhat following the war. In addition, the influx of African Americans from the South to northern cities refocused attention away from earlier issues. All these factors led to less attention paid by the media to the ethnic origins of Americans of European ancestry, including Italian Americans. This was true for baseball players as well; with African Americans and Latinos entering the Majors in increasing numbers, the ethnic differences among white players became less noteworthy. In the words of Bill James, once black players came into the league, "everybody else was just White."[1] For the most part Italian Americans were no longer ethnic curiosities, and the terms "dago" and "wop," once acceptable even in such mainstream publications as the *New York Times* and the *Sporting News*, all but disappeared over time.

In the years following the war more Italian Americans were known to the general public than ever before, though with few exceptions they were paid entertainers, in either sports or show business. In addition to baseball stars there were boxing champions Rocky Marciano, Jake LaMotta, and Rocky Graziano and football legends Vince Lombardi, Gino Marchetti, and Alan "the Horse" Ameche. Eddie Arcaro was a five-time Kentucky Derby–winning jockey and Willie Mosconi a fifteen-time world billiards champion. Popular music was largely dominated by singers of Italian descent for many years: Frank Sinatra, Mario Lanza, Al Martino, Perry Como, and Louis Prima, in addition to those who were not readily identifiable from their stage names: Tony Bennett (Anthony Benedetto), Vic Damone (Vito Farinola), Dean Martin (Dino Crocetti), and Connie Francis (Concetta Franconero).

Ironically, at the same time that these celebrities were highly visible, many Italian Americans were concealing or at least downplaying their ethnic identity as they sought to assimilate into the mainstream. Participation in the war effort modified not only the public perception of Italian Americans but also Italian Americans' own sense of identity. With the nation on the brink of unprecedented prosperity, the American Dream never seemed more within reach. The growing economy and the GI Bill provided unprecedented opportunities for education and subsequent social and economic mobility, which in time led to the dispersion of urban ethnic neighborhoods. Those who had been brought up in large cities began moving away, responding to the siren call of the suburban life that was quickly becoming the distinguishing mark of middle-class Americans. And when these "new immigrants" moved to the suburbs, their spouses were more and more likely to be non-Italians.[2] For historian Rudolph Vecoli the 1950s were "the end of the first chapter of the history of Italians in America.... The old immigrants were dying; their children were headed for the suburbs hell-bent upon becoming 100 per cent American."[3]

Assimilation did not wipe the slate entirely clean, however. No matter how prosperous and suburbanized Italian Americans became, the albatross that had haunted them since the late nineteenth century—their presumed association with criminality—not only survived but was also reinvigorated in the fifties and beyond. On the heels of the gangster films of the thirties and forties came *The Untouchables*, the television show in which G-man Elliot Ness never seemed to arrest anyone whose name didn't end in a vowel. Then came the double whammy of Mario Puzo's novel *The Godfather* (1969), followed by Francis Ford Coppola's movie trilogy beginning in 1972. The Mafia stereotype became even more firmly entrenched in the American psyche in the late nineties when the HBO series *The Sopranos* enjoyed enormous success. RIP Joe DiMaggio; conflicted mob boss Tony Soprano, living the good life in the New Jersey suburbs, was the new Italian American archetype. Nor did discrimination disappear. It was in this postwar period that Vince Lombardi, who, according to biographer David Maraniss, "had gone through life being called a dago and a wop and guinea because of his dark skin and southern Italian heritage," was convinced that, at age forty-two, he had never been given a head coaching position because he was Italian.[4] It was also at this time that both Yogi Berra and Dom DiMaggio were denied entry into country clubs.

Throughout the first half of the twentieth century the great majority of Italian Americans who played Major League Baseball grew up in homes in which both parents were Italian immigrants or first-generation Italian Americans and spoke the language, with each other if not with their children. For all the reasons cited above, this gradually became less and less true. Second- and third-generation players of Italian descent were increasingly likely to be the offspring of mixed marriages, to have little or no familiarity with the Italian language, and to consider themselves first and foremost "American." Of the twelve rookies in 1960 who self-identified as being of Italian descent, for example, nine listed a second ethnic lineage, with surnames such as James, McAuliffe, Murphy, and Stafford.

In addition, the rapid increase in the number of African American and Latino players in the fifties and sixties corresponded with a gradual decline in the number of Italian Americans in the Majors as other economic opportunities opened up for them. It was the latest manifestation of the ongoing pattern of ethnic succession. Late in the nineteenth century German and Irish players gradually moved into professional baseball alongside Anglo-Americans, to be followed in the thirties by South and East Europeans. As those at the bottom of the socioeconomic ladder, with limited options, moved into the professional ranks of baseball, others from previously struggling groups found other opportunities for advancement.

This is not to say that Italian American fans did not recognize and celebrate, at least on a local level, stars such as Rocky Colavito, Tony Conigliaro, Joe Torre, and Ron Santo. However, the media were much less likely to take note of a player's ethnic background, and as time went on the players were less likely to identify themselves as Italian Americans. One possible indication of the declining interest in ethnic origin was that beginning in the fifties, even the Yankees passed on signing promising Italian American prospects, including New York City natives such as future stars Frank Malzone, Rico Petrocelli, Joe Torre, and John Franco. Had Eugene Morris Jerome been a young fan in the mid-fifties or later, he never would have said, "All the best Yankees are Italians." Whereas the Italian stars of the immediate postwar era were playing almost exclusively for New York teams, the later standouts were scattered across the continent, playing for teams in Oakland, Cleveland, Chicago, and Boston.

The Rock

One of the local Italian Americans that the Yankees passed on was Bronx native Rocky Colavito. Signed instead by the Indians, the twenty-two-year-old outfielder established himself as one of the hottest young sluggers in the game in 1956, when he hit twenty-one home runs in 101 games. With his curly black hair, engaging smile, and willingness to sign countless autographs, the muscular, six-foot-three, 200-pound matinee idol slugger soon became a favorite of Indians fans, especially among the bobby-soxers.

The youngest of five children of Rocco and Angela Colavito, immigrants from a small town near Bari, Rocco Domenico Colavito was born on August 10, 1933. Asked if he was aware of Italian American ballplayers as a youngster, he said, "There was always something special about Italian ballplayers. My favorite was always Joe DiMaggio. It was just his demeanor. A lot of the Italians in the neighborhood loved him."[5] So enamored was he of his idol that he had to be convinced, in his first year in the Minors, to stop imitating the Yankee Clipper's batting stance and develop his own style.

Colavito's father wasn't particularly interested in baseball—Rocco's mother died when he was nine—but he didn't discourage his son from playing ball. "When I played on semi-pro teams he came to watch me," he said. "My father always thought you should make a living the best way you could as long as it was clean."

Colavito made a living hitting home runs. After hitting twenty-one homers in his abbreviated '56 season, he hit twenty-five and forty-one the next two years, then tied Harmon Killebrew for the league lead with forty-two in 1959. On June 10 that year, in an 11–8 win at Baltimore, Colavito became only the third American Leaguer (and eighth overall) to hit four home runs in one game.

Even before that '59 season "the Rock," as he was called in Cleveland, was a fan favorite and one of the most feared sluggers in the American League—all of which made the news that broke on April 17, 1960, shocking: in one of the more startling trades made to that time Cleveland general manager Frank Lane sent Colavito, the reigning

home run champ, to the Tigers for Harvey Kuenn, the reigning batting average champ. The trade triggered a firestorm of protest by
the fans. Colavito was, as the *Cleveland Plain Dealer* recalled in 1991,
the "favorite son of Cleveland's Italian community and the rock on
whom the Indians of the '60s were supposed to be built." The *Sporting News* reported that dummies of Lane "were strung from several
telephone poles on the city's streets." The editorial in the same edition
asked if the trade was in the best interest of the Indians, noting that
Colavito was "the most popular of the Indians, exemplifying young
American manhood at its best."[6]

Colavito hit thirty-five home runs his first year with the Tigers,
then followed that with a career-high forty-five in 1961. After four
years with the Tigers he was traded to Kansas City in 1964, then made
a triumphant return to Cleveland in 1965 before being traded to the
White Sox in 1967. He then split his final season, in 1968, between
the Dodgers and his hometown Yankees. In his fourteen-year career
Rocky Colavito hit 374 home runs and drove in 1,159 runs. He hit
thirty or more homers seven times and forty or more three times
and was in the league's top five seven times. Typical of the sluggers
who came into vogue in the fifties, he didn't hit for a high average
(.266 lifetime), and he struck out a lot (880). The right fielder also
possessed one of the strongest arms of his time. A six-time All-Star,
he finished in the top eight in the MVP vote four times.

Davey Nelson, who would spend ten years in the Majors, was a
nervous Minor Leaguer who had been invited to the Indians' spring
training camp in 1966. "They weren't real cordial to rookies," he
recalled. "Nobody was talking to me, but then Rocky came up, introduced himself, and said, 'Let's play some catch.' He made me feel
welcome. He was a genuinely great person, humble for a big star. He
was beloved in Cleveland. Their slogan was 'Don't knock the Rock.'"[7]

In 1976 fans chose Colavito as the "Most Memorable Personality in Indians History." When his baseball career ended, Colavito worked as a television analyst and served as a coach for the Indians and Kansas City Royals before retiring to his home in Bernville, Pennsylvania.

One of Colavito's teammates, with both Cleveland and Detroit, was Don Mossi. The lefthander from St. Helena, California, had a solid career, as both a starter and reliever, with a 101-80 record with fifty saves in twelve seasons (1954–65). Unfortunately Mossi is best remembered for his interesting face. Known as "the Sphinx," he had big ears, a large nose, and a generally wrinkled face. Bill James was merciless in his description: "Don Mossi was the complete five-tool ugly player. He could run ugly, hit ugly, throw ugly, field ugly and ugly for power. He was ugly to all fields." James justified his description by noting that while he would normally be reluctant to write this, "Don knows he's ugly."[8]

Another Cleveland teammate of Colavito was outfielder John Patsy "Tito" Francona. A classic journeyman ballplayer, the native of Aliquippa, Pennsylvania, spent fifteen years in the Majors with nine different teams, compiling a lifetime average of .272. His father, Carmen, was the son of an immigrant from the Abruzzo region, while his mother, Josephine, was of Polish descent but learned to speak Italian. Asked if he thought of himself as Italian as a child, Tito replied, "Very much so. My dad had two brothers and two sisters and they all spoke Italian, and we ate Italian food."[9]

Francona's son Terry followed in his father's footsteps as a journeyman outfielder, playing for five teams in ten years between 1981 and 1990. Terry's lifetime average of .274 was almost identical to that of his father, but he would go on to gain greater fame as the manager who led the Red Sox to their first World Series title in eighty-six years.

Unlike his father, Terry, born in 1959, did not identify with his Italian heritage. "My name is Italian, but I'm really not more Italian than anything else," he said, noting that three of his four grandparents were of Polish, German, and Irish descent. "We're past those times. I didn't live through that, never have given it a thought. I was raised to respect people, not to look at backgrounds. I'm proud of my name and my grandparents, but it doesn't really matter."[10]

Frank Malzone

After four years in the Minors and two in the army, it appeared that Frank Malzone was ready to play in the Majors when he hit .310 for the Red Sox Triple A club in 1955. But then, just before spring training in 1956, his fourteen-month-old daughter died. The distraught rookie began the season with the Sox but was sent to their new affiliate in San Francisco after appearing in twenty-seven games. The son of an immigrant father from Salerno and an Italian American mother, Malzone finally got a chance to play a full season in 1957, and he made the most of it. He was second in the league in hits, third in RBIs and doubles, was chosen for the All-Star team, and won a Gold Glove at third base. Considered by many the best third baseman in Red Sox history, Malzone spent eight more years with Boston before signing with the California Angels as a free agent in 1966, his final season. In his twelve-year career he was a six-time All-Star and won three straight Gold Gloves (1957–59) while compiling a lifetime average of .274 with 133 home runs and 728 RBIs. Following his retirement he served as a Red Sox advance scout for twenty-seven years.

Jerry Casale, a Brooklyn native who pitched in the Majors for parts of five seasons between 1958 and 1962, offered his own analysis of Malzone's career with Boston. "I have to believe there was an anti-Italian bias," he told me.[11] Regarding Malzone's demotion to San

29. Rocky Colavito, Yogi Berra, and Frank Malzone at the 1959 All-Star Game.
National Baseball Hall of Fame Library, Cooperstown NY.

Francisco in 1956, he said, "They kept Billy Klaus instead of Frank
Malzone. Frank was an All-Star third baseman in Louisville and hit
.314 [*sic*] in 1955, and I was an All-Star pitcher." Following what he
termed an outstanding spring training in 1956—"the papers were
calling me a phenom"—Casale was told by Manager Pinky Higgins

that he was being sent to the Minors. "I told him where he could go." Then he said to GM Joe Cronin, "You tore out my heart. Why'd you pull this shit on me?" Cronin explained that he was being sent to the team's new affiliate in San Francisco because "they've got a big Italian population in San Francisco." To which Casale replied, "What kind of bullshit are you giving me?"

That season Casale, Malzone, and infielder Ken Aspromonte were all sent to San Francisco, where they were key parts of the Seals lineup. When I spoke with Casale at his Manhattan restaurant in 2002, he was still bitter over the Red Sox decision to send him to San Francisco in 1956, especially because he fell one month short of qualifying for a pension when his career ended.

Casale had made the same claims about the Red Sox bias in an earlier interview, for Peter Golenbock's book *Fenway: An Unexpurgated History of the Boston Red Sox*. He claimed that he and Malzone were treated unfairly because Pinky Higgins and Joe Cronin "were bigoted Irishmen." When I asked Malzone about Casale's allegations, he said, "Who's to say? If it happened, I don't know about it." He did say that he didn't care for Joe Cronin but that he got along well with Pinky Higgins, even though "Pinky called me a dago, and I told him only another Italian could call me that."[12]

Tony C

Few Major Leaguers have ever burst on the scene as dramatically as Tony Conigliaro. By the time he was twenty years old, the Red Sox outfielder had won an American League home run title, and at twenty-two he had hit one hundred homers, the second youngest ever to do so. Beyond that he was a handsome local kid who had quickly become one of the all-time favorites of Boston fans. But when he was only twenty-two years old, an errant fast ball smashed into his face and changed a probable Hall of Fame career into a classic tale of a gifted young athlete cut down in his prime.

The oldest of three sons, Anthony Richard Conigliaro was born in Revere, Massachusetts, on January 7, 1945, and grew up in the Italian section of East Boston. There was more than a little squabbling in the Conigliaro home, between sons and parents and among the siblings, but there was always a strong sense of family unity. "I thank God for my parents," Conigliaro wrote in his autobiography. "I more than love them; without them I am nothing."[13]

A star athlete in baseball, football, and basketball at St. Mary's High School in Lynn, Massachusetts, Conigliaro was signed by the Red Sox in October 1962, when he was seventeen. After being named the MVP of the New York-Penn League in 1963, Conilgiaro joined Frank Malzone in the Red Sox starting lineup in 1964, at the age of nineteen. As a sign of things to come, in the first home game of the season he hit a home run in his very first time at bat in Fenway. His twenty-four home runs in that rookie season are the most ever hit by a teenager. As if being a hero for his hometown team wasn't enough, Conigliaro, never lacking in confidence, had thoughts of becoming a singing star. After cutting a record that sold well in New England, he was signed to a recording contract by RCA records prior to spring training in 1965, which only enhanced his standing as the idol of teenage girls throughout New England.

In his sophomore season Conigliaro hit thirty-two home runs to become, at age twenty, the youngest player ever to lead the league. He was living the dream, and in 1967 the Red Sox got to live their own dream. To say that they entered that season as a long shot to win the pennant would be a gross understatement. Since the league had expanded to ten teams in 1961, the Sox had never finished higher than sixth and had finished in ninth place in '66, losing ninety games.

But everything came together that year under new manager Dick Williams. It was to be the season of Red Sox renaissance, when New England once again got excited about its team.

In mid-July a ten-game winning streak put the Sox in the thick of the race. Then, on the night of August 18, Conigliaro stepped into the batter's box at Fenway in the fourth inning to face the Angels' Jack Hamilton. Hamilton threw a high, inside fastball to the Boston slugger, who, as always, was crowding the plate. The pitch hit Conigliaro on the left cheekbone, just below his eye, and he slumped to the ground.

"As soon as it crunched into me, it felt as if the ball would go into me and come out the other side," he would later say. Angels catcher Buck Rodgers said that when the ball hit, it sounded "like taking a bat to a pumpkin."[14] Conigliaro was rushed to the hospital, his eye swollen shut, his cheekbone fractured. He would play no more that season, the year that the Red Sox, led by Triple Crown winner Carl Yastrzemski, would realize the "Impossible Dream" by winning one of the more dramatic pennant races in history. But for Tony C the nightmare was just beginning.

When the damage to his eye proved more serious than originally diagnosed, Conigliaro was forced to sit out the entire 1968 season. He was even told he would never play again. But he made a triumphant return in 1969, hitting twenty home runs, driving in eighty-two runs, and winning the Comeback Player of the Year Award. (That year his brother Billy was in his rookie year with the Sox, the first of five seasons he would spend in the Majors.) In 1970 Tony was second in the league in RBIs (116) and fourth in home runs (thirty-six), both career highs. In spite of that performance, the Red Sox, convinced that Conigliaro's eyesight was deteriorating, traded him to the California Angels.

The Red Sox were right about his eyesight; after seventy-four

30. Tony and Billy Conigliaro, 1970. Courtesy of Boston Red Sox.

games with the Angels Conigliaro announced his retirement. In a press conference he announced that his eyesight had never returned to normal and that he had never told the Red Sox. "When the pitcher holds the ball, I can't see his hand or the ball," he said. "I pick up the spin on the ball late, by looking away to the side. I don't know how I do it."[15] He tried one more comeback, as a designated hitter with the Red Sox in 1975, but gave that up after twenty-one games and left the game for good at the age of thirty.

Conilgiaro went to work as a baseball broadcaster, but fate had more in store for him. On January 9, 1982, two days after his thirty-seventh birthday, he suffered a heart attack while being driven to the Boston airport by Billy. By the time they got to the hospital, Tony's heart had been stopped for at least six minutes and his brain deprived of oxygen, leaving him comatose for seven weeks. His parents, Sal and

Teresa, were by his side daily, there was a tremendous outpouring of sympathy and support from fans, and benefits were held to help pay the bills. His family remained optimistic and Tony made some modest improvements, surprising even the doctors, but he never fully recovered. He spent the rest of his days essentially bedridden, barely able to speak, and died at the family home on February 24, 1990, at the age of forty-five.

Even as a child, Conigliaro was supremely confident—cocky in the opinion of many—but he managed to charm even most of those who were initially put off by his demeanor. No one, not even his detractors, ever questioned his will to succeed. He was the type of power hitter made for Fenway Park, and he was, like Rocky Colavito, a home run hitter with a modest batting average and plenty of strikeouts. And as with Colavito, part of his appeal was due to his good looks and charisma; he was idolized by Red Sox fans and was a major reason for the resurgence of interest in the dormant franchise in the mid-sixties. The premature end to his career and his tragic illness and death at an early age endeared him to those fans even more.

In 1990 the Red Sox honored Conigliaro's memory by establishing the Tony Conigliaro Award, given annually to a Major League player who overcomes adversity "through spirit, determination and courage." And in 2007 the Sox opened "Conigliaro's Corner," a two-hundred-seat bleacher section located high above the right field area where Tony C once chased down fly balls.

Rico

Another key player on the Red Sox Impossible Dream Team of 1967 was shortstop Rico Petrocelli. Born in Brooklyn on June 27, 1943, Americo Peter Petrocelli was the youngest of seven children of immigrants from the Abruzzo region. Born when his father was fifty-one and his mother forty-two, he was much younger than his siblings, all of whom spoke Italian. "I think I was a surprise to my parents," he told me. "I was fortunate to be able to play baseball. My brothers and sisters had to work to help us survive." His father, who worked as a fireman for the Pennsylvania Railroad, was skeptical about Rico's interest in baseball. "Once in a while he would say, 'Go out and get a real job. There's no money in baseball.' But I told him I loved it, so he finally said, 'Go ahead.'"[16]

"Ours was a close family," Petrocelli said. "My brothers took me to ball games all the time. There was usually one [New York] team at least in the World Series, so that made me want to be a great ballplayer." One trip to Yankee Stadium left an indelible impression. "We were in the bleachers, and Joe DiMaggio was still playing. I looked around and noticed nobody was watching the pitcher throw the ball. Everyone was looking at DiMaggio. When he'd catch a ball, he'd lope after it. It was just beautiful to watch. I'll never forget it. The only thing my father knew about baseball was DiMaggio, Rizzuto, Berra, because he could relate to them. When you're struggling like my father was, then somebody makes it big, that gives others the confidence to go out and try to be successful"

Petrocelli, who broke into the starting lineup in 1965, was not the typical slick-fielding, weak-hitting shortstop. The six-foot, 180-pound power hitter did for the American League what Ernie Banks had done for the National League a decade earlier. Even in the Minors Petrocelli did not hit for a high average, but he did hit the long ball. That continued with the Red Sox. He set an American League record for shortstops by hitting 40 home runs in 1969 (a record that stood until 1998), then followed that with 29 and 28 homers the next two seasons. In his twelve full years with the Red Sox the two-time All-Star hit 210 home runs with 773 RBIs.

31. Rico Petrocelli. Courtesy of Boston Red Sox.

Petrocelli was also a better than average fielder. In 1969 his fourteen errors tied the record, since broken, for fewest errors by a shortstop. When he moved to third base in 1971 following the arrival of future Hall of Fame shortstop Luis Aparicio, he led the league in fielding percentage at his new position. A member of the Red Sox Hall of Fame—together with Malzone, Conigliaro, and Dom DiMaggio—he went on to manage in the Minor Leagues for four years between 1986 and 1992.

Asked if he encountered any prejudice as a professional ballplayer, Petrocelli recalled an incident in his first year in the Minors, when he played for Winston-Salem in the Carolina League: "One day we had four Italians in the infield, and this big, heavy guy in the stands said, 'Well, look at that, we got an all-guinea infield,' and 'Hey, the wops are coming.' He wouldn't let up. I heard things even early on in Boston, like 'Petrocelli, you wop.' The worst thing you could do was to acknowledge it, so you just kept your mouth shut. But it wasn't anything close to what the blacks had to go through." Unlike Jerry Casale, however, Petrocelli never sensed any bias on the part of the Boston brass. During his rookie year of 1965 he, Malzone, and Conigliaro were all in the starting lineup. "The management of the Red Sox has been almost exclusively Irish American over the years," he said, "but I never felt a prejudice against Italian American ballplayers during my years. I was treated very well." (By the time Petrocelli was signed in 1961, Joe Cronin, the general manager when Casale was with Boston, had left to become president of the American League.)

Like so many Major Leaguers, Petrocelli was celebrated by the local Italian community. "In the North End the Italians really made me feel welcome. They were great." He said that both he and Conigliaro were aware of their role in the community. "We knew that the Italian Americans who had struggled in other fields were proud of us, and we wanted to go out there and do a good job."

Peck's Bad Boy

When Joe Pepitone made his Major League debut in 1962, he became the first player of Italian descent to break into the Yankee lineup in many years. The Brooklyn-born Pepitone, who was signed out of high school in 1958, was seen as a player of unlimited potential who would become a Yankee star, maybe the next Mickey Mantle. But it proved to be a bumpy ride.

With his long, shaggy hair, mod clothing, and flamboyant personality, Pepitone, who was twenty-one when he joined the Yankees, was a nonconformist by the standards of Major League Baseball. Mantle was no choir boy, but in term of enjoying the good times, "Pepi" put him to shame. Sportswriters produced an avalanche of adjectives to describe him: colorful, volatile, unpredictable, fun-loving, happy-go-lucky. Pepitone attributed his devil-may-care attitude to two events that occurred while he was a senior in high school. First, he suffered an accidental gunshot wound while at school; then, soon after Pepi returned home from the hospital, his thirty-nine-year-old father, Willie, died of a heart attack. "Losing my dad put me in a mental depression," he later said. When the depression ended, "I made up my mind that I would never worry about anything again."[17]

New York was the right place for Pepitone to play Major League Baseball, both because of his native son status and because of New Yorkers' tolerance of, and fondness for, the unconventional. His blithe, carefree persona endeared him to many fans but irritated others who resented what they considered his indifferent approach to the game. When he applied himself, his talent was unmistakable. The rangy six-foot-two, 200-pound left-handed first baseman could hit and field. In 1963 he came into his own, slugging twenty-seven home runs, driving in eighty-nine runs, and starting in the All-Star Game. He was an All-Star again in 1964 and 1965, when he won the first of three Gold Gloves. While Pepitone continued to be a productive slugger, his performance was uneven, and the feeling was that he would never live up to his full potential. Eventually he wore out his welcome. In 1969, when he was traded to Houston, Joseph Durso of the *Times* called him "Peck's Bad Boy" and "the last and most controversial of the old imperial Yankees."[18]

The honeymoon in Houston didn't last long; after seventy-five games Pepitone left the team and was suspended indefinitely. Then on July 29 the Chicago Cubs claimed him off waivers. Playing now for Leo Durocher, himself a free spirit, Pepitone flourished in the Windy City. In fifty-six games he drove in forty-four runs and hit twelve homers, all while keeping his teammates loose in the clubhouse with his clowning. He had another good year in 1971, but hampered by injuries, he announced his retirement early in May 1972, only to come back at the end of June. After playing in only sixty-six games that year, he was traded to Atlanta in May 1973 but left that club after three games and retired permanently, at least from Major League Baseball. By mid-June he was in Japan, playing for the Yakult Atoms, but he left that team after appearing in fourteen games.

Pepitone's career numbers (219 home runs, 721 RBIs, .258 average in twelve years) are very similar to those of Rico Petrocelli. But when the Yankees traded Pepitone in 1969, General Manager Lee MacPhail summed up what would come to be the general assessment of his career: "He's been a real good player, but not as good as everyone hoped he'd be. He was colorful and he had the spirit of youth, and some of the problems that go with it."[19] Like Tony Conigliaro, Joe Pepitone was tall, dark, handsome, and charismatic. But whereas Tony C, who also liked to party, never let that interfere with his dedication to the game, Pepitone often lacked discipline, on and off the field. While Conigliaro became a victim of forces beyond his control, Pepitone struggled with his own inner demons.

Joe Torre

Yet another native of Brooklyn who made it to the big leagues was Joe Torre, whose success in managing the Yankees to four World

Series titles between 1996 and 2000 should not overshadow the fact that as a player, he was a nine-time All-Star with a batting title, Gold Glove, and MVP Award to his credit. But before he became a Major Leaguer, his older brother Frank beat him to it. Born in 1931, nine years before Joe, Frank spent seven years with the Braves and Phillies between 1956 and 1963. Though primarily a backup, Frank was the Braves' starting first baseman in their pennant-winning seasons of 1957 and '58.

Frank and Joe were two of five children born to Joseph and Margaret Torre. In his autobiography Joe described Margaret as a typical Italian mother: "She was a fabulous and prodigious cook (my early physique was a walking irrefutable testament to that talent) and a devout Catholic who always put her family first."[20] Their father, a New York detective, was not so nurturing. "My dad, who was born in the States, both physically and emotionally abused my mom," he told me. "Part of it was telling her she came from the other side and wasn't smart enough. He didn't allow her to be proud of her heritage. So she was, in essence, American because that way everybody would perceive her in a better light." This explained to Torre why, when he asked where in Italy she was from, his mother, a Neapolitan who had immigrated at the age of eight, replied, "We're American."[21]

Asked what effect this might have had on his own sense of identity, Joe said, "I knew what nationality I was, on both sides of the family, but mainly I was American. I'm proud of my heritage, proud of my mom, but I didn't feel any more closeness to someone because they're Italian. I know the Italians were prejudiced against, and still are in some circles, and I didn't like any of that. I grew up not having any prejudices, going to school with blacks and Jews. Looking back, it's probably the greatest exposure I had as a child."

The "early physique" to which Joe referred in his autobiography was a source of embarrassment to Torre and almost cost him his career as a ballplayer. Like many other future Major Leaguers from Brooklyn, Joe grew up playing ball on the diamonds of the Parade Grounds.[22] An outstanding hitter, he drew little interest from scouts because he was overweight and slow. Frank was ruthless in teasing him about his weight and telling him he was too fat to be a ballplayer. When, as a teenager, Joe went to Ebbets Field to work out with the Braves when they were in town, Frank encouraged his teammates to make fun of his kid brother. "Spahnie [pitcher Warren Spahn] called Joe 'spaghetti bender,'" Frank told me. But for all that, Joe credited his brother with giving him, a shy, overweight kid with little self-esteem, "the kick in the butt I needed to amount to anything in life. . . . I may not have had a father in my life then [his parents divorced when he was eleven years old], but I sure as hell had a hero."[23] It was only when Joe became a catcher, at the urging of Frank, that the scouts got serious about him.

Signed by the Braves in 1959, a relatively trim Joseph Paul Torre (six-foot-two and 215 pounds) was the MVP of the Northern League in 1960. By May 1961 he was the starting catcher for the Braves, and on August 11 that year he caught the 300th win by the same Warren Spahn who had mocked him a few years earlier. In eight full seasons with the Braves Joe twice hit over .300, won a Gold Glove in 1965, and was a five-time All Star. In those years he also married twice, in 1963 and 1968, with both marriages ending in divorce. "I was very immature, probably irresponsible," Torre said of his years with the Braves. "When I got traded to St. Louis [in 1969], a very successful franchise, I learned what competing was about, and I learned how to behave."[24]

Following the trade to the Cardinals, Joe moved to third base in

1970 and hit .325, second best in the National League. Then in 1971 he led the National League in average (.363), hits (230), RBIs (137), and total bases (352) and was the overwhelming choice as the league's MVP. Former teammate Ted Simmons recalled Torre's performance that year: "He had probably the single most incredible season as a hitter I ever saw," he said. "It seemed like every time he came to the plate, he got a hit."[25]

Torre spent the last three years of his career with the New York Mets, assuming the role of player/manager in 1977. A nine-time All-Star, he retired with a .297 lifetime average, 252 home runs and 1,185 RBIs. For all that he accomplished, Torre admitted that he didn't enjoy playing as much as he should have. "Baseball has been my whole life," he said. "It was always talked about in our family; just baseball, baseball, baseball. Everything was work to me. I had older brothers who both played baseball, and I felt a great deal of pressure to live up to whatever I had to live up to. I think it was because I didn't have a lot of self-esteem, probably based on a lot of abuse that was going on at home. I think my self-esteem was based on how I did on the baseball field."[26] As a manager, Torre would have many more opportunities to have his self-esteem tested.

The Other "Mr. Cub"

Ron Santo and Joe Torre first met as teenagers when they were on opposing teams in the Hearst All-Star Game in New York, Santo representing the state of Washington for the U.S. squad, Torre playing for the New York team. Being standout young ballplayers was not the only thing Santo and Torre had in common; both were born in 1940, both would begin their long Major League careers in 1960, and both had abusive fathers.

Born on February 25, 1940, to an Italian-born father (Louis, a native of Foggia) and a Swedish-born mother (Vivian Danielson), Santo grew up in the Italian district of Seattle known as "Garlic Gulch." "I'm half Italian, half Swedish, and all Italian," he told me. "My mother, even though she was Swedish, could speak Italian with my dad. Tuesday, Thursday, Sunday, it was spaghetti. We were definitely an Italian family."[27]

They were also a dysfunctional family. "My father was an alcoholic and an abusive man," said Santo. "He owned a couple of taverns, and he was a mean drunk. I was four years old, and I remember vividly; he'd be pounding the walls, and I'd jump on his back. I'll never forget the day that he never came back; he left when I was six years old, and I could finally sleep through the night. My stepfather, John Constantino, came into my life when I was nine, and I loved him. He took very good care of my mother, and he always came out and watched me play."

Santo excelled in both football and baseball in high school. "I had a couple of football scholarships, but baseball was my first love. I signed out of high school and went directly to Double A ball." In late June 1960, after less than two years in the Minors, Santo was called up to the parent club. "The Cubs were playing like horseshit," he said. The six-foot, 190-pound third baseman was in the starting lineup that same day, and he stayed there for the next fourteen seasons. When he came up, the Cubs were a perennial second-division team, never finishing higher than fifth since 1946. Nor did they improve in Santo's first years, finishing seventh in '61 and ninth in '62, the year the league expanded to ten teams. The worst came in 1966, when, under new manager Leo Durocher, they finished dead last, losing 103 games.

It looked like Leo "the Lip" would finally lead the Cubs to the promised land in 1969; they got off to a fast start, led the division from opening day, and were still there at the end of August. It was the year that baseball expanded to twenty-four teams and initiated divisional play, Neil Armstrong walked on the moon, and Dwight Eisenhower and Rocky Marciano died, but in Chicago it is remembered as the year the Cubs blew it. In mid-August they held a 9½-game lead, then lost seventeen of twenty-five and finished eight games behind the Mets. Even with future Hall of Famers Ernie Banks, Billy Williams, and Ferguson Jenkins, not to mention Santo, the Cubs could not shake the label of lovable losers. To the Wrigley faithful none was more lovable than Santo in 1969. After a Cubs win at home he would run down the left field line, jump in the air, and click his heels, at least until their late-season swoon.

In 1965, at age twenty-five, Santo was named team captain. Confident to the point of being cocky, he had no trouble taking on the responsibility of keeping his teammates focused, even when they were losing, as they did most of the time. A passionate and occasionally volatile competitor, he sometimes got into disputes with umpires, managers, and players. One writer called him "a throwback to an earlier era when players were rough and tough and asked no quarter." Durocher, himself a tough customer as player and manager who began his Major League career in 1928, called him "the best all-around third baseman I've ever seen."[28]

"There was something about Chicago, about Wrigley Field, that I loved," said Santo. "Being in Chicago and being Italian was unbelievable." Asked if other players acknowledged his Italian background, he said, "Oh, yes. In fact, my nickname was 'dago.' I didn't mind; they said it in a friendly way." Santo's ethnic heritage also attracted the attention of one fan in particular: Sam Giancana, reputed mob boss of Chicago. One day an usher at Wrigley Field told Santo there was

32. Ron Santo. National Baseball Hall of Fame Library, Cooperstown NY.

a gentleman in the box seats who wanted to talk to him. "I walked over, and this guy says, 'I'm Sam Giancana.' So I shook his hand. He came to five ball games and every time he'd yell to me, 'Hi, Ron,' and every time I'd hit a home run. So he invites me over to his house in Elmwood Park for dinner. He made his own spaghetti sauce, and he had the homemade wine. They find out and I had to go to the commissioner's office. Bowie Kuhn tells me, 'You can't associate with him.' So I had to tell him, and that was tough. But he understood."

Traded to the crosstown White Sox in 1974, Santo retired after a disappointing season. His fifteen-year record included 342 home runs, 1,331 RBIs, and a .277 average. A nine-time All-Star, he hit thirty or more home runs and drove in one hundred or more runs four times each and led the league in walks four times and on-base percentage twice. Though not as graceful as some, he was also an outstanding third baseman, winning five consecutive Gold Gloves and seven times leading the league in both putouts and assists by a third baseman.

Following his playing career, Santo was involved in a number of successful business ventures before returning to baseball in 1990 as the color analyst on Cubs radio broadcasts. He is no less passionate and emotional in the broadcast booth than he was on the field, a virtual cheerleader, at least when the team is doing well. Listeners are accustomed to hearing him shout, "Yes!" in response to a good play or, when a Cub messes up, sigh in disbelief, with a "Boy, oh boy, oh boy" thrown in for good measure. A particularly hideous play can evoke a loud "Nooo!" Pat Hughes, his broadcast partner since 1995, said, "I've been with Ronny eleven years, and I love the guy. He's one of the most iconic figures in the history of Chicago sports, but you forget that because he's so down to earth."[29]

Santo's life was marked by challenges and tragedies. In 1973 his mother and stepfather were driving to spring training to visit with Santo when they were killed in a collision with a truck. At age eighteen he was diagnosed with diabetes and is the first known player to play his entire Major League career with the disease. "Nobody knows what it's like to take insulin every day and go out there and bust your ass," he told me. Concerned that people would think he was using the illness as an alibi if he played poorly, he confided in the team doctor prior to the 1962 season but swore him to secrecy. Though many in the media did become aware eventually, it wasn't until "Ron Santo Day" in August 1971 that he publicly revealed the news, at which time he also began what became a lifelong commitment to raising funds for the cure of juvenile diabetes.

Complications resulting from his diabetes ultimately led to a series of medical procedures. At one point Santo underwent eleven operations in four months and suffered cardiac arrest during a hospital stay. Finally doctors determined that he had to have both legs amputated below the knee if he were to survive. Yet through it all he retained a sense of humor and a positive attitude. In a 2002 interview he said, "I am so happy, so lucky, so blessed. I really have everything that any 61-year-old person could want. The only thing that was taken away from me was a leg."[30]

The fact that Santo could recall the exact date of his call-up when I spoke with him thirty-eight years later says something about his desire to make it to the big leagues. But he had even higher aspirations. "I don't want to be average; I want to be a *great* ballplayer," he was quoted as saying early in his career. "You can go higher than the big leagues. You can go higher by being the best there is."[31] For a Major Leaguer ultimate recognition of being the best takes the form of election to the Hall of Fame, an acknowledgment that, at the time of this writing, has not been accorded to Santo. (In 2007 he came within five votes of election by the Veterans Committee.) His failure to be elected triggered endless debates; Santo himself, after years of waiting and hoping, became resigned.

On September 28, 2003, Ron Santo's uniform number 10 was retired as a flag bearing the number was hoisted up the left field foul pole at Wrigley Field. Five years later, during the Cubs' final 2008 visit to Milwaukee, Santo, sitting in the radio broadcast booth, spoke about the Hall of Fame issue. "My Hall of Fame was seeing that flag go up in Wrigley Field," he said. "It would mean more to me to see the Cubs win the World Series."[32] He sounded very believable.

14

The 1970s and Beyond

In the wake of the postwar boom in assimilation, just when it seemed as if European ethnicity was becoming a historical relic, suddenly there was an ethnic revival. Amid the social and political turmoil of the 1960s caused by the civil rights movement and the Vietnam War, descendants of European immigrants were expressing renewed pride in their heritage. As African Americans openly asserted their claims to full participation in American society, white ethnics became more assertive about their identity. Social scientists in turn debated the question as to whether this reawakening of ethnic pride was representative of the fundamental and abiding role of ethnicity in American life or a last gasp in what sociologist Richard Alba termed the "twilight of ethnicity." The ethnic revival, Alba argued, was really what Herbert Gans labeled "symbolic ethnicity," intermittent and a matter of individual choice rather than a fact of daily life.[1]

What is certain is that by the late twentieth century more and more Americans of Italian descent were far removed from the immigrant generation of their forebears. Economic, social, and geographic mobility, together with an increase in intermarriage, had combined to diminish the Old World family bond that for so long had characterized Italian Americans. Consequently, for many third- and fourth-generation Italian Americans, the level of association with their Italian ancestry was often tenuous and in some cases nonexistent. I found this to be true of many but certainly not all of the younger ballplayers I interviewed for this book. And when I asked older Italian Americans who were still involved with big league baseball if they thought there was less ethnic awareness among younger players, virtually all of them said yes.

In fact Italian American ballplayers active around the turn of the twenty-first century expressed a range of identity with their ethnic heritage. David Dellucci, a left-handed-hitting outfielder from Baton Rouge, Louisiana, whose family on both sides came from Sicily, was beginning his third year in the Majors when I spoke with him in 1999. "I take great pride in being Italian American," he said, "and to be an Italian American athlete is really something special. To follow in the footsteps of Joe DiMaggio and some of the legends, I feel privileged, and I hope the same for my son when he comes along." Sal Fasano, a catcher who broke into the Majors in 1996, grew up in the largely Italian neighborhood of Elmwood Park in Chicago. His parents had emigrated from Calabria, together with their respective parents, then met in Chicago. "It's a proud tradition, being Italian," he said. "I grew up speaking Italian, or actually Calabrese. It was a big deal when I moved away to Kansas [to play with the Royals]. I have two boys now, Enzo and Angelo. The main reason I moved back to Chicago was to be near the family; my parents and grandparents still live there." Mark DeRosa, a native of Passaic, New Jersey, whose career began in 1998, grew up in a large family where "Sundays were big pasta days, and all holidays were big Italian get-togethers. I think that's the key to an Italian family; everything revolves around a big meal." A Major Leaguer since 1995, infielder Mark Loretta's ties to Italy are more cultural than genetic.

Like Fasano's, his Italian roots were in Calabria. "I've got more English-Irish blood than Italian," he said, "but Italy's my favorite country to visit, and Florence is probably my favorite city in the world." At the opposite end of the spectrum from David Dellucci in terms of ethnic identity was Dustin Pedroia, the Red Sox second baseman who won the Rookie of the Year Award in 2007 and the MVP Award in 2008. "My dad's dad is full-blooded Italian, and my dad's mom is Portuguese, so I'm kind of a mixture," he said. "I know I'm Italian, Portuguese, and Spanish, but I just consider myself American."[2]

By the time the Dodgers and Giants moved west in 1957 the impact of Italian American players had passed its peak. One measure of the shifting demographics in the Major Leagues is the fact that between 1956 and 1965 eight of the twenty MVP Awards went to African American players. That corresponds exactly to the number of MVP Awards won by Italian Americans between 1947 and 1955. After 1955 it would be sixteen years before another Italian American, Joe Torre, would win the award, and another twenty-five years after that before Ken Caminiti would win in 1996. Among the players to break into the Majors in the 1940s were Rizzuto, Berra, Raschi, Furillo, Branca, Campanella, and Maglie, not to mention the large number of regulars with solid, lengthy careers. While there continued to be a number of rookies of Italian descent in the fifties (an average of seven per year, according to the Lee Allen data base on recruits), the number of impact players declined sharply. In 1952, for example, four of the nine American League starters in the All-Star Game were Italian Americans. Twenty years later six of the nine National League All-Star starters in 1972 were African Americans. In the entire decade of the seventies, in fact, only four Italian Americans (Joe Torre, Ron Santo, Larry Bowa, and Gene Tenace) started in an All-Star Game.

By the early seventies Major League Baseball itself had undergone a number of changes, especially on the economic front. Expansion, divisional play, the effects of the recently instituted amateur draft, salary arbitration, and increasing tensions between labor and management significantly altered the game and, for some time at least, the fans' perception of it. (Their perception of the men who played the game was also altered when, in 1970, Major League pitcher Jim Bouton published *Ball Four*, a best seller that for the first time provided a candid behind-the-scenes look at the seamy side of baseball.) In the meantime, professional football had flourished and was challenging baseball as the nation's favorite sport.

Concerned about falling attendance and what he perceived as his fellow owners' complacency, Charles O. Finley of the Kansas City Athletics took some unusual steps to draw more fans. A consummate promoter, Finley introduced such gimmicks as a mechanical rabbit behind home plate to deliver baseballs to the umpire, a mule named Charlie O as the team mascot, and green and gold uniforms with white shoes. But Finley was also a shrewd judge of talent. Bolstered by young stars such as Reggie Jackson, Vida Blue, Catfish Hunter, and Rollie Fingers, the A's, who moved to Oakland in 1968, became dominant, winning three straight World Series titles from 1972 to 1974. No one better represented the talent and individuality of that team than its captain, Sal Bando.

Born in Cleveland in 1944, Salvatore Leonard Bando was the grandson of four immigrants from Palermo, Sicily. He met his future wife, Sandy, while playing winter ball in Puerto Rico. "I called my mother and said, 'Ma, you'll never guess. I met an Italian girl, and I'm in love.'" True to the regional attitude characteristic of Italian life, his mother asked, "What part of Italy is her family from?"[3] Chosen by Kansas City in the 1965 draft, by 1968 the six-foot, 200-pound third baseman was in the starting lineup, and the next year he was the starting third baseman in the All-Star Game. It was about a month into that season when Manager Hank Bauer asked Bando, then twenty-five years old and in his second full year in the Majors, to be captain of the team.

The A's became an American League dynasty with their three consecutive championships, but they were anything but a harmonious team. As colorful as their green and gold uniforms, the mustachioed players fought with each other and even more so with the tightfisted Finley, who served as his own general manager from 1968 on. "We win because we have guys who love the challenge," said Bando at the time. "We have a nucleus of gutsy players who don't know how to lose."[4] No one stood up to the intrusive owner more than Captain Bando, who, like others on the squad, frequently clashed with Finley over salary issues. In 1976 Finley offered to trade one of his four stars to the Red Sox for a million dollars and Bando for half that amount. When Boston GM Dick O'Connell asked him, "Don't you like dagos?," Finley replied, "I don't like *him*."[5]

Bando was with the A's for eleven years before becoming one of the early free agents when he signed in 1977 with Milwaukee, where he spent the last five years of his career. Bud Selig, the Brewers' owner, was between general managers at the time, and it was his decision to sign Bando. "We had a lot of great young players," recalled Selig, "but we needed a leader. He brought a level of maturity, and his greatest contribution was off the field."[6] Following the 1981 season, Bando, a four-time All-Star, retired with a career average of .254 with 242 home runs and 1,039 RBIs, three times finishing in the top four in the MVP vote.

When Bando's playing career ended, Selig appointed him as a

33. Sal Bando, captain of the Oakland A's. Transcendental Graphics.

special assistant to GM Harry Dalton. Then following the 1991 season, Bando became the first general manager of Italian descent when he replaced Dalton. In Bando's first year the Brewers finished second in the AL East, but when they were on their way to a seventh straight losing season in 1999, he was dismissed. Looking back on the experience, Bando called it "the toughest eight years I've ever spent in my life. We were a small-budget team trying to compete and trying to get a new stadium. We did the best we could to stay competitive, but it was very difficult." Selig agreed, saying, "The nineties were impossible for small-market clubs. Sal was loyal and one of the finest human beings I've ever met."[7]

One of Bando's teammates with the A's was Gene Tenace, who was born Fiore Gino Tennaci. A catcher/first baseman from Russellton, Pennsylvania, Tenace had a modest offensive record in his fifteen-year career. He is best remembered for his remarkable performance in Oakland's first World Series win in 1972. He hit home runs in his first two times at bat in a World Series, the first player ever to do so, and drove in all three runs in the 3–2 A's win. He then hit home runs in the fourth and fifth games. In addition to his four homers, he hit .348, drove in nine of the sixteen runs the A's scored in the entire Series, and was selected as the Series MVP.

In 1975 the A's World Series streak was snapped when they lost the pennant to the Red Sox. It was in Game 6 of that year's Series, with the Sox trailing three games to two, that an otherwise obscure journeyman outfielder gained a spot in baseball history. In the bottom of the eighth, with the Sox trailing 6–3, there were two men on and two out when Bernardo "Bernie" Carbo was sent up to pinch-hit. With two strikes on him Carbo hit a home run to tie the game, setting the stage for Carlton Fisk's historic game-winning homer off the left field foul pole in the twelfth inning to end what many consider the most exciting World Series game ever.

No less fiery an infielder than Sal Bando was Larry Bowa. A native of Sacramento, he was the Phillies' starting shortstop for twelve years, from 1970 to 1981, before spending his final four seasons with the Cubs and Mets. Though his sixteen-year lifetime average was a modest .260, the switch-hitting Bowa had more hits in the seventies than all but six players. An excellent fielder, the five-time All-Star won two Gold Gloves and led the league in fielding average six times. Bowa modeled his play after Phil Rizzuto and Luis Aparicio. "They were scrappers," he said. "They didn't hit a lot of home runs, but they helped their team in a lot of ways. I didn't have a lot of talent, but if you have the desire and the work ethic, it can be done. I made myself a player. The bottom line is, you've got to respect the game."[8] Bowa went on to manage the Padres (1987–88) and Phillies (2001–04), compiling a record of 418-435.

Asked about his name, Bowa said, "Everyone used to say, 'That's not an Italian name.' They think I'm German or Polish. The family name was originally Bua. My grandfather, who came over from northern Italy, changed it in the twenties." When I asked Bowa if he thought there was less sense of ethnic identity among younger players, he said, "Yes. A lot of players, if you asked them, wouldn't know who Rizzuto was. There's no history involved. I'm not saying all of them, but most of them."

Like Bowa, second baseman Steve Sax was a five-time All-Star. National League Rookie of the Year in 1982, Sax was a fixture in the Dodger infield for seven years before going to the Yankees as a free agent in 1989. As his name indicates, Sax derived his Italian heritage from his mother; his father was of German descent. His grandfather, Luigi Colombani, emigrated from Bologna to Broderick, California, where he worked as a dairy farmer. Growing up, Sax considered himself an American, but he was very much aware of his Italian heritage. "We were the typical Italian family," he said. "All the houses on one street in Broderick belonged to my relatives. There was a lot of good food and affection, respect for your elders. Those were the values I grew up with. I got the same thing from the German side, but I'd say the Italians were more affectionate."[9]

In 1983, his sophomore season, Sax suddenly and inexplicably had trouble making routine throws to first base. By mid-August he had made thirty errors, most of them on errant throws. It got to the point that fans behind first base started wearing batting helmets, and Sax practiced by throwing blindfolded. The curious affliction, which came to be known as "Sax disease," lasted until 1985 before he regained control of his throws.

Another player not recognizable as Italian American from his name was Jack Clark. In his eighteen-year career (1975–92) he was a four-time All-Star and four times finished in the top ten in the MVP vote. A right-handed-hitting outfielder/first baseman from New Brighton, Pennsylvania, "Jack the Ripper" was with the Giants until 1985 before spending his final years with four other teams. Eight times he hit twenty-five or more homers, including in five of his last six seasons. For his career he hit .267 with 340 home runs and 1,180 RBIs.

Two More MVPs

One of the more inspiring, but ultimately tragic, baseball figures of the late twentieth century was Ken Caminiti. A Gold Glove–winning, power-hitting third baseman, he amazed people with his willingness and ability to play through numerous injuries, but his feel-good story turned into a tale that symbolized not only the dangers of substance abuse, which cut his life short, but also what would come to be known as baseball's steroid era.

A native of Hanford, California, Kenneth Gene Caminiti was a classic "gamer," a fearless competitor who would play whatever the physical cost. But he wasn't always so dedicated to the game. When I spoke with him in 1999, the stocky infielder with a neatly trimmed mustache and goatee and intense eyes said that if it hadn't been for his father's persistence, he would have given up baseball as a youngster. (A native of Chicago whose family had emigrated from Sicily, his father was a catcher who was drafted by the Cubs but went into the army instead.) "My father saw a lot of qualities in me I didn't see," said Caminiti. "I was really frustrated. My first year in college I had a bad year and I said, 'I don't like this game; it's not for me.' He said, 'Yes, it is. Give it one more year.' So I played on a winter league team and got a full scholarship [to San Jose State University]. From there I just went off. I started switch-hitting, and doors started opening."[10]

The Houston Astros opened the door to the Majors by drafting Caminiti in 1984, and by 1989 he was in the starting lineup. A durable player in spite of injuries, he put up respectable if not spectacular offensive numbers in his eight years with the Astros, but it was on defense that he excelled, winning three consecutive Gold Gloves from 1995 to 1997. Above all it was his gritty determination to play through pain that earned the respect and affection of his teammates and management. General Manager Kevin Towers called him "a warrior in every sense of the word. I can't tell you how many times I remember him hobbling into the manager's office, barely able to walk, and saying, 'Put me in the lineup.'"[11]

While in Houston, Caminiti became a favorite of the city's large Italian American community. "I'm a part of the Italian American Foundation in Houston," he told me. "In fact the year I got traded to San Diego, they gave me the Gold Glove Award. I hadn't won it, but they thought I deserved it, so they gave me a replica of the Gold Glove. I had tears in my eyes, it was such a great thing. I got three official Gold Gloves, but the one the Italian Americans gave me was probably more special."

After eight years with Houston, Caminiti went to San Diego in 1995. The next year he led the Padres to a division title as he soared to career highs in homers, RBIs, batting average, and slugging average, all of which made him the unanimous choice for the NL MVP Award. The "gamer" had blossomed into a star. Caminiti's triumphant season took on legendary overtones because of what happened on August 18 in Monterrey, Mexico, where the Padres were playing the Mets. Before the game Caminiti was stretched out on the floor of the manager's office, the victim of food poisoning. But after receiving two pints of intravenous fluid, he went out and hit two home runs. Unable to finish the game, he returned to the locker room, where after the game his teammates again found him on the floor with an IV in his arm.

When he ended his fifteen-year career in 2001, the three-time All Star had hit 239 home runs with 983 RBIs and a .272 average. The next year, in a *Sports Illustrated* cover story by Tom Verducci, Caminiti made the first public admission of steroid use by a baseball player. He said he began using them in his 1996 MVP season after playing in pain for several weeks with a torn rotator cuff, and he also admitted that he continued to use steroids periodically for the rest of his career. "I've made a ton of mistakes," he said. "I don't think using steroids is one of them. It's no secret what's going on in baseball. At least half the guys are using steroids." What had been suspected for years was now out in the open. Commissioner Bud Selig was quoted as saying, "No one denies that it is a problem. It's a problem we can and must deal with now." In 2003 Major League Baseball began testing for steroid use.[12]

Caminiti's substance abuse problems were not limited to steroids. In 2000 he checked into a rehab center to deal with alcohol abuse. In 2001 he was arrested in Houston on charges of cocaine possession and placed on probation for three years but was ordered to undergo drug treatment in 2003 after failing a drug test. On October 10, 2004, he was found dead in a Bronx apartment just days after admitting in a Houston court that he had tested positive for cocaine. The autopsy attributed his death to an overdose of cocaine and opiates, with coronary artery disease and an enlarged heart as contributing factors. Survived by three daughters and his former wife, Caminiti was forty-one. Craig Biggio, a Houston teammate for seven years, said of Caminiti, "We know he had some issues, but people need to remember him as a great guy, a great friend who would do anything for you."[13]

In 2000, four years after Caminiti won the National League MVP Award, Jason Giambi, a West Covina, California, native, became the fourth player of Italian descent to be named the American League MVP. Drafted by the Oakland A's in 1992, he became a regular in 1996, playing at both third and first. The six-foot-two, 200-pound left-handed-hitting first baseman was a rarity: a power hitter who hit for average. In his MVP season, for example, in addition to hitting forty-three home runs with 137 RBIs, he had a .333 average.

That 2000 season was special for another reason: his brother Jeremy, three years younger, joined the A's after two seasons with Kansas City. Then in 2002 Jason's fortieth home run, hit on September 24, combined with Jeremy's twenty, gave them the single-season record for home runs by brothers, surpassing Joe and Vince DiMaggio, who hit fifty-nine in 1937. "It's nice to have," said Jason of the record, "especially for my mom and dad. It keeps it in pinstripes and keeps it in the Italian family, too."[14]

Now one of the premiere hitters in baseball, Giambi became a free agent at the end of the 2001 season and headed east when the Yankees offered him a seven-year, $120 million dollar contract. Tabbed as the next Babe Ruth, Giambi was given a New York nickname: Giambino. He got off to a good start in trying to fill those big shoes by hitting forty-one homers in each of his first two seasons with the Yanks, but in 2004 he played in only eighty games, reportedly because of an intestinal parasite and a benign tumor on his pituitary gland. Then on December 2, 2004, the *San Francisco Chronicle* reported that according to the transcript of his testimony before a grand jury hearing evidence against the Bay Area Laboratory Co-Operative (BALCO), which was accused of distributing illegal substances to athletes, Jason Giambi admitted to using steroids and human growth hormone, as did his brother Jeremy.

After publicly denying the accusations, Jason Giambi was quoted in the May 23, 2007, issue of *USA Today* as saying, "I was wrong for doing that stuff. What we should have done a long time ago was stand up—players, ownership, everybody—and said: 'We made a mistake.' We should have apologized back then and made sure we had a rule in place and gone forward." On March 30, 2006, Commissioner Selig appointed former senator George Mitchell to head an investigation into the use of performance-enhancing drugs in Major League Baseball. When the Mitchell Report was released on December 13, 2007, a total of eighty-nine former and current players were named, including Jason and Jeremy Giambi.

Pitchers

According to a common premise, pitchers tend to mature later than position players. It appears this may be true for Italian American ballplayers as a whole. While there were fewer position players of great distinction after the fifties, not only did the number of pitchers of Italian descent with long and notable careers increase, but the list also included three Cy Young Award winners and some of the best relief pitchers in history.

Cy Young Award Winners

Frank Viola's big league career did not get off to a promising start. In 1982 the twenty-two-year-old rookie went 4-10 for the Minnesota Twins, then followed that with a 7-15 record. Things changed dramatically in 1984, when he won eighteen and lost twelve, beginning a five-year streak with at least sixteen wins each year. In 1987 the six-foot-four, 210-pound lefthander from Hempstead, New York, led the Twins to their first World Series title. After going 17-10 with a 2.90 ERA in the regular season, in three starts against the Cardinals Viola won the first and seventh games and was voted the Series MVP.

Known for his outstanding change-up, Viola had his career year in 1988, leading the league in wins with a 24-7 record. He was also the starting and winning pitcher in the All-Star Game. At the end of the season he became the first Italian American pitcher to win the Cy Young Award, earning twenty-seven of twenty-eight first-place votes. Following a trade to the Mets, "Sweet Music" went 20-12 with a 2.67 ERA in 1990, earning him a third-place finish in the Cy Young vote. The three-time All-Star went on to pitch for the Red Sox, Reds, and Blue Jays before ending his fifteen-year career with a 176-150 record and a 3.73 ERA.

Given his surname, John Smoltz, a native of Morris, Michigan, obviously inherited his Italian background from his mother's side of the family. Of his maternal grandmother, who lit candles and prayed whenever he pitched, Smoltz said, "She was a full-blooded Italian, the greatest cook in the world, and I loved her to death. She used to say that I'd never smile or have fun when I was on the mound."[15]

Smoltz probably didn't have a lot of fun as a twenty-one-year-old rookie with the Braves in 1988, struggling through a 2-7 record. But he would then go on to post double-digit wins in ten of the next eleven years as he became part of the celebrated trio of Atlanta starters, together with Greg Maddux and Tom Glavine. Unlike those finesse pitchers, Smoltz was a power pitcher, with a fast ball clocked in the mid-90s and a wicked slider. In 1996, after posting a 24-8 record with a career high 276 strikeouts and a 2.94 ERA, Smoltz became the second pitcher of Italian descent to win the Cy Young Award. The six-foot-three, 210-pound righthander was also a big-game pitcher, going 15-4 with an ERA of 2.64 in twenty-five postseason series between 1991 and 2009. His fifteen postseason wins were the most ever until Andy Pettitte reached eighteen in 2009. Smoltz continued to hold the postseason strikeout record with 199.

Still pitching at age forty-two in 2009, his twenty-first season, Smoltz was not only durable but versatile. After twelve years as a starter he became the Braves' closer in 2001. He led the league with fifty-five saves in 2002, followed by forty-five and forty-four the next two years. Then in 2005 he returned to the starting rotation and went 44-24 over the next three seasons. In twenty-one seasons he compiled a record of 213-155 with 154 saves and an ERA of 3.33. An eight-time All-Star, Smoltz twice led the league in wins, winning percentage, innings pitched, and strikeouts.

A Cy Young Award winner in 2002 at the age of twenty-four, and a seventeen-game loser at thirty, Barry Zito was one of the more fascinating figures to enter the big leagues near the end of the twentieth century. Even for a left-handed pitcher—the perennial "flakes" of the baseball world—Zito was unusually enigmatic, on and off the field. Both his father, Joe, who was once an arranger and conductor for Nat King Cole's band, and his mother, Roberta, a former backup singer for Cole, were into New Age theories, which young Barry absorbed and later openly espoused. He also practiced yoga and played the guitar, all of which set him apart from most of his big league peers.

In June 2007, six months after signing what was at the time the richest contract ever given to a pitcher, the Giants pitcher sat in front of his locker in the visitors' clubhouse in Milwaukee and spoke about his Italian heritage. "My father's father was a five-star general in the Italian army," he told me. "My father's sister was the godchild of Mussolini. My dad was born in the Bronx but grew up on a farm in upstate New York. He spoke Italian until he was about thirteen. I knew I was Italian for sure, but we never spoke Italian around the house." However, his mother, who is of German and English extraction, "learned all the Italian recipes from my dad's mother."[16]

Zito attributed his success in baseball to his father, who nurtured Barry's early interest in the game. "I started throwing a curve ball at seven, and he wanted to cultivate it. We started working in the back yard every day. He would always tell me, 'You're going to be a Major League pitcher,' and I believed him. He had no background in baseball. He just knew the ingredients of a champion, so he just applied that to baseball. He was like a professional dad; he took that responsibility like no one I've ever seen."

Drafted by the Oakland A's in the first round of the 1999 draft, Zito made his Major League debut one year later. After winning seventeen games in 2001, he skyrocketed to a 23-5 record in 2002, a performance that won him the Cy Young Award at age twenty-four and made him one of the most sought-after pitchers in the Majors. While the six-foot-four lefty with the best curve ball in baseball continued to be a durable pitcher, making at least thirty-four starts in each of the next four seasons, his 55-46 performance did not come close to Cy Young levels. Nevertheless, when Zito became a free agent in 2007, the Giants gave him a seven-year deal worth $126 million.

And that's where the on-field mystery begins. After an 11-13 record in his first season with San Francisco, things got worse for Zito in 2008; his seventeen losses were the most in the National League, and his ERA jumped to a career-high 5.15. Suddenly the once *wunderkind* of baseball was being booed for being a bust at thirty. While some blamed Zito's fall on complacency or his rock-star lifestyle, Dave Righetti, the Giants' pitching coach, had a more baseball-oriented explanation: Zito had lost five miles off his fast ball and control of his curve ball. "It's not physical," Righetti said. "It's a matter of confidence."[17]

At the time I spoke with him, Zito was in the third month of his first season with the Giants. When I asked him about his interest in New Age thought, he said that it served primarily to quiet his mind. "If everything's working the way it should, you go out and have easy games and effortless success. At other times, you fight yourself and complicate things, and it seems so much harder than it is, as in life." As for his reputation as a flake, he said, "I don't think I'm eccentric. I just think I'm a thinker, a regular person just a little bit more aware of things in general. I don't know the depths of anyone else's mind except my own, and I don't even know that."

Asked if he thought of himself as an Italian American, Zito said, "Definitely. I take a lot of pride in being Italian. The Italians have probably contributed more to the world than anyone else, in literature, art, food, architecture, music. I'm going to Europe for the first time in November, and I'll spend eight days in Rome."

Other Starters

Another outstanding pitcher who, like Smoltz, claims Italian heritage from his mother is Andy Pettitte. (The granddaughter of an immigrant from the Calabria region, her maiden name was Martello.)[18]

After making his debut with the Yankees in 1995, the six-foot-five, 235-pound lefty from Baton Rouge, Louisiana, produced thirteen straight winning seasons with New York and Houston. In only his second season with the Yankees he won twenty-one games, lost eight, and finished second in the Cy Young vote, then posted an identical 21-8 record in 2003. Through 2009 his fifteen-year record of 229-135 equated to an impressive .629 winning percentage. And by winning four playoff and World Series games for the Yankees that year, Pettitte set a new all-time record for postseason wins with eighteen.

When the Mitchell Report was released in December 2007, Pettitte and teammate Roger Clemens were two of the players named. Clemens denied the accusation, but Pettitte admitted to using human growth hormones (HGH) on two occasions in 2002 for an elbow injury. In February 2008 he told congressional investigators that he had also injected himself with HGH twice in 2004 because of an arm injury. With regard to the claim made by personal trainer Brian McNamee that he, McNamee, had provided Clemens with both HGH and steroids, Pettitte stated that Clemens, a close friend, had admitted using HGH. In a February press conference at the Yankees' spring training camp, Pettitte apologized to fans for his lack of judgment.

A few other pitchers merit mention here. After several years as a starter with Houston and St. Louis, Dave Giusti was converted into a reliever when he went to the Pirates in 1970. In that first year in his new role he had twenty-six saves, finished fourth in the Cy Young vote and sixth in the MVP vote, and was the *Sporting News* Fireman of the Year. He was an All-Star in 1973 and finished seventh in the Cy Young Award balloting. He retired in 1977 with a fifteen-year record of one hundred wins, ninety-three losses, 145 saves, and an ERA of 3.60. John "the Count" Montefusco was the NL Rookie of the Year in

1975, and in 1976 he led the league in shutouts and threw a no-hitter against Atlanta. In thirteen seasons the Long Branch, New Jersey, native compiled a 90-83 record with a 3.55 ERA. After two brief, unsatisfactory stays with the Brewers, Tom Candiotti turned his career around when he became a knuckleball specialist with Cleveland in 1986, winning sixteen games and leading the league with seventeen complete games. He ended his sixteen-year career in 1999, at age forty-one, with a record of 151-164 and a 3.73 ERA. In an eleven-year career with the Brewers and Mariners between 1986 and 1996, Chris Bosio compiled a 94-93 record with a 3.96 ERA. A burly righthander at six-foot-three and 235 pounds, he threw a no-hitter against the Red Sox in 1993.

Relievers

At the turn of the century Dave Righetti's grandfather emigrated from a village near La Spezia on the Italian Riviera to San Francisco. Many years later the family moved to San Jose, where David Allan Righetti was born in 1958. "I'm very proud of my heritage," Righetti told me. His father, Leo, was a star shortstop for the San Francisco Seals. "All my dad's best friends were Italians," he said, "including ex-ballplayers from the Seals. My kids are taking Italian, and we're definitely going to go to Italy to see my grandfather's town when I retire."[19]

Drafted by the Texas Rangers in 1977, Righetti was traded to the Yankees following the 1978 season. "I was lucky to be traded to the Yankees," he said. "Being Italian there, you felt some pressure, but it was great. It was something to live up to. I remember, after my first or second year, they put me in the Columbus Day parade, and that was pretty cool. I got invited to marriages, weddings, just about everything."

Righetti more than lived up to the expectations as an Italian American playing in New York. The twenty-two-year-old lefty won the Rookie of the Year Award in 1981 and pitched a Fourth of July no-hitter against the Red Sox in 1983 while winning fourteen games. Then in 1984 Manager Yogi Berra decided to send "Rags" to the bullpen to replace future Hall of Fame closer Goose Gossage. Righetti adapted quickly to his new role, saving thirty-one games that year, and went on to become one of the all-time great relief pitchers. In 1986 he set a new Major League record, later broken, with forty-six saves, and won the Rolaids Relief Award that year and the next. In his seven years as the Yankee closer (1984–90) Righetti averaged just under thirty-two saves a season, and he ranks second behind Mariano Rivera on the all-time Yankee list in both saves (224) and games (522). In 1991 he went to the Giants as a free agent and recorded twenty-four saves, in the process setting a new record for career saves by a lefthander, a record that stood until 1994. When his sixteen-year career came to an end in 1995, Righetti had recorded 252 saves, as well as eighty-two wins and seventy-nine losses.

Righetti was in his ninth year as the Giants' pitching coach when I spoke with him in 2008. When asked if he thought younger Italian American players still had a strong sense of ethnic identity, he said, "In some of the fishing towns on the West Coast you see a little bit more of that. But other than that it's breaking up because they're probably marrying outside of their background."

Born in Brooklyn in 1960, John Anthony Franco grew up in the predominantly Italian neighborhood of Bensonhurst. He told me that both his wife and their then eleven-year-old daughter spoke Italian. "I guess I'm the only one that never caught on," he said. "From what I understand, my picture is up in my wife's grandmother's house in Italy."[20] A 1999 article in the Bergen County (New Jersey) *Record* reported that Franco's pride in his Italian heritage permeated the Mets spring training clubhouse in Florida. The Mets "lift weights to Sinatra, do sit-ups to Dean Martin, dress to the music of Louis Prima, and steal time during the day to watch 'Goodfellas' in the clubhouse manager's office."[21]

Unlike Righetti, Franco spent his entire career as a reliever. In 1986 he made the first of four All-Star appearances over the next five years. In each of the next three seasons he had thirty-two or more saves before being traded in 1990 to the Mets, the team he had dreamed of playing for when he was a kid. The Mets gave Franco their biggest contract to that time—$7.6 million for three years—and he repaid them by leading the league with thirty-three saves, making the All-Star team, and winning the Rolaids Relief Award for the second time.

The five-foot-ten lefty spent the next fourteen years in New York, becoming both a fan favorite in his hometown and one of the most successful relievers ever. In his twenty-one-year career he led the league in saves three times and finished in the top five nine times. (In 1999, after Franco had picked up save number 400, Mayor Rudolph Giuliani gave him the key to New York.) His 424 saves are the most ever by a lefthander and, as of the end of the 2009 season, placed him fourth all-time. In addition, he holds the National League record with 1,119 games pitched, third most in Major League history. In 2006 Franco was the pitching coach for Team Italy in the World Baseball Classic.

Catchers

As the twentieth century was winding down, two players of exceptional talent and endurance emerged: Craig Biggio and Mike Piazza. For each decade from the thirties to the sixties a single Italian American appeared on Bill James's All-Star team of the decade. There were none in the seventies or eighties, but both Biggio and Piazza were on James's nineties' All-Star team, the only time that two players of Italian descent made the cut.[22] By the time they retired—Biggio in 2007, Piazza in 2008—both seemed destined for the Hall of Fame. They had one other thing in common: both had started their careers as catchers, among the most recent in a long line of Italian American catchers that continues to this day. In fact at no other position have Italian American players maintained such a strong tradition. Topped by Hall of Famers Ernie Lombardi, Yogi Berra, and Roy Campanella, the list includes such other notables as Gus Mancuso, Joe Torre, Mike Scioscia, and Joe Girardi. Among those with respectable, lengthy careers are John Boccabella, Chris Cannizzaro, Rick Cerone, Phil Masi, Jim Pagliaroni, Tom Pagnozzi, John Romano, Gene Tenace, Dave Valle, Mike DeFelice, and Paul Lo Duca. As this is written, Major League rosters include catchers named Mike Napoli, Sal Fasano, Chris Iannetta, and Jarrod Saltalamacchia, who happens to hold the record for the longest surname in Major League history.

Craig Biggio

For someone who didn't like to watch baseball as a kid—"It was boring, I hated it"—Craig Biggio did well by the game. Preferring football when he was growing up in Kings Park, New York, he won an award as one of the two best high school players on Long Island. "I could have gone to a lot of places on a football scholarship, but destiny brought me to Seton Hall University," he said.[23] Following his junior year at Seton Hall, he was drafted in the first round by the Astros in June 1987. One year later, at age twenty-two, Biggio was in an Astros uniform, which he would wear for the next twenty seasons. In 1989, his first full season, he won the Silver Slugger Award as the

34. Craig Biggio. National Baseball Hall of Fame Library, Cooperstown NY.

best-hitting catcher in the National League, and in 1991 he made his first of seven All-Star appearances.

Following the 1991 season, the Astros asked Biggio to make the extraordinary move from catcher to second baseman, a position he had never played. After thinking it over, he agreed. "I decided I would be the best second baseman I could be, and it worked out real well." So well that in 1992, his first year at the new position, he was again an All-Star and went on to win four consecutive Gold Glove Awards, from 1994 to 1997. Then in 2003, after eleven seasons at second, the thirty-seven-year-old Biggio moved to center field, making yet another seamless transition to a new position. On June 28, 2007, he reached one of baseball's premiere milestones when he got hit number 3,000 against Colorado's Aaron Cook.

When Biggio retired in 2007, his 3,060 hits ranked twentieth in Major League history. A seven-time All Star, four-time Gold Glove winner, and five-time Silver Slugger winner, he is the only player in Major League history to achieve all of these milestones: 600 doubles, 250 home runs, 2,700 hits, and 400 stolen bases. His 668 career doubles are the most ever by a right-handed hitter, and he is the only player other than legendary center fielder Tris Speaker to have 50 doubles and 50 stolen bases in the same season. He also holds the post-1900 record for most times being hit by a pitch (285) and the National League record for most leadoff home runs with 53. Calling Biggio "tremendously underrated," Bill James ranks him as the fifth best second baseman of all time.[24]

When I spoke with him in 2005, Biggio was thirty-nine years old and in his eighteenth season, but he still had the boyish face of someone years younger. "I've had some good genes," he said. His paternal grandfather emigrated from Italy, though Biggio wasn't sure from which region. "My grandfather was a typical short Italian," said Biggio, who himself stands five-foot-eleven. "He had rock hands and worked hard for a living, running a cement factory." His paternal grandmother was of German descent, and his mother is Irish, Swedish, and Lithuanian.

When I asked what motivated him to continue playing after eighteen seasons, Biggio said, "Just the game itself. You get to compete with the best players in the world, and I cherish that. Growing up in a small town on Long Island, I've exceeded my expectations. The biggest thing was to get here and survive. Now when you get compliments from other players, that's great." Phil Garner, the Astros' manager for the final four years of Biggio's career, also had some complimentary things to say. Known as "Scrap Iron" in his playing days, Garner admired Biggio's hard-nosed approach to the game. "He's like Robin Yount and Paul Molitor," he said. "They're throwbacks. He played hard every day, ran everything out. And he does the same thing today, twenty-five years later. And that's the highest compliment I can pay anybody. He's been a great player, and you won't ever hear anybody say anything bad about Craig."[25]

Off the field Biggio was active in community service. Throughout his career he was involved with the Sunshine Kids Foundation, dedicated to providing support for children with cancer. In 2007 he was the recipient of the Roberto Clemente Award, given annually to the Major League player who best exemplifies the game of baseball, sportsmanship, community involvement, and the individual's contribution to his team. Not only was his uniform number 7 retired on August 17, 2008, but also a life-sized statue of him was erected outside Minute Maid Park while he was still an active player.

Mike Piazza

Standing on the top step of the dugout, Mike Piazza was shouting encouragement to his teammate at the plate as Italy played the Dominican Republic in the 2006 World Baseball Classic. What impressed me as I stood next to him—I was serving as the team interpreter—was how totally involved he was in the game, as if it were a Major League pennant showdown. Here was the man widely considered to be the greatest offensive catcher ever, playing with an assortment of Italian American Major and Minor Leaguers, none of whom approached him in fame or ability, and five young players from Italy's professional league. He was the marquee attraction for the underdog Italian team, which was eliminated in the first round by world powers Venezuela and the Dominican Republic. The young native Italian players were clearly in awe of him, but they were no less impressed by the humility and friendliness of this baseball idol who was well known in Italy.

For Mike Piazza to be anyone's idol was something no one could have imagined when he was a nineteen-year-old hopeful that nobody wanted. If there were an award for most unlikely rise from obscurity to stardom, Piazza would win hands down. A sixty-second round draft pick becomes one of the game's all-time greats—not even a wily Hollywood agent could sell that script. Piazza himself may not have pursued the dream had it not been for his father, himself a frustrated ballplayer. "He had aspirations to play professionally," said Piazza, "but he had to work to support his family. My dad bought me a batting cage and pitching machine when I was eleven. Times when I didn't want to practice, he kind of forced me to go out there. He knew that I had talent, and looking back now, I have to thank him for being very stern and making me practice. Even if I had never made it in baseball, it taught me responsibility and discipline."[26]

Even though Piazza was the MVP in both his high school and American Legion leagues, scouts ignored him, as they did after two lackluster years of college ball. Finally, thanks to a request by Dodger manager Tommy Lasorda, a close friend of Piazza's father, the Dodgers picked him in the 1988 draft, after 1,389 other players had been selected.[27] Piazza, now converted from first base to catcher, initially struggled in the Minors, almost quit, but persevered. By 1992 he had become the Dodgers' Minor League Player of the Year with Triple A Albuquerque. The next year the twenty-four-year-old catcher made the first of ten consecutive All-Star appearances and was the unanimous choice as Rookie of the Year.

At six-foot-three and 200 pounds, the right-handed-hitting catcher generated great bat speed, which enabled him to launch prodigious home runs. But he was also one of those rare sluggers who hit for average. Over each of the next four years he hit between twenty-four and forty homers and hit .319 or higher. His best overall offensive performance came in 1997, when, in addition to hitting forty home runs and driving in 124 runs, he had a career-high average of .362, the highest in Los Angeles history. Amazingly that .362 average was only good enough for third place in the league, behind Tony Gwynn and Larry Walker. Aware of baseball history, Piazza told me, "I really wanted to be the first catcher since Ernie Lombardi to win the batting title. I never figured that hitting .362 as a catcher I'd finish third."

It was assumed that Piazza, a Dodger legend after five outstanding seasons, would, like Lasorda, be wearing Dodger blue for his entire career. But in 1998 the Dodgers suddenly traded him to the Florida Marlins following a contract dispute. A week later the cash-strapped Marlins traded him to the Mets, who, at the end of the 1998 season, gave the one-time draft afterthought a franchise-record seven-year deal worth $91 million.

On September 21, 2001, Piazza hit a two-run game-winning homer against the Atlanta Braves in the first professional sporting event in New York after the September 11 terrorist attacks. In ceremonies marking the closing of Shea Stadium in September 2008, that home run was chosen as the second-greatest moment in the stadium's history. On May 5, 2004, Piazza hit home run number 352 to pass Carlton Fisk and establish a new career record for home runs by a catcher.

35. Mike Piazza. National Baseball Hall of Fame Library, Cooperstown NY.

In his sixteen-year career Piazza was a twelve-time All-Star (ten times the starting catcher), won ten consecutive Silver Slugger Awards, and four times finished in the top five in MVP voting. He had a lifetime average of .308 with 427 home runs (including a record 396 as a catcher), 1,335 RBIs, and a .545 slugging average. Of the sixteen catchers currently in the Hall of Fame only Mickey Cochrane and Bill Dickey have higher averages, and only Yogi Berra and Johnny

Bench (both of whom had longer careers) have more RBIs. None has hit as many home runs or has a higher slugging average.

For all his offensive prowess, Piazza faced criticism for his defensive play as a catcher. Though considered competent in other areas, he was ineffective at throwing out runners. "The glory of defensive catching is purely throwing," he said. "If you call a good game or if you block a ball, those things don't get the glory. I'll be the first to admit I haven't been the most prolific thrower, but I don't think I've been the worst ever. Sometimes in my career I've been a little self-conscious about it; it isn't as if I haven't applied myself."

Asked what he learned in overcoming the early doubts about his ability to play the game, he said, "I didn't let anybody discourage me because it's easy [to be discouraged] when you have expert scouts telling you to go back to school. I just want to relay to people that you don't have to be the most highly regarded athlete or highly regarded student. You might have to work twice as hard as the next guy, but I find pleasure in that because the work keeps you grounded and makes you more able to deal with anything that comes your way."

To anyone who spent any time with Team Italy during that 2006 World Baseball Classic, Piazza's total involvement made it clear that his participation was not a pro forma appearance to satisfy someone's request. Rather, he was there because of an awareness of, and loyalty to, his Italian American heritage. He was not playing for money or for personal glory but for the pride of representing the country where his grandparents were born. "I wouldn't have missed this for the world," he told me at the time. "It's important to reconnect with your roots."[28]

Michael Joseph Piazza was born in Norristown, Pennsylvania, in 1968. His grandfather, Rosario, had emigrated from Sciacca, Sicily, and his grandmother, Elisabetta, from Naples. "My grandfather took a lot of criticism for marrying a 'foreigner,'" Piazza said with a smile. His father, Vince, dropped out of high school and sold used cars, eventually building a string of auto dealerships. "My dad was a little scrutinized for marrying a Slovak, but by then those stereotypes of having to marry an Italian had eased. That's kind of nice and obviously the melting pot of this country."

For all his accomplishments, not to mention his on-field swagger, in person Mike Piazza was anything but arrogant. Pulitzer Prize–winning *New York Times* columnist Ira Berkow wrote, "I liked Mike Piazza—he was sensitive, intelligent and accomplished. And, perhaps with the perspective of once having been one of the very last players selected in the Major League draft, he had a disarming humility. Also, unlike many athletes who seem rooted to their invisible pedestal, he was adult, and to a great extent understood the role of the press and remained cooperative with us."[29]

Piazza was aware of his place in baseball history but seemed humbled by it. "Being of Italian descent and knowing how people, especially other Italian Americans, respond to that, is very flattering," he said. "Obviously there are a lot of predecessors who have a great tradition and have contributed a lot to baseball. With what Joe DiMaggio stood for, it's almost impossible to measure up to that as far as talent and legacy. I think Italian Americans are ever searching for the next Joe DiMaggio. I can only say I'm very much inspired by DiMaggio, and if people put me in that category, it's very flattering."

In 2002 Piazza made his first trip to Italy, where, as part of Major League Baseball's effort to internationalize the game, he conducted clinics for young Italian players. "I went to Rome for a few days, and that whetted my appetite to go back," he said. "I've been back several times since. I've always looked for a bridge between the Italians who stayed and the people who migrated here. We grew up in the United States and we love this country, but we're very proud of our ancestry, the fact that Italy is a country of historical tradition. That's what I find fascinating."

Meanwhile, as Biggio and Piazza were rekindling memories of past greatness on the diamond, other Italian Americans were making their mark on baseball off the field.

15

From Labor to Management

Even after Italian Americans began assimilating in greater numbers than ever after the war and sharing in the general prosperity of the era, they continued to be perceived as blue-collar workers. With few exceptions, for much of the twentieth century the only Americans of Italian descent widely known to the public came from the worlds of sports, entertainment, and, sad to say, organized crime. Notorious figures such as Al Capone, Lucky Luciano, and John Gotti often garnered as much press as Joe DiMaggio or Frank Sinatra.

By the early 1980s, however, Italian Americans had attained such executive positions as chairman of Chrysler (Lee Iacocca), president of Avis (Joseph Vittoria), president of Yale (A. Bartlett Giamatti), and governor of New York (Mario Cuomo). With mass media fanfare the "official" arrival of Italian Americans as part of the mainstream was heralded by a front-page story in the *New York Times Magazine* of May 15, 1983. Featured on the cover, like so many debutantes at a coming-out party, were portraits of the four individuals listed above, as well as those of eight others prominent in science, politics, the arts, and the Catholic Church. These personalities represented, according to the text of Stephen S. Hall's article, "merely the brightest lights in a general fluorescence of Italians in American life."[1]

In describing "the quiet yet spectacular rise of Italian-Americans in the United States today," Hall noted that while they had sometimes been regarded as "slow to assimilate and climb America's social ladders," they now "swell the ranks of the middle class, mass power and wealth, and help set the decade's social and political agenda as never before." Compared to individuals like DiMaggio, Sinatra, and La Guardia, who attained success in "highly circumscribed worlds," Italian Americans had now become "prominent players with national impact as well as a national following, taking the initiative in crucial political and social issues."[2]

As in other fields the evolution from labor to management in Major League Baseball was gradual. With the exception of Oscar Melillo's brief stint as manager of the St. Louis Browns at the end of the 1938 season, no Italian American was entrusted with a managerial position until Phil Cavarretta in 1951, more than two decades after large numbers of players had begun appearing on Major League rosters. And, with one exception, it would be some time after that before they rose to baseball's equivalent of white-collar administrators as general managers and owners. But like their counterparts in other business endeavors, Italian Americans gradually became more visible and prominent in a variety of baseball-related positions, not only as administrators but also as journalists, broadcasters, and umpires.

Sportswriters

Inevitably the ability of Italian Americans to move into more prestigious positions had been linked to their level of education. Many early immigrants distrusted education as one of the threats to family loyalty and unity, so there was little incentive for their children to pursue even a high school diploma. But especially in the years after World War II one aspect of the increased mobility of young Italian

Americans was their pursuit of higher education. (According to the 2000 census, 18.5 percent of Italian Americans had a bachelor's degree, compared to 15.5 percent nationally.) More education was certainly one characteristic of those who moved into the higher echelons of baseball administration as general managers and owners, but it was also true for those in sports journalism.

The first noteworthy sportswriter of Italian descent was Paul Gallico (1897–1976), the son of an Italian concert pianist and an Austrian mother. After graduating from Columbia in 1921, the New York native was named sports editor of the *New York Daily News* in 1924. A pioneer of participatory sports journalism, he boxed with Jack Dempsey, played golf with Bobby Jones, and hit against Dizzy Dean. He was also the founder of the Golden Gloves boxing tournament. One of the bright lights of the golden age of sports, Gallico retired from full-time sportswriting in 1936 to become a freelance writer. Among his forty-one books were *Farewell to Sport*, in which he denounced racism in sports, and *Lou Gehrig: Pride of the Yankees*, which was made into what is widely considered one of the best baseball movies.

Apart from Gallico no sportswriter of Italian descent attained national prominence until Bill Gallo in the 1960s. Born in Manhattan in 1922, the World War II combat veteran attended Columbia University and the School of Visual Arts before joining the sports department of the *New York Daily News* in 1960. A twenty-time recipient of the Page One Journalism Award from the New York Newspaper Guild, he also received the James J. Walker Award from the Boxing Writers Association and was inducted into the International Boxing Hall of Fame. But Gallo gained his greatest fame as a sports cartoonist, receiving the National Cartoonist Society Milton Caniff Lifetime Achievement Award in 1998. In 1977 Mike Lupica joined Gallo at the *Daily News*, becoming, at age twenty-five, the youngest columnist ever at a New York newspaper. As a syndicated columnist, he went on to become one of the most widely read sportswriters in the country. In addition, he has been a panelist on ESPN Television's *Sports Reporters* and has written numerous nonfiction books and novels.

After receiving a degree in journalism from Penn State, Tom Verducci spent ten years as a sports reporter for *Newsday*, where he was the national baseball columnist. In 1993 he became the lead baseball writer for *Sports Illustrated* and its online magazine, si.com. He also co-wrote two books with Joe Torre: *Chasing the Dream: An Autobiography* (1997) and *The Yankee Years* (2009). Other contemporary writers of note are *Boston Globe* baseball columnists Nick Cafardo and Tony Massarotti.

Two writers of Italian descent have been awarded the prestigious J. G. Taylor Spink Award, whose recipients are chosen by the Baseball Writers' Association of America and are recognized in the "Scribes and Mikemen" exhibit in the National Baseball Hall of Fame. In 1981 the award went to Bob Addie (1910–1982); the son of an immigrant, he anglicized the family name of Addonizio. Addie covered baseball as a reporter and columnist for the *Washington Times-Herald* and *Washington Post* for almost forty years and served as president of the Baseball Writers' Association of America. The 1995 recipient of the Spink Award was Joseph Durso (1924–2004). A *magna cum laude* graduate of New York University, Durso broadcast his *Sports of the Times* radio show on WQXR in New York for twenty-seven years. A writer, editor, and columnist for the *New York Times* from 1950 to 2001, he was the author of fourteen books, including *DiMaggio: The Last American Knight*.

Broadcasters

Recipients of the Ford Frick Award for broadcasters, which is presented annually for "major contributions to baseball," are also recognized in the "Scribes and Mikemen" exhibit in the Hall of Fame. There have been two honorees of Italian descent: Harry Caray (1989) and Joe Garagiola (1991). Garagiola, whose broadcasting career was discussed above, was one of the first of the former ballplayers to find success behind the microphone. Caray, born Harry Carabina in St. Louis in 1914, began his career in 1945 with the Cardinals. Broadcasting on powerful KMOX radio, Caray brought Major League Baseball to towns throughout the Midwest, as well as several western states. Then after one year with the Oakland A's and eleven years with the Chicago White Sox, in 1982 Caray moved across town to the Cubs. There with his trademark cry of "Holy Cow!" and his singing of "Take Me Out to the Ball Game" during the seventh inning stretch, he gained national prominence thanks to the countrywide reach of WGN television. With his oversized glasses, boisterous personality, and boundless enthusiasm for the game, Caray was a fan favorite wherever he worked. Following his death in 1998, the Cubs erected a life-sized statue of Caray outside Wrigley Field.

Umpires

Umpires play a prominent, if often underappreciated, role in baseball, responsible as they are for maintaining the integrity of the game. While there have been several of distinction, the overall number of umpires of Italian descent has been small relative to coaches and managers, who come and go with much greater frequency. It is simply more difficult for umpires to make it to the Majors, both because there are few slots available at any given time and because umpires, once appointed, tend to stay on the job for many years.

Babe Pinelli, the first Italian American to work in the big leagues, enjoyed a long and successful twenty-two-year career from 1935 to 1956. However, notwithstanding Pinelli's example, by the time he retired only six other umpires of Italian descent had appeared on Major League diamonds. Art Passarella was the first to follow Pinelli; hired in 1941, he served in World War II, returned in 1945, and worked until 1953. Only two other Italian Americans were appointed in the forties: Joe Paparella in 1946 and Frank Dascoli in 1948. Nor did the number of new umpires increase in the fifties, when only three were appointed: Augie Donatelli (1950), Augie Guglielmo (1952), and Frank Tabacchi (1956).

Another handful were hired in the sixties and seventies, but it appears that there were none hired in the eighties, at least judging by surnames. Of the fifty umpires hired by the Major Leagues in the nineties, however, six are readily identifiable as Italian American: Phil Cuzzi, Mike DiMuro, Larry Poncino, Tony Randazzo, Ed Rapuano and Dan Iassogna. On August 13, 2002, in a game between the White Sox and Rangers in Arlington, Texas, for the first time in Major League history the entire crew was made up of umpires from the same ethnic background: Rapuano (home), Poncino (first), Randazzo (second), and Iassogna (third).[3]

According to the old adage, you know an umpire is doing a good job when you don't notice him. August J. "Augie" Donatelli, however, was hard to miss. In his twenty-four-year career (1950–73) he was animated on the field and never reluctant to eject players and managers. Donatelli, who had worked alongside his father in the coal mines of western Pennsylvania, was also instrumental in the formation of the National League Umpires Association in 1963, the forerunner of the Major League Umpires Association. Former umpire Harry Wendelstedt was quoted as saying, "Augie's the man who made all the good things possible in umpiring today."[4]

Another who did not shy away from calling attention to himself was Ron Luciano. An American League umpire from 1969 to 1980,

Luciano was an inveterate talker and showman on the field; he would routinely punctuate an out call with repeated arm pumps or even fire an imaginary gun at the runner. He also served as president of the Major League Umpires Association. "He did a great job [as president]," said former umpire Bruce Froemming, who also noted that not all of Luciano's colleagues appreciated his on-field humor as much as the fans did. "Ronnie entertained fans and players and himself," Froemming said, then added diplomatically, "but he did things that you would never see now."[5] Sad to say, Luciano took his own life in 1985, at the age of fifty-seven.

Steve Palermo was another umpire who gained public attention, but for a different reason. Hired in 1977, he was recognized as one of the best in the business. But his on-field career came to an early end in July 1991, when, in attempting to break up a robbery outside a Dallas restaurant, he was shot and seriously wounded. In 2000 he was named a supervisor of Major League umpires. "He was going to be a star," said Froemming. "He absolutely loved umpiring; he had a lot of hustle and great judgment."[6]

Coaches

To the best of my knowledge, Tony Lazzeri became the first Italian American to coach in the Majors when Cubs owner Phil Wrigley hired him away from the Yankees in 1938 to be a player/coach. Many former players would go on to become baseball "lifers" as managers, coaches, or scouts. It was Lazzeri's former double play partner, Frank Crosetti, who set the standard for coaches, serving for twenty-four years, twenty-two as the Yankees' third base coach. Among others who enjoyed long coaching careers were Joe Amalfitano, Leo Mazzone, and Matt Galante.

Amalfitano, a one-time Giants bonus baby, managed the Cubs for parts of three seasons between 1979 and 1981. Before and after that he spent sixteen years coaching for the Cubs, Giants, Padres, and Reds. From 1983 to 1998 he was a Dodger coach under Tommy Lasorda. "That was fun," Amalfitano told me. "I'd be in the third base coach's box, and he'd just yell out the signals in Italian." Amalfitano took great pride in having been a coach for thirty-one years. "In terms of longevity on the lines, I've gone by Frank Crosetti, which is important to me because I knew who he was."[7] In 2008, then entering his fifty-fourth year in professional baseball, he was named a roving instructor and special assignment scout by the Giants.

A left-handed pitcher who never got beyond the Minors, Leo Mazzone went on to become recognized as one of the top pitching coaches in the game. (He was also known for his trademark habit of rocking back and forth while watching his pitchers from his seat in the dugout.) In his sixteen years with the Atlanta Braves (1990–2005), he coached one of the greatest rotations ever, headed by Greg Maddux, Tom Glavine, and John Smoltz, who won a combined six Cy Young Awards during Mazzone's tenure. In that time ten different Atlanta pitchers were named to the All-Star team. Mazzone also had a reputation for transforming pitchers who had been mediocre with other teams into good or outstanding ones in Atlanta.

A native of Brooklyn, Matt Galante attended St. John's University before playing ball in the Yankee system. "My parents made sure I graduated," said Galante. "They said, 'How can you make a living at baseball?'"[8] Galante made a living managing in the Minors for eleven years, then coaching for the Houston Astros from 1985 to 2001 (except for 1997, when he managed their Triple A team in New Orleans). After coaching for the Mets from 2002 to 2004, he returned to Houston as a special assistant to the general manager. In 2006 he was selected to manage Team Italy in the inaugural World Baseball Classic.

Galante commented on the decline in ethnic identity within his family. "My parents came from Castellamare del Golfo in Sicily, so we got some of that tradition handed down," he said. "Then we got a little lax, and our kids are more Americanized. My daughter has three kids, and she's going to pass down even less of it. Each generation loses a little bit, and that's sad." He also noted the decrease in the number of ballplayers of Italian descent. "We've had great Italian Americans in baseball. I don't think we have enough of them now. There are other things for them to do."

Managers

By the first decade of the twenty-first century, Italian American managers were not only numerous, but they were also at the top of their profession. Three of the four teams in the league championship finals in 2000 were managed by Italian Americans: Joe Torre, Tony La Russa, and Bobby Valentine. In 2004, the year Terry Francona led the Red Sox to their first World Series title in eighty-six years, two of the other three managers in the league championship series were again Torre and La Russa. In 2008 Torre led the Dodgers to the NL West division title, while Francona's Red Sox lost the American League title to the upstart Tampa Bay Rays, managed by American League manager of the year Joe Maddon, whose family name was originally Madonnini.[9] In fact between 1996 and 2009 Italian American managers were in the World Series every year except 1997 and 2005, and in 2000 and 2004 both teams were managed by Italian Americans. Between 1998 and 2009 six were named manager of the year: Torre, La Russa, Maddon, Larry Bowa, Mike Scioscia, and Joe Girardi. But for all the success they have achieved in recent years, the chance for an Italian American to lead a Major League team was a long time coming.

As his Major League career was winding down, Tony Lazzeri made it known that he would welcome the opportunity to manage. He did go on to manage in the Minor Leagues for several years, but he was never given a chance at the Major League level, even though he was acknowledged as one of the smartest men in baseball. The same year that Lazzeri became a Cubs coach, Oscar "Spinach" Melillo became the first Italian American to manage in the big leagues when, at the end of the 1938 season, he replaced Gabby Street as skipper of the hapless St. Louis Browns, who went 2-9 in Melillo's brief stint. It would be another thirteen years before Phil Cavarretta would become the first Italian American to manage for a full season.

Following Cavarretta's two and a half seasons as manager of the Cubs between 1951 and 1953, Cookie Lavagetto became the second full-time manager of Italian descent in May 1957, when he took over the last-place Washington Senators. In Lavagetto's first three years at the helm Washington continued to live up to its tradition of being "first in war, first in peace, and last in the American League." In 1961, when the team moved to Minneapolis, Lavagetto became the first manager in Twins history, but his first season in the Twin Cities was also his last. With his team in ninth place Lavagetto was fired in June, replaced by Sam Mele. By 1965 Mele had led the Twins to the franchise's first pennant since 1933 and their only hundred-win season to date (102-60). When Mele was dismissed early in the 1967 season, the Twins had compiled a 524-436 record under his leadership.

In a preview of things to come Billy Martin led the Twins to a divisional title in 1969, his first year as a manager, only to be fired at the end of the season. His replacement, Bill Rigney, was replaced in turn by Frank Quilici midway through the 1972 season. Quilici, who managed through 1975, was the Twins' fourth manager of Italian descent since the franchise moved to Minnesota. In fact in the nineteen years between 1957, when Lavagetto was hired, and 1975, Quilici's final year, the Senators/Twins were managed by Italian Americans in all or part of sixteen seasons, including eleven in a row between 1957 and 1967.

Two other clubs that have shown a fondness for Italian American managers are the Cubs and Phillies. In addition to Phil Cavarretta, Cubs skippers have included Herman Franks (1977–79), Joe Amalfitano (1979–81), Frank Lucchesi (1987), and Joe Altobelli, interim manager for one game in 1991. Lucchesi was also the first Italian to pilot the Phillies (1970–72), followed later by three consecutive Italian American managers over a span of fourteen years: Jim Fregosi (1991–96), Terry Francona (1997–2000), and Larry Bowa (2001–4). After four losing seasons in Philadelphia, Francona went to Boston in 2004, winning a World Series in his first year and another in 2007.

Joseph Salvatore Altobelli was a Cubs coach in 1991 when he stepped in as interim manager for a single game. Before that the Detroit native had managed the Giants to fourth- and third-place finishes in 1977 and 1978 before being replaced late in the 1979 season. In 1983 he was named manager of the Baltimore Orioles, succeeding the legendary Earl Weaver. In his first year Altobelli became the third Italian manager (after Billy Martin and Tommy Lasorda) to win a World Series when the Orioles beat the Phillies in five games. After Baltimore fell to fifth place the next year, Altobelli's brief stay ended fifty-five games into the 1985 season.

Yogi Berra

In 1964, his first year as Yankee skipper, Berra became the first Italian American manager to win a pennant. Before the season the skeptics had predicted he would fail. He was, they said, too close to the players, and there were questions whether he had the intelligence to be a manager. But Berra remained patient, and the Yankees rallied late to clinch the pennant on the next-to-last day of the season. Nevertheless, the day after the Yankees lost the World Series to the Cardinals, Berra was fired. The Yankee bosses had decided that Yogi was not enough of a disciplinarian to control the team.

Berra wasn't out of baseball for long. The New York Mets, a National League expansion team in 1962, were eager to capitalize on Berra's popularity with the fans and hired him as a player/coach in 1965. Seven years later he was named the Mets manager on April 6, 1972, four days after Manager Gil Hodges died suddenly. The Mets won a pennant under Berra in 1973, but after a losing season the next year, he was fired in August 1975.

Again Berra landed on his feet, becoming a Yankee coach under Billy Martin. He held the job for eight years, amid all the turmoil created by owner George Steinbrenner, who made eight managerial changes in that period. When Steinbrenner fired Martin (for the third time) in December 1983, he replaced him with the easygoing Berra, leading everyone to wonder how long the marriage would last. Berra's future did indeed look doubtful after the Yankees finished third in 1984, but the owner publicly announced during spring training that his manager's job was safe for the entire season, no matter what. Then sixteen games into the 1985 season Steinbrenner fired Berra, his preseason vote of confidence so much smoke in the wind, and brought back Martin for his fourth try at pleasing "the Boss." Berra's public response was one of gracious stoicism, but privately he was incensed that the owner had dispatched his general manager, Clyde King, to break the news. He vowed that he would never return to Yankee Stadium as long as Steinbrenner was in charge. True to his word, he maintained his self-imposed exile for fourteen years; following an apology from Steinbrenner, he returned to throw out the first pitch on opening day of the 1999 season.

Billy Martin

When Yogi's former teammate Billy Martin was hired by Minnesota in 1969, he set the tone for his entire sixteen-year managerial career. He took the Twins from a seventh-place finish in 1968 to the Western Division title, but not before getting into an alley fight in August with pitcher Dave Boswell. In spite of the team's success Martin quickly wore out his welcome and was fired at the end of the season. The long, torturous journey had begun.

Hired by the Tigers in 1971, Martin again transformed a losing team into a winner, taking it from a fourth-place finish in 1970 to second place in '71, then a division title in 1972. But again he was unable to stay out of trouble, getting into an altercation with a fan in Baltimore in April 1972. Martin was fired on September 2, 1973, only to be named six days later as manager of the Texas Rangers, where he continued to work his magic. The Rangers jumped from sixth to second place in 1974, earning Martin the first of four Associated Press Manager of the Year Awards. But the honeymoon was brief yet again, and Martin was fired in July 1975. Now the real fun began.

One month later Martin was hired by the Yankees, beginning the tumultuous relationship between the gifted but volatile manager and Steinbrenner, the intrusive, win-at-all-costs owner. What appeared to be a doomed marriage from the start proved to be a love-hate connection with numerous breakups and reconciliation attempts, punctuated by championships, public accusations, and constant tension. In 1976, his first full season in New York, Martin justified Steinbrenner's trust by leading the Yankees to their first pennant since Berra had managed in 1964, and the first of three straight. Then in 1977 he became the first Italian American manager to win a World Series when the Yanks beat Tommy Lasorda's Dodgers in six games.

That was the year that Steinbrenner had hired high-priced free agent Reggie Jackson, in spite of Martin's objections. The addition of Jackson to the mix meant there were now three huge egos in the Yankee family, which only heightened the tension. The following year the tension boiled over in July, when Martin publicly called Jackson "a born liar" and Steinbrenner (who had pled guilty to making illegal contributions to Richard Nixon's 1972 campaign) a "convicted" one. The next day Martin, reportedly under pressure from management, resigned from his dream job. But the first of many reconciliations came quickly; when the team got off to a slow start in 1979, Martin was returned to the fold.

The reconciliation was predictably short-lived. In October, after the Yankees finished fourth and two days after Martin punched a marshmallow salesman outside a Minneapolis bar, Steinbrenner fired him. The next year he was back in the dugout, this time in Oakland, and again turning a loser into a winner, taking the A's from seventh to second place. In the strike-shortened 1981 season the A's, employing the aggressive running style known as "Billy Ball," won the Western Division. But again the revival was temporary, and when the team fell to fifth in 1982, Martin was gone.

Three more times Martin walked through the Yankees' revolving door; he was hired and fired in 1983, again in 1985, and yet again in 1988. Meanwhile, Martin, seemingly in a constant struggle with his inner demons, continued to drink and to get into fights with various bar patrons. On Christmas Day 1989, after drinking at a local bar, he was killed when the pickup truck in which he was either the driver or a passenger crashed at the entrance to the driveway of his home near Binghamton, New York.[10]

For all his brilliance as a tactician Martin wore on people, both players and management, because of his intensity, volatility, and disdain for authority. Davey Nelson, who played for Martin in Texas, saw this firsthand. "I learned a lot and enjoyed playing for him," said Nelson. "There was probably not a better strategist in the game. He could take a team that struggled and make them better, but then it would wear off. He motivated through intimidation, which has a short-term effect. It was a good philosophy for the young kids, but a lot of the veteran players had confrontations with him."[11]

Martin certainly made his share of enemies, both as a player and as a manager. Regardless of his human frailties, he led his teams to three pennants and two World Series titles and elicited great respect for his skill. Few if any managers in history have been better at turning a team around quickly, and no other manager has ever led four different teams to the postseason. Like other combative managers, Martin motivated some players to unprecedented levels of performance, alienated others, and to some did both. Jim Fregosi, who played for Martin in Texas and later managed against him, expressed an opinion shared by many. "He was a rambunctious little guy, I'll tell you that. Probably, overall, the best between the lines I've ever seen." Former umpire Bill Haller said simply, "Billy Martin was the best manager I ever saw."[12]

Jim Fregosi

Fregosi was a thirty-six-year-old infielder in 1978, playing for the Pittsburgh Pirates in his eighteenth Major League season, when he got a phone call from General Manager Buzzie Bavasi and Gene Autry, owner of the California Angels. "They asked me if I was interested in managing the team," Fregosi said. "I told them, 'The way I'm hitting, I'll take any job I can get.' I managed the Angels the next day."[13] Fregosi was no stranger to the Angels, having begun his playing career with the expansion franchise in its 1961 inaugural season. A fan favorite in Anaheim, he spent the first eleven of his eighteen Major League seasons playing shortstop for the Angels before moving on to the Mets, Rangers, and Pirates. In 1998 the Angels retired the six-time All-Star's number 11.

In 1979, his first full season, Fregosi led the Angels to their first Western Division crown in their nineteen-year existence, but after the team fell to sixth place the next year, he was replaced midway through the 1981 season. He took the reins of the White Sox in 1986 but was let go after three straight fifth-place finishes. He led the Phillies to the National League pennant in 1993 before three straight losing seasons cost him his job in 1996, then led the Blue Jays to winning seasons in his two-year stay in 1999–2000. By the time his career ended Fregosi had managed in four decades with a record of 1,028-1,095.

Fregosi's grandfather was an immigrant from Tuscany who worked in the produce business in South San Francisco, where his father later owned an Italian deli. "My father spoke Italian," said Fregosi, "but he didn't want us to speak the language. 'You're American, speak English,' he said. Every time I hit a home run in the big leagues, when the store opened in the morning, all the old Italians would come in and have a shot of whiskey with my dad."

When I spoke with him in 2005, Fregosi, then a special assistant to the general manager of the Atlanta Braves, looked back on his forty-six years in professional baseball. "I was fortunate to play at a time when it was still a game," he said. "I loved the years when I played. There was a different type of camaraderie. You spent more time with newspaper men, with umpires, with other players. When we played, we were all fans of the game. It's been a labor of love for me. I had the opportunity to play in the Major Leagues, to manage, to work in the front office. I feel as fortunate as anyone could ever be, to be involved in something you love."

Tommy Lasorda: the Ultimate Italian

As a player, coach, manager, and executive with the Dodgers for many years—sixty as of 2009—Tommy Lasorda was so dedicated to the franchise that he was said to bleed Dodger blue. But even more essential to his sense of self was the Italian blood that flowed through his veins. He may not have won more games, pennants, or World Series than any other Italian American manager, but there is little question that he was the most "Italian." In the words of Frank Torre, "Lasorda would like all the managers in baseball to be Italian." When Torre received a heart transplant in October 1996, Lasorda sent him a note saying, "I hope you got an Italian heart."[14]

Thomas Charles Lasorda was born in 1927 in Norristown, Pennsylvania. His father, Sabatino, was an immigrant from Tollo, a small town in the Abruzzo region, and his American-born mother, Camilla, was also of Abruzzese origin. During a visit to Italy in 1979 to conduct baseball clinics Lasorda visited his father's hometown. With characteristic understatement, he said to the residents of Tollo: "To walk the streets my father walked on, to see the faces of so many proud relatives, to cry tears of joy with my *compaesani* . . . this is something my wife Jo and I will never forget."[15]

Memories of Lasorda's own hometown were less heartwarming. "We were practically all Italians in the East End," he told me, "but the people in the West End didn't like Italians. The girls wouldn't dance with us because we were Italian. Some people in town changed their names, but our name was gold to us. Why would we change our name if we loved our father's and mother's heritage?"[16]

Lasorda's father, who drove a truck in a sand quarry, wanted his five sons to go to school, but all Tommy wanted to do was play baseball. "In high school I made the varsity, but the coach said I had to have baseball shoes," Lasorda recalled. "My father said he could barely afford regular shoes and he wasn't going to buy me baseball shoes. I cried, and the next day when I came home from school, there was a box on the table. It was a pair of baseball shoes three sizes too big. My dad said he wasn't going to buy another pair in a year, so I had to pack them with cotton."[17]

Drafted by the Dodgers in 1948, Lasorda had a stellar Minor League career as a left-handed pitcher, but his Major League career with the Dodgers and Athletics consisted of twenty-six games and an 0-4 record. In 1973, after managing in the Minors for several years, he was named the third-base coach under longtime Dodger manager Walter Alston. When Alston resigned in September 1976, Lasorda began his twenty-one-year run as skipper. From the start his primary strength was his ability to motivate players. He approached his work with the fervor of a television evangelist, one whose relentlessly optimistic message was the promise not of redemption but of victory. He was quoted as saying, "I don't care if it's the World Series or just a spring training game. I hate to lose."[18] Giving new meaning to the term "hands-on managing," Lasorda made it a point to hug his players after a win or a big play. "A lot of opposing players didn't like the hugging," said Davey Lopes, a mainstay of Lasorda's infield. "I think he was the first manager to hug his players. I think it has something to do with his heritage. That's his style; either you like it or you don't."[19]

In 1977, Lasorda's first full season, the Dodgers won the pennant, but then, in the first World Series in which both managers were of Italian descent, they lost to Billy Martin's Yankees. Lasorda again lost to Martin in 1978, but in 1981 he won his first Series title, this time beating a Yankee team managed by Bob Lemon. Seven years later Lasorda won a second championship when he willed a squad of

36. Tommy Lasorda celebrates during a Dodgers-Giants game at Candlestick Park, 1990. Otto Greule Jr./Getty Images.

overachievers to the pennant and an upset win over Tony La Russa's powerhouse Oakland A's.

Lasorda led the Dodgers to two more divisional titles before resigning in 1996 (reportedly with a nudge from owner Peter O'Malley) after suffering a mild heart attack. Over his twenty-one-year career the Dodgers won eight division crowns, four pennants, and two World Series. Only Connie Mack, John McGraw, and Walter Alston managed one team for more years, and only Casey Stengel managed more postseason games—sixty-three to Lasorda's sixty-one. Lasorda was twice named manager of the year (1983 and 1988), and in 1997 he was inducted into the Hall of Fame, the seventh Italian American and the fourteenth manager to be so honored.

The indefatigable Lasorda was hardly the retiring type. After managing the U.S. Olympic team to a gold medal in 2000, at the age of seventy-two, he was appointed as a special adviser to Dodgers owner Frank McCourt. In 2006 he was named ambassador-at-large for the inaugural World Baseball Classic, and in December 2008 the emperor of Japan awarded him the Order of the Rising Sun in recognition of his contributions to the development of Japanese baseball. A gregarious, gifted raconteur and eternal optimist, Lasorda became one of the best known figures in baseball and a goodwill ambassador for the game.

Lasorda's dual passions, for baseball and his Italian heritage, as well as his motivational style, were never more evident than in the pep talk he gave to Team Italy prior to its game against the powerful Venezuela squad in the 2006 World Baseball Classic. With the team gathered in the clubhouse, Lasorda reminded the underdogs that "It's not always the fastest man who wins the race, and it's not always the best team that wins the game. You've got to want this game today more than they do. You've gotta believe; self-confidence is the first step to success." Then, with his voice rising in a crescendo, he said, "If you win today, they'll be dancing in the streets of Florence! They'll even be dancing in the Vatican!"[20] With that the fired-up players cheered, marched out of the clubhouse, and headed for the field to vanquish the foe. That day, however, not even a Tommy Lasorda speech was enough to keep the better team from winning.

Bobby Valentine

A first-round draft choice, infielder/outfielder Bobby Valentine was in Lasorda's starting lineup for two years in the early seventies before playing for four other teams in his ten-year career. Six years after retiring as a player, the thirty-five-year-old Valentine was named manager of the Texas Rangers early in the 1985 season. Following a seventh-place finish that year, Valentine did his best Billy Martin imitation, moving the Rangers up to second place in 1986. But in six subsequent seasons they never finished higher than third, and Valentine was fired early in the 1992 season. Near the end of the 1996 season Valentine went to the Mets, who secured a wild card spot in 1999. (It was during that season that Valentine, after being ejected from a game, reappeared in the dugout thinly disguised in sunglasses and a Groucho Marx-like painted-on mustache.) Valentine took the Mets to the World Series in 2000, losing to Joe Torre's Yankees, then was not renewed after the team fell to fifth place in 2002.

Before being hired by the Mets, Valentine had taken his managerial skills overseas in 1995 to manage the Chiba Lotte Marines of the Japanese Pacific League. When he was let go by the Mets in 2002, he returned to the Lotte Marines, a perennial second-division team. By 2005 he had led them to the Japanese championship, becoming the only man to manage in both the World Series and the Japan Series. Valentine, who had learned to speak Japanese and was always a fan favorite, was now a national star, with a burger, a beer, and a street named after him.[21]

Valentine told me in an interview that his family name had originally been Valentini. His grandfather, who was originally from a town near Naples, lived for a time in England. "That's probably where the name was changed," he said. "He and his wife sailed from Liverpool in 1907." While acknowledging that "some of the greatest guys I've met in the game are those, like Tommy Lasorda, who wanted to be proud of their heritage and accepted me as one of theirs," Valentine, whose wife Mary is the daughter of Ralph Branca, was ambivalent about his heritage. "I always thought there was more rivalry and competition among Italians," he said. "That's the way we do things, strangely enough. There's not a real bonding."[22]

Throughout his managerial career Valentine was recognized as a smart strategist, but his outspoken, provocative manner led to accusations that he was arrogant and smug. A *Sports Illustrated* feature on the four managers in the 2000 league championship series (La Russa, Torre, Valentine, and Lou Piniella) described them as "among the best of the current skipper class, in achievement and outsized reputation." The placid Torre was "the very picture of Zen," and La Russa "the grey streaked professor." As for Valentine, "He is—as he'd gladly tell you—one of the most astute baseball minds of our time."[23]

Mike Scioscia

A stereotypical slow-footed catcher, the six-foot-two, 220-pound native of Upper Darby, Pennsylvania, spent his entire thirteen-year playing career with Lasorda's Dodgers. While his offensive production was modest, he was considered the heart and soul of the team, distinguishing himself with his skill at handling pitchers, exceptional plate-blocking ability, and baseball smarts. Many regarded him as a future manager, perhaps even the successor to Lasorda. But Scioscia was one Dodger-bred player who went to another franchise, moving across town in 2000 to replace Joe Maddon as manager of the Anaheim Angels, who had lost ninety-two games in 1999. He quickly turned the Angels into a winning team. In 2002, when they won the World Series for the first time in their forty-one-year history, Scioscia was named AL manager of the year. Over the next seven seasons the Angels won five divisional titles, earning Scioscia recognition as one of the best managers in the game—he won his second AL Manager of the Year Award in 2009—as well as making him a hero in Anaheim.

In many ways Mike Scioscia typifies the Italian American of his generation: he is aware of his ethnicity but primarily because of his parents' background. His father and mother were both children of immigrants, and they both spoke Italian, but they did not pass that on to their children. His father would point out Italian American Major Leaguers to him, but, Scioscia said, "I admired Johnny Bench because he was a catcher and I was a catcher. I think that reflects the melting pot that the United States is. It's not like it was with my dad's generation, where, being the first generation Italian in this country, he really identified with it. Where I grew up, my friends were German and Irish. It wasn't an Italian ethnic neighborhood. It was more of a diverse culture, which was great. I think it adds a lot to your personality and understanding." Following the 1997 season, Scioscia went to Italy for the first time to conduct baseball clinics at the invitation of the Italian Baseball Federation. "I do have pride in being Italian," he said. "It's a great culture, and going to Italy really revitalized that feeling."[24]

Tony La Russa

In his study of the intricacies of the game, *Men at Work: The Craft of Baseball*, Pulitzer Prize–winning columnist George Will profiled three players who were among the best at their respective specialties—pitching, hitting, and defense—and one manager, Tony La Russa. Will noted that La Russa's mother was of Spanish descent and spoke Spanish, that his father also spoke Spanish, and that La Russa himself spoke Spanish before he spoke English.[25] In fact many people have assumed that La Russa is Latino. What Will did not mention is that La Russa's father, Antonio, is of Italian descent. "My dad's family comes from the Catania province of Sicily," La Russa told me. "My mother's family came from Spain. My dad speaks Italian and Spanish, so we spoke Spanish in the home. My nickname as a kid was 'Tonin' [Italian for Little Antonio]. I was raised in a Latin American, Italian American community with a bunch of people who really loved baseball."[26]

Anthony La Russa Jr. was born in Tampa, Florida, in 1944. "My father was a fanatic about baseball," La Russa said. "He was a pretty good catcher but never played much because his father would require him to do chores. We never had a lot of extra money, and he worked so hard [as a wholesale milk salesman], but he always gave me every opportunity to play because he didn't want me to be frustrated like he was."

La Russa made it to the Majors, but like so many successful managers, he had a marginal career as a player, appearing in 132 games in six seasons. He recalled that he felt a sense of camaraderie with other Italian American players. He was an eighteen-year-old rookie infielder in 1963 when Rocky Colavito, then with the Tigers, said to him, "It's nice to have another Italian in the league." One of his roommates when he was with the A's was Sal Bando. "Because we had Italian backgrounds, there were a lot of similarities about beliefs and family."

Recognizing his limitations as a player, La Russa decided to pursue a law degree. "I always loved reading and problem solving, and I had friends who were lawyers, so that seemed like a good thing to do," he explained. He ultimately got the degree and passed the Florida bar exam in 1979—but not before being given the chance to manage in the White Sox organization in 1978.[27] After managing in the Minors for less than two full seasons, La Russa became, at thirty-four, the youngest manager in the Majors when the White Sox promoted him late in the 1979 season.

The same interests that led him to study law—reading and problem solving—have served La Russa well in his chosen profession. His reading material consists of statistical analysis and the strategies of opposing managers, both of which help him solve the problem of how to win games. And win he has. As of the end of 2009, in his thirty-one years with the White Sox, A's, and Cardinals, La Russa had won twelve divisional titles, five pennants, and two World Series. (When the Cardinals beat the Tigers to win the 2006 World Series, he became only the second manager—after Sparky Anderson—to win the Series in both leagues.) He has also won an unprecedented four Manager of the Year Awards, three in the NL, one in the AL. He also stood third on the all-time list of career wins. The only managers with more wins than La Russa's 2,552 through 2009 were the legendary duo of Connie Mack and John McGraw. After thirty-one years of managing, La Russa himself had become legendary, considered by many the best in the game. Roland Hemond, a baseball executive since 1961, was the White Sox GM who gave La Russa his first managerial job in 1979. "Tony La Russa," said Hemond, "is one of the brilliant minds of our game that I've come across."[28]

La Russa is quick to acknowledge managers who helped him at the start. "There were giants in the league then, guys like Sparky Anderson, Billy Martin, Chuck Tanner, Earl Weaver. All those guys

37. Tony La Russa. National Baseball Hall of Fame Library, Cooperstown NY.

answered a bunch of questions. Later on you realize just how great
their advice was."

Intensely focused, intelligent, and articulate, Tony La Russa does
not suffer fools gladly, a trait that has not endeared him to many

in the media. During a game he is either pacing like a restless cat or sternly surveying the action on the field, always searching for one more detail that might give his team an edge. In *Men at Work* George Will wrote that his book is about "men who are happy in their work."[29] Given his intensity and the edginess he displays throughout a game, La Russa does not appear to be someone happy in his work. But when I asked him what kept him motivated after all those years and more than 4,500 games, his answer made it clear that for all the anxiety and frustration that his job can inflict, it's what he was born to do. "As long as I get excited, I figure this is what I should be doing," he replied. "The key is, you've got a responsibility and an opportunity to put people in the right places and try to win games. If the fire keeps burning, I'm going to do it. If it doesn't, it would be cheating, and I don't want to cheat."

Joe Torre

As of 2009 of all Italian American managers, only La Russa had more career wins than Joe Torre, whose 2,246 victories placed him fifth on the all-time list. Thirty-six years old and in his third season playing for the Mets, Torre was named player/manager on May 31, 1977. His managerial debut did not go well, as the Mets never finished higher than fifth in five seasons. By the time he was fired in 1981, the consensus was that he had not done a good job, playing too much by the book. Notwithstanding his 286-420 record in New York, Torre was given a three-year contract by the Atlanta Braves in 1982, bringing him back to the franchise where he had started his playing career twenty-two years earlier. Things got off to a much better start in Atlanta, with a divisional title in his first year. But when the Braves fell to an 80-82 record two years later, Torre was fired again. Almost six years passed before he was given another shot with the Cardinals in August 1990. After logging winning records in his first three full seasons, in June 1995, with the Cardinals in fourth place, Torre was fired for a third time.

A year later Torre was hired to manage the Yankees, a move met with widespread skepticism in New York. Why hire this guy who had only five winning seasons in fourteen years? How long could he last under a win-now owner like Steinbrenner? Torre made believers of many of the skeptics in his first year by leading the Yankees to their first World Series title since Billy Martin's squad had won in 1978. The Series was made all the more dramatic and heartwarming by the story of Joe's older brother, Frank, who was on a life support machine in a New York hospital waiting for a heart transplant. On October 25, the day after the Yankees took a 3–2 lead over the Braves, the team for which he and his brother had played, Frank got his new heart.

If Torre's first championship made him less suspect, by 2000, when the Yankees won their fourth title in five years, he was an icon in his hometown. Torre, the AL manager of the year in 1996 and 1998, was always known as a players' manager, and this was never more true, or more effective, than when he piloted the Yankees. He had a veteran squad of professionals, and his low-key approach earned their respect and loyalty. His demeanor in the dugout became something of a signature. He sat there, impassive, inscrutable, his cap pulled down low over his dark, thick eyebrows, his heavy-lidded eyes focused on the field. No less recognizable was his slow, stiff-legged walk to the mound, as if he were in no hurry to bring the bad news to his pitcher. There were those who downplayed Torre's success, noting that he had never won with previous teams and benefited from Steinbrenner's deep pockets. (Of course Steinbrenner's deep pockets had failed to bring New York a title for seventeen years before Torre's arrival.) On the other side of the ledger, Torre provided calm, steady leadership

38. Joe Torre. National Baseball Hall of Fame Library, Cooperstown NY.

to a franchise so frequently unsettled by Steinbrenner's volatility and penchant for impulsive changes.

Ultimately winning was what kept you in "the Boss's" good graces, and even though Torre had taken the Yankees to the postseason every year of his tenure, the failure to win a World Series after 2000 was unacceptable. When the Yankees offered their longtime manager a one-year contract for 2008, with a pay cut, an insulted Torre walked away. His twelve years as Yankee manager (with a record of 1,173-767) equaled Casey Stengel's mark and was surpassed only by Joe McCarthy's fifteen-plus years. Soon after Torre declined the offer, Roger Angell wrote of him in the *New Yorker*: "He, at last, supplied the touch of class, the Augustan presence, that the Yankees had so persistently proclaimed for themselves and have now thrown away."[30] Two weeks after spurning the Yankees, the sixty-seven-year-old Torre accepted a three-year offer from the Dodgers, then led them to division titles in 2008 and 2009.

Joe Girardi, a Yankee catcher from 1996 to 1999, was hired to replace Torre in 2008. For someone who wore the so-called "tools of ignorance" for fifteen Major League seasons, Girardi brought to his profession an unlikely background. A native of Peoria, Illinois, he received a degree in industrial engineering from Northwestern University, where he was a three-time Academic All-American in baseball. In 2006, three years after his playing career ended, he was named manager of the Florida Marlins, who bounced back from being twenty games below .500 in May to finish at 78-84. As a result Girardi was named the NL manager of the year, only the third rookie to win the honor, but differences with management led to his dismissal at the end of the season. Girardi's first year as Torre's successor in New York was a disappointment, as the team finished third, failing to make the postseason for the first time since 1994. In 2009, Girardi's third year as a Major League manager, he led the Yankees to their twenty-seventh World Series title.

Girardi's paternal grandparents were from Turin, his maternal grandparents from Rome. Asked about his sense of ethnic identity, he said, "It's who I am; it's where my family is from. I feel blessed to have come from a home where both parents worked very hard to make our lives better." As for baseball, "Times have changed," he said. "Before, there were a lot more Italians in the game. Education is stressed more for athletes today. I was fortunate that my parents made me understand that school was first."[31]

Beginning with the arrival of Tony Lazzeri in 1926 and continuing with Crosetti, DiMaggio, Rizzuto, Berra, Raschi, and Martin, players of Italian descent had prominent roles with the great Yankee teams from the mid-1920s to the late 1950s. Then in the thirty-four years between 1975, when Martin was first hired, and 2009, with Girardi at the helm, the Yankees were managed by Italian Americans for all or part of twenty-three years. Given Berra's pennant win in 1964, Martin's World Series title in 1977, Torre's four championships, Girardi's World Series win in 2009, and the popularity they all enjoyed with the fans, it was as managers, not as players, that Italian Americans made their mark with the Yankees in the second half of the twentieth century.

16

Executive Suite

Seventy years passed from the time that Nicholas Apollonio was elected as the figurehead president of the Boston franchise in 1874 before there was another baseball executive of Italian descent. Coincidentally it was the very same Boston franchise that Lou Perini bought in 1944, becoming the first Italian American Major League owner. Seven years later, in 1951, Buzzie Bavasi became the first Italian American to be named general manager of a Major League franchise. At that time, however, Perini and Bavasi were the exceptions that proved the rule; there would not be another owner of Italian descent until 1972 and no general manager until 1991. But eventually, just as they did in other professions, increasing numbers of Italian Americans moved into executive positions in baseball in the 1970s and beyond. And in 1989 one of them rose to the game's highest position as commissioner.

General Managers

Emil "Buzzie" Bavasi was the son of a French immigrant from Marseilles and an Italian American named Rosaria Maggio. (It was his sister Iola who gave him his nickname because he was always "buzzing" around.)[1] According to Bavasi's son Peter, "Even though he was one-half French, Buzzie very much thought of himself as an Italian American. And to his colleagues in baseball, Buzz was Italian. And so are we, his four sons."[2]

Born in New York on December 12, 1915, Bavasi began his long career in baseball in 1939, when he was hired by the Dodgers as an assistant to the traveling secretary. Following two years of service in World War II—he was awarded the Bronze Star after seeing action on the Italian front—he became general manager of Brooklyn's Class B club in Nashua, New Hampshire, in 1946. (It was Bavasi who agreed to take Roy Campanella and Don Newcombe after another Dodger farm team had refused.) After three years as GM of the Triple A Montreal affiliate, he was named general manager of the Dodgers in 1951, a position he held until 1968. During his tenure as GM, which included the postwar glory years and the move to Los Angeles, the Dodgers won eight National League pennants and four World Series. Roger Kahn, who covered the Dodgers as a beat writer in 1952 and '53, said that Bavasi "had a little of the Sinatra quality, poised, good-looking, always would pick up the check, was fun to be with."[3]

In 1968 Bavasi parted company with the Dodgers to become half owner of the expansion San Diego Padres, serving as president and general manager. Not surprisingly, the new franchise struggled, never finishing above .500 or higher than fourth place in the eight years of Bavasi's stewardship. After heading north to become GM of the California Angels in 1978, Bavasi was replaced in September 1984, ending his thirty-four consecutive years as a Major League executive.

Acknowledged as one of the game's great executives and an astute judge of talent, Bavasi made one series of moves that proved unpopular with one observer in particular. During his time in San Diego, where money was always a concern, he received a phone call after trading three players: Al Santorini, Al Ferrara, and Ed Spiezio. When he answered, the caller asked, "Am I next?," then hung up. Realizing it was his mother, he called her back to ask what was wrong. "Well," she said, "you sold three Italians in a row. I figured I was next."[4]

Two of Bavasi's four sons followed in his footsteps. After four years as farm director of the Padres, Peter Bavasi replaced his father as GM in 1973, a position he held through 1976. In 1977 he became the executive vice president and GM of the expansion Toronto Blue Jays and from 1979 to 1981, their president; from November 1984 to January 1987 he served as president of the Cleveland Indians. His brother, Bill, was director of the Angels Minor League Operations from 1983 to 1993 before being promoted to GM in 1994. He then served as director of player development for the Dodgers in 2002–3 and as GM of the Seattle Mariners for four and a half years before being replaced in June 2008.

In 1998, seven years after Sal Bando had become the second general manager of Italian descent, Joe Garagiola Jr. was named GM of the expansion Arizona Diamondbacks. Garagiola typifies the generation of postwar Italian Americans who were able to pursue higher education and move into the professions. A graduate of Notre Dame, he received a law degree from Georgetown in 1975 and spent two years as an in-house attorney for the Yankees before venturing out on his own as an agent. After moving to Arizona in 1982, he became involved in the effort to bring Major League Baseball to the Phoenix area, working with Jerry Colangelo, majority owner of the NBA Phoenix Suns. When the franchise was awarded in 1995, he accepted Colangelo's offer to work full time with the expansion Diamondbacks. Garagiola served as the team's GM from their initial season in 1998 until August 2005, when he was appointed by Major League

Baseball as senior vice president of baseball operations. In Garagiola's seven-plus years as GM the Diamondbacks won three division titles and the 2001 World Series.

In a 1999 interview in Phoenix Garagiola spoke about his heritage. "My dad's parents were immigrants from Inveruno, a little town outside Milan," he said. "What courage they had. Somehow my grandfather makes his way from Inveruno to Milan to wherever the boat left from, takes the boat to New York, gets on the train, and rides one thousand miles into the heart of this country, where he can barely speak the language. Two generations later, here I am. That's what I think about in terms of what being an Italian American means and how fortunate I am to be able to stand on his shoulders and on my dad's."[5]

Some of the general managers younger than Garagiola were often not only college graduates, but also part of a new breed of technologically savvy baseball people more comfortable with a laptop than with a radar gun or stopwatch. Disciples of Bill James, the founding father of the statistical analysis of baseball known as sabermetrics, they put more faith in numbers than did their predecessors, who relied more heavily on the observations and instincts of their scouting staffs. The prototype of the techno GM was Billy Beane of the Oakland A's, whose success in finding young talent overlooked by others and building a winning team on a minimal budget was celebrated in Michael Lewis's 2003 book, *Moneyball: The Art of Winning an Unfair Game*.

According to Lewis, pivotal to Beane's success was a young assistant he hired in 1998 named Paul DePodesta, a 1995 cum laude graduate of Harvard with a degree in economics. Even before he was hired by Beane, DePodesta had "plugged the statistics of every baseball team from the twentieth century into an equation and tested which of them correlated most closely with winning percentage," concluding that on-base percentage and slugging average far outweighed other factors.[6] Lewis also credits DePodesta with adapting and refining the analytical techniques of James and others into a model capable of predicting how draft-potential amateurs might perform as professional ballplayers, giving the A's an edge in recruitment and player development. In his five years with Oakland the team had a record of 392-255, which tied the best winning percentage in the Majors over that period.

In February 2004 DePodesta was named general manager of the Dodgers, becoming, at thirty-one, the fourth youngest GM ever. (He had turned down an offer from the Blue Jays to be their GM when he was only twenty-eight.) In his first year in Los Angeles DePodesta helped assemble the roster that won the NL West division title, but when the team fell to a 71-91 record in 2005, he was fired by owner Frank McCourt. When catcher Paul Lo Duca, considered by many to be the heart and soul of the team, was traded in July 2004, DePodesta incurred the wrath of fans. Some sportswriters also vilified him, fueling speculation that they had been skeptical from the start about a young sabermetrician GM they perceived as a computer nerd. In 2006 DePodesta was hired by the San Diego Padres as vice president and special assistant for baseball operations.

DePodesta was replaced as the Dodgers GM by Ned Colletti, who had previously served for nine years as the Giants assistant GM. A Chicago native and graduate of Northern Illinois University, Colletti had begun his baseball career in 1982 with the Cubs, first in media relations, then in baseball operations. The Dodgers rebounded under Colletti, who was more old school than new breed, winning the NL West division title in 2008, the year that he had hired Joe Torre as manager.

When Billy Beane was playing for the Mets' Class A team in Little Falls, New York, one of his teammates was J. P. Ricciardi. Neither came close to making the big leagues as players, but when Beane became the A's GM in 1997, he named Ricciardi director of player personnel. A protégé of Beane's sabermetric approach to talent evaluation, Ricciardi was hired as the Toronto Blue Jays' GM prior to the 2002 season in the hope that he could bring the same kind of success to another small-budget franchise. At the time of Ricciardi's hiring noted baseball analyst Peter Gammons wrote that the Blue Jays had gotten "the man who just might be the single best evaluator of talent in the major leagues today."[7] Success did not come immediately, but after losing seasons in three of Ricciardi's first four years in Toronto, the Blue Jays put together three consecutive winning seasons in the tough AL East Division. However, another losing season in 2009 led to Ricciardi's dismissal.

Owners

One of the true innovators of the game, Lou Perini was not only the first Major League owner of Italian descent, but he was also an early proponent of expansion and the first owner to move a franchise since 1900. It was an unlikely résumé for someone who became a construction worker before he ever got to high school. Born in Ashland, Massachusetts, in 1903, Perini was one of thirteen children born to Bonfiglio and Clementina Perini. Bonfiglio was part of the early wave of immigrants, coming to America in the 1880s from his hometown of Gottolengo in the northern Italian province of Brescia. A stonemason, he formed his own construction company in 1892. As a youngster, Lou Perini played sandlot ball in Ashland, but his playing days ended when he left school after the eighth grade to work in his father's company. When Bonfiglio died in 1924, Lou, then twenty-one, became president of what would become one of the largest construction companies in the nation.

Perini never lost his love for baseball, and if he couldn't play the game, he would do the next best thing: buy a Major League team. "He was an inherent entrepreneur," said his son David in a telephone interview. "When he became interested in the Braves in the late thirties, they were a floundering team, but he saw the potential. It became like a challenge for him; he was a real risk taker."[8] In fact the Braves had been a second-division team for nine straight years when, together with two other local contractors, Guido Rugo and Joe Maney, Perini purchased the Braves in January 1944. They became known as the "Three Little Steam Shovels," though it was Perini, the youngest of the three at forty, who was the principal owner. In 1951 Perini and his two brothers, Charles and Joseph, became full owners of the Braves.

Initially the Braves continued to struggle under their new owners, but in 1948, led by the pitching duo of Johnny Sain and Warren Spahn, they won their first pennant since 1914 before losing to the Indians in the World Series. The success was short-lived, however, and by 1952 the Braves had fallen to seventh place. The fall in attendance was no less dramatic; from a high of 1.4 million in 1948 it had plummeted to a little over 281,000 in 1952. That was when Perini made his historic decision to move the team to Milwaukee, the first franchise shift since 1900. David Perini described the response to the move as traumatic. "My father got a lot of hate mail, and the press was after him," he said. "He just felt in his heart that the demographics weren't right for two teams and that the Red Sox would always outdraw the Braves. It took a lot of guts."

The move proved to be an immediate success for the Braves, who drew 1.8 million fans in 1953, then topped 2 million the next four years. The team also flourished on the field. Led by future Hall of Famers Warren Spahn, Eddie Matthews, and Hank Aaron, they beat the Yankees in the 1957 World Series before losing to them the next year. Eventually attendance sagged, and in 1962 Perini sold the club to a group of Chicago investors.

No less important than the move itself was the ripple effect it had on Major League Baseball. By disrupting the status quo that had existed in baseball's alignment for more than a half century, Lou Perini opened the door for further franchise shifts and ultimately for the expansion of Major League Baseball. The year after the Braves' shift, the St. Louis Browns moved to Baltimore and became the Orioles, and one year later the Philadelphia Athletics moved to Kansas City. Then in 1958 the Dodgers and Giants transferred to the West Coast, certainly encouraged by Perini's sudden success in Milwaukee.

Perini had tried to shake up the baseball world even before he made the move to Milwaukee. The front-page headline in the April 25, 1951, issue of the *Sporting News* read: "12-Club Major Loops Urged by Perini." A strong proponent of air travel, he envisioned the expansion of each league to twelve teams, with franchises located not only on the West Coast, but possibly even in Canada and Mexico. "Can the major leagues afford to stand still?" he asked. "Maybe, after all, we haven't yet begun to scratch the surface for ways and means to spread the gospel of America's National Game."[9]

Perini, who made several visits to Italy, was also ahead of his time in promoting the international development of the game. Even before the war he had proposed sending Major League teams to Italy to play exhibition games, and it was reported in 1952 that he was sending uniforms and equipment to Italy "so the Italian youth may learn the thrills of America's national pastime."[10] In 1958, at the invitation of Baseball for Italy, a nonprofit organization co-chaired by Perini and television personality Ed Sullivan, Prince Steno Borghese, commissioner of Italian baseball, came to the United States to request aid in developing the sport in his country.[11]

On some of his trips to Italy Perini visited his father's hometown of Gottolengo. "There's a street there named after my grandfather," said David Perini. "He would send money to an orphanage there after he became successful in the construction business. My father was extremely proud of his heritage, and he never let us forget our humble roots."

In 1972, twenty-eight years after Perini bought the Braves, Cleveland native Nick Mileti became the second owner of Italian descent. (Born Nicolo Mileti, he was the son of Vincenzo and Giuseppina Mileti, immigrants from Alcara Li Fusi, Sicily.) A graduate of Bowling Green State University and Ohio State Law School, Mileti practiced law in Cleveland, but in the late sixties he turned his attention to sports. In 1968 he bought the Cleveland Barons of the American Hockey League, and two years later he was awarded an NBA expansion team, which he named the Cleveland Cavaliers. Meanwhile, the Cleveland Indians were losing games (102 in 1971), attendance, and money. Concerned that owner Vernon Stouffer was about to move the team, Mileti headed a group of investors that purchased the franchise in March 1972. After opening the twenty-two-thousand-seat Richfield Coliseum in 1974 to house the Cavaliers, he sold his interest in the Indians in 1975. In 2002 *Cleveland Magazine* named Mileti one of Cleveland's thirty most influential people of the last thirty years. After moving to Hollywood, where he produced and financed plays and movies, Mileti retired in 1989 and moved to Rome, where for three years he immersed himself in the study of Italian culture.

Five years after Mileti sold the Indians, Edward DeBartolo's bid to buy the Chicago White Sox was rejected by the other owners. The son of immigrant parents, Anthony and Rose Paonessa, DeBartolo was born in Youngstown, Ohio, in 1919. After his father died, he took the name of his stepfather, Michael DeBartolo, an immigrant from Bari. A graduate of Notre Dame in civil engineering, DeBartolo made his fortune by developing shopping malls across the country. In 1977 he purchased the NFL franchise San Francisco 49ers, which, under the direction of his son, Edward DeBartolo Jr., won four Super Bowl championships. In 1980 DeBartolo Sr. attempted to buy the White Sox from Bill Veeck, who agreed to sell the team for $20 million. But the other owners rejected DeBartolo's offer, purportedly because he owned a racetrack and because he would be an absentee owner. (At the time Yankee owner George Steinbrenner was an owner of Florida Downs and lived in Tampa.) In his study of the business of baseball, *Lords of the Realm*, John Helyar wrote that the owners had been encouraged to reject DeBartolo's bid by Commissioner Bowie Kuhn: "The real reason was that he was reputed to have some un-savory associations—Italian-American, don't you know. As Bowie Kuhn put it over cocktails while lobbying a baseball executive, 'He's not RP.' Come again? 'Right people.'"[12] What remained unspoken were the innuendos that DeBartolo had links to organized crime figures, even though law enforcement investigations never turned up any evidence. DeBartolo died in December 1994.

Jerry Colangelo: From the NBA to MLB

When Jerry Colangelo was just starting to gain notoriety as a high school athlete in the Chicago area, an old-timer he described as a "kind of neighborhood counselor" said to him, "You know, you're going to have to change your name." When Colangelo asked him why, he said, "Because they're going to hold you back because of your name. You have to change it or shorten it, Americanize it." To which Colangelo replied, "I'll never do that. I'm too proud of my heritage."[13]

In spite of his friend's warning, by all indications Colangelo's name did not hold him back. After starring in basketball at the University of Illinois, he went on to become one of the most influential figures in professional sports. In 1968, at age twenty-eight, he became the general manager of the expansion Phoenix Suns in the NBA. When he and others purchased the franchise in 1987, he became president and CEO. (His son Bryan served as general manager of the Suns for eleven years before being named president and general manager of the NBA Toronto Raptors in 2006.) Colangelo was also instrumental in the construction of the nineteen-thousand-seat America West Arena, which opened in 1992, and he brought to Phoenix a WNBA team (the Phoenix Mercury) and an arena football team (the Arizona Rattlers). A four-time NBA executive of the year, he was inducted into the Basketball Hall of Fame in 2004. As managing director of the USA Basketball Men's Senior National Team, he assembled the coaches and players of the Olympic squad that won the gold medal at the 2008 games in Beijing.

In 1995 Colangelo brought Major League Baseball to Arizona when he and his fellow investors were awarded an expansion team. With Joe Garagiola Jr. as their GM, the Arizona Diamondbacks made their debut in 1998. Success came quickly. The very next year the newcomers won one hundred games and the NL West division title. In 2001, only their fourth season, the Diamondbacks became the youngest franchise to win a World Series, beating the defending champion Yankees in seven games. But success came at a high price. Colangelo spent heavily on expensive players like Randy Johnson and Curt Schilling in those first years, resulting in substantial debt, which in turn led his partners to replace him as CEO in 2004. For his role in bringing professional sports to the state, the *Arizona Republic* named him the most influential sports figure in Arizona of the twentieth century.

Born in 1939, Colangelo was the grandson of Giovanni and Rosina Colangelo, immigrants from a village east of Naples. He grew up in the "Hungry Hill" section of Chicago Heights, in the house his grandfather built using material from railroad boxcars. Describing "Hungry Hill" as a "blue-collar, lunch-pail neighborhood," he said, "I have great memories of that childhood, growing up in a poor ethnic neighborhood. We were thankful for whatever we had." On the day his grandfather died, Colangelo, fifteen at the time, was scheduled to pitch in a game. Told by his parents that his grandfather would have wanted him to play, he threw a no-hitter. "In the last inning I was crying the whole time because I wanted to do it for him."

Colangelo had lived in Arizona for more than thirty years when I met with him in his office at the America West Arena in 1999. But there were obvious reminders that he had not lost touch with his heritage. Within a few feet of his desk was what he called his "roots corner," which included a photo of his boyhood home, which by then stood on a street named Colangelo Way in his honor. Below the picture was the accordion on which he had played Italian tunes for his grandfather. On a nearby credenza, among several small statues depicting athletes in action, stood a statue of Christopher Columbus.

"Being born here, we're Americans," Colangelo said. "But we shouldn't lose sight of the fact that we're of Italian heritage, and we should be proud of that. And we should be proud of those who've been able to achieve in this world, many against great obstacles. Baseball offered an opportunity for people of all descents. If they showed they had the physical ability, they had a chance."

Another indication of Colangelo's connection to his heritage is the role he played in the development of the National Italian American Sports Hall of Fame in Chicago. Its founder and chairman, George Randazzo, is a native Chicagoan and the grandson of immigrants from Sicily. After initially establishing the Italian American Boxing Hall of Fame in 1977, he expanded the project the following year to honor Italian Americans in all sports. Among its first inductees in 1978 were Joe and Dom DiMaggio. In 1998 Randazzo enlisted the help of Colangelo (a 1994 inductee) in raising funds to build a new facility in the Little Italy section of Chicago on Taylor Street. Calling on friends in the sports world, Colangelo was able to raise almost $2 million, enabling the new building to be dedicated in 2000 as the Jerry Colangelo Center. "We couldn't have put up the building without the help of Jerry," said Randazzo."[14]

By 2008 the Italian American Hall of Fame had honored more than two hundred inductees. Across the street from the hall is Piazza DiMaggio, a gift from the City of Chicago, featuring a statue of the Yankee Clipper. In his statement on the hall's Web site as chairman of the National Leadership Committee, Colangelo writes the following: "The Hall of Fame seeks to pass on the values that drove Italian American immigrants to succeed to the next generation of young men and women, supporting community outreach and contributing over $6 million to scholarship programs that promote diversity, education, and the discipline and perseverance necessary to succeed both in sports and in life."[15]

At the same time that Colangelo secured a franchise for Phoenix, Vince Naimoli did the same for Tampa Bay. The son of a second-generation Italian American, the New Jersey native received an engineering degree from Notre Dame and an MBA from Fairleigh Dickinson

University. At a 1995 news conference Naimoli explained that the new team would be named the Devil Rays because devil rays are "so gentle they'll let humans ride them and pet them." Jerry Colangelo, on the other hand, offered a different rationale for the name of his team. "We're a little more aggressive in Arizona," he said. "You don't pet and you don't ride diamondback rattlesnakes. We wanted to put some bite into our name."[16]

There was little bite to the Devil Rays, however. In the five years of Naimoli's ownership, from 1998 to 2005, they finished last in the AL East each year, losing at least 91 games and as many as 106 in 2002. Equally feeble was their ability to draw fans. After a first-year total of 1.5 million, attendance fell off dramatically, ranking last in the American League from 2001 to 2007. In addition, there were rumors of bankruptcy in 2001, and there was concern that the team would be eliminated when Major League Baseball was considering contraction in 2002. At the end of the 2005 season Naimoli's share in the team was bought out by new owner Stuart Sternberg.

Recent Owners

In the old days one of the common images of Italian immigrants was that of the fruit and vegetable peddlers hawking their wares out of small push carts on crowded city streets. One example of how far Italian Americans have come since then is the Castellini Group of Companies. Now one of the nation's largest distributors of fresh produce, it was started in Cincinnati in 1896 as J. J. Castellini Fruits and Vegetables. In January 2006 the company's chairman, Robert Castellini, became the newest owner of the oldest team in professional baseball. When he and his partners purchased the Cincinnati Reds, Castellini became the CEO of a franchise whose history dates back to 1869, when the Red Stockings became the first openly professional team in the country.

A Cincinnati native, Castellini had long been involved with Major League Baseball, having been a partner in the Texas Rangers and the Baltimore Orioles and an investor in the St. Louis Cardinals. Like many business executives, Castellini, with a degree in economics from Georgetown and an MBA from the Wharton School, proved to be a decisive owner. Wasting no time in shaking up a team that had endured five straight losing seasons, he replaced the team's general manager only three days after taking over, then made another change two years later.

At a 2007 panel discussion at the Wharton School on "Leadership Lessons Learned from Sports," Castellini said that his model for building a team depended on finding players with both character and a winning attitude and coaches able to motivate them. He also pointed out something that Tommy Lasorda had told him: "While it's important to have chemistry in the clubhouse, if you don't have the talent, you don't win."[17] After contending for much of the season and climbing to third place in 2006, the Reds fell back to fifth place the following two seasons, and the storied franchise was still looking for its first winning season since 2000.

One recent owner whose team had more immediate success is Mark Attanasio. He was a native New Yorker who operated his business out of Los Angeles, but it was in the Midwest that he made his mark on baseball, investing new money, and instilling new life, into the Milwaukee Brewers. In 2005 the then forty-seven-year-old executive of a money management firm purchased the team brought to Milwaukee in 1970 by a group led by Bud Selig, who relinquished the day-to-day operations of the club to his daughter, Wendy Selig-Prieb, when he became commissioner in 1998. Born in the Bronx in 1957, Attanasio came from a middle-class family; both his father Joseph, an engineer, and his mother Connie (Greco) were college educated. Mark himself got an Ivy League education, graduating from Brown in 1979 and receiving a law degree from Columbia in 1982. The great-grandson of immigrants from Positano on Italy's Amalfi coast, Attanasio retains his ties to his roots by taking his family, including his parents, to Italy each summer. "My father is conversational in Italian and loves the country," he said in a 2005 interview. "My mother, on the other hand, is fluent in Italian."[18]

At the time Attanasio became the principal owner, it had been twelve years since the Brewers, a classic small-market team, had had a winning season and twenty-six years since they were in the post-season. In 2005 the Brewers' payroll of $40 million ranked twenty-seventh among the thirty Major League franchises, but by 2008 the Brewers had moved to the middle of the pack with a payroll of $81 million. That was the year GM Doug Melvin made a midseason deal that brought to Milwaukee the reigning Cy Young Award winner, "CC" Sabathia, who went on to an 11-2 record in leading the Brewers to a wild-card spot. In four years under new ownership the Brewers' payroll doubled, and the team ended a twenty-six-year playoff drought.

Larry Lucchino: Rediscovering His Roots

By the time he became president and CEO of the Red Sox in 2002, Larry Lucchino had been involved in Major League Baseball for twenty-eight years and had served as president and CEO of both the Orioles (1988–93) and Padres (1995–2001). No stranger to winning teams, having won a pennant with the Padres and a World Series with the Orioles, Lucchino, along with partners John Henry and Tom Werner, helped guide the Red Sox to their first World Series title in eighty-six years in 2004, followed by another championship in 2007.

Lucchino got his start in professional sports when he went to work at the law firm founded by famed trial attorney Edward Bennett Williams. When Williams bought the Orioles in 1979, he named Lucchino vice president and general counsel and, in 1988, president. From 1992 to the end of the '93 season Lucchino was president and CEO, then held that same position with San Diego before moving to Boston.

This is an impressive résumé for the grandson of immigrants from the southern Italian region of Calabria who settled in Pittsburgh and were city employees. Both of Lucchino's parents, Dominic and Rose (Rizzo) Lucchino, were born in Pittsburgh, as was Lucchino in 1945. "My father was one of six and my mother one of seven children, so there were always plenty of uncles and aunts around," he told me. "There was definitely a sense of Italian food, culture, and family values that permeated our home."[19] An all-city basketball player in high school, Lucchino graduated with honors from Princeton, where he played on the 1965 Final Four team that starred future basketball Hall of Famer and senator Bill Bradley.

Like many second- and third-generation Italian Americans, Lucchino and his brother were the first in the family to attend college. "I was a bit of a black sheep in that I went off to college and lived in other cities," he said. "My older brother, Frank, a judge, still lives in Pittsburgh. He's more of a typical Italian American. I left a multiethnic community, surrounded by Italians, Germans, and Croatians, and went to Princeton. As I was making that transition, I saw that I was different because of my name. I had an ethnic name as opposed to an old-line American name."

Things were different when he went to law school at Yale. "I liked New Haven because it had a very strong Italian culture and community. There I had one foot in town and one in gown, and I felt comfortable in both. I was a person in transition from an ethnic enclave to a broader American society, and I think I lost some sense of ethnic identity. I began to recover it in New Haven." The recovery of his identity continued when, right after law school, Lucchino visited his maternal grandmother's hometown of Motta Santa Lucia in Calabria and stayed with relatives. "I stayed in a farmhouse built in the sixteenth or seventeenth century, with frescoes on the wall," he recalled. "It was like a scene out of a movie. I was welcomed with open arms. I sent a card to my parents letting them know I was going to find an Italian girl to marry."

Lucchino's experience as a young Italian American growing up after the war was not unlike that of many of his generation. "My grandmother lived with us, and she spoke Italian to my mother," he said. "I regret that I didn't learn the language, but at that time I wanted to be an American. The older and wiser I get, the more I recover a sense of my ethnic identity. I have a keen sense of pride in my heritage." One thing of which Larry Lucchino is clearly aware is that his success was made possible by the sacrifices of those who came before him. "Italian Americans faced perils," he said, "but America has provided opportunities, in spite of the early difficulties."

The Commissioner

No one, I think, better epitomizes the culmination of the evolution of Italian Americans in baseball—or in American society, for that matter—than Angelo Bartlett Giamatti. The grandson of an immigrant laborer, Giamatti became the president of Yale, then president of the National League before ascending to the office of Commissioner of Major League Baseball. Granted, Giamatti's heritage was mixed—on his mother's side he was descended from New England Yankees—but he understood better than most the nature and significance of the immigrant experience, and he wrote about it eloquently, as he did about baseball. In fact the significance of his impact on baseball is not just that he rose to its highest office, but that he was also one of its most passionate and articulate exponents.

Giamatti's paternal grandparents immigrated at the turn of the century to New Haven, Connecticut, from Telese Terme, a small town northeast of Naples. Angelo Giammattei (as the family name was originally spelled) worked as a laborer at the New Haven Clock Company. His son Valentine, who earned a bachelor's degree from Yale and a PhD from Harvard, became a professor of Italian at Mount Holyoke College and married Mary Claybaugh Walton, a descendant of New England sea captains and shoe manufacturers. Angelo Bartlett Giamatti, named for both his Italian and Yankee grandfathers, was born in Boston, while his father was at Harvard, on April 4, 1938. In 1940 the family moved to South Hadley, Massachusetts, when Valentine was hired at Mount Holyoke. At home Giamatti absorbed Italian culture from his father, but the world outside his front door was that of a classic Yankee New England town, complete with village green, whose history dated to 1662. (Having grown up only a few miles from South Hadley, I knew it as a place inclined more to Calvinist sobriety than to Mediterranean exuberance.) Growing up, Bart, as he preferred to be called, spent two years in Italy, when he was nine—while his father was on sabbatical—and again when he was in high school. In his dual biography of Giamatti and Pete Rose, James Reston Jr. quoted Giamatti as saying that his time in Italy "gave him a 'bifocal sense, a doubleness of view' . . . making him an 'amalgam' of both Italian and American cultures."[20]

Unlike Valentine Giamatti, who turned away from the blue-collar work of his father to pursue an academic career, Bart Giamatti did follow in his father's footsteps by going to Yale and becoming a professor of literature. But he hedged his bet somewhat on the ethnic issue. Rather than focusing solely on Italian literature and Dante, as his father had done, he received a PhD in comparative literature from Yale, specializing in English and Italian literature, as if to mirror the duality of his ethnic heritage. Even the fact that he identified himself as A. Bartlett Giamatti, rather than as Angelo, suggests some ambiguity about his ethnic identity or about his reluctance to be perceived as too "Italian."

Whatever ambivalence he may have had, in at least one way Giamatti expressed his affinity for his Italian heritage as a youngster. A passionate baseball fan, he compiled his own Italian American All-Star team: Berra was the catcher; Camilli, Lazzeri, Crosetti, and Rizzuto made up the infield; the DiMaggio brothers, Mele, Zarilla, and Furillo were in the outfield; and Raschi and Maglie were his pitchers.[21] It was a team inevitably heavy with Yankees, but Giamatti was devoted to the Red Sox, and especially to his personal hero, second baseman Bobby Doerr. His dream of emulating Doerr ended when he failed to make his high school team. Instead he became the team manager, an early forecast of his future as an administrator.

After receiving his PhD in 1964, Giamatti taught at Princeton for two years before returning to Yale. A popular teacher and active scholar, he published works, such as *Exile and Change in Renaissance Literature*, that reflected his interest in the influence of Italian Renaissance writers on English literature. He also strode across campus wearing a Red Sox cap. Then in December 1977, in the same city where his immigrant grandfather had worked in a factory, Angelo Bartlett Giamatti was named president of Yale, that bastion of the old-stock American establishment. At thirty-nine, he was the youngest ever to hold that post, as well as the first "ethnic." A *New York Times* article noted that Yale "has moved away from traditional stereotypes in regard to leadership of the university," adding, "Many people have interpreted Dr. Giamatti's Italian background as a further sign of relaxation of the old criteria."[22]

It was while he was president of Yale that Giamatti was one of the twelve prominent Italian Americans featured on the cover of the May 15, 1983, issue of the *New York Times Magazine*. Three years later, in June 1986, the Renaissance scholar with the neatly trimmed goatee and irreverent wit was named the twelfth president of the National League. It was almost the job that he had always wanted; when he was a candidate for president of Yale, he was quoted as saying that the only thing he had ever wanted to be president of was the American League. When the opportunity came along, he readily gave up one of the most prestigious positions in academia to become a baseball administrator. When asked at a press conference what Dante, the author of *The Divine Comedy*, would have thought about his move, he said, "He would have been delighted. He knew very well the nature of paradise, and what preceded it. After all, baseball was first played in the Elysian Fields, in Hoboken, N.J., in 1845."[23] It was while he was president of the National League that Giamatti demonstrated his knowledge of the history and character of Italians and Italian Americans in his lengthy 1987 "Commentary," written for a documentary volume entitled *The Italian Americans*.[24]

On April 1, 1989, Giamatti succeeded Peter Ueberroth as Commissioner of Major League Baseball. Within two generations the grandson of an Italian immigrant had risen to the pinnacle of America's national game, the same game that most immigrants once considered a waste of time. Not gifted with the talent to play the game, Giamatti found another way to realize the dream of becoming a Major Leaguer that he shared with so many of his generation.

39. Angelo Bartlett Giamatti, Commissioner of Major League Baseball. National Baseball Hall of Fame Library, Cooperstown NY.

As commissioner, Giamatti was no less a traditionalist than he had been as a teacher and scholar. For him sports are an attempt to return to a lost paradise, a place always envisioned as "an enclosed, green space," much like the green field of a baseball park. "*Paradise*," the word later applied to the Garden of Eden, "derives from the Avestan word *paridaēza*, for enclosure, meaning the enclosure or park of the King."[25] At the same time that he rhapsodized about the metaphysical implications of baseball, Giamatti championed the simple pleasures of the game as he assumed the role of watchdog over its integrity. Artificial turf, the designated hitter, exploding scoreboards: these were all anathema to his perception of the way the game should be played. On the occasion of being named president of the National League, he had told the gathered press, "I favor the fundamental grid, the geometric beauty, the fundamental structure of the history of baseball, and I think it ought to be tampered with very gingerly."[26]

Giamatti's brief term as commissioner was primarily consumed by the issue of alleged gambling on baseball by Pete Rose, one of the most popular players in the game and the holder of the all-time record for career hits. While the question as to whether Rose had in fact bet on baseball was not officially resolved, a six-month investigation did conclude that Rose had associated with known gamblers and drug dealers. When Giamatti announced, on August 24, 1989, his decision to ban Rose from baseball for life because of "a variety of acts which have stained the game," he called it "the sad end of a sorry episode." Baseball, he added, "because it has such a purchase on our national soul, has an obligation to the people for whom it is played—to its fans and well-wishers—to strive for excellence in all things and to promote the highest ideals."[27] Nine days after that announcement Giamatti died of a heart attack at his summer home on Martha's Vineyard, five months to the day after he had become commissioner. He was fifty-one years old.

There is of course no way to know how Giamatti would have fared as commissioner had he lived. Given his conservative stance about the structure of the game and knowing how radically that structure would change with the advent of expansion and divisional play, one wonders how he would have eventually fared in dealing with owners. An essay Giamatti wrote for the *New York Times* op-ed page during the baseball strike of 1981 suggests a possible collision course with owners and/or players had his term as commissioner continued. Calling the strike a "triumph of greed over the spirit of the garden," he appealed, with characteristic rhetorical flourish, to both owners and players to resolve their differences: "O, Sovereign Owners and Princely Players, masters of amortization, tax shelters, bonuses and deferred compensation, go back to work. . . . Reassume your dignity and remember that you are the temporary custodians of an enduring public trust."[28]

Even though Giamatti had little chance, beyond his ruling on the Rose case, to demonstrate what his concrete contributions might have been, his love of the game, demonstrated in both his defense of its traditions and his eloquent celebrations of its meaning, were enough to convince many of his unique status in the game. *New York Times* columnist Ira Berkow speculated that Giamatti, "this most cultured and civilized and warm and generous and witty man . . . might have become the best baseball commissioner we've ever had. He had brains, sinew, and the best wishes of the game." George Will wrote that Giamatti "was to the Commissioner's office what Sandy Koufax was to the pitcher's mound: Giamatti's career had the highest ratio of excellence to longevity." Former umpire Bruce Froemming said, "I loved Bart. I think he would have done a terrific job down the line." Bud Selig, who would later become commissioner himself, chaired the search committee that selected Giamatti for that post in 1988. "I was stunned at how much he knew about the game itself, its inner workings," Selig told me. "I remember saying to myself, 'How could we find anybody else so smart, so articulate?' He was one of the most remarkable human beings I've ever met."[29]

Not surprisingly for a student of literature, Bart Giamatti was given to symbolic thought. For him, the ultimate fan who saw in the game he loved a clear expression of the national psyche, baseball became a metaphorical expression of the American Dream, not as material fulfillment but as a spiritual quest for home. The basic rhythm of baseball—the going out and the subsequent quest to return home— is "part of America's mysterious, underlying design . . . the plot of the story of our national life." That plot is "the story of going home after having left home, the story of how difficult it is to find the origins one so deeply needs to find." And, to return to a point first raised in the introduction to this volume, "The concept of home has a particular resonance for a nation of immigrants, all of whom left one home to seek another."[30] Elsewhere Giamatti wrote that baseball is "no game but a work of art fashioned to remind us that we all began in the great green Elysian Field of the New World, with all its terrors and promises."[31]

Giamatti's immigrant grandparents, like mine and all those who came in the great wave of migration, endured the terrors they encountered in America in the hope that their new home would fulfill its promise of providing a better life for those who came after them. One goal of this book has been to document the many ways that the descendants of those immigrants enriched baseball throughout the twentieth century, both on and off the field. However, no claim is made here that Italian Americans fundamentally changed the way the game is played. Instead this book is more about the impact the game has had on Italian Americans, as both participants and spectators, in terms of their sense of self identity.

As it was for immigrants from all nations, baseball was a symbol of the possibility of success and acceptance, either directly for those who played the game at the highest level or indirectly for those who were inspired by the success of others to see the possibility that the promise of America might indeed be both real and realized. Along with that promise came the other reality of making it in America—a certain willingness to sacrifice at least a part of the Old World traditions inherited from the first generation, to weaken if not sever the strong bond of family unity that had been the core value transplanted from the country of origin. No judgment need be passed on the choice to venture out of the safe harbor that the family provided into the larger world. That choice is simply part of the historical pattern of American life, the evolution from being an outsider to becoming part of a larger, more heterogeneous culture. It is the bargain we strike in becoming part of the great American experiment, an experiment that is continually modified and renewed by all those who come here from other lands in search of a new home.

Notes

Introduction

1. Giamatti, "Baseball and the American Character," 41–42; *Take Time for Paradise*, 92.

2. Levi, *Christ Stopped at Eboli*, 4.

3. Carr, "The Coming of the Italians," 419.

4. Gambino, *Blood of My Blood*, 71.

5. Mormino, "The Playing Fields of St. Louis," 8.

6. Sweeney, "Mental Tests for Immigrants," *North American Review* 215 (May 1922): 611, quoted in Guglielmo, *White on Arrival*, 61; Diggins, *Mussolini and Fascism*, 12.

7. Quoted in Richards, *Italian American*, 175.

8. Salvatore Mondello, "Italian Immigration to the U.S. as Reported in American Magazines 1880–1920," *Social Science* 29 (June 1964): 131–42; quoted in Diggins, *Mussolini and Fascism*, 12n. On the issue of Italians being perceived as non-white, see Vecoli, "Are Italian Americans Just White Folks?" and Guglielmo, *White on Arrival*.

9. Di Salvatore, *A Clever Base-Ballist*, 437n.

10. Covello, *The Heart Is the Teacher*, 43; Joe Torre, interview with author, June 7, 2005.

11. Fullerton, "Fans," 465; Lieb, "Baseball," 393.

12. *Sporting News*, December 6, 1923, 4.

13. "Forever Baseball," PBS, American Experience series, November 7, 1989.

Chapter 1. Ed Abbaticchio

1. Reynolds, "The Frisco Kid," 22.

2. *New York Times*, March 28, 1936, 20.

3. In the National Italian American Sports Hall of Fame in Chicago, Lewis Pessano "Buttercup" Dickerson, who played in the National League and American Association between 1878 and 1885, is honored as the first Italian American Major Leaguer. However, according to Charles Weaver of Baltimore, who has done extensive research on Dickerson, including interviews with his granddaughters, there is no evidence that Dickerson was of Italian descent. In a telephone interview on June 13, 2001, Inez Cardiges, one of the granddaughters, told me that Dickerson's parents, William Porter Dickerson and Mary Larmore, immigrated from England, though they may have been from Scotland originally. Cardiges, who lived with her grandmother (after Dickerson died) until she, Cardiges, was in her twenties, also said she was not aware of any Italian connection in the family. As for Dickerson's middle name of Pessano, she said that it was a custom in their family to give to the boys as a middle name the name of the doctor who delivered them.

4. According to the Web site of Princeton University, it was Alec Moffatt, captain of the football team in the mid-1880s, who created the spiral punt. Http://mondrian .princeton.edu/CampusWWW/Companion/football.html. Thanks to William McColly for calling this source to my attention.

5. Abbaticchio played football against another early two-sport star, Christy Mathewson, who was a fullback and kicker with the Pittsburgh Stars in 1900. Recalling those days, Abbaticchio later said, "I played against Matty when we both were fullbacks. What a ballplayer that fellow was!" (quoted in *Fort Lauderdale Daily News*, May 13, 1952). Also see Grosshandler, "Two-Sport Stars."

6. I am indebted to the Abbaticchio family for providing biographical information and documentation not available elsewhere. Sources not otherwise identified are from the family; newspaper clippings are frequently untitled and without page numbers.

7. Burk, *Never Just a Game*, 160.

8. *Sporting Life*, October 10, 1908, 9.

9. James, *The Baseball Book, 1990*, 167–68.

10. *Sporting News*, September 1, 1906, 2.

11. On Italian-Irish relations, see Femminella, *Italians and Irish in America*. Also see Puleo, *The Boston Italians*.

12. Http://us.history.wisc.edu/hist102/pdocs/lodge_immigration.pdf.

13. Daniel, "Viva Italia!" 347. In that same article, Daniel identified Cubs short-stop Joe Tinker, of Tinker-to-Evers-to-Chance fame, as the first Major Leaguer of Italian descent but provided no evidence to support his claim. Murray McGee, of Ottawa, Kansas, has done extensive research on Tinker's biography but has been unable to identify Tinker's ethnic background.

14. Spalding, *America's National Game*, 205.

15. *Total Baseball*, 6th ed., 2,496.

16. I am indebted to Bob Richardson for the biographical information on Apol-lonio; he in turn drew on the original research of Tom Shea. As for the discrepancy in Apollonio's first name, Richardson notes that Harold Kaese, in his Putnam his-tory of the Boston franchise, mistakenly used "Nathaniel" rather than "Nicholas" and surmises that Kaese may have found the wrong name in a newspaper account of a stockholders' meeting. Richardson also points out that the only Apollonios listed in the Boston city directories in the 1870s were Nicholas and his father and brothers; there was no Nathaniel.

17. Letter in Garoni's Hall of Fame file.

Chapter 2. The Boys from San Francisco

1. Alexander, *Our Game*, 5. Also see Ivor-Campbell, "The Many Fathers of Baseball," 10, and Dobbins and Twichell, *Nuggets on the Diamond*, 15. Based on newspaper reports from the period, Angus Macfarlane ("The Knickerbockers") speculates that baseball may have been introduced to San Francisco in 1851 by other members of the New York Knickerbockers who had transferred to San Francisco.

2. Zingg and Medeiros, *Runs, Hits, and an Era*, 2; Seymour, *Baseball*, 44, 195.

3. Gumina, *Italians of San Francisco*, 5; Cinel, *From Italy to San Francisco*, 19.

4. Gumina, *Italians of San Francisco*, 11.

5. Cinel, *From Italy to San Francisco*, 19, 162.

6. Riess, *City Games*, 104.

7. Dario Lodigiani, interview with author, October 2, 2000.

8. Dobbins and Twichell, *Nuggets on the Diamond*, ix.

9. At least through the thirties, Oakland and San Francisco exceeded all other cities in producing Major League ballplayers in excess of their proportion of the total white population of the United States. See Lehman, "The Geographic Origins of Professional Baseball Players."

10. Quoted in Mackey, *Barbary Baseball*, 190.

11. Quoted in *Sporting News*, December 27, 1961, 40.

12. *Spalding's Official Base Ball Guide*, 47.

13. Farrell, *My Baseball Diary*, 28.

14. Dario Lodigiani, telephone interview with author, May 25, 2001.

15. *New York Daily Mirror*, March 28, 1948.

16. Quoted in Creamer, *Babe*, 221.

17. Quoted in *Sporting News*, December 27, 1961, 40.

18. Quoted in Creamer, *Babe*, 213.

19. Quoted in Creamer, *Babe*, 222.

20. *Sporting News*, December 27, 1961, 40; *New York Times*, March 8, 1918, 8.

21. *Sporting News*, December 27, 1961, 40; *New York Times*, December 19, 1961, 29.

22. *Sporting News*, December 27, 1961, 40; *New York Times*, December 19, 1961, 29.

23. Joseph Pezzolo, telephone interview with author, August 16, 1999. The comment by Mr. Pezzolo in the following paragraph is from this same interview.

24. Quoted in Graham, "Hidden-Ball King," 53.

25. Pinelli, *Mr. Ump*, 11.

26. Pinelli, *Mr. Ump*, 8.

27. Pinelli, *Mr. Ump*, 7.

28. Undated clipping, Pinelli file, Baseball Hall of Fame Library.

29. Pinelli, *Mr. Ump*, 66–67.

30. Pinelli, *Mr. Ump*, 73.

31. Lane, "'Babe' Pinelli," 395.

32. *Sporting News*, November 29, 1934, 5.

33. Quoted in Pinelli, *Mr. Ump*, 77.

34. Pinelli, *Mr. Ump*, 95.

35. Pinelli, *Mr. Ump*, 116. Here Pinelli's recollection is faulty; both years he played in the American League, 1918 and 1920, Bodie was also in the league.

36. Quoted in Will, *Men at Work*, 64.

Chapter 3. Where Are the Italians?

1. Lewis Allen, *Only Yesterday*, 208.

2. Creamer, *Babe*, 16.

3. Lieb, "The Italian in Sport," 16.

4. Calling the Carnera fiasco "the most shameful chapter in all boxing," sportswriter Paul Gallico portrayed the Italian fighter as a guileless victim of unscrupulous handlers, "a helpless lamb among wolves who used him until there was nothing more left to use." Gallico, "Pity the Poor Giant," 321–22.

5. Riess, *Touching Base*, 192.

6. On the subject of town teams and their social significance, see Seymour, *Baseball*, 188–98.

7. Quoted in Carr, "The Coming of the Italians," 429.

8. *Spalding's Official Base Ball Guide*, 23.

9. On efforts to Americanize immigrants, see Higham, *Strangers in the Land*, 234–63. For responses to efforts to Americanize Italian American children, see Alba, *Italian Americans*, 53–54. On the concept of organized sport as a means of acculturating Jewish youth early in the twentieth century, see Levine, *Ellis Island to Ebbets Field*, passim.

10. Seymour, *Baseball*, 48.

11. *Arena*, April 1897; quoted in Moquin, *A Documentary History of the Italian Americans*, 53.

12. Quoted in Cooper, *The John Fante Reader*, 29.

13. Mangione, *Mount Allegro*, 1.

14. Generational conflicts over participation in sports existed in other ethnic communities as well. See, for example, Levine, *From Ellis Island to Ebbets Field*, 93–95.

15. Dolph Camilli, quoted in Mackey, *Barbary Baseball*, 189; Phil Rizzuto, interview with author, June 12, 1993.

16. Frank Crosetti, telephone interview with author, September 4, 1998.

17. Joe Amalfitano, interview with author, April 22, 1998.

18. Burk, *Much More Than a Game*, 32. Burk's figures are based on data compiled by Hall of Fame historian Lee Allen, found in Lee Allen Research Papers, 1921–1929.

19. Aulick, *America's National Game*, no pagination.

20. Lieb, "Baseball," 393.

21. *Sporting News*, December 6, 1923, 4.

22. *Sporting News*, January 26, 1931.

23. Burk, *Never Just a Game*, 9, 93.

24. Zoss and Bowman, *Diamonds in the Rough*, 125.

25. Mackey, *Barbary Baseball*, 3.

26. Cinel, *From Italy to San Francisco*, 19.

Chapter 4. The Tony Lazzeri Era

1. *Il Progresso Italo-Americano*, October 3, 1926, 3; my translation. All subsequent quotations from *Il Progresso* will also consist of my translations of the original Italian.

427

2. Levine, *Ellis Island to Ebbets Field*, 116.

3. Quoted in *Sporting News*, December 11, 1930.

4. The story of the origins of Lazzeri's nickname and its coverage by Derks appeared in the *Salt Lake Tribune*, October 3, 1993, C1-3. Thanks to Larry Gerlach for bringing the article to my attention.

5. Notarianni, "Italianità in Utah," 323–24.

6. Barrow, *My Fifty Years in Baseball*, 147.

7. *Sporting News*, December 31, 1925, 1.

8. *Sporting News*, April 8, 1926, 2.

9. Barrow, *My Fifty Years in Baseball*, 145.

10. Graham, *The New York Yankees*, 114.

11. Quoted in Ritter, *The Glory of Their Times*, 236.

12. *New York Times*, October 11, 1926, 1.

13. Lane, "'Poosh-Em-Out' Tony Lazzeri," 501.

14. Lane, "A Great Natural Ball Player," 305; Gallico, *New York Daily News*, October 9, 1927; quoted in Fleming, *Murderers' Row*, 384.

15. *New York Graphic*; quoted in Fleming, *Murderers' Row*, 281; *New York Times*, September 9, 1927, 20.

16. In various publications Lazzeri's death has been attributed to injuries suffered in a fall following an epileptic seizure, but his death certificate lists acute cardiac arrest as the cause.

17. *New York Sun*, August 25, 1927; quoted in Fleming, *Murderers' Row*, 317.

18. *New York Times*, August 9, 1946, 23.

19. Graham, *The New York Yankees*, 115.

20. Frank Crosetti, telephone interview with author, September 4, 1998. Unless otherwise noted, all quotations are from this interview.

21. *Sporting News*, August 14, 1946, 14; *New York Times*, August 8, 1946, 21.

22. Phil Rizzuto, quoted in Trachtenberg, *The Wonder Team*, 72.

23. Frank Crosetti, quoted in Trachtenberg, *The Wonder Team*, 74.

24. Bouton, *Ball Four*, 23.

25. *New York Times*, October 5, 1968, 42.

26. Quoted in *Sporting News*, November 30, 1963, 28.

27. *Sporting News*, November 30, 1963, 28; Adomites and Wisnia, *Best of Baseball*, 322.

28. Quoted in *Sporting News*, February 4, 1932, 5.

29. Quoted in *Sporting News*, September 21, 1968, 36.

30. *Sporting News*, February 4, 1932, 5, and September 21, 1968, 36.

31. According to www.imdb.com, Ernie was still working as a stunt coordinator in 2008; Frank, who was Arnold Schwarzeneger's double in the 1984 hit *The Terminator*, died in December 2004. The family tradition continued with Ernie's son, Noon Orsatti, a film and TV stunt man and coordinator. He in turn, is the father of stunt performers Allie and Rowbie Orsatti.

Chapter 5. The Turning Point

1. For an overview of baseball in the Depression, see Alexander, *Breaking the Slump*. Also see Tygiel, *Past Time*, ch. 5, and Rossi, *The National Game*, ch. 6.

2. For a brief history of Slavs in baseball, see Pease, "Diamonds out of the Coal Mines." For a history of Jewish athletes in all sports, see Levine, *Ellis Island to Ebbets Field*. Brief general discussions of the arrival of players of South and East European background can be found in Alexander, *Breaking the Slump*, 191–95, and Zoss and Bowman, *Diamonds in the Rough*, 121–25.

3. Mancuso had appeared in eleven games in 1928 but technically was a rookie in 1930.

4. *Sporting News*, September 7, 1933, 1.

5. *New York Times*, March 25, 1937, 32.

6. Taped interview, National Baseball Hall of Fame Library, BL-8073.91.

7. H. Johnson, *Who's Who in Major League Baseball*, 130. On July 5, 1935, Tony and his younger brother Al (an infielder who played in fifty-four games for the Giants in his only big league season) both hit home runs in a Dodgers-Giants game.

8. *Sporting News*, August 10, 1939, 1.

9. Quoted in Bartell, *Rowdy Richard*, 95.

10. Quoted in Westcott, *Diamond Greats*, 97, 99.

11. Tallulah Bankhead, quoted in Dawidoff, *Baseball*, 240.

12. *USA Today*, December 12, 1997, 6C.

13. Casso, "Zeke Bonura," 7.

14. Quoted in *Sporting News*, March 23, 1987, 46.

15. *Washington Post*, March 24, 1938, x27, and April 2, 1938, x16. The Nats, short for "Nationals," was a popular nickname for the Senators.

16. Garrett, "But He Can Hit," 44.

17. Quoted in Goldstein, *Spartan Seasons*, 247.

18. *Washington Post*, April 6, 1943.

19. Quoted in Bingham, "Not Such a Tough Cookie," 43.

20. Bingham, "Not Such a Tough Cookie," 39.

21. *Sporting News*, October 14, 1967, 16.

22. *Baseball Magazine*, March 1934, 463–64.

23. With the exception of Paul Gallico, who stopped writing about sports in 1936 to become a freelance writer, none of the prominent sportswriters at the time were of Italian descent.

24. *Sporting News*, January 29, 1931, 1.

25. *Sporting News*, July 9, 1931, 4.

26. *Literary Digest*, July 2, 1932, 37.

27. Undated clipping in Baseball Hall of Fame Library files.

Chapter 6. Viva Italia!

1. Daniel, "Viva Italia!," 347.

2. Daniel, "Viva Italia!," 347.

3. *Sporting News*, May 21, 1936, 3.

4. Daniel, "Viva Italia!," 379.

5. Daniel, "Viva Italia!," 348.

6. *Sporting News*, March 26, 1936, 3.

7. In some sources Daniel's name is listed as Markowitz, but in the Library of Congress catalog and the Web site of the International Jewish Sports Hall of Fame, it is Margowitz (http://www.jewishsports.net/).

8. *Sporting News*, March 19, 1936, 1.

9. Angelo Giuliani, interview with author, June 8, 2001.

10. *Il Progresso Italo-Americano*, March 25, 1936.

11. Undated taped interview of Dallessandro with Eugene Murdock in Cleveland Public Library.

12. Quoted in *Sporting News*, May 5, 1938, 3.

13. *Sporting News*, May 5, 1938, 3.

14. *Sporting News*, December 31, 1977, 59.

15. Dario Lodigiani, telephone interview with author, March 2, 1999.

16. Dario Lodigiani, interview with author, October 2, 2000. Subsequent quotations are from this interview.

17. Nino Bongiovanni, telephone interview with author, November 30, 2005. Unless otherwise noted, all quotations are from this interview.

18. Nino Bongiovanni, taped interview by Ed Attanasio, January 11, 2005, San Jose, California.

19. *Sporting News*, September 28, 1939, 3.

20. *Sporting News*, September 28, 1939, 3.

21. Povich, *The Washington Senators*, 225.

22. *Sporting News*, January 14, 1948, 15.

23. Quoted in Peary, *We Played the Game*, 74.

24. *Sporting News*, March 17, 1948, 18.

25. Herman Franks, telephone interview with author, June 8, 2001. All quotations are from this interview.

26. Sibby Sisti, interview with author, March 21, 2002.

27. Johnny Antonelli, interview with author, March 21, 2002.

28. Quoted in *Pittsburgh Tribune-Review*, June 4, 2006.

29. Herman Franks, telephone interview with author, June 8, 2001.

30. Burk, *Much More Than a Game*, 32.

31. Lee Allen Research Papers, 1929.

32. Burk, *Much More Than a Game*, 44–49.

33. List based on data compiled by author from Allen, Research Papers, 1920, 1930, 1935, 1939.

34. Italian American players were identified by reviewing the rosters of all Major League teams for these given years as recorded by Neft and Cohen in *The Sports Encyclopedia: Baseball* and confirming their ethnic identity by cross-checking in Lee Allen's data on Major League recruits. Percentages were calculated on the basis of Major League roster totals provided by Retrosheet, courtesy of David Smith.

In *Touching Base*, Steven Riess reported that "By 1941, about 8 percent of the big leaguers were Italian" (192). However, Riess's calculation was based on the 1941 edition of the *Baseball Register*; in that year the *Register* did not list all Major Leaguers but only the top four hundred players, and this listing would account for the inflated percentage cited by Riess. According to my calculations, in 1941 there were thirty-seven Italians in the Major Leagues, a number that represented 6.8 percent of all Major Leaguers.

Chapter 7. The First MVPS

1. *Sporting News*, January 29, 1931, 1.

2. Bubbles Hargrave, also with Cincinnati, is credited with winning the batting title in 1926 (he hit .353), even though he had only 326 official times at bat. In 1886 King Kelly won the NL title with a .388 average, but he caught in only 53 of the 107 games in which he played.

3. Lee Allen, The *Cincinnati Reds*, 264.

4. Quoted in *Sporting News*, October 15, 1977, 51.

5. Lombardi quoted in *Sporting News*, October 15, 1977, 51; Sibby Sisti, interview with author, March 21, 2002.

6. Quoted in *Sporting News*, July 15, 1967, 8.

7. Grantland Rice, quoted in *Louisville Courier Journal*, February 8, 1977.

8. Quoted in *Sporting News*, July 6, 1974, 10.

9. Quoted in *New York Daily News*, August 3, 1986.

10. Quoted in Steadman, "Dolph Camilli," 80.

11. *Sporting News*, March 10, 1938, 1.

12. Quoted in *San Francisco Chronicle*, November 2, 1997.

13. Phil Cavarretta, telephone interview with author, April 29, 2001. All quotations are from this interview.

14. According to Goldstein, *Spartan Seasons*, xiii, only 32 of the 128 players who were starters in 1945 were still playing regularly for the same clubs in the first postwar season.

Chapter 8. To War and Back

1. Creamer, *Baseball in '41*, 4.

2. *New York Times*, June 30, 1941, 20.

3. *Sporting News*, July 17, 1941, 4.

4. DiMaggio, *Real Grass*, 127.

5. *Washington Post*, July 2, 1941, 20.

6. Gould, "The Streak of Streaks"; quoted in Dawidoff, *Baseball*, 591.

7. *Time*, July 14, 1941, 44.

8. *Washington Post*, July 2, 1941, 10, and April 15, 1941, 20.

9. Len Merullo, telephone interview with author, December 16, 2001. Merullo's grandson Matt, a catcher, played for three teams in his six-year Major League career between 1989 and 1995.

10. *Chicago Tribune*, September 14, 1942, 25.

11. Neft and Cohen, *The Sports Encyclopedia*, 228–29.

12. Quoted in *Boston Globe,* September 24, 2000.

13. Povich, *Washington Post*, May 11, 1942, 18, and May 18, 1942, 15; Cramer, *Joe DiMaggio*, 202.

Chapter 9. Postwar New York

1. Tygiel, *Past Time*, 149.

2. *Il Progresso Italo-Americano*, September 30, 1947. A *Sporting News* article on

October 15, 1947, 28, noted that of the fifty-four players eligible to play in the Series, nine were of Italian descent. Frank Crosetti, a player/coach, was not eligible to play in the Series.

3. There were four other Italian American players on the Yankee roster in 1947, including Crosetti, but none of them played in the Series. Ken Silvestri, a backup catcher, appeared in three regular-season games, and infielder Johnny Lucadello in twelve games. Rinaldo "Rugger" Ardizoia, a right-handed pitcher born in Oleggio, Italy, made his one and only Major League appearance on April 30, giving up four hits and two runs in two innings of relief.

4. *New York Times*, October 1, 1947, 31.

5. *New York Times*, October 3, 1947, 53.

6. Quoted in *New York Times*, October 4, 1947, 11.

7. Quoted in *New York Daily News*, August 13, 1990, 44, and *New York Times*, October 4, 1947, 11.

8. Kahn, *The Era*, 116.

9. Golenbock, *Bums*, 179; Al Gionfriddo, personal correspondence with author, December 10, 1998.

10. *New York Times*, October 6, 1947, 29.

11. Http://ezinearticles.com/?Famous-Sports-Radio-Broadcasts—Keep-the -Thrills-Alive&id=1626513.

Chapter 10. The DiMaggio Brothers

1. In his essay on "Baseball Families" Larry Amman wrote, "In terms of balanced, outstanding achievement, no group of three or more brothers can match the DiMaggios" (215). Other Italian American Major League brothers include Bob and Ken Aspromonte, Sal and Chris Bando, Lou and Dino Chiozza, Tony and Billy Conigliaro, Al and Tony Cuccinello, Danny and Al Gardella, Phil and Ralph Gagliano, Jason and Jeremy Giambi, and Gus and Frank Mancuso.

2. Dom DiMaggio, interview with author, July 8, 2002. Unless otherwise noted, all quotations by him are from this interview.

3. *New York Daily News*, April 6, 1936.

4. *Time*, July 13, 1936, 43–44. Michael died in 1953 at the age of forty-four, when he drowned after falling from his boat.

5. M. Allen, *Where Have You Gone, Joe DiMaggio?*, 52–53.

6. *Sporting News*, October 15, 1936, 8.

7. Busch, "Joe DiMaggio," 62, 63, 68.

8. *New York Times*, February 8, 1949, 33.

9. Quoted in *New York Daily News*, December 12, 1951.

10. Like other right-handed sluggers, DiMaggio was penalized by playing in Yankee Stadium, where so many warning-track outs would have been home runs in other parks. In 880 games at home he hit 148 homers, compared to 213 on the road in 856 games. See R. Johnson and Stout, *DiMaggio*, 264.

11. Jerry Coleman, interview with author, September 1, 2005.

12. Willams, *My Turn at Bat*, 209–10.

13. "The Great DiMagg'"; unsigned column in the *Washington Post*, July 2, 1941; Coleman, interview with author, September 1, 2005.

14. Johnny Pesky, interview with author, April 22, 1990.

15. Quoted in Kiersh, *Where Have You Gone, Vince DiMaggio?*, 257, 260.

16. Quoted in *Sporting News*, August 24, 1949, 6.

17. Quoted in Talese, "The Silent Season of a Hero," 9.

18. Quoted in Bamberger, "Dom DiMaggio," 110.

19. In *Creating the National Pastime*, chapter 8, G. Edward White examined the impact both DiMaggio and Hank Greenberg had on attitudes toward ethnicity in baseball. Having proved their patriotism by serving in the military during World War II, these two superstars came to be seen as "'American' role models . . . confirmations of the melting pot theory of ethnicity in America" (249). Also see Yoseloff, "From Ethnic Hero to National Icon."

20. Gomez quoted in M. Allen, *Where Have You Gone, Joe DiMaggio?*, 29; Graham, *The New York Yankees*, 226.

21. Both quotations in *New York Daily News*, March 9, 1999.

22. Lasorda, interview with author, January 19, 2001; Machi, interview with author, March 12, 2006.

23. Quoted in *New York Daily News*, March 9, 1999.

24. In his astute analysis of contemporary Italian American identity, Thomas J. Ferraro writes, "No one has ever been more important to Italian America's sense of itself—outside the family—than Frank Sinatra" (*Feeling Italian*, 92). However, given its focus on the arts, the book does not take into consideration DiMaggio or sports in general.

25. Quoted in the *New Yorker*, September 15, 2003, 38.

26. Quoted in Bamberger, "Dom DiMaggio," 110.

Chapter 11. Italian Yankees

1. Simon, *Brighton Beach Memoirs*, 6.

2. Jerry Coleman, interview with author, September 1, 2005.

3. Phil Rizzuto, interview with author, June 12, 1993. Unless otherwise noted, all quotations by Rizzuto are from this interview. In this interview Rizzuto attributed the quotation to Dodgers manager Casey Stengel, but it has been shown that Stengel was not in New York at the time of Rizzuto's tryout. In a *Sporting News* interview in May 1941 Rizzuto attributed the words (in a slightly different version) to a Giants coach. Gene Schoor identified the coach as Pancho Snyder of the Giants (*The Scooter*, 7).

4. Quoted in *Sporting News*, May 1, 1941, 4.

5. According to testimony by Bernardo Pasquel, *New York Times*, June 9, 1946.

6. For Gardella's challenge of the reserve clause, see Marshall, *Baseball's Pivotal Era*, and Mandell, "Danny Gardella."

7. In a later version Frishberg substituted the name of umpire Art Passarella for that of Campanella. See Frishberg, "Van Lingle Mungo," 143–44.

8. *New York Times Book Review*, April 4, 1993, 26.

9. Jerry Coleman, interview with author, September 1, 2005; Stengel quoted in Creamer, *Stengel*, 237.

10. Atlanta Braves telecast, TBS, April 4, 2005.

11. Berra and Fitzgerald, *Yogi*, 49.

12. Yogi Berra, telephone interview with author, February 17, 1999.

13. Berra and Fitzgerald, *Yogi*, 55. There are other versions of the origins of the nickname, but this is the one Berra himself most often cites.

14. In June 2003 the 5400 block of Elizabeth Avenue was renamed Hall of Fame Place in honor of Berra, Garagiola, and Cardinals broadcaster Jack Buck, who lived on the block in the late 1950s.

15. Berra, *Ten Rings*, 51.

16. Rocky Colavito, telephone interview with author, May 4, 1998; Jim Fregosi, interview with author, September 11, 2005.

17. Jerry Coleman, interview with author, September 1, 2005.

18. Virgil Trucks, interview with author, February 13, 2004.

19. James, *The Bill James Historical Baseball Abstract*, 325.

20. *Sporting News*, April 30, 1947, 1, 4.

21. Craig Biggio, interview with author, May 28, 2005; Phil Garner, interview with author, July 22, 1999.

22. Berra and Fitzgerald, *Yogi*, 215–16, 231.

23. Yogi Berra, telephone interview with author, February 17, 1999.

24. Daniel, "Viva Italia!" 348.

25. Henrich, *New York Times*, February 23, 1954, 31; Coleman, interview with author, September 1, 2005; Stengel quoted in Creamer, *Stengel*, 327.

26. Raschi quoted in Honig, *Baseball between the Lines*, 175; Berra, *Ten Rings*, 115.

27. Quoted in Honig, *Baseball between the Lines*, 173.

28. Honig, *Baseball between the Lines*, 179.

29. Santina Gilday, cited in undated article from *Springfield Republican*, in files of Hamden County (Massachusetts) Historical Society.

30. Quoted in Honig, *Baseball between the Lines*, 180.

31. Martin and Golenbock, *Number 1*, 48.

32. Martin and Golenbock, *Number 1*, 204.

Chapter 12. Interborough Warfare

1. Goodwin, *Wait 'Til Next Year*, 125.

2. Kahn, *The Era*, 98.

3. Ralph Branca, interview with author, July 8, 2002.

4. Quoted in Turner, *When the Boys Came Back*, 216.

5. Delillo, *Underworld*, 14. The prologue to *Underworld*, in which Delillo probes the soul of America in the second half of the twentieth century, is set against the backdrop of the "shot heard 'round the world" game.

6. Quoted in Vincent, *We Would Have Played for Nothing*, 28.

7. Quoted in *Sporting News*, September 13, 1969, 23.

8. Prager would later expand his article into a book: *The Echoing Green: The Untold Story of Bobby Thomson, Ralph Branca and the Shot Heard Round the World*.

9. In both my original telephone interview with Franks (June 18, 2001) and a follow-up (June 20, 2008), he declined to discuss the incident. As for Yvars, the native New Yorker was the son of a Spanish father and an Italian mother from Calabria. See Prager, *The Echoing Green*, 333.

10. Quoted in Vincent, *We Would Have Played for Nothing*, 31; *New York Times*, October 1, 2001, D12.

11. Ralph Branca, interview with author, July 8, 2002.

12. Roland Hemond, interview with author, June 26, 2008.

13. Eig, *Opening Day*, 223.

14. *Chicago Defender*, September 20, 1947, 19; Robinson, *I Never Had It Made*, 68; *Pittsburgh Courier*, June 21, 1947; cited in Eig, *Opening Day*, 163.

15. Eig, *Opening Day*, 229.

16. Lord, *In the Year of the Boar*, 93, 133.

17. Prince, *Brooklyn's Dodgers*, 10; *New York Times*, October 8, 2006.

18. Joe Garagiola, telephone interview with author, March 15, 1999. For other accounts of the incidents, see Kahn, *The Era*, 96–98, and *New York Times*, June 2, 1950, 36.

19. Joe Garagiola, telephone interview with author, March 15, 1999.

20. Kessner, *Fiorello H. La Guardia*, 526, 532.

21. Heaphy, *The Negro Leagues*, 196.

22. Campanella, *It's Good to Be Alive*, 288.

23. *Chicago Defender*, April 3, 1948.

24. Campanella, *It's Good to Be Alive*, 131. For a discussion of the differences between Campanella and Robinson see Tygiel, *Baseball's Great Experiment*, 326–27.

25. Campanella, *It's Good to Be Alive*, 202. His second marriage, in 1945, to Ruthe Willis, with whom he had three children, was another casualty of his injury; they separated in 1960. Following her death in 1963, Campanella married Roxie Doles in 1964.

26. Quoted in Campanella, *It's Good to Be Alive*, 236.

27. Kahn, *The Boys of Summer*, 303.

28. Carl Furillo Jr., telephone interview with author, July 26, 2008.

29. Kahn, *The Boys of Summer*, 303.

30. Quoted in Golenbock, *Bums*, 357.

31. Jon Furillo, telephone interview with author, July 21, 2008.

32. Quoted in Golenbock, *Bums*, 284.

33. Quoted in Kahn, *The Boys of Summer*, 312.

34. Herman Franks, telephone interview with author, November 28, 2005.

35. Quoted in Testa, *Sal Maglie*, 217.

36. Carl Erskine, e-mail, July 28, 2008.

37. Eig, *Opening Day*, 41–44; Kahn, *The Era*, 34; Tygiel, *Baseball's Great Experiment*, 170–71.

38. Eig, *Opening Day*, 44; Kahn, *New York Times*, January 29, 1989.

39. Jon Furillo, telephone interview with author, July 21, 2008; Campanella, *It's Good to Be Alive*, 279.

40. Kahn, *The Boys of Summer*, 304.

41. Carl Erskine, e-mail, July 26, 2008.

42. Carl Furillo Jr., telephone interview with author, July 26, 2008; Jon Furillo, telephone interview with author, July 21, 2008.

43. Quoted in *New York Times*, January 26, 1989.

44. *New York Herald Tribune*, April 19, 1954; Kahn quoted in Testa, *Sal Maglie*, 225.

45. *Sporting News*, June 27, 1994, 18.

46. Testa, *Sal Maglie*, 80.

47. Ed Fitzgerald, "The Barber of the Giants," *Sport*, September 1952;, quoted in Testa, *Sal Maglie*, 127.

48. Kahn, *Memories of Summer*, 189. For all his sensitivity to ethnic slights, Kahn, who also found Furillo's nickname of "Skoonj" to be offensive, was not immune to stereotyping. Later in the book (pp. 258–59), he refers to Maglie as "glowering like a movie mafioso."

49. Maglie and Boyle, "The Great Giant-Dodger Days," 47.

50. Quoted in Kahn, *The Boys of Summer*, 130.

51. Testa, *Sal Maglie*, 267–68; Shapiro, *The Last Good Season*, 138.

52. Maglie and Boyle, "The Great Giant-Dodger Days," 47.

53. Maglie and Boyle, "Baseball Is a Tough Business," 80.

54. Antonelli, interview with author, March 21, 2002; Franks, telephone interview with author, November 28, 2005.

55. Testa, *Sal Maglie*, xviii.

56. John August Antonelli is not to be confused with John Lawrence Antonelli, an infielder with the Cardinals in 1944–45.

57. Antonelli, interview with author, March 21, 2002; unless noted, all subsequent quotations are from that interview.

58. Both quotations from Hirshberg, "Johnny Antonelli," 53.

59. Kahn, *The Era*, 286.

60. *New York Times*, October 9, 1957.

61. *New York Times*, September 25, 1957.

Chapter 13. The Last "Italians"

1. James, *The Bill James Historical Baseball Abstract*, 210.

2. According to the data in Lee Allen's files in the Hall of Fame, of the nine Italian American rookies in 1955, only three married women of Italian descent, and of the twelve in 1960, none did.

3. Vecoli, "Are Italian Americans Just White Folks?" 76.

4. Maraniss, *When Pride Still Mattered*, 242, 165.

5. Rocky Colavito, telephone interview with author, May 4, 1998. All quotations are from this interview.

6. *Cleveland Plain Dealer*, August 4, 1991; *Sporting News*, April 27, 1960, 3, 12. Four years after the Colavito/Kuenn trade the Cubs and Cardinals announced what many consider the most lopsided trade ever. On June 15, 1964, the Cubs traded outfielder Lou Brock, at the time a .260 hitter over two seasons, to the Cardinals for an Italian American pitcher named Ernie Broglio. In 5½ seasons with the Cards Broglio had won seventy games and led the NL in wins in 1960 (21-9), but in 2½ years in Chicago he went 7-19. Brock, on the other hand, went on to a nineteen-year, Hall of Fame career.

7. Davey Nelson, interview with author, August 2, 2007.

8. James, *The Bill James Historical Baseball Abstract*, 220.

9. Tito Francona, telephone interview with author, July 21, 2008.

10. Terry Francona, personal interview with author, March 14, 2008.

11. Casale, interview with author, October 11, 2002. Unless otherwise noted, all quotations are from this interview.

12. Frank Malzone, interview with author, March 12, 2008.

13. Conigliaro and Zanger, *Seeing It Through*, 238.

14. Quoted in Cataneo, *Tony C*, 107.

15. Quoted in *Sporting News*, October 9, 1971, 16.

16. Rico Petrocelli, interview with author, February 12, 2004. All quotations are from this interview.

17. Quoted in *Sporting News*, August 23, 1969, 19.

18. *New York Times*, December 6, 1969, 56.

19. Quoted in *New York Times*, December 6, 1969, 56.

20. Torre, *Chasing the Dream*, 17.

21. Joe Torre, interview with author, June 7, 2005. The following quote from Torre is also from this interview. In 2002 Torre and his wife Ali founded the Joe Torre Safe at Home Foundation to educate the public about domestic violence.

22. Part of Prospect Park, the Parade Grounds were the site of several diamonds that attracted thousands of spectators as well as scouts to watch future Major Leaguers such as the Torre brothers, Ken and Bob Aspromonte, Joe Pepitone, Sandy Koufax, and Manny Ramirez.

23. Frank Torre, interview with author, July 21, 1997; Torre, *Chasing the Dream*, 37.

24. Joe Torre, interview with author, May 14, 2008.

25. Ted Simmons, interview with author, May 31, 2008.

26. Joe Torre, interview with author, May 14, 2008.

27. Ron Santo, interview with author, June 15, 1999. Unless otherwise noted, all quotations are from this interview.

28. Quoted in *Sporting News*, September 6, 1969, 3.

29. Pat Hughes, interview with author, August 8, 2008.

30. Quoted in *USA Today Baseball Weekly*, March 6–12, 5.

31. Quoted in Watson, "A Boy and a Dream," 21.

32. Ron Santo, interview with author, September 14, 2008.

Chapter 14. The 1970s and Beyond

1. Alba, *Italian Americans*, 159. Also see Herbert Gans, "Symbolic Ethnicity." For a different perspective see Glazer and Moynihan, *Beyond the Melting Pot*, and Novak, *The Rise of the Unmeltable Ethnics.*

2. David Dellucci, interview with author, March 18, 1999; Sal Fasano, interview with author, May 17, 2006; Mark DeRosa, interview with author, April 4, 2007; Mark Loretta, interview with author, August 19, 2008; Dustin Pedroia, interview with author, March 13, 2008.

3. Sal Bando, interview with author, July 29, 2008. Unless otherwise noted, all quotations are from this interview.

4. Quoted in *Time*, August 18, 1975.

5. Quoted in Helyar, *Lords of the Realm*, 185.

6. Bud Selig, interview with author, December 22, 2008.

7. Bud Selig, interview with author, December 22, 2008.

8. Larry Bowa, interview with author, May 13, 2008.

9. Steve Sax, telephone interview with author, December 30, 2008.

10. Ken Caminiti, interview with author, September 26, 1999. Unless otherwise noted, all quotations are from this interview.

11. Quoted in *New York Times*, October 12, 2004.

12. *Sports Illustrated*, June 3, 2002, 34.

13. Craig Biggio, interview with author, May 28, 2005.

14. Quoted in *New York Times*, September 25, 2002.

15. *Atlanta Journal-Constitution*, April 4, 2006.

16. Barry Zito, interview with author, June 19, 2007. All subsequent quotations are from this interview.

17. Quoted in *Play: The New York Times Sports Magazine*, September 2008, 41.

18. Andy Pettitte, interview with author, April 9, 2004.

19. Dave Righetti, interview with author, April 6, 2008. All quotations are from this interview.

20. John Franco, interview with author, August 4, 1999.

21. Quoted in *Bergen Record*, March 16, 1999, s8.

22. James, *The New Bill James Historical Baseball Abstract*, passim.

23. Craig Biggio, interview with author, May 28, 2005. All quotations are from this interview.

24. James, *The New Bill James Historical Baseball Abstract*, 486–87.

25. Phil Garner, interview with author, August 20, 2006.

26. Mike Piazza, interview with author, June 6, 2006. Unless otherwise noted, all quotations are from this interview.

27. Lasorda has often been identified as Piazza's godfather, but in fact he was godfather to Tommy, Piazza's youngest brother.

28. Mike Piazza, interview with author, March 6, 2006.

29. Ira Berkow, e-mail to author, December 26, 2008.

Chapter 15. From Labor to Management

1. Hall, "Italian-Americans," 31.

2. Hall, "Italian-Americans," 28, 31.

3. Thanks to George Randazzo for bringing this to my attention.

4. *Chicago Tribune*, May 27, 1990.

5. Bruce Froemming, interview with author, April 27, 2008.

6. Bruce Froemming, interview with author, April 27, 2008.

7. Joe Amalfitano, interview with author, April 22, 1998.

8. Matt Galante, interview with author, September 26, 1999. All quotations are from this interview.

9. The family name was changed by Maddon's father. A *Sports Illustrated* article of October 6, 2008, listed the name as Maddoninni, but that spelling does not exist in Italy.

10. It was initially reported that William Reedy, a friend, was driving, but Peter Golenbock, in his biography, *Wild, High and Tight*, concluded that Martin was behind the wheel.

11. Davey Nelson, interview with author, August 2, 2007.

12. Jim Fregosi, interview with author, September 11, 2005; Bill Haller, speaking at the Society for American Baseball Research convention, July 28, 2007.

13. Jim Fregosi, interview with author, September 11, 2005. All quotations are from this interview.

14. Frank Torre, interview with author, July 21, 1997; *New York Daily News*, October 30, 1996.

15. Quoted in *Sporting News*, March 8, 1980, 6.

16. Tommy Lasorda, interview with author, November 12, 2005.

17. Tommy Lasorda, interview with author, January 19, 2001.

18. *Sporting News*, July 15, 1978, 9.

19. Davey Lopes, interview with author, August 2, 2000.

20. From my tape of the speech.

21. *New York Daily News*, May 11, 2008.

22. Bobby Valentine, interview with author, April 10, 1998.

23. *Sports Illustrated*, October 16, 2000, 39.

24. Mike Scioscia, interview with author, April 21, 1998.

25. Will, *Men at Work*, 27.

26. Tony La Russa, interview with author, May 12, 2008. All quotations are from this interview.

27. Only four other Major League managers received law degrees: Monte Ward, Hughie Jennings, Miller Huggins, and Branch Rickey. All are in the Hall of Fame.

28. Roland Hemond, interview with author, June 26, 2008.

29. Will, *Men at Work*, 6.

30. *New Yorker*, November 5, 2007, 34.

31. Joe Girardi, interview with author, September 1, 2006.

Chapter 16. Executive Suite

1. *New York Times*, May 2, 2008, A19.

2. E-mail to the author, December 4, 2008.

3. Roger Khan, quoted in Golenbock, *Bums*, 333. Bavasi was succeeded as Dodger GM by Al Campanis. Though his father was reportedly Italian, Campanis, who was born in Greece, was raised by his Greek mother and always expressed pride in his Greek heritage. Two former general managers, Roland Hemond and Peter Bavasi, both of whom knew Campanis well, told me they never heard him mention an Italian background.

4. Quoted in *New York Times*, May 2, 2008.

5. Joe Garagiola Jr., interview with author, March 14, 1999.

6. Lewis, *Moneyball*, 127.

7. Espn.go.com/gammons/s/2001/1114/1278229.html.

8. David Perini, telephone interview with author, December 4, 2008. All quotations are from this interview.

9. *Sporting News*, April 25, 1951, 2.

10. Quoted in *Sporting News*, February 6, 1952, 6.

11. *New York Times*, December 1, 1958, 44.

12. Helyar, *Lords of the Realm*, 242.

13. Jerry Colangelo, interview with author, March 15, 1999. Unless otherwise noted, all quotations are from this interview.

14. George Randazzo, telephone interview with author, December 29, 2008.

15. http://www.niashf.org/index2.cfm?ContentID=55.

16. Quoted in *New York Times*, March 12, 1995.

17. Quoted on Web site http://knowledge.wharton.upenn.edu/article.cfm ?articleid=1728.

18. Mark Attanasio, interview with Mario Ziino, *Italian Times* (Milwaukee), April 2005.

19. Larry Lucchino, telephone interview with author, October 10, 2008. All quotations are from this interview.

20. Reston, *Collision at Home Plate*, 18.

21. Halberstam, *Summer of '49*, 116.

22. *New York Times*, December 21, 1977, 35.

23. Quoted in *New York Times*, June 11, 1986, D27. During his tenure as National League president, Giamatti was instrumental in the effort to expand the Baseball Hall of Fame Library. On July 26, 1998, the A. Bartlett Giamatti Research Center was dedicated in the new wing of the library.

24. Giamatti, "Commentary," 9–23.

25. Giamatti, *Take Time for Paradise*, 42–43.

26. Quoted in *New York Times*, June 11, 1986, D27.

27. Quoted in *New York Times*, August 25, 1989.

28. Quoted in *New York Times*, June 16, 1981, A19.

29. Berkow, *New York Times*, September 2, 1989, 41; Will, *Men at Work*, 4–5; Froemming, interview with author, April 27, 2008; Selig, interview with author, July 3, 1997.

30. Giamatti, *Take Time For Paradise*, 81, 90, 92.

31. *New York Times*, June 16, 1981, A19.

Bibliography

Baseball statistics are from *Total Baseball*, 6th ed. (New York: Total Sports, 1999), and www.baseball-reference.com.

Adomites, Paul, and Saul Wisnia. *Best of Baseball: A Collection of Greatest Players, Teams, Games, Ballparks, and More*. 1996. Reprint, Lincolnwood IL: Publications International, 1997.

Alba, Richard D. *Italian Americans: Into the Twilight of Ethnicity*. Englewood Cliffs NJ: Prentice-Hall, 1985.

Alexander, Charles C. *Breaking the Slump: Baseball in the Depression Era*. New York: Columbia University Press, 2002.

———. *Our Game: An American Baseball History*. New York: Henry Holt, 1991.

Allen, Frederick Lewis. *Only Yesterday: An Informal History of the Nineteen-Twenties*. New York: Harper and Brothers, 1931.

Allen, Lee. *The Cincinnati Reds*. New York: Putnam, 1948.

———. Lee Allen Research Papers. Cooperstown NY: National Baseball Hall of Fame Museum.

Allen, Maury. *Where Have You Gone, Joe DiMaggio?* New York: Dutton, 1975.

Amman, Larry. "Baseball Families." In *Total Baseball*, ed. John Thorn et al., 215–21, 6th ed. New York: Total Sports, 1999.

Aulick, W. W. *America's National Game*. New York: Publisher's Printing, 1912.

Bamberger, Michael. "Dom DiMaggio." *Sports Illustrated*, July 2, 2001, 107–10.

Barrow, Edward Grant, with James M. Kahn. *My Fifty Years in Baseball*. New York: Coward-McCann, 1951.

Bartell, Dick, with Norman L. Macht. *Rowdy Richard: A Firsthand Account of the National League Baseball Wars of the 1930s and the Men Who Fought Them.* Ukiah CA: North Atlantic Books, 1987.

Berkow, Ira. "The Extraordinary Life and Times of Ping Bodie." In *Reaching for the Stars: A Celebration of Italian Americans in Major League Baseball,* ed. Larry Freundlich. New York: Ballantine, 2003.

Berra, Yogi, with Dave Kaplan. *Ten Rings: My Championship Seasons.* New York: Morrow, 2003.

Berra, Yogi, and Ed Fitzgerald. *Yogi: The Autobiography of a Professional Baseball Player.* Garden City NY: Doubleday, 1961.

Bingham, Walter. "Not Such a Tough Cookie." *Sports Illustrated,* May 15, 1961, 38–40, 43–44.

Bouton, Jim. *Ball Four: My Life and Hard Times Throwing the Knuckleball in the Big Leagues.* New York: World Publishing, 1970.

Burk, Robert Frederick. *Much More Than a Game: Players, Owners, and American Baseball since 1921.* Chapel Hill: University of North Carolina Press, 2001.

———. *Never Just a Game: Players, Owners, and American Baseball to 1920.* Chapel Hill: University of North Carolina Press, 1994.

Burr, Harold C. "The Brothers DiMaggio." *Baseball Magazine,* July 1941.

Busch, Noel F. "Joe DiMaggio: Baseball's Most Sensational Big League Star." *Life,* May 1, 1939, 62–69.

Campanella, Roy. *It's Good to Be Alive.* 1959. Reprint, Lincoln: University of Nebraska Press, 1995.

Carr, John Foster. "The Coming of the Italians." *Outlook* 82 (February 24, 1906): 419–31.

Casso, Evans J. "Zeke Bonura, A Legendary Hero." *Italian-American Digest,* Summer 1981, 7–8.

Cataneo, David. *Baseball Legends and Lore.* 1991. Reprint, New York: Galahad Books, 1995.

———. *Tony C: The Triumph and Tragedy of Tony Conigliaro.* Nashville TN: Rutledge Hill Press, 1997.

Cinel, Dino. *From Italy to San Francisco.* Palo Alto: Stanford University Press, 1984.

Conigliaro, Tony, and Jack Zanger. *Seeing It Through.* New York: Macmillan, 1970.

Cooper, Stephen, ed. *The John Fante Reader.* New York: Morrow, 2002.

Covello, Leonard, with Guido D'Agostino. *The Heart Is the Teacher.* New York: McGraw-Hill, 1958.

Cramer, Richard Ben. *Joe DiMaggio: The Hero's Life.* New York: Simon and Schuster, 2000.

Creamer, Robert W. *Babe: The Legend Comes to Life.* 1974. Reprint, New York: Penguin, 1983.

———. *Baseball in '41: A Celebration of the Best Baseball Season Ever—In the Year America Went to War.* New York: Viking, 1991.

———. *Stengel: His Life and Times.* 1984. Reprint, Lincoln: University of Nebraska Press, 1996.

Daniel, Daniel M. "Viva Italia!" *Baseball Magazine*, July 1936.

———. "Watch Those Walloping Wops." *Jack Dempsey's All Sports Magazine*, June 1938.

Dawidoff, Nicholas, ed. *Baseball: A Literary Anthology.* New York: Library of America, 2002.

Diggins, John P. *Mussolini and Fascism: The View from America.* Princeton NJ: Princeton University Press, 1972.

Delillo, Don. *Underworld.* New York: Scribner, 1997.

DiMaggio, Dom, with Bill Gilbert. *Real Grass, Real Heroes: Baseball's Historic 1941 Season.* 1990. Reprint, New York: Zebra Books, 1991.

Di Salvatore, Bryan. *A Clever Base-Ballist: The Life and Times of John Montgomery Ward.* New York: Pantheon Books, 1999.

Dobbins, Dick, and Jon Twichell. *Nuggets on the Diamond: Professional Baseball in the Bay Area from the Gold Rush to the Present.* San Francisco: Woodford Press, 1994.

Eig, Jonathan. *Opening Day: The Story of Jackie Robinson's First Season.* New York: Simon and Schuster, 2007.

Farrell, James T. *My Baseball Diary.* New York: A. S. Barnes, 1957.

Femminella, Francis X. *Italians and Irish in America: Proceedings of the Sixteenth Annual Conference of the American Italian Historical Association.* Staten Island NY: AIHA, 1985.

Ferraro, Thomas J. *Feeling Italian: The Art of Ethnicity in America.* New York: New York University Press, 2005.

Fleming, Gordon H. *Murderers' Row.* New York: Morrow, 1985.

Freundlich, Larry, ed. *Reaching for the Stars: A Celebration of Italian Americans in Major League Baseball.* New York: Ballantine, 2003.

Frishberg, Dave. "Van Lingle Mungo." In *The National Pastime: A Review of Baseball History* 27 (2007): 143–44.

Frommer, Harvey. *New York City Baseball: The Last Golden Age, 1947–1957.* Orlando FL: Harcourt Brace Jovanovich, 1980.

Fullerton, Hugh. "Fans." *The American Magazine* 74 (May–November 1912): 462–67.

Gallico, Paul. "Pity the Poor Giant." Originally in *Farewell to Sport,* 1938. Repr. in *The Thirties: A Time to Remember,* ed. Don Congdon, 321–32. New York: Simon and Schuster, 1962.

Gambino, Richard. *Blood of My Blood: The Dilemma of the Italian-Americans.* Garden City NY: Doubleday, 1974.

Gans, Herbert. "Symbolic Ethnicity: The Future of Ethnic Groups and Cultures in America." *Ethnic and Racial Studies* 2 (January 1979): 1–20.

Garrett, C. W. "But He Can Hit." *Collier's,* July 22, 1939.

Gerlach, Larry. *The Men in Blue: Conversations with Umpires.* New York: Viking Press, 1980.

Giamatti, A. Bartlett. "Baseball and the American Character." In *A Great and Glorious Game: Baseball Writings of A. Bartlett Giamatti,* ed. Kenneth S. Robson, 41–65. Chapel Hill NC: Algonquin, 1998.

———. "Commentary." In *The Italian Americans,* ed. Allon Schoener, 9–23. New York: Macmillan, 1987.

———. *Take Time for Paradise: Americans and Their Games.* New York: Summit Books, 1989.

Glazer, Nathan, and Daniel Moynihan. *Beyond the Melting Pot: The Negroes, Puerto Ricans, Jews, Italians, and Irish of New York City.* Cambridge MA: MIT Press, 1970.

Goldstein, Richard. *Spartan Seasons: How Baseball Survived the Second World War.* New York: Macmillan, 1980.

Golenbock, Peter. *Bums: An Oral History of the Brooklyn Dodgers.* New York: Putnam, 1984.

———. *Fenway: An Unexpurgated History of the Boston Red Sox.* New York: Putnam, 1992.

———. *Wild, High and Tight: The Life and Death of Billy Martin.* New York: St. Martin's Press, 1994.

Goodwin, Doris Kearns. *Wait 'Til Next Year: A Memoir.* New York: Simon and Schuster, 1997.

Gould, Stephen Jay. "The Streak of Streaks." *New York Review of Books*, August 18, 1988, 8–12. Repr. in Dawidoff, *Baseball*.

Graham, Frank. *The Brooklyn Dodgers: An Informal History*. New York: Putnam, 1945.

———. "Hidden-Ball King: Pinelli." *Baseball Digest*, November 1948, 53–55.

———. *The New York Yankees: An Informal History*, rev. ed. New York: Putnam, 1958.

Grosshandler, Stan. "Two-Sport Stars." In *Total Baseball*, ed. John Thorn and Pete Palmer, 237–43. New York: Harper Collins, 1993.

Guglielmo, Thomas A. *White on Arrival: Italians, Race, Color, and Power in Chicago, 1840–1945*. New York: Oxford University Press, 2003.

Gumina, Deanna Paoli. *Italians of San Francisco, 1850–1930*. New York: Center for Migration Studies, 1968.

Halberstam, David. *Summer of '49*. 1989. Reprint, New York: Avon Books, 1990.

Hall, Stephen S. "Italian-Americans: Coming into Their Own." *New York Times Magazine*, May 15, 1983.

Heaphy, Leslie A. *The Negro Leagues, 1869–1960*. Jefferson NC: McFarland, 2003.

Helyar, John. *Lords of the Realm: The Real History of Baseball*. New York: Villard Books, 1994.

Higham, John R. *Strangers in the Land: Patterns of American Nativism, 1860–1925*. 1955. Reprint, New York: Atheneum, 1972.

Hirshberg, Al. "Johnny Antonelli: From Bonus Baby to Big Leaguer." *Sport*, June 1955, 48–56.

Honig, Donald, ed. *Baseball between the Lines: Baseball in the Forties and Fifties as Told by the Men Who Played It*. 1976. Reprint, Lincoln: University of Nebraska Press, 1993.

———. *The Cincinnati Reds: An Illustrated History*. New York: Simon and Schuster, 1992.

Ivor-Campbell, Frederick. "The Many Fathers of Baseball." In *The American Game: Baseball and Ethnicity*, ed. Lawrence Baldassaro and Richard Johnson, 6–26. Carbondale: Southern Illinois University Press, 2002.

James, Bill. *The Baseball Book, 1990*. New York: Villard Books, 1990.

———. *The Bill James Historical Baseball Abstract*. New York: Villard Books, 1986.

———. *The New Bill James Historical Baseball Abstract*. New York: Free Press, 2001.

Johnson, Harold, ed. *Who's Who in Major League Baseball*. Chicago: Buxton, 1937.

Johnson, Richard A., and Glenn Stout. *DiMaggio: An Illustrated Life*. New York: Walker, 1995.

Kahn, Roger. *The Boys of Summer*. 1971. Reprint, New York: Signet, 1973.

———. *The Era: 1947–1957, When the Yankees, the Giants and the Dodgers Ruled the World*. New York: Ticknor and Fields, 1993.

———. *Memories of Summer: When Baseball Was an Art and Writing about It Was a Game*. New York: Hyperion, 1997.

Kessner, Thomas. *Fiorello H. La Guardia and the Making of Modern New York*. New York: McGraw-Hill, 1989.

———. *The Golden Door: Italian and Jewish Immigrant Mobility in New York City, 1880–1915*. New York: Oxford University Press, 1977.

Kiersh, Edward. *Where Have You Gone, Vince DiMaggio?* New York: Bantam, 1983.

Lane, F. C. "'Babe' Pinelli, a Colorful Descendant of the Ancient Romans." *Baseball Magazine*, February 1926.

———. "A Great Natural Ball Player Is Tony Lazzeri." *Baseball Magazine*, December 1927.

———. "'Poosh-Em-Out' Tony Lazzeri and His Colorful Record." *Baseball Magazine*, April 1927.

Lehman, Harvey. "The Geographic Origins of Professional Baseball Players." *Journal of Educational Research* 34 (October 1940): 130–38.

Levi, Carlo. *Christ Stopped at Eboli*. Translated by Frances Frenaye. New York: Farrar, Straus, 1963.

Levine, Peter. *Ellis Island to Ebbets Field: Sport and the American Jewish Experience*. New York: Oxford University Press, 1992.

Lewis, Michael. *Moneyball: The Art of Winning an Unfair Game*. New York: Norton, 2003.

Lieb, Frederick G. "Baseball—The Nation's Melting Pot." *Baseball Magazine*, August 1923.

———. "The Italian in Sport." *The Ring*, March 1924, 16–17.

Lord, Bette Bao. *In the Year of the Boar and Jackie Robinson*. New York: Harper and Row, 1984.

Macfarlane, Angus. "The Knickerbockers: San Francisco's First Baseball Team?" *Base Ball: A Journal of the Early Game* 1 (Spring 2007): 7–21.

Mackey, R. Scott. *Barbary Baseball: The Pacific Coast League of the 1920s.* Jefferson NC: McFarland, 1995.

Maglie, Sal, and Robert H. Boyle. "Baseball Is a Tough Business." *Sports Illustrated*, April 15, 1968.

———. "The Great Giant-Dodger Days." *Sports Illustrated*, April 22, 1968.

Mandell, David. "Danny Gardella and the Reserve Clause." *National Pastime*, 26 (2006): 41–44.

Mangione, Jerre. *Mount Allegro.* 1943. Reprint, New York: Columbia University Press, 1981.

Mangione, Jerre, and Ben Morreale. *La Storia: Five Centuries of the Italian American Experience.* New York: HarperCollins, 1992.

Maraniss, David. *When Pride Still Mattered: A Life of Vince Lombardi.* New York: Simon and Schuster, 1999.

Marshall, William. *Baseball's Pivotal Era: 1945–1951.* Lexington: University of Kentucky Press, 1999.

Martin, Billy, and Peter Golenbock. *Number 1.* New York: Dell, 1980.

Moore, Jack B. *Joe DiMaggio: Baseball's Yankee Clipper.* New York: Praeger, 1987.

Moquin, Wayne, with Charles Van Doren. *A Documentary History of the Italian Americans.* New York: Praeger, 1974.

Mormino, Gary Ross. "The Playing Fields of St. Louis: Italian Immigrants and Sports, 1925–1941." *Journal of Sport History* 9 (Summer 1982): 5–19.

Neft, David S., and Richard M. Cohen. *The Sports Encyclopedia: Baseball.* New York: St. Martin's Press, 1997.

Notarianni, Philip C. "Italianità in Utah: The Immigrant Experience." In *The Peoples of Utah*, ed. Helen Z. Papanikolas, 303–31. Salt Lake City: Utah State Historical Society, 1976.

Novak, Michael. *The Rise of the Unmeltable Ethnics: The New Political Force of the Seventies.* New York: Macmillan, 1971.

Peary, Danny, ed. *We Played the Game: Memories of Baseball's Greatest Era.* New York: Black Dog and Leventhal, 2002.

Pease, Neal. "Diamonds out of the Coal Mines: Slavic Americans in Baseball." In *The American Game: Baseball and Ethnicity*, ed. Lawrence Baldassaro and Richard A. Johnson, 142–61. Carbondale: Southern Illinois University Press, 2002.

Pinelli, Babe, as told to Joe King. *Mr. Ump*. Philadelphia: Westminster Press, 1953.

Pluto, Terry. *The Curse of Rocky Colavito: A Loving Look at a 33-Year Slump*. New York: Simon and Schuster, 1995.

Povich, Shirley. *The Washington Senators*. New York: Putnam, 1954.

Prager, Joshua. *The Echoing Green: The Untold Story of Bobby Thomson, Ralph Branca and the Shot Heard Round the World*. New York: Pantheon Books, 2006.

Prince, Carl E. *Brooklyn's Dodgers: The Bums, the Borough, and the Best of Baseball, 1947–1957*. New York: Oxford University Press, 1996.

Puleo, Stephen. *The Boston Italians: A Story of Pride, Perseverance, and Paesani, from the Years of the Great Immigration to the Present Day*. Boston: Beacon Press, 2007.

Reston, James, Jr. *Collision at Home Plate: The Lives of Pete Rose and Bart Giamatti*. 1991. Reprint, Lincoln: University of Nebraska Press, 1997.

Reynolds, Quentin. "The Frisco Kid." *Collier's*, June 13, 1936.

Richards, David A. J. *Italian American: The Racializing of an Ethnic Identity*. New York: New York University Press, 1999.

Riess, Stephen A. *City Games: The Evolution of American Urban Society and the Rise of Sports*. Urbana: University of Illinois Press, 1989.

———. *Touching Base: Professional Baseball and American Culture in the Progressive Era*. Westport CT: Greenwood Press, 1980.

Ritter, Lawrence. *The Glory of Their Times: The Story of the Early Days of Baseball Told by the Men Who Played It*. New York: Macmillan, 1966.

Roberts, James B., and Alexander G. Skutt. *The Boxing Register: International Boxing Hall of Fame Official Record Book*, 2nd ed. Ithaca NY: McBooks Press, 1999.

Robinson, Jackie, as told to Alfred Duckett. *I Never Had It Made*. New York: Putnam, 1972.

Rossi, John P. *The National Game: Baseball and American Culture*. Chicago: Ivan R. Dee, 2000.

Santo, Ron, and Randy Minkoff. *Ron Santo: For Love of Ivy*. Chicago: Bonus Books, 1993.

Schoor, Gene. *The Scooter: The Phil Rizzuto Story*. New York: Scribner, 1982.

Seymour, Harold. *Baseball: The People's Game*. New York: Oxford University Press, 1990.

Shapiro, Michael. *The Last Good Season: Brooklyn, the Dodgers, and Their Final Pennant Race Together*. New York: Doubleday, 2003.

Sheed, Wilfrid. "Joe DiMaggio: The Making of a King." In *Reaching for the Stars: A Celebration of Italian Americans in Major League Baseball*, ed. Larry Freundlich, 87–103. New York: Ballantine, 2003.

Simon, Neil. *Brighton Beach Memoirs*. New York: Random House, 1984.

Spalding, A. G. *America's National Game*. 1911. Reprint, Lincoln: University of Nebraska Press, 1992.

Spalding's Official Base Ball Guide. New York: American Sports Publishing, 1912.

Steadman, John. "Dolph Camilli: An Old-Time Star Recalls the Babe." *Baseball Digest*, June 1977, 78–80.

Stout, Glenn, and Richard A. Johnson. *Red Sox Century: One Hundred Years of Red Sox Baseball*. Boston: Houghton Mifflin, 2000.

Talese, Gay. "The Silent Season of a Hero." *Esquire*, August 1966. Repr. in *The Best American Sports Writing of the Century*, ed. David Halberstam. Boston: Houghton Mifflin, 1999.

Testa, Judith. *Sal Maglie: Baseball's Demon Barber*. DeKalb IL: Northern Illinois University Press, 2007.

Torre, Joe, with Tom Verducci. *Chasing the Dream: My Lifelong Journey to the World Series*. New York: Bantam, 1997.

Trachtenberg, Leo. *The Wonder Team: The True Story of the Incomparable 1927 New York Yankees*. Bowling Green OH: Bowling Green State University Popular Press, 1995.

Turner, Frederick. *When the Boys Came Back: Baseball and 1946*. New York: Henry Holt, 1996.

Tygiel, Jules. *Baseball's Great Experiment: Jackie Robinson and His Legacy*. New York: Oxford University Press, 1997.

———. *Past Time: Baseball as History*. New York: Oxford University Press, 2000.

Vecoli, Rudolph. "Are Italian Americans Just White Folks?" In *The Review of Italian American Studies*, ed. Frank M. Sorrentino and Jerome Krase, 75–88. Lanham MD: Lexington Books, 2000.

Verducci, Tom. *Inside Baseball: The Best of Tom Verducci*. New York: Sports Illustrated Books, 2006.

Vincent, Fay. *We Would Have Played for Nothing: Baseball Stars of the 1950s and 1960s Talk about the Game They Loved*. New York: Simon and Schuster, 2008.

Watson, Emmett. "A Boy and a Dream." *Sport*, July 1962, 86–88.

Westcott, Rich. *Diamond Greats: Profiles and Interviews with 65 of Baseball's History Makers*. Westport CT: Meckler Books, 1988.

White, G. Edward. *Creating the National Pastime: Baseball Transforms Itself, 1903–1953.* Princeton NJ: Princeton University Press, 1996.

Will, George F. *Men at Work: The Craft of Baseball.* 1990. Reprint, New York: Harper Perennial, 1991.

Williams, Ted, as told to John Underwood. *My Turn at Bat: The Story of My Life.* 1969. Reprint, New York: Pocket Book, 1970.

Yoseloff, Anthony. "From Ethnic Hero to National Icon: The Americanization of Joe DiMaggio." *International Journal of the History of Sport* 11 (September 1999): 1–20.

Zingg, Paul, and Mark D. Medeiros. *Runs, Hits, and an Era: The Pacific Coast League, 1903–58.* Urbana: University of Illinois Press, 1994.

Zoss, Joel, and John Bowman. *Diamonds in the Rough: The Untold History of Baseball.* 1989. Reprint, Chicago: Contemporary Books, 1996.

Source Acknowledgments

Portions of some chapters previously appeared in the following books and journals.

Chapter 1, in "Ed Abbaticchio: Italian Baseball Pioneer," NINE: A Journal of Baseball History and Social Policy Perspectives 8:1 (1999): 18–30.

Chapter 2, in "Go East, Paesani: Early Italian American Major Leaguers from the West Coast," in Italian Immigrants Go West: The Impact of Locale on Ethnicity, ed. Janet Worrall, Carol Bonomo Albright, and Elvira DiFabio, 100–108 (Cambridge MA: American Italian Historical Association, 2003).

Chapters 1 and 2, in "Before Joe D: Early Italian Americans in the Major Leagues," in The American Game: Baseball and Ethnicity, ed. Lawrence Baldassaro and Richard A. Johnson, 92–115 (Carbondale: Southern Illinois University Press, 2002).

Chapter 7, in "Ernie Lombardi's Bum Rap," in Reaching for the Stars: A Celebration of Italian Americans in Major League Baseball, ed. Larry Freundlich, 131–48 (New York: Ballantine Books, 2003).

Portions of the interview with Phil Rizzuto in chapter 11 appeared in "Schmoozing with the Scooter: A Conversation with Phil Rizzuto," Elysian Fields Quarterly, 13:3 (1994): 70–81.

Lyrics from "Mrs. Robinson" copyright 1968 Paul Simon. Used by permission of the publisher, Paul Simon Music.

Index